POLITICS AND THE BUREAUCRACY
POLICYMAKING IN THE FOURTH BRANCH OF GOVERNMENT

FOURTH EDITION

POLITICS AND THE BUREAUCRACY
POLICYMAKING IN THE FOURTH BRANCH OF GOVERNMENT

FOURTH EDITION

KENNETH J. MEIER
Texas A&M University

Harcourt College Publishers

Fort Worth   Philadelphia   San Diego   New York   Orlando   Austin   San Antonio
Toronto   Montreal   London   Sydney   Tokyo

Publisher	Earl McPeek
Executive Editor	David C. Tatom
Market Strategist	Steve Drummond
Project Editor	Joyce Fink
Art Director	Chris Morrow
Production Manager	Serena Barnett

ISBN: 0-15-505523-2
Library of Congress Catalog Card Number: 99-61383

Portions of this work were published in previous editions.

Address for Domestic Orders: Harcourt College Publishers, 6277 Sea Harbor Drive, Orlando, FL 32887-6777
800-782-4479

Address for International Orders: International Customer Service Harcourt, Inc., 6277 Sea Harbor Drive, Orlando, FL 32887-6777 407-345-3800 (fax) 407-345-4060 (e-mail) hbintl@harcourtbrace.com

Address for Editorial Correspondence: Harcourt College Publishers, 301 Commerce Street, Suite 3700, Fort Worth, TX 76102

Web Site Address:
http://www.harcourtcollege.com

Printed in the United States of America

9 0 1 2 3 4 5 6 7 8   066   9 8 7 6 5 4 3 2 1

Harcourt College Publishers

....

To: Marvin York
a politician with honor.

PREFACE

Bureaucracy has never been a popular institution in the United States, but for the last few decades it has come under continual siege. Presidents, interest groups, members of Congress, and the public at large have blamed their problems on bureaucracy. At the same time the bureaucracy serves as the political scapegoat in the United States, the expectations for and demands on bureaucracy continue to escalate. The reinventing government movement has institutionalized the demand for higher performance with fewer resources. Contracting out has become the latest panacea designed to cure bureaucracy.

This book addresses two audiences. First, it serves as an introduction to politics and the bureaucracy. Bureaucracy, just as the president, Congress, or the Supreme Court, is a political institution. It must build political support for its actions, and it uses that political support to interact with the other political institutions to make public policy. Bureaucracy is the least visible of all our political institutions, so a separate book is often necessary to introduce students to the intricacies of bureaucratic politics in the United States.

Second, the book is designed to serve as a reference for scholars. I have made a serious effort to include cutting edge research on bureaucracy within each of the chapters. This task has become more difficult. When the first edition was published in 1979, fewer than a dozen empirical scholars of bureaucracy and public policy were publishing research. The 1980s saw an explosion of research on bureaucracy. A large and growing group of scholars have focused their work on the political role of bureaucracy. At the present, it is one of the most dynamic fields in political science. Much of this work is cited in the bibliography.

The book's general structure remains the same, but I have rewritten and updated virtually all parts of the book. New examples have been used in place of old ones. Significant changes have taken place in several chapters. Chapter 3 has again grown. What was an empirical theory with only case study support in 1979 has become an empirical theory with solid multivariate research. Much material on state and local bureaucracy has also been added. Chapter 5, for the first time, was not restructured. The public's expectations of bureaucracy are complex and contradictory; we need to understand how bureaucracies deal with such expectations.

Chapter 6 continues to expand. The growth area in public administration has been political control of the bureaucracy. There is, I think, no longer any question that other political institutions can control the bureaucracy if they wish to do so. The new question has become, can they control the bureaucracy without doing it serious harm?

Chapter 7 also has undergone additional changes. The discussion of administrative ethics was expanded. Studies of administrative ethics have blossomed. My own reading suggests that we now pay more attention to ethics than at any time since the original work of Paul Appleby. Chapter 7 also contains an expanded discussion of public choice as a control on bureaucracy. My personal bias is that public choice is a normative theory of bureaucracy, and I have treated it as such. I have included other public choice research only where the research examined real data. I had originally planned to drop Chapter 8 and propose a radical alteration of the political system, but, in the end, that was a different book and I have made only incremental changes.

Over the course of three editions, I have benefited from the comments and critiques of several colleagues. The first edition was read and critiqued by David Brady, Scott Harris, Jeremy Plant, Chuck Jones, and John Wanat. Detailed reviews of the first edition by David Lowery, Bill Browne, Eric Herzik, Tom Lauth, Larry Hill, and Harry Holloway formed the basis for the second edition. Helpful comments on that edition were also provided by Jim Campbell, Frank Thompson, and Pat Ingraham. The second edition was reviewed by Larry Hill, David Kozak, David Lowery, and John Wanat for the transition to the third edition. I would like to thank the following reviewers of the third edition for their suggestions: Brian P. Janiskee, California State University at San Bernandino; John J. Hindera, Texas Tech University; and S.K. Schneider, University of South Carolina. Joe Cooper provided me admirable instruction on the legislative veto and on why my position is wrong. Larry Hill and Paul Sabatier have greatly influenced my thinking on bureaucracy, especially about using the book as a showcase for research. Jim Anderson always reads each edition carefully and sends me a list of the mistakes that I have made. Numerous conversations with Dan Wood and George Krause have sharpened my thinking about bureaucracy. I would like to thank all these individuals, and to show my appreciation, Paul Sabatier has agreed to buy them all beer at the next convention. George Waller, Alesha Doan, Warren Eller, Matthew Eshbaugh-Soha, and Scott Robinson all provided research assistance to update the fourth edition. The standard statement about all the remaining errors in the book being the responsibility of Paul Sabatier holds.

College Station, TX
December 1998

ABOUT THE AUTHOR

Kenneth J. Meier (Ph.D.Syracuse) is currently the Charles Puryear Professor of Liberal Arts, professor of political science, and coordinator of the Program in American Politics at Texas A&M University. Meier is also the director of the Texas Educational Excellence Project, which conducts research on educational policies that affect disadvantaged students. He has served as president of the Southwest Political Science Association as well as the Public Administration, the Public Policy, and the State Politics sections of the American Political Science Association. He was a member and chair of the Oklahoma State Ethics and Merit Commission and a member of the Governor's Commission on Professional Licensing and Discipline (Wisconsin) and the Task Force on Property and Liability Insurance (Wisconsin). He is the author or coauthor of several books, including *Applied Statistics for Public Administration* (Harcourt Brace, 1999), *The Case Against School Choice* (M. E. Sharpe, 1995), *The Politics of Sin: Drugs, Alcohol and Public Policy* (M. E. Sharpe, 1995) and *The Politics of Hispanic Education* (State University of New York Press, 1991). His hobbies include serving as the resident humorist for the discipline and seeking the perfect California zinfandel.

TABLE OF CONTENTS

CHAPTER 5
BUREAUCRACY AND THE
PUBLIC'S EXPECTATIONS   103

CHAPTER 6
CONTROLLING THE BUREAUCRACY: EXTERNAL
CHECKS BY POLITICAL INSTITUTIONS   123

CHAPTER 7
CONTROLLING BUREAUCRACY: ETHICS AND PARTICIPATION 165

CHAPTER 8
REFORMING THE BUREAUCRACY 195

....

INDEX   247

....

LIST OF TABLES

LIST OF FIGURES

CHAPTER I

BUREAUCRACY AND POLITICS

The United States was founded on a philosophy of limited government. That government which governed least was assumed to govern best. The core functions of a limited government—collecting taxes, maintaining law and order, and dispensing justice to the contractually and criminally aggrieved—are now only minor aspects of modern government. The eclipse of limited government by "positive" government has added functions to the nation-state totally foreign to nineteenth-century and early twentieth-century governments. In the past three decades the national government has taken responsibility for protecting the environment, solving the problems of the homeless, regulating the health and safety of the nation's workforce, curing AIDS and other dangerous diseases, and protecting society from the ill effects of drug abuse. Even radical conservatives in the twenty-first century demand a larger government to ban abortions, permit prayer in schools, and root out pornography.

The growth of positive government has exacerbated another trend—the growth in the major instrument of positive government, bureaucracy.[1] Each new government function has spawned a corresponding bureaucracy to administer that function. With the advent of President Lyndon Johnson's Great Society programs, the Department of Health and Human Services grew from a budget of $5 billion in 1963 to $770 billion in 1998 (including Social Security). To coordinate the nation's energy policies in the wake of the Arab oil embargo, the Office of Emergency Preparedness was dusted off and charged with energy responsibilities. When this small office appeared inadequate, the Federal Energy Office (FEO) was created in the executive office of the president. Even the FEO pales in comparison to its son, the Federal Energy Administration, and its grandson, the Department of Energy. Although the federal government abandoned most of its energy policies in the 1980s, the Department of Energy continued to survive. Concern for workers' health and safety gave rise to the Occupational Health and Safety Administration (OSHA), and the needs of consumers were entrusted to the

---

[1] This book uses the term "bureaucracy" to refer to government organizations and "bureaucrat" to refer to government employees. Both terms are used in a neutral way to describe specific organizations or individuals. The reader should not infer anything pejorative from their use.

Consumer Product Safety Commission (CPSC). Other examples in the recent past are far too numerous to mention.

When faced with acute crises, chronic problems, or even apathy, the positive state responds; and the response usually includes a bureaucracy. Even under President Ronald Reagan, a vigorous public advocate of less government, the elaborate bureaucratic structure of the positive state remained intact. Although the Reagan administration created few new agencies, it did not eliminate any old ones.[2] Under Reagan the total number of federal government employees actually grew from 2,821,000 in 1981 to 3,065,000 in 1989, and the federal budget breached $1 trillion for the first time.

Only under President Bill Clinton with Vice President Al Gore's initiative on reinventing government did the size of the federal government decline. Total federal employees dropped from 3.128 million in 1990 to 2.765 million by March 1998. The reduction, however, was essentially blue smoke and mirrors. It was achieved by simply contracting out functions to private organizations, organizations often staffed by former federal employees. Republican members of Congress also made some token efforts in this direction in the mid-1990s when they abolished a few minor agencies, the most notable being the Interstate Commerce Commission.

Recent events notwithstanding bureaucracy has grown both in size and the quantity of resources it consumes and also in a qualitative sense. Few aspects of a citizen's life are immune from the tentacles of government bureaucracy. Today's citizens awake in the morning to breakfasts of bacon and eggs, both certified as fit for consumption by the U.S. Department of Agriculture (although the Department of Health and Human Services would urge you to eat a breakfast lower in cholesterol). Breakfast is rudely interrupted by a phone call; the cost of phone service is determined by a state regulatory commission. When our citizens drive to work, their cars' emissions are controlled by a catalytic converter mandated by the Environmental Protection Agency. The cars have seat belts, padded dashboards, collapsible steering columns, and perhaps air bags required by the National Highway Traffic Safety Administration. When our citizens stop for gasoline, they pay a price that is partly determined by energy policies (or a lack thereof) administered by the Department of Energy. To take their minds off the numerous bureaucracies regulating their lives, the bureaucratic citizens turn on their radios. Each radio station is licensed by the Federal Communications Commission, and all advertising is subject to the rules and regulations of the Federal Trade Commission. When our citizens arrive at work (say, at a bureaucracy such as a university), they enter a handicapped accessible building (required by federal law) in a building built with federal funds to report to jobs financed in large part by the Department of Education.[3]

Although our hypothetical citizens have been awake only a few hours, at least nine federal, state, and local bureaucracies have touched their lives. The normal citizen in

---

[2] The Civil Aeronautics Board was abolished, but that was scheduled under President Carter. The termination of the Law Enforcement Assistance Administration in 1982 had been planned under Carter. The Community Services Administration was eliminated under Reagan, but by the time of its elimination the CSA had few actual programs.

[3] My students are fond of noting that all this contact with bureaucracy so early in the day will produce a painful headache. The remedy, of course, is two headache tablets regulated by the Food and Drug Administration.

the United States works in a government bureaucracy (one of every six workers) or in a private bureaucracy that is regulated obtrusively or unobtrusively by a government bureaucracy, eats bureaucratically inspected food, wears bureaucratically regulated clothes, plays in bureaucratically sanctioned places and ways, and will definitely be buried in a bureaucratically approved manner.

Few aspects of a person's life are left untouched by bureaucracy. According to the Office of Management and Budget, Americans spend 785 million hours per year filling out federal government forms. One-third of the nation's land and 400,000 buildings are owned by the federal government and managed by its bureaucracies (*National Journal,* 1982: 436).

This chapter discusses the development of bureaucracy as a government power center. First, the dissatisfaction with bureaucracy in the United States is examined. Second, this dissatisfaction is traced to the phenomenon of administrative power. Third, the use of administrative power by four federal government agencies is discussed to illustrate the range of bureaucratic action. Fourth, the term "administrative power" is explicitly defined as it is used in this book.

....

BUREAUCRACY: A FAVORITE TARGET

The growth of bureaucracy has not been without dissent. In a nation that pays lip service to notions of individual liberty and limited government, the growth of bureaucracy is viewed at best as a threat and at worst as un-American. Bureaucracy has become a favorite target of both politicians and citizens (see Hill, 1989b). In 1976 then-President Gerald Ford made the size and responsiveness of the bureaucracy a political issue. He attacked several regulatory agencies including the Civil Aeronautics Board (since abolished) and the Interstate Commerce Commission, as inefficient and harmful. Ford's war on bureaucracy was extended to other agencies such as the Food and Nutrition Service, which was charged with incompetence and uselessness. Ronald Reagan, both in his 1976 primary race against Ford and in subsequent successful runs for the presidency, was equally critical of government bureaucracy and its efficiency. In 1980 Reagan proposed that both the Department of Energy and the Department of Education be abolished.

In the past the bureaucracy could dismiss such criticisms as right-wing rhetoric, but increasingly politicians of the center and the left have also denounced the evils of bureaucracy (Kaufman, 1981). Democratic members of Congress indignantly criticized the Defense Department for purchasing $640 toilet seat covers, $659 ashtrays, and $7,000 coffee makers (Sussman, 1985: 37). Former Senator William Proxmire (D.-Wis.) continued to give his "Golden Fleece" award to National Science Foundation grants and other examples of bureaucratic waste even after his retirement from office in 1989. In 1976 Democrat Jimmy Carter ran for president on the pledge to reorganize the federal bureaucracy to make it more streamlined and efficient. The Clinton-Gore reinvention effort merely uses different terms to undercut and restrict government bureaucracy.

Constant criticism of bureaucracy by politicians was both recognized and accepted by the general public. Business leaders led a chorus attacking the costs and restrictions of government regulation. In 1982 the President's Private Sector Survey on Cost Control, known as the Grace Commission, issued a 47-volume report on government waste. The Grace Commission made 2,478 recommendations designed to achieve greater efficiency in government that according to the commission would save $424 billion over a three-year period (Goodsell, 1984). Although a subsequent analysis of the Grace Commission's recommendations concluded that such savings were grossly over-estimated (Goodsell, 1984), the general public accepted its claims as fact. A 1985 *Washington Post* poll found that people thought 42 cents of every federal tax dollar were wasted (Sussman, 1985: 37). In an earlier *Washington Post* poll, 57 percent of the American public believed that government was more responsible for inflation than business or labor (*Washington Post Poll*, 1982: 22). When asked, "In your opinion which of the following will be the greatest threat to the country in the future—big business, big labor, or big government?" nearly 50 percent answered, big government (reported in Hill, 1989b). As one observer noted, fear of bureaucracy had become a "raging pandemic" (Kaufman, 1981).

A detailed analysis of these criticisms of bureaucracy would reveal that they posses a common core—the belief that bureaucracy is inefficient. Bureaucracy, the argument goes, hinders the effective operation of the market economy that efficiently allocates resources; therefore, the impact of bureaucracy will always be harmful (see Stokey and Zeckhauser, 1978).

CRITICISM AND RHETORIC

The broad criticism of bureaucracy indicates that something is wrong with the bureaucracy. Only an idealist would be so foolish as to contend that government bureaucracy is an unmixed blessing for modern society. The contemporary criticism, however, must be classified more as rhetoric than conclusive evidence for two reasons.

EFFICIENCY: AN UNTESTED HYPOTHESIS

First, the contention that government bureaucracy is inefficient is essentially not a testable proposition. If efficiency is defined as delivering goods and services at the least possible cost, then efficiency standards are meaningful only when one organization is compared with another. Since we can never know what the least cost of producing any good or service is (such things change over time with new technologies), the only valid comparison is to compare one organization with another doing the same thing. In the private sector, efficiency comparisons are often possible because many firms produce the same item. Firms producing a specific item at lower costs can be termed more efficient. Many government bureaus, however, cannot be compared with other organizations or with each other because each bureau produces a unique product. Only the Department of Defense, for example, "produces" a national defense. As a result, descriptions of government bureaucracy as inefficient rarely have a solid comparative foundation.

The argument for government inefficiency is often based more on assumption than on fact. The critic of bureaucracy often uncritically accepts the assumption of classical economic theory that competition leads inevitably to efficiency through competitive allocation of scarce resources. Applying this assumption, the critic reasons, "If there is no competition to force efficient production, then the organization must be inefficient."[4] To support the claim of inefficiency, the critic usually presents a bureaucratic horror story, cites past mistakes made by the bureaucracy, or denounces bureaucratic red tape. Never are we told the extent of the condemned behavior, its frequency, or whether the bureaucracy has taken corrective action.

An excellent example of such rhetoric is the publicity campaign started by J. Peter Grace after the Grace Commission released its final report. A subsequent analysis by the General Accounting Office found that two-thirds of the Grace Commission's claims had no factual support. Many other proposals were, in fact, policy recommendations disguised as efficiency proposals. For example, the commission proposed saving several million dollars by abolishing the Rural Electrification Administration, clearly a policy proposal rather than just an efficiency measure (Rauch, 1985b: 749).

Examples of bureaucratic inefficiency whether cited by the Grace Commission or by others demonstrate little because all large-scale formal organizations, whether public or private, make mistakes. Ford Motor Company's decision to produce the Edsel and perhaps the Pinto rivals the Defense Department's ill-fated Sergeant York gun. Sperry Rand, in the early 1950s, concluded that no market existed for computers and consequently gave up its technological advantages in the field, a forecasting error as large as predicting that Iraq would not invade Kuwait. Coca-Cola's decision to alter its basic formula in 1985 generated as much public resentment as did the Department of Transportation's decision in 1974 to prevent cars from starting unless seatbelts were buckled; both decisions were reversed. These examples do not prove that Ford, Sperry Rand, or Coca-Cola are inefficient; they show only that large-scale organizations make mistakes. Without some information about the frequency of the mistakes, judgments about efficiency cannot be made. Because most claims of inefficiency in public sector bureaucracy are not based on solid comparative evidence, the "bureaucracy is inefficient" hypothesis has not been adequately tested.

IS EFFICIENCY A GOAL?

In some instances measures are available to judge the efficiency of a bureaucracy, but these measures are applicable only to a small portion of the government's activities and may involve assuming that efficiency is a bureau's only goal. The Postal Service, some defense procurement, the Government Printing Office, and, at the local level, garbage

---

[4] The reader should note that the critic's logic is fallacious. The critic assumed that if there is competition, then there will be efficient allocation of resources. Observing a basic fact of government bureaucracy, that there is no competition, the critic concludes that the bureaucracy must be inefficient. The critic has denied the antecedent, one of the most elementary of logical fallacies.

collection and street repair are government activities that are often assessed in terms of efficiency.

To make this assessment, however, we must assume that the primary goal of these organizations is to deliver services as efficiently as possible. Many times the goal of government agencies is universal service rather than efficient service. More efficient postal delivery, for example, could be achieved by shifting the tasks of small post offices to large mechanized centers where economies of scale could operate. Efficiency could be increased if the Postal Service merely assigned every citizen within a hundred-mile radius a post office box in a single building and had citizens pick up their own mail. The cost of delivering mail under these circumstances would be greatly reduced while the speed of "delivery" would increase. By definition, this type of service is more efficient. The public, however, would probably reject such efficient service.

Despite the constraints of universal service, the widely criticized Postal Service has received little credit for its efficiency gains. In 1970, 741,000 postal workers delivered 85 billion pieces of mail; in 1997, 764,000 postal workers delivered 176.8 billion pieces of mail (*National Journal,* 1989: 98). From 1970 to 1982 productivity in the Postal Service increased by 48.2 percent, a gain significantly greater than the private sector improvement (Vittes, 1985: 508). In 1989 the Postal Service delivered 94 percent of local mail the next day to the appropriate post office and 74 percent to the addressee; it also delivered 87 percent of nonlocal mail (81 percent to the addressee) within three days (Priest, 1990: 37). Unlike such competitors as United Parcel Service, the Postal Service attained this record while serving all areas of the country.

In some areas government agencies perform services identical with those of private organizations, and efficiency comparisons may be appropriate. Examining a variety of studies comparing garbage collection, hospital operation, urban transportation systems, utilities, colleges, and insurance, Charles Goodsell (1983: 48–55) found that in some cases private organizations were more efficient and in other cases government organizations were more efficient. On the average government and private organizations were about equally efficient. Using a broader definition of efficiency that included quality concerns, Poister and Henry's (1994) survey of public and private sector services found no significant differences between the two. Assessing a series of contracting studies, Boyne (1998), concludes that most studies were too poorly designed to be able to support the conclusion that private sector service delivery was more efficient.

From a different perspective, Crewson (1995) compared the relative quality of public sector and private sector individuals who worked in similar jobs. His conclusion, based on a battery of tests, was that public-sector individuals were consistently better qualified. The implication of Crewson's finding is that public sector organizations may well be able to outperform private sector organizations given that they attract higher quality human resources.

If efficiency is a difficult concept to apply to the few areas of government that perform quasi-private functions such as delivering the mail, then for most government functions efficiency is at best a minor goal. Government programs have goals of equity, justice, fairness, and other similar values that take precedence over the goal of efficiency. According to former EPA administrator Douglas Costle (1980: 3), if efficiency were the predominant goal of government, then "the Washington Monument ought to be torn down and replaced by condominium apartments."

In other areas of public policy, efficiency concerns are irrelevant. How does one measure the efficiency of health research, or environmental protection, or even occupational safety in an unambiguous manner? "Efficiency" is a foreign term in these and other areas of government (despite the efforts of economists to apply the term), because the tasks we demand that government perform are more complex than the tasks we demand of the private sector. The objective of building Ford Escorts must pale before the goal of curing cancer; protecting environments is much more complex than designing a computerized payroll system; protecting worker safety is not amenable to the same standards of profit measurement as the production of tires. Because the goals and objectives of public programs are more complex and require different and possibly more sophisticated expertise, the public sector rarely has the regularity and predictability needed to apply a simple standard such as efficiency to its operations.

Perhaps the best assessment of efficiency and organizational form is that of Nobel Laureate Herbert Simon (1998: 10):

> The idea that there is one form of organization—specifically, the private corporation—that has a unique capacity of efficient action is simply a myth that ignores both the motivations at work in organizational behavior and the limits on our capacities for measuring consequences and converting them into costs and demand prices.

ADMINISTRATIVE POWER AS POLITICAL POWER

Although the argument that the public is dissatisfied with bureaucracy because it is inefficient lacks credibility, dismissing the complaints against bureaucracy would be too hasty. While the bureaucracy may not be peopled with incompetents eager to infringe on the economic and political freedoms of the American people, neither are they neutral angels without political objectives of their own.

To understand the criticism of bureaucracy in American society, bureaucracy and its functions must be examined. What does bureaucracy do to cause the American people to reject it? Bureaucracy, in the case of our hypothetical bureaucratized citizens, affects all aspects of their lives. Bureaucracy regulates our behavior, it redistributes our income, it distributes benefits of society; in short, bureaucracy allocates societal resources.

The influence that bureaucracy has on our lives is authoritative. In most cases it is perceived as legitimate and backed by the coercive power of the state. By authoritatively allocating values, bureaucracy is engaging in politics of the first order (Easton, 1965). As a political institution, the bureaucracy is subject to the same criticism levied at all American political institutions. Recent public opinion polls (see Table 1–1) demonstrate that all government institutions, and bureaucracy is no exception, lack the confidence of a large number of people. This lack of confidence is probably related to bureaucracy's need to make hard political choices. Current politics is what Lester

• TABLE 1-1 •

PEOPLE'S LEVEL OF CONFIDENCE IN VARIOUS LEADERS

As far as the people running various institutions are concerned, would you say you have a great deal of confidence?

PERCENTAGE OF PUBLIC WITH A GREAT DEAL OF CONFIDENCE IN	THE LEADERS OF THE
44	Military
37	Education
38	Medicine
37	U.S. Supreme Court
14	Press
10*	State Government
17**	Local Government
17	Executive Branch
12	Congress
13	Organized Labor

*Last asked in 1989.
**Last asked in 1988.

SOURCE: Harris Poll, February 11, 1998.

Thurow (1980) calls zero-sum politics; for every person who benefits from public policy, another person must pay for those benefits. Bureaucracy's exercise of political power quite naturally leads to criticism by political elites and the public at large who favor different policies.

To a person used to viewing bureaucracy as a neutral instrument for implementing others' political choices, the concept of bureaucracy as a political power is a difficult one. The following four cases are included to illustrate the political nature of bureaucracy in a variety of different policy areas.

CASE 1: FEDERAL HOUSING

The Federal Housing Administration (FHA), an agency within the Department of Housing and Urban Development (HUD), seeks to improve the quality of housing in the nation through construction and rehabilitation (see Boyer, 1973; Wolman, 1971). In 1937 Congress assigned the FHA the goal of improving housing but left much of the goal's implementation to the FHA's discretion. The FHA's approach was to set standards of acceptable housing. To enforce those standards, the FHA guaranteed mortgages for houses that met their standards. In effect the FHA offered positive benefits for compliance with their housing standards.

Before 1967 the FHA also required that all mortgage loan guarantees be economically sound. The value of the house underwritten had to have a market value high enough to compensate the government's loss if the homeowner defaulted. Within these narrow bounds, the FHA program was a spectacular success. Millions received the loan guarantees necessary to purchase homes, making the single-family dwelling the norm for middle-class American families. The agency's fiscally conservative management produced a loan default rate of less than one-half of 1 percent.

Although the FHA's method of implementing congressional housing policies is an exercise in political decision making, the policy's implications clearly demonstrate the FHA's influence on national priorities. In order to limit the losses from defaulted mortgages, certain localities in every city were redlined; that is, they were designated as areas where mortgages would be poor risks because of the nature of the neighborhood and other factors. No mortgages were insured in redlined areas. Many of the nation's inner-city and ghetto areas were redlined, and no federal mortgage guarantees were available in these areas. Because federal mortgage guarantees lowered housing costs by eliminating the hazards of default, permitting FHA-loan guarantees in the "economically sound" areas only encouraged the white middle-class to move to the suburbs where FHA-mortgage guarantees were available. Redlining also contributed to inner-city decay by denying the financial support needed to undertake rehabilitation through increased ownership.

The actions of the Federal Housing Administration were redistributive in every sense of the word. Housing benefits were redistributed from the poor and minorities in the cities to the middle class in the suburbs through selective granting and denial of benefits. Loan guarantees redistributed income from other social needs to housing but only to the portion of the housing market used by the middle class. Financial institutions wisely invested their funds in completely safe FHA loans rather than in myriad other uses.

This redistribution was the status of housing policy prior to 1967. With the creation of the Department of Housing and Urban Development in 1965, the Federal Housing Administration was transferred to HUD. Transferring the fiscally conservative FHA to the Department of Housing and Urban Development, with its social welfare orientation, had a profound impact on the goals of the FHA. The FHA was charged with correcting the impact of past policies; the FHA was to house the nation's poor.

With this new goal, policy implementation was again left to the FHA because the complexities of housing policy were beyond the ken of many HUD executives and members of Congress. The FHA moved to eliminate the practice of redlining inner-city areas. Unfortunately, the agency's new goal was counter to the standard operating procedures of lower-level agency personnel. Newspapers reported case after case of FHA appraisers estimating the market value of houses from their cars because they were afraid to step out into the ghetto to appraise the housing in a standard and adequate fashion (Boyer, 1973; Wolman, 1971). The results were disastrous. Through both fear and corruption thousands of shoddy houses worth at most a few hundred dollars were each appraised at thousands.[5] Individuals could purchase these houses with

---

[5] The charge of corruption has been documented by Boyer (1973), and there have been several investigations by newspapers and congressional committees. By May of 1973, 116 indictments had been handed down in cases involving the FHA program, naming some 250 people in more than 300 charges. Despite the low priority placed on these cases by local prosecutors, 46 convictions were returned by May 1973.

a down payment of a few hundred dollars. When the inadequacies of a house became known to the owner and the costs for repairs exceeded the owner's ability to pay, the house was abandoned. With abandonment came default, and the Federal Housing Administration became the proud owner of a defective house with no market value.

The redistributive nature of post-1967 FHA policies is evident. The FHA used its discretion and adopted an implementation strategy that increased inner-city deterioration. The poor, the intended beneficiary of the policy, suffered most because the amount of housing declined (in many cases after the FHA failed to resell a house, it was destroyed). The policy's beneficiaries were the real estate brokers who were able to sell the houses and the bankers who were able to make risk-free investments at the expense of the government.

CASE 2: THE CUBAN MISSILE CRISIS

National security policy, especially during a crisis such as the Cuban Missile Crisis, is a policy area where we expect bureaucracy to be subservient (see Ripley and Franklin, 1991). Military bureaucracies have strong norms of hierarchy and obedience. As Oliver North remarked to Congress during the Iran-Contra hearings, if the president told him to go stand in the corner, then this lieutenant colonel would go stand in the corner. Power in such situations should pass to the president and his close circle of advisors. The Cuban Missile Crisis, in fact, had at least two characteristics that Richard Neustadt (1960) deemed necessary for the exercise of presidential power: presidential involvement was clear, and the other actors had no doubt about the president's ability to act. The bureaus involved, the Central Intelligence Agency and the armed services, are also hierarchically structured organizations designed to carry out presidential orders quickly.

When President Kennedy and his advisors learned with certainty that the Soviet Union had placed offensive missiles in Cuba, they narrowed their response to two options—a surgical air strike against the missiles and a blockade of the island (Allison, 1971). The U.S. Air Force claimed that a surgical strike was not feasible. To be effective and to be certain of success, the air force argued that they must bomb all missile sites, storage depots, airports, and artillery batteries. Since that option was clearly beyond the level of force the president was willing to unleash, the advice of the air force effectively foreclosed one of the president's two options.

With the decision for the blockade, the initial details were left to the navy's discretion. The navy, to ensure the safety of its mission, initially established the blockade out of the range of the Cuban Air Force, five hundred miles from Cuba. The president, feeling that this gave the Soviets too little time to think and react, requested that the ships be moved closer to the Cuban coast. When the navy balked at the suggestion, Secretary of Defense Robert McNamara made the request a direct order.

Although the decision makers felt their order had been implemented, when the first ships were intercepted, it was clear that the navy had followed its own conscience. The first ship was intercepted some five hundred miles off the coast of Cuba. To avoid the appearance of direct disobedience, the navy permitted at least one ship to slip through its blockade (Allison, 1971). Clearly in the Cuban Missile Crisis the air force and the navy exercised political power. The air force through its advice foreclosed one option of the president; the navy chose to ignore an order of the secretary of defense and in the process increased the risks of confrontation. However political power is defined, increasingly the risk of war must be included as an exercise of that power.

CASE 3: THE NATIONAL HEALTH SERVICE CORPS

The National Health Service Corps was a program designed by Congress in 1970 to encourage physicians to practice in rural areas that lacked adequate health care (Thompson, 1982b). The brief four-page law gave the Health Services Administration (HSA) little guidance about implementation, although the intent was clear: physicians were to be placed in areas that could economically support a physician. HSA administrators loosely defined what an area lacking in physician services was and allowed exceptions to the "shortage" requirement if the area had a low use of health services (Thompson, 1982b: 433).

By 1978 health care professionals administering the program were placing physicians in urban sites where HSA-sponsored group practices were already established. Rather than serving as a method of providing physicians to rural areas, therefore, the program funneled physicians into inner-city areas. The agency had moved from "fighting geographic barriers inhibiting medical care availability to fighting economic barriers" (Thompson, 1982b: 435).

This fundamental change in the program goals of the National Health Service Corps resulted, not because Congress changed program goals, but rather because individual bureaucrats did so. The Health Service Administration accepted the values of delivering health services to the disadvantaged; it did not perceive its goals to include establishing physicians in private practice. Through the implementation process, therefore, the National Health Service Corps was transformed into a program more consistent with the goals of the administering agency.[6]

CASE 4: THE FEDERAL TRADE COMMISSION

The Federal Trade Commission (FTC) was created in 1914 as an independent agency charged with maintaining a "strongly competitive enterprise as the keystone of the American economic system." The FTC has several tools to pursue this goal, including the antitrust laws, consent decrees, cease and desist orders, and informal bargaining; but the FTC was given little guidance regarding where to act or what specific policies to follow.

For a long time the FTC was regarded as an agency with little life or power. In 1969 an exposé by the Nader organization, written in part by President Nixon's future

---

[6] During the 1980s, this program was reduced dramatically as part of the Reagan budget cutbacks. The number of medical personnel placed dropped from a high of 1,600 in 1985 to a low of 215 in 1989. Congress, by law in 1987, endorsed the idea of urban group practices at government facilities and created a loan revolving fund to continue this program (General Accounting Office, 1990a).

son-in-law Edward Cox, revealed the agency to be generally incompetent (Cox, Fellmuth, and Schulz, 1969). Nixon appointed Casper Weinberger, who under the guise of a reorganization proceeded to fire one-third of all FTC employees and began to recruit bright, young, consumer-oriented lawyers (Clarkson and Muris, 1981).

With some encouragement from Congress, the FTC embarked on an aggressive, consumer-oriented program that affected major business interests. Antitrust suits were filed against the major oil companies and the largest cereal makers, the suits against the latter under the innovative legal concept of a shared monopoly. Rules were issued to prevent anticompetitive practices in the eyeglass industry. Along with the Justice Department, the FTC vigorously attacked professional associations of accountants, engineers, and physicians who prohibited advertising and other competitive behaviors. The FTC started major investigations involving advertising on children's television shows (the kidvid study), practices in the insurance industry, competition in the funeral industry, deception in the used-car market, and numerous other areas.

Although Congress had encouraged consumer activism (Pertschuk, 1982), the specific policies pursued by the FTC were its own. Such an aggressive move by a small agency against some of the major industries of the nation, however, did not go unnoticed. Used car dealers, funeral directors, large agricultural cooperatives, physicians, attorneys, and others affected by FTC actions or proposed actions demanded that Congress rein in this runaway bureaucracy (see Weingast and Moran, 1983). The FTC continued its pro-consumer actions despite yearly battles in Congress that threatened to restrict or even abolish the agency (Meier, 1985: 112).

Not until the election of Ronald Reagan and his appointment of James Miller to head the FTC was the regulatory fervor of the FTC quenched. Under Miller's leadership the FTC became a strong advocate of market-oriented solutions to consumer problems. As an example, the FTC declined to force a manufacturer to recall defective survival suits used in ocean situations. The FTC reasoned that the heirs of individuals who drowned while wearing these suits would sue and, thus, be compensated for their losses (Wines, 1983a: 223).

The FTC example illustrates the major changes in public policy undertaken by agency employees. The agency was transformed from a passive observer of the market place to an aggressive consumer advocate between 1969 and 1980. Under Miller the agency was changed yet again into an organization more concerned with market efficiency than with traditional methods of consumer protection. Recent evidence suggests that under Presidents Bush and Clinton the FTC has again become a more aggressive consumer advocate, although not to the extent of the 1969–1980 era.

The four case studies show not only the exercise of administrative power but also the breadth of policy areas affected by it. Many policy analysts divide most public policy into three categories—regulatory, distributive, and redistributive—with several other policies falling into a more general fourth category (Lowi, 1972; Ripley and Franklin, 1991; see Chapter 4 for a detailed discussion of policy areas). Our cases present evidence of bureau power in each of the four major policy areas: the Federal Housing Administration operates in a sphere of redistributive policy; the Federal Trade Commission is a regulatory agency; the Health Services Administration's policies are distributive; and the Department of Defense and national security policy are in the more general category.

Our cases do not demonstrate that administrative power is necessarily harmful. For every FHA policy that may pursue objectives in the narrow self-interest of its clientele, an FTC policy may seek a broader consumer interest despite organized opposition. For every navy admiral who may directly disobey an order of the secretary of defense, an administrator in the HSA may allocate health personnel to areas that need them more. The objective of the citizen in a state where bureaucracy exercises a great deal of political power, and the United States is such a state, should not be to condemn and destroy bureaucratic power but to structure it so that the benefits of bureaucracy can be attained without some of its negative consequences. Simply to denounce the growth of bureaucracy, as many politicians have done, is to ignore the positive contributions that bureaucracy has made to the nation.

ADMINISTRATIVE POWER: A DIFFICULT TERM

Until now administrative power has not been precisely defined. To be a useful concept, administrative power must be defined more carefully. Administrative power is the ability of a bureaucracy to allocate scarce societal resources. Administrative power, in this definition, is nothing more than political power exercised by a government bureaucracy when it determines, in Lasswell's (1936) words, who gets what, when, and how. Administrative power, and political power for that matter, has two requisites—resources and autonomy. Administrative power is not possible without access to resources—legislative authority, money, trained personnel, and other tools necessary to make and carry out political decisions. One bureau, therefore, is more powerful than another when it extracts more resources from its environment.

Having access to resources or rather having the ability to extract resources, however, is not by itself sufficient to create a powerful bureaucracy. The National Institutes of Health (NIH) and the Social Security Administration (SSA) are both successful in extracting resources from their environments, but the Social Security Administration, especially the retirement system, is rigidly bound by rules and legislation passed by Congress to restrict the SSA's discretion (Schick, 1971). To become powerful, an agency must have autonomy, the discretion to make decisions concerning agency activities. Having autonomy without resources, however, is as moderating as having resources without autonomy, because an agency with only a high degree of autonomy will not have the money, personnel, or authority to enforce the decisions it makes. The Internal Revenue Service, for example, estimates that it could collect $60 billion more annually in unpaid taxes if it had the resources to pursue these cases (Broder, 1990: 4). As the 1997–1998 Congressional hearings on IRS abuses demonstrated, however, Congress is unlikely to authorize more resources for the IRS.

Resource extraction and autonomy in the use of resources are two distinct dimensions of administrative power. Agencies can have a great deal of resources with little

• TABLE I-2 •

DIMENSIONS OF ADMINISTRATIVE POWER

AUTONOMY	RESOURCE EXTRACTION	
	HIGH	LOW
HIGH	National Institutes of Health	Internal Revenue Service
LOW	Social Security Administration	Equal Employment Opportunity Commission

discretion, as the Social Security Administration has in its retirement programs, or agencies can have few resources but a great deal of autonomy, as the Internal Revenue Service has. Some agencies are fortunate to have both, as in the case of the National Institutes of Health, while others are so unlucky as to have neither, as in the case of the Equal Employment Opportunity Commission (EEOC). Resources and autonomy are two distinct dimensions of administrative power, and agencies can have varying combinations of either (see Table 1–2).

SUMMARY

This chapter discussed the phenomenon of administrative power. The public displeasure with bureaucracy was noted and tied to the growth of bureaucracy as a powerful political institution. The policymaking power of the bureaucracy was illustrated with case studies of the Federal Housing Administration, the Cuban Missile Crisis, the National Health Service Corps, and the Federal Trade Commission. The chapter concluded with a definition of administrative power.

The remainder of this book will examine the exercise of bureaucratic power in a democracy. Chapter 2 presents a descriptive background of the federal bureaucracy so that the reader has a core of knowledge essential for understanding the remainder of the book. Chapter 3 discusses the reasons why some bureaus develop political power and others do not; the discussion focuses on the political environment of federal agencies. Chapter 4 examines the policymaking process in the bureaucracy in an attempt to determine how different agencies affect public policy. With Chapter 5 the focus shifts to control of administrative power. Chapter 5 discusses the expectations that people have for bureaucracy, focusing on two major dimension—competence and responsiveness. Chapters 6 and 7 examine a series of proposals for controlling the political power of bureaucracy. Chapter 8 provides some concluding comments about the role bureaucracy plays in the policymaking process of a democratic nation.

CHAPTER 2

THE STRUCTURE OF AMERICAN BUREAUCRACY

Bureaucracy is by far the least known of all U.S. political institutions. The president, a highly visible actor, is constantly in the public eye whether his activities are official or personal. Congress also maintains high visibility both as a focal point for opposition to the president and as a policymaking body in its own right (Hibbing and Theiss-Morse, 1995). Even the courts periodically receive public attention when they rule on significant cases. Although bureaucracy directly affects the lives of many citizens (Chapter 1), it rarely receives the public attention that other political institutions do.

Because general knowledge about the bureaucracy is lacking, this chapter describes the federal bureaucracy in detail and state and local bureaucracy briefly in order to provide a foundation for the arguments in later chapters. It examines several characteristics of American bureaucracy including the organization of the federal government (the types of departments, agencies, and other organizations that comprise the federal bureaucracy), the size of government bureaucracy, the government's personnel system (the different types of government employees and how they are recruited to government), and the role of state and local bureaucracies in the federal system.

THE ORGANIZATION OF THE FEDERAL GOVERNMENT

In theory the federal government's organization is relatively simple. The U.S. government has three co-equal branches—the executive, the legislative, and the judicial. The bureaucracy is officially responsible to the president under his constitutional charge to take care that the laws of the nation are faithfully executed (see Figure 2–1). In reality the federal bureaucracy, despite its formal subordinate status, is a relatively autonomous policymaker. Both the president and Congress, partly in response to the growth of bureaucratic power, have developed bureaucratic organizations of their own. This section outlines the major organizational features of the federal bureaucracy and discusses the political bureaucracies of the president and Congress.

• FIGURE 2-1 •

THE GOVERNMENT OF THE UNITED STATES

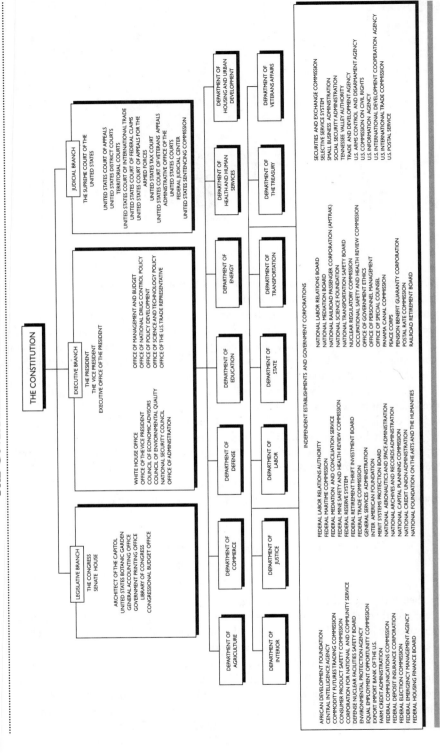

SOURCE: *U.S. Government Manual, 1998/1999.*

DEPARTMENTS

The first level of organization below the president is the fourteen executive departments, each headed by a cabinet secretary (see Table 2–1). The departments contain 65 percent of all federal employees and conduct many important policy activities. Individual departments were established by Congress over a 200-year period with department structures and functions reflecting the political forces present during their creation.

Departments Performing Essential Government Functions

The Departments of State, Treasury, and War were created in 1798 as the three essential functions of government.[1] Both the State and War Departments were initially perceived as presidential departments because they performed the functions of diplomacy and national defense and the president is designated as chief diplomat and commander-in-chief of the armed forces. The Department of the Treasury, on the other hand, was initially perceived as a congressional department closely related to Congress's power to tax. Currently the State Department conducts the nation's diplomacy and coordinates a variety of U.S. programs that affect other nations. The Treasury Department through its bureaus collects the nation's taxes, prints the nation's money, finances

• **TABLE 2–1** •

SIZE OF U.S. GOVERNMENT EXECUTIVE DEPARTMENTS 1998:
CIVILIAN PERSONNEL AND BUDGET

DEPARTMENT	PERSONNEL	BUDGET ($BILLIONS)
Agriculture	99,000	55.0
Commerce	38,300	4.1
Defense	731,000	251.4
Education	4,600	30.7
Energy	17,100	14.4
Health and Human Services	124,200	769.6
Housing and Urban Development	10,400	31.0
Interior	67,600	7.9
Justice	119,800	15.5
Labor	16,700	32.1
State	22,900	5.3
Transportation	64,900	40.5
Treasury	146,000	387.2
Veterans Affairs	206,000	43.1

SOURCE: *Budget of the U.S. Government, FY 1999.*

---

[1] A good description of the formation of federal executive departments can be found in Van Riper (1958) and White (1948; 1951; 1954; 1958). A good brief summary that this section relies on is Diamond et al. (1970: 255–262).

the national debt, and dispenses federal grant funds to other governments. The War Department went through a variety of organizational permutations; in its last major reorganization in 1947 the Department of Defense was created by merging the Department of War and the Department of the Navy.

Departments Reflecting the Needs of a Growing Nation

Congress created two departments in response to national growth, the Department of Justice and the Department of the Interior. In the first cabinet President Washington had an attorney general, but at this time the attorney general was simply a private lawyer hired to serve the government. As the legal needs of the nation grew, so did the attorney general's tasks; and in 1870 Congress created the Department of Justice. The Department of Justice is composed of several legal units that represent the United States in court on legal matters concerning antitrust, criminal law, civil law, civil rights, tax law, and land and natural resources law. The Department also contains the nation's federal law enforcement agencies (for example, the FBI), the immigration service, and the federal prisons. The Department of Justice was the fastest growing federal department in the late 1980s as it expanded to fight President Reagan's war on drugs.

A second federal department created in response to growing national needs was the Interior Department.[2] Creating an Interior Department was a major political issue from 1789 to 1849 because the states feared that a federal department on the order of the British Home Department would interfere with states' rights. Proposals to create a Department of the Interior were either proposed or debated in Congress several times before one finally passed in 1849. The Interior Department initially included such internal affairs programs as patents, public lands, and Indian affairs. Currently the department no longer has jurisdiction over patents but has added parks, recreation, and some natural resources programs. Soon after its creation, the Department of the Interior established strong ties to interest groups interested in public lands, recreation, and reclamation (Culhane, 1981). These ties with clientele groups established a pattern that served as a blueprint for the next three departments established.

Clientele Departments

The "clientele" departments are the Departments of Agriculture, Commerce, and Labor. These departments were not created to serve the general needs of government but rather in response to interest group pressure. Created in 1862, the U.S. Department of Agriculture (USDA) was the first of the clientele departments. The USDA began as a research organization devoted to developing new agricultural techniques. During the 1930s the department was transformed into a subsidies and regulation department designed to limit farm production and raise farm income. Currently many USDA programs concern marketing agricultural goods for domestic and foreign markets and distributing food (food stamps, school lunch programs, etc.). Its

---

[2] The Post Office Department was created in the nineteenth century in response to government needs, but it was changed to a government corporation in the 1970s and is discussed in the government corporations section of this chapter.

most recognized program, farm subsidies, is scheduled to be phased out (Wrinkle and Meier, 1998).

The Commerce Department was established in 1903 and at one time may have been the dominant department of the federal government. During the 1920s the Commerce Department was a major force in shaping domestic policies of economic growth. With the rise of labor unions and the growth of government in other areas, the Commerce Department has lost influence. Today Commerce contains several diverse programs including business promotion, the Census Bureau, the Patent Office, and the National Oceanic and Atmospheric Administration.

The Department of Labor was originally part of the Department of Commerce but was separated from it in 1913. The current Labor Department monitors worker health and safety, employment standards, unemployment compensation, and programs to create additional jobs. For several decades after the creation of the Department of Labor, no new departments were established. Government expansion during the New Deal and World War II took place either within exiting department organizations or in the form of independent agencies such as those discussed in the next section.

Departments Reflecting National Priorities

The next four federal departments were all established to respond to pressing national needs or to recognize the priority of certain problems. The Department of Health and Human Services (HHS) was created (initially as the Department of Health, Education, and Welfare) out of the Federal Security Administration and other programs to signify the priority of these functions. The present HHS operates programs that distribute funds for health research, health care (Medicaid, Medicare), welfare, and social security.

The Department of Housing and Urban Development (1965) reflected President Lyndon Johnson's commitment to urban problems. The department administers the federal mortgage guarantee programs, the public housing programs, as well as programs designed to address problems of urban life. It is perhaps best known for a major corruption scandal in the late 1980s involving political favoritism. The Department of Transportation, containing most federal government transportation programs affecting railroads, airlines, highways, and the Coast Guard, was established in 1967 to emphasize the need for comprehensive approaches to transportation problems. Finally, the Department of Energy was created in 1977 in response to growing concern about the nation's energy shortage and President Carter's request for a unified approach to energy problems. Although most of the department's funds are devoted to nuclear energy, the department also contains research, development, and regulation functions for other forms of energy.

The New Clientele Departments

Being an executive department (rather than an agency; see below) confers prestige on the organization and its clientele. The two most recent cabinet departments were both established as the result of political pressure from clientele groups. Initially, education programs were part of the Department of Health, Education, and Welfare (a precursor to Health and Human Services), but in 1979 education functions were elevated to a separate department. The Department of Education was established to redeem President Carter's campaign promise to the National Education Association that he would create such an organization. Although the Department of Education contains many federal education programs, it is not the home of several others, including Head Start, the school lunch program, and Indian schools (Stephens, 1983: 653). The Department of Veterans Affairs was created in 1989 in response to demands from veterans groups. Although the old Veterans Administration (VA) had a reputation as poorly managed and unresponsive to new needs, elevating the VA to department status was a politically popular move for both the president and Congress.

Department Bureaus and Agencies

The fourteen executive departments of the federal government are not monolithic units. Each department is composed of several smaller bureaus and agencies that administer the department's programs. In some departments such as the Department of Housing and Urban Development, the department exercises relatively close control over the bureaus and agencies so that they operate with less autonomy vis-à-vis the department. Other federal departments are not really departments at all; they are holding companies. In a holding company department, power resides at the bureau and agency level. The Department of Health and Human Services is a good example of a holding company. Some of the units in HHS such as the Public Health Service were in existence long before the department was created. These bureaus have their own clientele, were established by legislation different from the law that established the department, and operate with little departmental control.

A good example to illustrate the nature of department agencies and bureaus is the U.S. Department of Agriculture. As the USDA organization chart shows (see Figure 2–2), the first level of organization under the secretary of agriculture is the undersecretary and assistant secretary level. In the USDA, the assistant secretary for Marketing and Regulatory Programs is in charge of an administrative apparatus designed to monitor the actions of three bureaus. The bureau level is one level down—the Agricultural Marketing Service, Animal and Plant Health Inspection Service, and the Grain Inspection, Packers and Stockyards Administration. These bureaus and agencies in the USDA have substantial autonomy and actually administer the programs and make the policy choices.

The assistant secretary or the undersecretary is a political appointee. Bureau chiefs may be either career civil servants or political appointees depending on the legal requirements. In actual practice, however, three types of persons become bureau chiefs. Approximately one-third of bureau chiefs are **politicians** who have been appointed by the president to fill these positions (Meier, 1980). These men and women have long records of service in the president's party. Their average age is approximately 50, and they were appointed initially as a bureau chief or held at most one other position in the agency before assuming the top spot. The average politician spends less than four years in the agency and less than two years in the top position. During the Reagan administration, the average political appointee served only twelve months as a bureau chief (Ban and Ingraham, 1990).

Another one-third of bureau chiefs are career civil servants although many hold positions that are designated as political appointments. The careerist bureau chief is

• FIGURE 2-2 •

U.S. DEPARTMENT OF AGRICULTURE: HEADQUARTERS ORGANIZATION

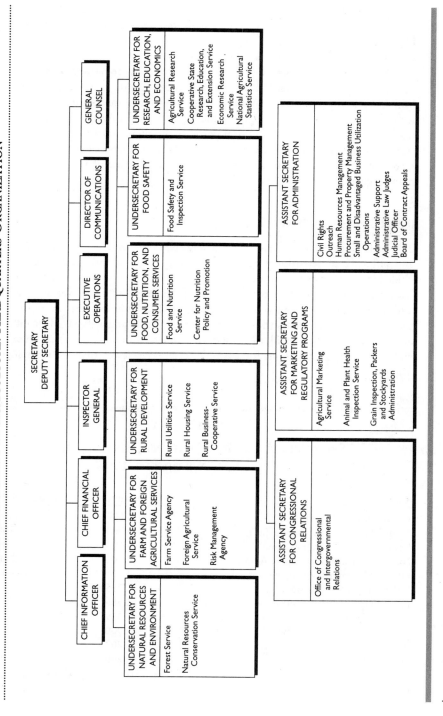

slightly older (56) than the politician. Unlike the politician, the **careerist** entered the federal service at a young age, spending an average of twenty-three years in the agency. Despite the longer career of the careerist, the average careerist bureau chief had been a bureau chief less than five years (Meier, 1980).

The remaining one-third of the bureau chiefs may be termed **professionals**. The professional pursues a scientific or technical career outside of government. After establishing reputations in their profession, these individuals are appointed to top-level bureau positions, moving up to bureau chief in a few years. Although some professionals may be associated with one political party or the other, they do not necessarily have strong party ties. Professionals (average age about 50) tend to head bureaus with research or scientific missions such as the National Institute of Health. In recent years many regulatory agencies have been headed by professionals.

INDEPENDENT AGENCIES

The Federal government has approximately sixty independent agencies, similar in size and influence to department agencies and bureaus. These agencies, which are not included in the fourteen major departments, report directly to the president or directly to Congress. An independent agency may be fairly large, as is the National Aeronautics and Space Administration (NASA), which has 20,000 employees, more than four of the executive departments (Education, Energy, HUD, and Labor). Most independent agencies, however, are small; the American Battle Monuments Commission or the Federal Maritime Commission, for example, each have fewer than 400 employees (see Table 2–2).

• **TABLE 2–2** •

SELECTED MAJOR INDEPENDENT AGENCIES OF THE FEDERAL GOVERNMENT 1998

AGENCY	EMPLOYEES	BUDGET ($MILLIONS)
Environmental Protection Agency	18,000	6,400
Federal Emergency Management Agency	4,700	3,700
General Services Administration	14,100	900
National Aeronautics & Space Administration	19,600	13,700
Office of Personnel Management	3,000	46,400
Federal Trade Commission	795	107
Equal Employment Opportunity Commission	2,586	250
National Foundation on the Arts/Humanities	319	233
National Labor Relations Board	1,900	176
National Science Foundation	1,200	3,200
Smithsonian Institution	4,269	331

SOURCE: *Budget of the U.S. Government, FY 1999.*

Independent agencies are established outside the jurisdiction of the executive departments for a variety of reasons. President Franklin Roosevelt created many agencies outside the executive departments because he felt the departments were tied to old ways of approaching policy problems (Seidman and Gilmour, 1986). Other independent agencies were created to avoid clientele pressures in departments with strong clientele ties. Others still including the independent regulatory commissions (for example the Consumer Product Safety Commission) were made independent to avoid presidential control (Renfrow, 1980). Still other agencies, such as the National Aeronautics and Space Administration, were made independent because their function did not fit within any of the existing departments.

THE GOVERNMENT CORPORATION

Government corporations are business corporations established by the federal government to carry out some government task (Mitchell, 1998). As such they are located in a gray area where the distinction between government and the private sector blurs. To isolate the corporations from politics, they are usually headed by boards or commissions with bipartisan membership and long terms of office. Congress creates government corporations for a variety of political reasons; the corporate form permits Congress to shift responsibility to a "nonpartisan" arena and also to hide the cost of the program by removing it from the budget (Tierney, 1984: 78–79). A recent example of a government corporation was the creation of the Resolution Trust Corporation in 1989 to sell assets recovered from failed thrifts (i.e., savings and loans).

The isolation from politics, in theory, allows the corporations to employ efficient, businesslike procedures. Government corporations have separate personnel systems, can borrow money, can undertake projects without congressional approval, and can even operate at a profit. The Federal Reserve System, for example, operates at a profit of several billion dollars a year. Some government corporations go so far as to sell stock and accord their stockholders certain rights that private sector shareholders have (for example, COMSAT, created to operate communications satellites, see Moe and Stanton, 1989).[3] On occasion government corporations are even sold to the private sector, as Conrail (a corporation that operated railroads in the northeastern United States) was in 1987 (Henig, 1989: 649).

Government corporations exist in numerous areas. The Tennessee Valley Authority operates power systems, reclamation projects, and a variety of other enterprises in the Tennessee River Valley. The Federal Deposit Insurance Corporation insures deposits in national and state financial institutions. The Postal Service delivers the nation's mail. Government corporations may be either independent agencies, as are the Postal Service, the Tennessee Valley Authority, and the Federal Deposit Insurance Corporation, or within a department, as are the Commodity Credit Corporation and the Federal Crop Insurance Corporation (both within the Department of Agriculture).

---

[3] COMSAT in all respects is no different from a private corporation; it even owns a National Hockey League team.

Government corporations closely resemble another type of institution that is neither a public nor a private sector organization. Federally Funded Research and Development Centers (FFRDCs) are private research centers established throughout the country and funded by the federal government to conduct government research (Lambright, 1976). These institutions may run solely on federal money or may combine federal money with private money.

The difference between FFRDCs or the Postal Service and private corporations that rely on government to provide most of the demand for their products is minor. Some corporations such as North American Rockwell and General Dynamics receive such large percentages of their income in federal government contracts that they cannot be considered private organizations. In comparison, the Postal Service and the Federal Reserve receive far less (often nothing) of their operating funds from the federal government than does General Dynamics. Because these companies have argued that they perform a role not unlike federal labs, they want government to guarantee that they do not suffer financial collapse. In such cases the distinction between government organizations and private organizations is unclear. This book does not deal with the problems of private sector bureaucracy even though those problems are as pressing as the problems of public sector bureaucracies.

When the terms *agency* and *bureau* are used in the remainder of this book, they will refer to department agencies, independent agencies, and government corporations. Departments will be referred to only by the term *department*. These four organization forms are the dominant forms of government organizations, but they do not exhaust the total variety of governmental units (see Seidman and Gilmour, 1986). Other forms include the federal advisory committee and the minor boards, commissions, and committees.

THE ADVISORY COMMITTEE

Numerous federal programs and agencies have advisory committees to provide expert advice on a variety of topics. These committees may be either temporary and used for a single purpose or permanent with a multitude of purposes. Without restraints, advisory committees proliferate because such committees serve to link agencies with their clientele and to provide the president with prestigious patronage appointments. In 1975 the federal government had more than 1,500 advisory committees. As part of his reorganization efforts, President Carter abolished about 700 of these committees. With Carter gone from the White House, advisory committees again proliferated, growing to 928 by late 1984 (*National Journal,* 1985: 1320).

MINOR BOARDS, COMMITTEES, AND COMMISSIONS

The federal government has more than sixty minor boards, committees, and commissions established by Congress or the president for a specific purpose. These are not really agencies, since they are usually staffed by temporary personnel, lack program responsibilities, are extremely small, or only have the power to recommend action.

Perhaps the most newsworthy commission recently was the Grace Commission, which made a series of recommendations to cut the size of the federal government in 1984. Other minor boards are less conspicuous. The Harry S. Truman Scholarship Fund, for example, is administered by the Harry S. Truman Scholarship Foundation. Another committee exists to encourage federal employees to purchase U.S. savings bonds. President Clinton's commission on race relations has been in the news frequently in the past few years. The bulk of these committees, boards, and commissions are relatively unimportant and will not be discussed in this analysis.

THE POLITICAL BUREAUS OF THE PRESIDENT AND CONGRESS

Both Congress and the president have institutionalized; that is, they have developed a system of supporting bureaucracies (Ragsdale and Theis, 1997). In part the institutionalization of Congress and the president was in response to the growing role of the federal bureaucracy in policymaking. To combat the power of the bureaucracy, alternative bureaucracies were created. Accordingly, these "political" bureaus are not just staff agencies designed to answer letters, but actual agencies that assist their sponsors in policymaking activities. The political bureaus of the president and Congress are important because they are often used in efforts to control the remainder of the federal bureaucracy.

The Presidential Bureaucracy

The bureau nearest the president is the White House Office; it provides staff assistance to the president. The White House Office contains the president's congressional lobby, the press secretaries, and the president's special assistants. Within the Executive Office of the President are a series of other bureaus designed to assist in policymaking activities. The first among equals is the Office of Management and Budget (OMB). The OMB prepares the federal budget and evaluates legislation to determine if it is in accord with the president's program (Pfiffner, 1979). President Richard Nixon added the responsibility for federal management improvement and bureaucratic oversight to the OMB. President Carter lodged his government reorganization team in the OMB, and President Reagan placed his regulatory analysis unit there. In all administrations, the Office of Management and Budget is a power broker of the first order.

On roughly the same organizational level as the OMB, the presidency has several policy councils. The National Security Council advises the president on a wide range of foreign policy and defense issues. Although the NSC was a major policymaking force under McGeorge Bundy and Henry Kissinger, it has had less influence in recent years. The Council of Economic Advisors and its staff provides assistance in economic matters; its influence depends on the president's confidence in it.

The executive office also contains a group of lesser bureaus. In 1999 these units included the Office of the U.S. Trade Representative, the Council on Environmental Quality, the Office of Science and Technology Policy, the Office of National Drug Control Policy, and the Office of Administration. These units advise the president and assist in formulating policies in their specialized areas. At times these agencies become well known; William Bennett, President George Bush's first drug czar, was head of the

Office of National Drug Control Policy. The president's bureaucracy also includes one nonstaff agency, the Central Intelligence Agency, the lead intelligence agency for the U.S. government.

The size of the president's political bureaucracy is difficult to determine. Approximately 1,650 people exclusive of the CIA and the foreign assistance program are listed in the federal budget, but this figure can be augmented by detailing. The president can request that other agencies "detail" personnel temporarily to presidential agencies. Detailing has been used extensively to increase the president's policymaking resources.

The Congressional Bureaucracy

The congressional bureaucracy is more complex than the president's. Congress and its staff was the fastest growing bureaucracy in Washington, D.C., during the 1970s; it has grown little since 1980. Each member of Congress has a personal staff whose size depends on the size of the member's district/state and the member's access to funds. Personal staff are augmented by committee staff who assist members in their committee work. A reasonable estimate of total personal and committee staff is about 18,000 people (Ornstein et al., 1990: 130).

Congress supplements these staff members with a group of information-gathering bureaus. The Library of Congress, particularly its Congressional Research Service, provides general information on current policy issues. Established by the Congressional Budget Reform and Impoundment Control Act of 1974, the Congressional Budget Office (CBO) performs the same budget analysis for Congress that the OMB performs for the president. In recent years the CBO has acquired a reputation for objective analysis of the budget and economic trends. The General Accounting Office (GAO) audits and analyzes federal programs for Congress.

Congress also has several bureaus with nonpolicy functions. The Government Printing Office prints not only Congress's heavy volume of documents but also many other bureaus' publications. The Architect of the Capitol maintains the buildings and grounds of Congress and plans its physical expansion. Even the Botanic Gardens is a congressional agency. Exclusive of the Government Printing Office, these nonpolicy, congressional bureaus employ approximately 15,000 people (Ornstein et al., 1990: 130).

THE SIZE OF THE BUREAUCRACY

The size of the federal bureaucracy is the subject of more misinformation than probably any other topic. A common perception holds that the federal bureaucracy is growing rapidly and threatening to engulf us all. Although the federal budget is growing by leaps and bounds, the number of people employed by the federal government is not. Current total federal civilian employment is 2.76 million people, and only 2.4 million are full time; this figure includes all civilian defense employees as well as all postal workers. Although 2.76 million people is not a small number, the size of the federal bureaucracy has declined by nearly 400,000 persons in recent years (Figure 2–3); before that it had not changed dramatically over the previous thirty-five years. In 1998

· **FIGURE 2–3** ·

FEDERAL EMPLOYMENT, 1940–1997

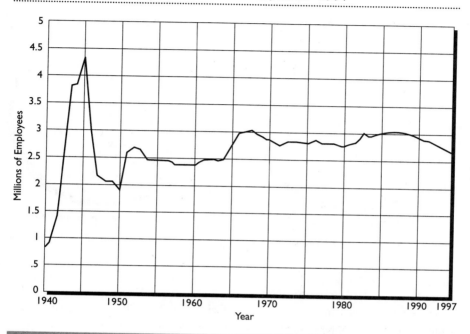

the federal bureaucracy was 17 percent smaller than it was in 1980 and fully 30 percent smaller than it was at the end of World War II.

The relative size of the U.S. bureaucracy can best be gauged in comparison to those of other nations. All governments in the United States (state, local and federal) employ about 18.3 percent of all workers in the United States. Compared to the nations of Western Europe, this is a small number. Governments employ 31.4 percent of the workforce in Great Britain, 32.6 percent in France, 25.8 percent in Germany, and 38.2 percent in Sweden (Rose, 1985: 6). Since 1951 the U.S. bureaucracy has grown only slightly faster than the U.S. population, whereas the bureaucracies of Western Europe have grown twice as fast as their respective populations (Rose, 1985: 11).

Although the U.S. federal bureaucracy has generally decreased in size since World War II, it fluctuates in response to environmental conditions. During wars, recessions, and other crises (e.g., drug wars), the bureaucracy grows as government attempts to deal with these problems. During quiet periods the bureaucracy goes through a period of fasting with gradual reductions in size. The recent shrinkage in size, however, is unprecedented.

Most federal bureaucrats are not located in Washington but are decentralized throughout the nation. Of the 2.76 million civilian employees, only 204,000 or 8 percent work in the District of Columbia. This percentage has been relatively constant

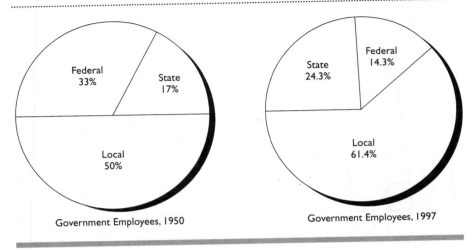

• FIGURE 2–4 •

RELATIVE SIZE OF FEDERAL, STATE, AND LOCAL BUREAUCRACIES

Government Employees, 1950   Government Employees, 1997

through history. The relatively small number of capital city bureaucrats can be understood in comparison. The 204,000 federal bureaucrats in Washington are fewer than the number of federal employees located in California (295,000) and less than half the number of people employed by New York City (425,000).

The number of federal civil servants is actually dwarfed by the number of state and local bureaucrats in this country. Since 1950, the federal bureaucracy has grown 31 percent to include 2.76 million people. At the same time, the 50 state bureaucracies have grown 301 percent to 4.7 million people. Local government bureaucracies have ballooned 244 percent to 11.9 million people. The total federal civilian bureaucracy is now smaller than the combined state and local bureaucracies of California, New York, and Texas.

Figure 2–4 shows the relative decline in the size of the federal bureaucracy compared to the growth of state and local bureaucracies. One of every three bureaucrats worked for the federal government in 1950 (over one-half worked for the federal government in 1945), while about one in seven bureaucrats in 1998 were employed by the federal government.

BUDGETARY GROWTH

Even though federal employment stayed relatively constant, the federal budget has grown greatly from $46.2 billion in 1950 to $1.7 trillion in 1998. Budgetary growth without personnel growth is possible because the federal government engages in proxy administration. Proxy administration is nothing more than the federal government providing money to other organizations and governments and having those organizations actually provide the services (Kettl, 1988). Such programs as environmental protection, unemployment insurance, food stamps, family planning, and many others operate with federal funds and state personnel. Proxy administration permits the federal government to expand without increasing employment.

What causes the growth in government budgets is subject to some dispute. Buchanan and Tullock (1977) present the cynical view that government bureaucrats are strong advocates of greater growth based on the assumption that bureaucrats seek to maximize their budgets (see Niskanen, 1971). These demands coupled with the growing voting strength of government employees fuels the growth in budgets. A less cynical view of growth is presented by Baumol (1967); he argues that because the public sector is labor intensive it cannot take advantage of many technologies that increase productivity in the private sector. According to Baumol, capital-intensive processes have an inherent productivity advantage over labor-intensive processes.

Unfortunately for these advocates, the theories of neither Baumol nor Buchanan and Tullock are supported by evidence. In a series of studies of government growth, Berry and Lowery (1984a; 1984b; Lowery and Berry, 1983) found no support for these explanations of growth. Other studies have linked the growth in government to changes in demographic composition, changes in economic situations, changes in military tensions, and a variety of other factors (Lewis-Beck and Rice, 1985). At the state level, education budgets rise and fall in response to the number of school-age children (Dye, 1988). This literature is consistent with the common-sense view that government grows because people demand that government do things (Berry and Lowery, 1987). They demand better health care, a financially secure old age, safer workplaces, cleaner environments, and numerous other benefits. Politicians respond to these demands (Page and Shapiro, 1983), and part of the response is the expenditure of funds, which in turn increases the size of either the federal or the state/local bureaucracies. Government grows, in short, because people demand more government goods and services.

THE FEDERAL PERSONNEL SYSTEM

People in the public service are key actors in bureaucratic policymaking. The methods used to recruit bureaucrats are discussed because public service selection processes influence the type of bureaucrats hired. Public servants are recruited via a variety of different government personnel systems with each system designed to meet different needs. The largest system is the competitive civil service. Created in 1883, the civil service system, according to the predominant view, was established in response to the evils of the spoils system which led in part to the assassination of President Garfield by a disappointed office seeker (F. C. Mosher, 1982). A minority view holds that the merit civil service was created to protect the job security of partisan appointees who faced dismissal (Meier, 1981).

Whatever the reason for creating a merit-based civil service system in federal government, it gradually spread to most government agencies. In addition to the **career**

civil service, the federal government has four other personnel systems. Several federal agencies do not use the competitive civil service but rely on their own **agency merit systems**, which incorporate principles similar to those of the civil service system. These separate merit systems provide more specialized personnel than does the competitive civil service. The **senior executive service** (SES) is a special personnel system designed for higher level management positions. The **excepted service** provides for patronage employees and other personnel hired on a noncompetitive basis. The **executive schedule** encompasses the political leadership of the bureaucracy. Each of the five personnel systems—the civil service system, the separate merit systems, the senior executive service, the excepted service, and the executive schedule—has characteristics that affect the values held by the bureaucrats and, therefore, their role in policy process.

THE CAREER CIVIL SERVICE

Containing three-fifths of all civilian federal employees, the career civil service system is governed by the Office of Personnel Management (OPM) and the Merit Systems Protection Board (MSPB) along with the Office of the Special Counsel. These agencies were created by the Civil Service Reform Act of 1978, which split the old Civil Service Commission into two agencies. The OPM has a rapidly declining staff (6,200 in 1993 to 2,800 in 1997) who set personnel policy and oversee the process of hiring, training, promoting, and terminating personnel. The system is built around merit principles: individuals are hired based on qualifications, promoted based on job performance, and given tenure in their jobs. The OPM's role is to be a staff arm of the president and to manage government personnel. Under President Carter's director, Alan K. Campbell, much of the day-to-day work of the civil service system was delegated to individual agencies, with the OPM focusing on overall personnel policy questions. Under Reagan's first OPM director, Donald Devine, some effort was made to recentralize such functions in the OPM (Ban and Marzotto, 1984: 103). At the present time the agency has been so radically downsized that some observers question whether it can be an effective personnel agency (Marshall 1998). Personnel administration was considered a nonpartisan process under the old Civil Service Commission; with the creation of the OPM more political appointees were slotted to the agency, and partisan concerns were more prevalent (Rosen, 1986: 209).

The MSPB and the Office of the Special Counsel are designed to be watchdogs over the OPM; their function is to enforce merit principles and protect civil servants from arbitrary treatment. Civil servants who are disciplined or fired can appeal to the MSPB. Since its creation in 1978 the MSPB has been able to process cases reasonably well, but it has also been characterized by weak leadership and a general reputation for ineffectiveness (Ban, 1984; Vaughn 1988: 356). Bernard Rosen (1986: 212), a former high-level federal personnel administrator, has gone so far as to term the MSPB "irrelevant" and a "mirage." The Office of Special Counsel, far from being an aggressive defender of the rights of civil servants, has become a passive agency with little influence. A more recent study of the MSPB (West and Durant 1998; Durant and West 1998) gives it more positive remarks. It has established a reputation as a generally fair and impartial monitor of the disciplinary process. It has not had a major policy role, but the organization tends to see itself as an adjudicator of complaints rather than a policymaker.

The career civil service contains two merit systems. Blue-collar employees are hired under the OPM's wage board schedule based on local wages in the private sector. Because wage board employees are not policy making personnel for the most part, they will not be discussed here. Wage board employees are often union members, and these unions are active in federal personnel issues.

The more important career system is the general schedule (GS) for clerical, administrative, and professional personnel. The general schedule has fifteen grades from GS1 to GS15, and within each grade are steps based on seniority, time-in-grade, or scarcity of the person's skill (see Table 2–3).[4] The lower four grades of the general schedule are for clerical personnel, the clerks, administrative aides, and secretaries that perform the day-to-day nonpolicy tasks of the government. Grades 5, 7, and 9 are the professional entry level grades. A college graduate normally enters the civil service at GS5; if the graduate has a good undergraduate record or other qualifications, he or she might enter at GS7 level. A job applicant with a needed masters degree or a master of public administration degree would normally expect to enter at GS9. Grades 6, 8, and 10 are usually reserved for executive secretaries; most professional personnel skip these grades

• **TABLE 2–3** •

FEDERAL PAY SCHEDULE: ANNUAL SALARY IN DOLLARS

	STEPS									
GRADE	1	2	3	4	5	6	7	8	9	10
1	12,960	13,392	13,823	14,252	14,685	14,938	15,362	15,791	15,809	16,214
2	14,571	14,918	15,401	15,809	15,985	16,455	16,925	17,395	17,865	18,335
3	15,899	16,429	16,959	17,489	18,019	18,549	19,079	19,609	20,139	20,669
4	17,848	18,443	19,038	19,633	20,228	20,823	21,418	22,013	22,608	23,203
5	19,969	20,635	21,301	21,967	22,633	23,299	23,965	24,631	25,297	25,963
6	22,258	23,000	23,742	24,484	25,226	25,968	26,710	27,452	28,194	28,936
7	24,734	25,558	26,382	27,206	28,030	28,854	29,678	30,502	31,326	32,150
8	27,393	28,306	29,219	30,132	31,045	31,958	32,871	33,784	34,697	35,610
9	30,257	31,266	32,275	33,284	34,293	35,302	36,311	37,320	38,329	39,338
10	33,320	34,431	35,542	36,653	37,764	38,875	39,986	41,097	42,208	43,319
11	36,609	37,829	39,049	40,269	41,489	42,709	43,929	45,149	46,369	47,589
12	43,876	45,339	46,802	48,265	49,728	51,191	52,654	54,117	55,580	57,043
13	52,176	53,915	55,654	57,393	59,132	60,871	62,610	64,349	66,088	67,827
14	61,656	63,711	65,766	67,821	69,876	71,931	73,986	76,041	78,096	80,151
15	72,525	74,943	77,361	79,779	82,197	84,615	87,033	89,451	91,869	94,287

SOURCE: *U.S. Office of Personnel Management.*

---

[4] The general schedule once had eighteen grades, but the top three grades were moved into the Senior Executive Service under the Carter civil service reforms.

with two grade promotions such as from GS9 to GS11. Grades 13, 14, and 15 are the civil service's midlevel management positions; pay increases at this level are linked to performance on the job (Ingraham and Ban, 1984; Perry, 1988).

The general schedule contains a broad cross-section of the American people. The two groups compare favorably in terms of region of origin, occupation, education, income, social background, and race (Meier and Nigro, 1976). For many of these characteristics, the American people and the federal bureaucracy are replicas of one another. The differences are modest. Civil servants, for example, are slightly better educated and have slightly higher status occupations than the rest of the American people; but, as Charles Goodsell (1983) concludes, they are mostly "ordinary people." If the American people and the civil service differ on any significant dimension, it is partisanship. As would be expected, civil service employment appeals more to Democrats than to Republicans (Garand, 1990: 31) although this may be changing (Aberbach and Rockman, 1995). Republicans with their strong beliefs in smaller government are more likely to be attracted to private sector employment (Garand, Parkhurst and Seoud, 1991a: 205–7; Aberbach and Rockman, 1976: 459).

THE SENIOR EXECUTIVE SERVICE

Under the Civil Service Reform Act of 1978 most GS16, 17, and 18 positions became part of the senior executive service (SES). The SES contains 7,900 upper-level managers; of these 10 percent can be filled via political appointments, and the remainder must be careerists promoted from the career civil service system. SES members do not have the job protection rights that general schedule personnel do. SES members can be transferred to different positions both within their agency and in other agencies. If an SES member receives two consecutive poor performance evaluations, that member is dismissed from the SES. In compensation for reduced job security, a system of bonuses for exceptional performance and generally higher pay levels were envisioned (Ingraham and Ban, 1984). Although these financial rewards were generally not forthcoming (Newland, 1983), the creation of the SES gave the president and his appointees more flexibility in managing the bureaucracy.

THE SEPARATE MERIT SYSTEMS

Thirty percent of federal employees work for agencies that operate their own merit systems. The largest of these separate merit systems governs the U.S. Postal Service. Other agencies with separate merit systems include the Department of State for its foreign service officers, portions of the Public Health Service, the Department of Veterans Affairs for scientists and doctors, the Tennessee Valley Authority, the Federal Bureau of Investigation, and a portion of the Department of Energy that was once the Atomic Energy Commission. Separate systems are established to make public employment more attractive to professionals, to give the agency greater freedom in hiring and firing employees, or to allow greater employee screening before and during employment.

Each agency with a separate merit system establishes its own personnel procedures, thus making each merit system somewhat unique. Frederick Mosher (1982), however, has discovered some similarities in these separate merit systems. In these agencies employment is usually considered a career rather than a short period of employment. People joining the FBI or the Department of State are expected to remain with the agency until retirement. To ensure adequate promotion opportunities, which are considered to be automatic, these organizations permit little lateral entry (hiring at other than the entry level). Sometimes the systems have an up-or-out promotion system whereby an individual passed over for promotion is involuntarily retired.

THE EXCEPTED SERVICE

The excepted service is often considered the patronage area of the public service. In reality few members of the excepted service are patronage appointments despite the absence of competitive entry procedures and merit system principles. The excepted service includes four separate groups: schedule A, schedule B, schedule C, and the noncareer senior executives.

Schedule A includes those jobs for which recruiting personnel through competitive civil service procedures is not practical and the positions are not of a "policymaking" nature. Approximately 100,000 positions are included under schedule A. One major occupational category in schedule A is attorneys because the Office of Personnel Management is prohibited by law from spending any funds to examine or rate attorneys for public employment. Attorneys are hired by the individual agencies through noncompetitive procedures; that is, attorneys apply and the agencies select those they wish to hire without an exam or explicit rating system. Also included under schedule A are chaplains, undercover narcotics agents, and certain seasonal workers.

Schedule B includes additional jobs where recruiting persons through competitive civil service procedures is not practical and where the positions are not policymaking positions. The difference between schedule B and schedule A is that schedule B employees in order to be hired must take a noncompetitive exam while schedule A employees do not have this restriction. Relatively few people were hired under schedule B before 1980 (approximately 1,700). Good examples of schedule B personnel at that time were Treasury Department bank examiners and air force communications intelligence personnel.

Schedule B became important in 1982 when the Office of Personnel Management settled a discrimination lawsuit. In the court case *Luevano* v. *Devine*, minorities charged that the federal PACE exam (the entrance exam for administrators and professionals) discriminated against minority applicants. At the time the PACE exam was the major recruiting device for administrative and professional people at entrance levels and was used for 116 job classifications. As part of the settlement, the federal government abolished the PACE exam and promised to create valid exams for the 116 job classes. As an interim measure, agencies were authorized to use schedule B to hire entry level professional and administrative personnel. Unfortunately, the OPM did not quickly develop new exams, and as of 1985 only one of the 116 exams had been put in place; by 1988 six exams covered 52 percent of former PACE positions. Schedule B, as a result, was a major method of recruitment for several years. In 1987 in response to a court order, executive order 12596 converted these schedule B personnel to career civil service status (Ban and Ingraham, 1988: 711). The court order also blocked future use of schedule B for these positions (Havemann, 1987: 31). Two prominent scholars of federal personnel administration have concluded that the use of schedule B along with the decentralized hiring process resulted in hiring persons with narrower skills than the PACE exam would have. They feel this will benefit the agencies in the short run but will reduce the quality of federal management in the long run (Ban and Ingraham, 1988: 715).

Schedule C includes about 1,400 positions at GS15 and below that the president uses for patronage purposes. President Dwight Eisenhower created schedule C in response to perceived problems with the 1950s civil service. By 1953 a large majority of civil servants had not been appointed through competitive exams but were hired in a variety of ways including partisan preference and were later "blanketed in" (designated as civil servants without ever taking an exam). Since these civil servants were likely to be Democrats, President Eisenhower created schedule C so that he could appoint some Republican loyalists to lower-level bureau positions. Despite their patronage origins, schedule C employees have valid administrative functions in a nation that demands a responsive public service. Schedule C employees can provide "unbiased" information to the president so that he can determine if programs are working and if other bureaucratic information is accurate. Agency heads appoint schedule C personnel at their own discretion (with the assistance of the White House personnel office) without any civil service restrictions.

Noncareer senior executives are those members of the SES who are appointed by the president or agency heads; they perform jobs similar to schedule C personnel but at a higher level. Noncareer senior executives include some 700 policymaking positions. A noncareer SES person will usually either head a small bureau or serve in a staff unit that reports directly to an agency or department head. The agency head normally appoints noncareer SES persons, but the person's qualifications must be approved by the Office of Personnel Management.

THE EXECUTIVE SCHEDULE

The executive schedule includes those positions of a policymaking nature that the president appoints either with or without senatorial confirmation. Approximately 800 positions are in the executive schedule, and these positions have a pay schedule different from the rest of the public service. The executive schedule has five salary levels although most of the positions in the two lower levels were moved into the senior executive service in 1978. Level 1 is reserved for cabinet secretaries and their equivalents; level 2 positions are usually held by department undersecretaries or heads of major subcabinet agencies such as the Department of the Army. Levels 3, 4, and 5 are used for agency-head positions, with the exact level based on the size and prestige of the agency. Normally the chair of a regulatory commission would be a level 3, while the head of a bureau or independent agency would be a level 5. The status of these rankings is reflected by J. Edgar Hoover's successful effort to acquire a level 2 position to head the Federal Bureau of Investigation despite the fact that its size merited no more than a level 3 position.

Although this chapter has included the executive schedule, the noncareer Senior Executive Service, and schedule C in this discussion of personnel, they should not be considered part of the bureaucracy. They are part of the president's management and policy team. As such they are politicians not bureaucrats. Bureaucrats have a long-term attachment to specific agencies; politicians generally do not. This distinction is especially important when evaluating the quality of the bureaucracy (see Chapter 5). Many perceived failings of bureaucracy are, in fact, failings of the political system, not the bureaucracy.

....

DISMISSALS

No description of the federal personnel system would be complete without a discussion of the termination of federal employees. A common perception exists that civil servants cannot be fired; or if they are, the process takes an excessive amount of time. President Carter in 1978 made the misleading statement that only 226 people of the 2 million federal employees (not counting the Postal Service) had been fired for incompetence or inefficiency (*Washington Post*, March 3, 1978: A-18).

Although civil servants leave the public service at approximately one-half the rate of persons who leave private sector jobs, a large number of public employees leave government service. In fiscal year 1996 356,000 persons were separated from the federal service. Many leave involuntarily. A study by the Merit Systems Protection Board (1982) found that 12,078 persons were dismissed from the federal service for performance-related reasons in a single year. In addition, they estimated that perhaps another 5,000 persons were dismissed during their probationary periods (court decisions require that such dismissals be confidential so numbers can only be estimated). Although 17,000 is a significant number of dismissals, it clearly is an underestimate. In many cases individuals who would be dismissed are given the opportunity to resign or are transferred to other positions and subsequently resign. Most experienced managers know a variety of ways to eliminate inadequate employees without going through formal termination hearings. The 17,000 cases referred to by the Merit Systems Protection Board are probably only the difficult cases in which less conspicuous methods of termination were not possible.

A General Accounting Office (1991c) study confirmed these expectations. Their survey of supervisors revealed that 5.7 percent of all employees (about 89,500 persons) were performing at less than "fully successful" levels at some time during the year. Of these 38 percent improved their performance and were no longer a problem. Some 22 percent (or about 19,700 persons) voluntarily agreed to demotions, retirements, resignations, or other forms of discipline. Of the remaining 40 percent, disciplinary action was taken against about one-third (12,500 persons). The rest remained poor performers and were still employed. Combining these two studies suggests that about 37,000 federal employees are terminated or disciplined for performance reasons in any given year. Clearly these studies how that federal civil servants can be fired or disciplined for poor performance.

....

STATE AND LOCAL BUREAUCRACIES

Although this book focuses on the federal bureaucracy, the important role of state and local bureaus in the policy process must be discussed. As stated earlier, state and local bureaucracies have grown rapidly while the size of the federal bureaucracy has increased only slightly. The reasons for this growth and the importance of state and local bureaus to federal policymaking are related to the nation's federal system.

State and local government bureaucracies have grown in part because federal policy encourages that growth. Under a system of proxy administration, federal programs are implemented via federal government grants to state and local agencies that actually oversee the program. Proxy administration permits the federal government to use its superior ability to collect resources and its national scope to attack problems yet avoid the political embarrassment of a growing federal bureaucracy. The pattern of federal funds with state administration developed as early as the 1860s with the Department of Agriculture. The Department of Agriculture gave federal grants to state colleges and local governments to develop agriculture research and to disseminate the research through county extension agents. Garand (1988) has demonstrated that federal grants are a major factor in explaining the growth of state government.

Much federal policy, including most federal redistribution programs (see Chapter 4), is designed to include state implementation. An example is welfare. Spending federal money (with some matching state funds), states determine, within limits, the amount of benefits, eligibility, and other implementation questions. Actual benefits are then distributed by state agencies or local government agencies. The food stamp program is another federally funded program with the actual distribution of food stamps by local employees. Highway construction, Medicaid, and some health care programs are also administered in this manner.

State and local bureaucracies are often miniature federal bureaucracies in form and substance. These bureaus are generally organized functionally along the same lines as the federal government. Most states have both the executive departments and a variety of independent agencies that report directly to the governor similar to the federal government. Government corporations are also prevalent at the state and local level; Mitchell (1990: 930) counts 6,350 state and local government corporations that provide housing, economic development, and variety of other functions. All states and many localities have independent merit systems that range from more comprehensive than the federal system to token efforts covering only a small percentage of employees.

State and local bureaucracies are subject to the same political influences that affect the federal bureaucracy. Agencies such as the Wisconsin Department of Transportation set policy and develop clientele support among those they serve. Although generalizations about the relative influence of state and local bureaucracies are difficult to make, they are probably less powerful than federal bureaucracies because they are weaker on the dimensions that contribute to bureau power (see Chapter 3; Fox, 1974; Grady, 1989). Despite the present level of state and local bureau influence, the impact that these bureaus have on public policy is likely to increase as a result of federal policies. Under proxy administration the federal government grants money to state agencies with restrictions concerning the use of the money; often the money is given directly to a state bureau charged with administering the program at the state level. Because these state agencies may receive more money from the federal government than they do from the state legislature, they naturally develop close relationships with the federal bureau that controls its funds. The end result is that such state bureaus gain resources from the federal government and establish autonomy in the use of those resources because their funds are not subject to the control of the state governor or legislature (Hedge, 1983: 149; Hale and Palley, 1979: 16). State governments lose control over these state bureaucracies, and the bureaus are able to develop independent power bases just as federal bureaus do. According to former North Carolina Governor Terry Sanford (1967), who termed this relationship "vertical functional autocracies," the federal bureau to state bureau relationships weaken state governments by isolating state bureaus from political control. Sanford believed the independence of state and local bureaucracies created by the federal relationship was one of the major dangers facing state government.

SUMMARY

This chapter serves as a descriptive introduction to the federal bureaucracy so that the reader will have an adequate background for the remaining chapters. Common misperceptions about the size of the federal bureaucracy were discussed. The federal bureaucracy is not growing rapidly; in fact, it is actually decreasing in size. The recent growth in bureaucracy has taken place at the state and local levels, where the size of these bureaucracies has doubled in the past fifty years. The growth of state and local bureaucracies is, in part, a function of federal policy that emphasizes the use of federal funds and state administrative organizations to combat public policy problems.

The chapter also discussed the organization of the federal government and the federal personnel system. The federal government is organized functionally into fourteen departments. Each was created to meet different needs at different points in the nation's history. Despite the functional organization preference of the federal government, several other organizational forms exist at the federal level. Many independent agencies were created to avoid biases and problems of department organizations. A variety of third-sector institutions—government corporations, advisory boards, and so forth—blur the normal distinction between the public sector and the private sector. These organizations operate with the powers of government and the flexibility of business.

The federal personnel system is designed to meet the goals of merit performance and political responsiveness. The bulk of federal employees enter through the merit system either by competitive or noncompetitive exams and are promoted on the same basis. A small percentage of employees enter via patronage procedures to guarantee a cadre of public servants loyal to the president.

CHAPTER 3

BUREAUCRATIC POWER AND ITS CAUSES

According to Chapter 1, bureaucracy often exercises the political power normally reserved for others in the American polity. The existence of bureaucratic power raises two immediate questions. First, why do bureaucracies take over political functions and exercise the power that in traditional political theory is granted only to the "political" branches of government? Second, given the general causes of administrative power, why do some agencies such as the U.S. Army and the National Institutes of Health have political power and other agencies such as the Bureau of Public Debt and the Selective Service System struggle along without it?

This chapter discusses these two questions. Before controlling the bureaucracy can be discussed (see Chapters 6–8), knowledge about how both bureaucracy in general and specific bureaus in particular acquire resources and autonomy is necessary. First, a framework for assessing bureau power in relation to bureau environments is presented. Second, using this framework, the reasons why bureaucracy becomes a separate political force is discussed. Third, the reasons why some bureaus are able to act relatively autonomously within their own policy spheres is examined.

A FRAMEWORK FOR THE STUDY OF BUREAUS

Examining a bureau in isolation reveals little about how the bureau operates and why it acts as it does. Many students of bureaucracy believe that organizations can be understood only in terms of their environment and their relationships with that environment (Perrow, 1972; Rourke, 1984; Rainey, 1991). To understand the causes and consequences of bureaucratic power, therefore, a framework relating bureaucracy to its relevant environment must be constructed.

An open systems model for analyzing bureaus is presented in Figure 3–1. Although the model oversimplifies reality, it contains the major environmental influences on a bureau. A bureau receives from its environment a series of inputs that can be classified generally as demands and supports. The model postulates that the proximity of the

• FIGURE 3–1 •

THE ENVIRONMENT OF A BUREAU

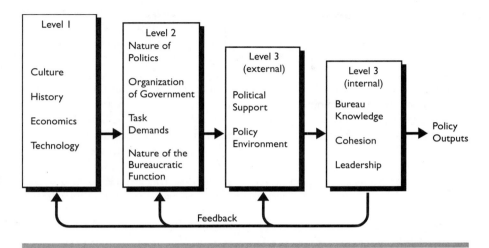

inputs to the organization is crucial in the bureau's power setting. Level 1 inputs from the environment have little impact on bureau power but rather establish the conditions necessary for bureaucracy to exist. A nation's culture, economics, history, and technology combine to favor the development of bureaucracy. Max Weber (1946) argued that the development of bureaucracy was related to the emergence of the money economy and that bureaucracy often formed by routinizing the charisma of a dominant leader. The impact of these level 1 factors on bureaus are relatively remote and will not be considered specifically in this analysis because they should be common to most developed or developing nations of the world. Our concern is with the more proximal factors.

The environmental influences in level 2 are more direct than those in level 1. An examination of level 2 influences will reveal why bureaucracy gains political influence at the expense of the other political institutions. Briefly, four factors (each discussed below) in the environment contribute to bureaucracy assuming political functions: (1) the nature of politics—what questions are considered in the realm of politics and what questions are the sphere of professionals and administration? (2) the organization of government—how is the political power of the state distributed among governmental institutions? (3) task demands—what tools are necessary to perform the tasks of government effectively? and (4) the nature of the bureaucratic function—how does implementation generate additional power for bureaucracy?

Level 3 environmental inputs determine whether or not a specific bureau has political power. These factors may be divided into two types, the bureau's external environment and its internal characteristics. The relevant portions of a bureau's external environment are its political support and its policy environment. A bureau's political support includes support from both citizens and government officials who deal with the bureau or are affected in some way by its operation. The policy environment of a bureau concerns the type of public policy—regulatory, distributive, redistributive, or other forms—that the bureau administers. The policy environment affects both political support and a bureau's internal sources of power. The internal sources of power are three: (1) knowledge—the information and expertise possessed by the agency; (2) cohesion—the commitment of the bureau's personnel to the organization and its goals; and (3) leadership—the effectiveness of the agency chief in managing the agency.

To some extent the distinction between level 2 and level 3 inputs to a bureau is artificial. Each of the level 2 inputs influences the level 3 inputs and, thus, is indirectly related to bureau power as well as the transfer of political functions to the bureaucracy. The organization of government, the nature of politics, and the function of bureaucracy, for example, combine to determine the political support of the bureau. The task demands of government policy and the bureaucratic function determine a bureau's knowledge. Leadership is a function of the organization of government and the nature of politics, while cohesion is directly related to the task demands of government policy. The distinction between level 2 and level 3, although partially artificial, is heuristically valuable, since level 2 inputs can effectively explain the transformation of bureaucracy into a political institution and level 3 inputs contribute directly, not through other factors, to the enhancement of the power of individual bureaucracies.

A final observation about the model in Figure 3–1 is in order. A bureau makes decisions, establishes policies, and delivers goods and services; these actions feed back to the environment. In this way a bureau affects the nature of the environment it occupies so that a bureau not only responds to its environment but over time can shape the environment that influences its power base (see Krause, 1996). The Department of Agriculture, for example, was active in forming the American Farm Bureau and developing the National Farmers' Union, giving the department a strong, unified clientele; the department could then cite Farm Bureau demands as evidence of public support (Baldwin, 1968; Brown, 1989). Similarly the Women's Bureau in the Department of Labor played a supportive role in the development of feminist groups during the 1960s (Duerst-Lahti, 1989). Most attempts to control bureaucracy (see Chapter 6) occur because bureaucracy has acted in such a way to influence other political institutions (Krause, 1996). O'Leary (1995) even documents a case in which lower and midlevel managers shaped the political environment; these lower level bureaucrats were able to marshal political support to enact federal legislation that authorized them to protect more wetlands in Nevada. These efforts were undertaken against the wishes of their hierarchical superiors. The open systems aspect of bureaus, therefore, is very important. Bureaus interact with the environment, and both the agency and the environment change as the result of the interaction.

WHY BUREAUCRACY IS A POLICYMAKING INSTITUTION

Bureaucracy is a fourth branch of government. The four level 2 factors within the environment that cause bureaucracy to assume political functions are (1) the nature of politics—the distinction between political and administrative questions; (2) the organization of government—the distribution of political power among government institutions; (3) task demands—the tools that are necessary to perform the tasks of government; and (4) the nature of the bureaucratic function.

THE NATURE OF AMERICAN POLITICS

The nature of American politics determines what questions will be resolved by the political branches of government, and this determination contributes to bureaucratic power. Early twentieth-century government theorists recognized a politics/administration dichotomy that required Congress or the president to decide policy questions. Bureaucracy's role according to Woodrow Wilson (1887) and Frank Goodnow (1900) was to neutrally implement policy determined elsewhere.

Even though it was never a realistic description of the political process (Appleby, 1949), the politics/administration dichotomy greatly influenced academic thoughts about bureaucracy. The growth of the positive state, however, contributed to the intellectual demise of the politics/administration dichotomy. People demanded that government solve economic, environmental, health, and numerous other problems. Congress, faced with demands for action and a lack of expertise to adequately design public policy to remedy perceived ills, turned to the bureaucracy.[1] The bureaucracy was delegated difficult public policy problems with little or no guidance. The Department of Energy, for example, is charged with resolving the nation's energy problems with the only requirement that programs be "equitable." The Environmental Protection Agency is charged with making waters fishable and swimmable by requiring the "best available technology." If determining future energy questions and regulating pollution involves political choices, then administrative agencies are forced to decide political questions.

The nature of politics in the United States blurs the distinction between political and administrative functions. Congress is no longer the dominant arbitrator of policy questions but rather shares this power with the federal bureaucracy and others. Congress gains in this process. By setting other policymaking mechanisms in action, Congress can produce better policies because the bureaus have access to more specialized knowledge than does Congress. The courts have sanctioned this situation with a series of court rulings upholding the delegation of legislative authority to administrative agencies even under vague standards (Davis, 1971).

Today "political" questions in the United States differ from "administrative" questions only by who decides them. Political questions are decided by Congress and the president, while administrative questions are decided by the bureaucracy. In content, political and administrative decisions do not differ. Congress, for example, sets pollution control emissions standards for automobiles but delegates the task of setting

---

[1] Congress turned to bureaucracy for reasons other than insufficient expertise. If a question was politically sensitive, delegating it to a bureau shifted the pressure from Congress to the bureau. Congress also delegates authority because it is unsure about the direction policy should take. The bureau can try several alternatives with Congress retaining a "veto" over the final policy.

pollution control standards for industry to the Environmental Protection Agency. The National Highway Traffic Safety Administration sets safety standards for motor vehicles, but in 1974 Congress decided that those standards could not include a seatbelt ignition interlock system. In many practical situations such as these, congressional action and administrative action deal with similar problems even though the scope of congressional lawmaking *can be* greater than the scope of administrative discretion (I cannot conceive that a bureau could decide the nation should have a social security system and then legitimately adopt one).

As Wolin (1960) notes, the United States, by permitting political abdication of policymaking, has sublimated political issues into professional, technical, and administrative questions. Since the American people perceive politics as basically corrupt and evil, the removal of policy from the political institutions has public support. In fact, the argument that sublimation is good appears frequently in the history of the nation; the merit system was created to remove personnel functions from the evils of spoils system politics; city manager government was established to free the city from the corruption of politics; the reform movement in education substituted professional control for political control.

Efforts to separate politics from administration enhance the autonomy of bureaucracy. Bachrach and French (1981) found that the establishment of merit principles and competitive exams in Belgium did more to establish administrative autonomy over the personnel process than to improve the competence of the civil service. Similarly in the United States, Nelson's (1982) history of the bureaucracy argues that attempts to control bureaucracy via merit systems actually lead to greater bureaucratic autonomy.

A good contemporary example of the sublimation of the politics is the nation's school system. The subjects and values taught in the nation's school system are of vital concern to the government because they establish the deep public support for the government that allows it to operate successfully. But the mere suggestion that government, particularly the federal government,[2] should have a say in what is taught in the nation's schools would be met with vocal and perhaps violent opposition. If a professional administrator decides curriculum content, however, that is permissible despite the fact that the end result is the same. Politicians can set general goals (e.g., higher test scores) but not specific policies (e.g., the appropriate social studies curriculum).[3] The public's preference for decisions by administrators, professionals, and technicians rather than by politicians undermines the legitimacy of politics. Politicians, as a result, lack the public support to be the major arbitrator of all political questions.

The nature of American politics, therefore, transforms bureaucracy into a political institution in two ways. First, the political branches of government acquiesce in the exercise of policymaking by bureaucracy. Second, by granting autonomy to bureaucratic institutions, political institutions grant legitimacy to bureaucratic institutions that they deny to themselves. Together these factors strengthen the hand of bureaucracy in the policy process.

---

[2] A recent manifestation of this opposition is the current resistance to a national performance exam for all students.

[3] One exception might be the recent prohibition of bilingual education by the state of California.

THE ORGANIZATION OF GOVERNMENT

American government is structured to require large policymaking bureaucracies. If any ideal other than private property was sacred to the founding fathers, it was the concept of limited government. Since the founders felt that everyone was subject to the corrupting temptations of power, the power that any one individual could exercise was severely limited. Government at the federal level was fragmented by the separation of political power into executive, legislative, and judicial branches, with each branch given the means to check the other two.

In dividing political power the fragmentation at the national level was augmented by a federal system with the federal and state governments exercising different powers. In the era of strong state government, the individual states provided a powerful check on the actions of the national government. Even today when the federal government is the dominant partner, it must rely on the states to implement many of its policies (Kettl, 1988). In the process states can limit the impact of federal policies (see Chapter 6; Scholz and Wei, 1985; Marvel, 1982; Thompson and Scicchitano, 1985; Wood, 1992).

If the formal fragmentation of American government was not sufficient, informal mechanisms also developed that further limited each political actor. Courts, by accepting the doctrine of judicial self-restraint, have sometimes limited their role in the policy process. Presidents have specialized in defense and foreign policy, areas where their impact is likely to be greater. The emergence of the United States as a world power means presidents spend most of their time on foreign policy to the neglect of domestic policy, a pattern that held even for a domestic advocate such as Lyndon Johnson. Congress, discovering that its size made action difficult if not impossible, divided itself into tens of committees and hundreds of subcommittees, all more or less independent of Congress as a whole. As a result Congress evolved into 535 separate political actors each pursuing different goals.

Politics, the unifying force in English government and American cities with political machines, does not unify American national government. Despite their increasing concern with political issues and the recent increase in party unity, American parties are broker parties; that is, they are broad coalitions more concerned with winning office than enacting specific policies. Candidates can run for office independently of the party organization and feel no need to follow the party's lead (if the party even has a position) on most issues. Without the disciplinary authority to purge mavericks and deny party nominations, the parties remain loose coalitions incapable of unifying the fragmented American policy process. The most recent effort at party control, the 1994 Republican "Contract with America," remained only a vague memory five years later.

Fragmentation permits loose coalitions of interests to dominate the policy process; most such coalitions contain at their core what has been termed a subsystem. A subsystem is a triumvirate of a bureau, congressional subcommittees, and the relevant interest groups who in normal political times can act independently of the major political institutions. The reason subsystems exist is that the nature of American politics ensures that bureaucracy has a role in determining political questions. After a policy question is shifted from a "political" to an "administrative" area, organized groups and others interested in the policy do not abandon their advocacy and return home simply because the area has become administrative (Truman, 1951). Interest groups remain to develop relationships with bureaucrats. These bureaus and interest groups are monitored by congressional subcommittees with functional interests similar to the bureaus. Long-term bureau–subcommittee relationships develop because most substantive committees and subcommittees are staffed with members of Congress who have a direct interest in the agency policy that they oversee (Freeman, 1965; Cater, 1964). Students of state government have identified similar patterns at the state level (Thompson, 1987: 764).

Together congressional subcommittees, interest groups, and bureaus have all the necessary political resources to satisfy each other's needs *as long as other political actors acquiesce.* Bureaus supply services or goods to organized groups but need resources to do so. Congressional committees supply the bureau with resources but need electoral support to remain in office and political support to win policy disputes in Congress. The interest groups provide political support to members of Congress but need government goods and services to satisfy members' demands. The result can be a tripartite relationship that has all the resources necessary to operate in isolation from politics if other interests are not adversely affected. The subsystem, therefore, can continue to satisfy each member's demands only if extensive political interest is not focused on the policy area. If the subsystem's activities become important to political leaders as the farm credit system did in 1985 when serious financial problems threatened the agricultural sector or as the savings and loan crisis of 1989 did, then the president and other members of Congress have incentives to intervene in the subsystem.[4] The best interests of all subsystem participants, therefore, demand that they resolve disagreements within the subsystem and limit the scope of any conflict.

Even though all members of a policy subsystem benefit from the relationship, the three participants are not necessarily equal (McCool, 1989). Veterans' organizations and congressional committees clearly dominate the Department of Veterans Affairs. Some research implies that agriculture agencies tend to dominate their clientele; as a result clientele provide a great deal of support but receive few tangible benefits (Meier, 1978). At the state level insurance companies and the regulatory agency often overwhelm legislative committees (Meier, 1988).

The openness of subsystems to outside influences is a key variable in policymaking. With the growth of entitlement programs and large national deficits, policy has taken on a distinctive zero-sum quality whereby benefits to one group can result in denial of benefits to others (Thurow, 1980). The structure of many subsystems has changed in this political environment with a variety of other actors more or less interested in subsystem decisions. Heclo (1978) terms the new-style policy system that has developed an "issue network" that includes state agencies, journalists, other federal agencies, academics/policy analysts, key executive branch personnel (such as OMB), and congressional staff members. Such a network might well contain two or more

---

[4] The breakup of subsystems has received a great deal of study recently under the rubric of agenda setting. Baumgartner and Jones (1993) argue that subsystems are in a period of equilibrium and that changes in the agenda open up subsystems to outside forces. Eventually, subsystem stability reasserts itself, but the new subsystems can look a lot different from the old subsystems.

advocacy coalitions pressing different issue positions within the subsystem (see Sabatier, 1988; Sabatier and Jenkins-Smith, 1993).

Perhaps the best way to view bureau–committee–interest group relationships is as a continuum with policy subsystems at one pole and issue networks at the other. Despite a recent academic preference for issue networks, McCool (1989: 264) identifies two political trends that increase the likelihood of policy subsystems. First, Congress and policymaking in general has become more decentralized; with decentralization, issue networks/policy subsystems are likely to become more homogeneous, have fewer policy disputes, and thus move toward the policy subsystem's pole. Second, requirements to consult with and accommodate others (e.g., state agencies, citizens) have increased. With increased accommodation, agencies have more choice in selecting specific groups and responding to them. A rational agency will respond to groups with interests similar to its own. Again the end result is more likely to be a policy subsystem than an issue network.

A third change that is also likely to foster more subsystems is the recent change in budgeting. As the result of an aggressive monetary policy and a good economy, the United States now faces a future with budget surpluses rather than deficits. Surpluses take away the zero-sum game that works against subsystem politics because the demands of one subsystem need not be traded off with that of another.

Actors in a policy network retain strong incentives to create or recreate subsystems if they can. Browne's (1990) work in agriculture shows that groups seek out niches that are not occupied by other interests and seek to avoid competition. At the state level, the work of Gray and Lowery (1996) shows a similar process. Subsystems offer the promise of stable, long term benefits, and political actors see this as the best of all possible worlds. Bickers and Stein (1994) found that federal agencies with grant programs systematically reduced the diversity of their recipients in the 1980s to facilitate supportive (read subsystem) group actions.

Bureaucracy is a key policy actor with opportunities to exercise political power whether the policy arena resembles a policy subsystem or an issue network. Because bureaucracies are permanent and because political power is too fragmented to give overall direction to public policy (Long, 1949), bureaucracies occupy a strategic position and can create coalitions in support of specific policy options. Bureaucracies generally have greater influence in subsystems, but they retain an influential role in issue networks. Recent work by Sabatier and Zafronte (1999), for example, shows that bureaucracies participate in advocacy coalitions on both sides of the issues in environmental policy.

TASK DEMANDS

A third reason why public bureaucracy has enjoyed a position of political power in the United States is the task demands of public policy. Most public policy is no longer so simple that legislative decrees are self-implementing (see Mazmanian and Sabatier, 1983). The complexities of modern public policy demand functions that can only be performed by large-scale formal organizations. No other institution can rival bureaucracy in its ability to perform the tasks of positive government.

The first task demand of current public policy is the ability to organize large projects. In a nation of more than 270 million people, few public policies are small scale. Making air travel safe requires traffic controllers monitoring millions of flights a year at thousands of airports. Maintaining a social security system means that every month 48 million checks are processed and a 173 million accounts credited. A clean environment requires that the Environmental Protection Agency define what the best available pollution control technology is for every type of manufacturing plant in the United States. Bureaucracy has several characteristics that permit it to organize large tasks effectively. The hierarchical nature of bureaucratic authority allows thousands of individuals to be coordinated indirectly by a few persons. If the Department of the Army is any indication, bureaucratic organizations can expand almost indefinitely. Bureaucracies also have continuity; permanent employees deal with the same problems day after day. As the bureaucracy becomes accustomed to its tasks, it develops standard operating procedures and shortcuts for handling problems. Thus a bureaucratic organization learns and becomes more effective as time passes (Sabatier, 1988; Kettl, 1990: 415; Lebovic, 1995; Meier and Keiser, 1996). Bureaucracies also have permanence, which, combined with continuity, gives the bureaucracy the advantage of time. Unlike the president who must conduct foreign policy in the morning, tax policy in the afternoon, and regulatory policy after dinner, a bureaucracy can concentrate on a single problem or series of problems. A bureaucracy, as a result, is under no pressure to solve a problem immediately; it can nibble away at the problem until an adequate solution is found.

A second task demand of government is the need for expert knowledge when dealing with public policy problems. The average person does not have knowledge and training to understand the intricacies of tax policy, the limits of health care research, or the technicalities of weapons development. Compared to other political institutions, this task demand is best met by bureaucracy because the large size, continuity, and permanence of bureaucracy permit specialization. Specialization allows bureaucracy as an entity to know more about a public policy than any individual or institution that lacks its size, continuity, and permanence (that is, everyone else). Despite years of concentration even the House Ways and Means Committee must occasionally defer to the tax experts in the Internal Revenue Service. That any collection of individuals knows more about government bonds than the Federal Reserve is difficult to believe. Specialization also means that many bureaucrats are highly trained professionals—tax experts, doctors, scientists, accountants, and so forth. Fifty-eight percent of the federal government's white-collar employees are classified as professionals by the Office of Personnel Management. Professionalization further augments influence because, as politics becomes sublimated into administration, politicians will defer to experts. While alternative sources of expertise exist in think tanks and in the other political institutions, they usually cannot match the bureaucracy's knowledge.

A third task demand of public policy that contributes to bureaucratic influence is the need for fast, decisive actions. Policymakers want clean air as soon as possible, schools to be desegregated with all deliberate speed, and a cure for AIDS now. If bureaucracy is structured hierarchically and if the bureaucracy has norms of obedience and discipline, it possesses the ability to act quickly. Although bureaucracy is often cited for its slow procedures, too many counterexamples exist to condemn all bureaucracies as slow especially when compared to other policymaking institutions. The

Defense Department quickly deployed troops and implemented the 1991 war with Iraq. The Food and Drug Administration set records for fast rulemaking when it required tamper-proof containers in the wake of the Tylenol poisonings and when it "fast-tracked" experimental drugs for AIDS. In response to congressional mandates, the Department of Agriculture's Women, Infants and Children (WIC) nutrition program expanded by 60 percent in only six months (Rauch, 1984: 2199).

The task demands of public policy, therefore, increase the bureaucracy's influence in the policy process. The need to perform large tasks, the need for expert knowledge, and the need for fast, decisive action are all needs where bureaucracy can perform better than other political institutions. Because it holds a quasimonopoly on the tools to meet these needs, bureaucracy may be the only way to deliver the goods and services demanded by the public.

THE NATURE OF BUREAUCRACY'S FUNCTION

Bureaucracy gains political power relative to other institutions of government from the nature of the bureaucratic function. Although bureaucracy is involved in all stages of the policymaking process—writing legislation, adopting policy through rulemaking, and evaluating policy—bureaucracy's primary function is to implement public policy (Anderson, 1997; Jones, 1984). Most astute analysts of public policy have given up the idea that implementation is unimportant; it contains the roots of additional power (O'Toole and Mountjoy, 1984; Mazmanian and Sabatier, 1983; Goggin et al., 1990).

The initial reason why implementation contributes to the power base of all bureaucracies is that law or policy statements can never be specific enough to cover all future applications. The function of bureaucracy is to fill in the gaps of official policy, and filling in the gaps means the exercise of discretion. Congress has passed laws prohibiting deceptive advertising, but the Federal Trade Commission must decide if a given commercial is deceptive. Similarly Congress has decreed that health and safety hazards in the workplace should be limited, but the Occupational Safety and Health Administration both defines what the hazards are and enforces the safety and health regulations concerning them (Thompson and Scicchitano, 1985). According to Theodore Lowi (1969), administrative discretion is increasing because our laws are less specific than they were in the early twentieth century. As a result, bureaucrats have more discretion; and policy implementation decisions have a greater impact on public policy.

During the implementation process, changes in the policy environment also require bureau discretion. The Department of Agriculture in the 1960s was charged with maintaining farm income by decreasing the supply of farm goods. After large Soviet grain purchases resulted in severe commodity shortages in the early 1970s, the USDA's priorities changed to increasing production. As the fruits of the 1970s policy were harvested, the department's priorities changed again to restricting farm production in hopes of raising farm income (Anderson, Brady, Bullock, and Stewart, 1984).

A special case of change in the policy environment is the discovery of new information. If the National Institutes of Health discovered a radical new cure for AIDs tomorrow, we would expect them to pursue this cure with new research rather than await political action. When effective performance requires changes in policy as the result of new information, discretion must be given to bureaucrats. If Congress or the president had to adopt new policies whenever the environment changed, they would be swamped with decisions. Congress and the president set priorities, and bureaucrats consider them but are granted sufficient discretion to make effective policy.

Another reason for discretion in policy implementation is the uncertainty of political forces. Congress may desire some action but be unsure about specifics. In that case giving discretion to an agency permits the agency to bargain with interested parties and to try out several policies without lobbying Congress for changes. In other circumstances with unsettled political forces, Congress or the president may wish to take action on a problem but have no preferred solution (for example, energy policy from 1973 to 1977, Kash and Rycroft, 1984), so they establish an agency charged with solving the problem subject to congressional review. Discretion with post hoc review provides both action and flexibility.

Implementing public policy, the task of bureaucracy, is not a simple process. Other political elites and possibly even the public are not satisfied if implementation is the strict application of a detailed law. They expect and demand implementation that includes flexibility, creativity, and responsiveness to changing needs (see Chapter 5). Only if the bureaucracy is granted discretion can it perform according to expectations.

Clearly Max Weber (1946) was correct; bureaucracy is a power instrument of the first order. Bureaucracy has become a powerful force in American politics because the nature of politics thrusts bureaucracy into policymaking, because the organization of government requires bureaus to acquire power, because the task demands of current policy require qualities that bureaucracy monopolizes, and because bureaucratic policy implementation entails discretion. Several factors basic to the American political process, therefore, contribute to the strengthening of bureaucracy and require that bureaucracy be a coequal fourth branch of government.

SOURCES OF BUREAU POWER

Although bureaucracy in general has become a powerful political institution, individual bureaus vary a substantially in their influence over public policy. Powerful agencies such as the Defense Department, the Environment Protection Agency, and the National Institutes of Health have both resources and autonomy; but other agencies such as the Selective Service System, the Arms Control and Disarmament Agency, the American Battle Monuments Commission, and the Bureau of the Mint have neither. The level 2 (see Figure 3–1) political and technical environment of American politics that permits the growth of bureaucracy as a political institution also affects whether or not an individual bureau has power. Bureau power is a function of the policy environment, public support, the bureau's special knowledge, the cohesion of bureau personnel, and bureau leadership.[5]

A bureau's policy environment actually interacts with the other four causes of bureau power, determining which of them are significant. Because the policy environment

---

[5] The following discussion draws heavily on Rourke (1984). The analysis contains Rourke's four determinants of bureau power—constituency support, expertise, leadership, and vitality, although the variables have been regrouped and integrated into the general model presented earlier in the chapter.

has such an impact on all these factors and also affects the policymaking process within a bureau, discussion of the policy environment will be deferred to Chapter 4. The remainder of this chapter discusses the political support, knowledge, cohesion, and leadership of government bureaus.

EXTERNAL SOURCES OF BUREAUCRATIC POWER: POLITICAL SUPPORT

A bureau's political support is its relative balance of support to opposition among the people and groups affected by the bureau's actions (Downs, 1967; Rainey, 1991). Because a bureau's clientele can provide political support that other policymaking elites need to perform effectively in office, public support can be a source of bureau power. A political elite who opposes a bureau's position must bear the wrath of that bureau's supporters. Many political elites will also respond to a bureau's supporters for nonelectoral reasons. Groups supporting or opposing bureaus are perceived as representing legitimate interests that government should satisfy (Zeigler and Peak, 1972). American political elites do not respond to the merchant marine because they fear the electoral consequences of that small group, but rather because maintaining a U.S. shipping capacity is a valid political interest worthy of representation.

Bureaus develop public support in response to three level 2 environmental conditions that make bureaucracy a political institution (Figure 3–1). The nature of American politics, by sublimating political questions into administrative ones, makes the bureau decide questions of concern to interest groups. The organization of American government, with its fragmentation and issue networks, forces bureaus to come to terms with their clientele because neither Congress nor the president provide the support necessary for a bureau to impose its wishes on its clientele. Finally, the nature of the bureaucratic function also facilitates the development of a positively balanced power setting by allowing the bureau to exercise discretion in policy implementation, discretion that can be used to build political support.

A bureau's public support ranges from diffuse support for the bureau's general function to specific support for individual programs. This section examines the various sources of public support for agencies beginning with the most diffuse and proceeding through the more specific.

Public Opinion

On the diffuse end of the public support continuum is the general public opinion concerning the agency and its functions. Public opinion can either support an agency (e.g., the Environmental Protection Agency) or oppose an agency (e.g., Internal Revenue Service). Individual agencies, however, vary greatly in public visibility; a public opinion poll found that 80 percent of the public felt they understood the functions of the Food and Drug Administration, 66 percent understood the Environmental Protection Agency, and 59 percent understood the Consumer Product Safety Commission, while only 39 percent and 30 percent respectively understood the functions of the Federal Trade Commission and the Securities and Exchange Commission (Barringer, 1981). Without some understanding of what an agency does, public opinion in regard to the agency is meaningless. Agencies recognize this relationship and often seek to create a favorable image via public relations efforts. Yarwood and Enis (1982: 39) found that the U.S. government was the 25th largest advertiser in the nation, ranking ahead of J.C. Penney, ITT, and Colgate-Palmolive. The Department of Agriculture alone annually issues 3,000 publications and distributes 9.3 million bulletins (Yarwood and Enis, 1982: 38). In 1981 federal agencies spent an estimated $1 billion on public relations (Relyea, 1986).

In situations in which few individuals have feelings one way or another about an agency, the public opinion most relevant to an agency is public opinion concerning the agency's general function, for example, agriculture, foreign aid, defense, health, and so forth. The public's regard for the agency's function affects the value other political elites place on the agency and, thus, its relative position of power.

Wlezien (1995) contends that public opinion acts like a thermostat for public policy. Whenever policy diverges from opinion or opinion changes, policy is then readjusted to conform with public opinion. Agencies are swept along with other political institutions in the adjustments of this thermostat process.

Defense spending provides a good example of Wlezien's argument. Figure 3–2

• FIGURE 3–2 •

DEFENSE BUDGETS AND PUBLIC OPINION

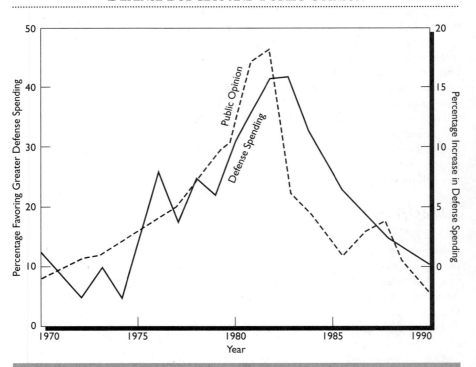

SOURCE: Gallup polls, cited in *Public Opinion,* and federal budgets.

shows public opinion on defense spending and the growth of the Defense Department's budget. Beginning in the late 1960s public opinion turned against defense spending, and defense budgets suffered a decline. After several years the public began to oppose cuts in the defense budget, and the defense budget began to grow again. With the rise of $200 billion annual deficits in the 1980s, public opinion again favored restrictions on defense spending; and efforts were made to reduce this budget. Although many other factors affected the Defense Department's budget from 1960 to 1990, general trends in public opinion and defense spending were often similar.

A bureau basking in the warm glow of diffuse public support should be able to press its claims for resources with more authority. The Environmental Protection Agency was able to achieve major budget growth during the strong environmental movement of the early 1970s. Later energy programs grew rapidly after the 1973 Arab oil embargo. During the late 1980s, drug control programs mushroomed. Table 3–1 presents the 1996 national spending priorities of the American people. These figures suggest that bureaus able to tie their programs to education, health care, drug abuse, environmental protection, crime and perhaps social security should fare reasonably well. Bureaus in the areas of foreign aid, space exploration, defense, and welfare generally face a hostile public.

Bureaus recognize that public opinion can be influenced by a favorable media image and, thus, seek to cultivate members of the media. The FBI's J. Edgar Hoover

---

• **TABLE 3–1** •

NATIONAL PRIORITIES

We are faced with many problems in this country, none of which can be solved easily or inexpensively. I'm going to name some of these problems and for each one I'd like you to tell me whether you think we're spending too much money on it, too little money, or about the right amount.

POLICY AREA	% TOO LITTLE	% ABOUT RIGHT	% TOO MUCH
Space exploration	11.74%	37.94%	50.32%
Protecting the environment	60.06%	30.86%	9.08%
Health care	62.08%	31.85%	6.07%
Problems of big cities	52.03%	30.72%	17.25%
Combating crime	70.93%	23.40%	5.68%
Drug addiction	63.68%	28.72%	7.60%
Education	59.43%	32.87%	7.70%
The condition of blacks	33.54%	44.69%	21.78%
The military	22.58%	44.20%	33.21%
Foreign aid	4.85%	20.93%	74.22%
Welfare	19.97%	28.83%	51.20%
Social security	53.57%	40.01%	6.41%
Highways	40.22%	51.31%	8.47%
Parks and recreation	32.09%	61.62%	6.29%

SOURCE: National Opinion Research Center, General Social Survey, June 18, 1996 release.

was the bureaucratic master of media influence; Hoover's public-enemy campaigns (designating certain criminals as public enemies) generated massive media attention. Hoover also hired a ghost writer to author books for him and was instrumental in getting favorable treatment of the FBI in motion pictures and television shows (Poveda, 1990). The FBI also sought jurisdiction over kidnapping and bank robbery, highly visible crimes that were relatively easy to solve. Although Hoover's media skills have yet to be matched by other bureaucrats, efforts to influence media are fairly universal among agencies. The Defense Department, for example, obviously learned a great deal about media and its impact in the 1980s; the Persian Gulf War generated far more immediate favorable publicity than did the invasion of Grenada or Panama.

The precise impact of public opinion on bureaucracy and public policy is subject to some debate. Some scholars contend public opinion has a dominant impact on public policy. Page and Shapiro examined 357 significant changes in public opinion over an extended period of time. In instances where good output measures of public policy existed and when the change in public opinion was lasting, Page and Shapiro (1983: 180) found that policy shifted to be congruent with public opinion 87 percent of the time. Examining tax and education policies at the state level, Lowery, Gray, and Hager (1989) also found policies over time became more consistent with public opinion. Peters and Hogwood (1985) linked public opinion more directly to bureaucratic growth. They identified issue cycles when certain public opinion issues became salient and found that during the high point of these cycles bureaucratic activities also increased (Peters and Hogwood, 1985: 250). The issue cycles they found included public works, commerce, and agriculture in the 1930s; defense, international relations, and housing during the 1940s; social welfare and transportation during the 1960s and environmental protection in the 1970s.

Although favorable diffuse support can be used to extract resources from other political elites, public opinion is fickle; it changes, sometimes rapidly. An agency dependent on the whim of public opinion is in a precarious position. The public, for example, strongly supported the U.S. space program in the early 1960s, but by 1965 and more so by 1971 the space program's public support had dissipated and NASA faced funding problems. Support increased again during the 1980s but dropped after the *Challenger* explosion and the problems with the Hubble telescope. Support in the mid-1990s rose briefly with the *Sojourner* mission to Mars. The drastic nature of public opinion swings is shown by the overwhelming support for increased defense expenditures (63 percent) in 1950 compared to the small support for defense expenditures in 1969 (8 percent). Given the transitory nature of public opinion, a bureau is well advised to seek more reliable support to ensure its continued survival.

Clientele Support

Bureaus can gather specific support from their clientele—the people who directly benefit or suffer from the programs that the bureau administers. The Environmental Protection Agency, for example, affects a wide variety of people including environmental groups such as the National Wildlife Federation and the Sierra Club, business organizations that must install pollution control devices, state pollution control agencies that implement EPA rules, scientists who study environmental problems, journalists who cover the area, and other agencies with related problems such as the Forest Service or the Bureau of Land Management. Since clientele may be either supportive or hostile, it behooves the bureau to have more support than opposition. Even members of Congress recognize this necessity; in one survey of members 73 percent stated that bureaus should have close relationships with their clientele (Aberbach and Rockman, 1978: 820). Favorable clientele support means some portion of an elected policymaker's constituency benefits from bureau programs and feels they are worthwhile. If a bureau has clientele support, a rational elected official will respond by granting the bureau more resources or permitting it to operate with greater autonomy.

Although clientele are, all things considered, better to have than not, clientele vary in their contribution to a bureau's political support. Clientele groups range in size from the gigantic American Federation of Labor-Congress of Industrial Organizations (AFL-CIO) to the relatively small American Soybean Producers. Generally the literature argues that, all things being equal, the larger a bureau's clientele is, the more weight clientele support is given in allocating resources (Rourke, 1984; Stigler, 1971). Size implies that the clientele can influence, more or less effectively, electoral consequences (in terms of votes and contributions) for other political elites. In addition, the larger a specific clientele group is, the easier the group can argue that its demands are broad enough to be considered a "public interest" rather than a narrow private interest. Despite the difficulties in defining the "public interest," a clientele group's ability to tie its demands to the public interest benefits the agency.

Although the hypothesis concerning size makes theoretical sense, empirical studies of politics have found that clientele size is rarely relevant. In insurance regulation those states with larger insurance industries do not establish regulation more favorably to the industry (Meier, 1988). The Environmental Protection Agency faces a political environment where the regulated industry always has more resources than the proenvironmental forces, yet many times the EPA expressly favors environmental groups (Ringquist, 1993; Vig and Kraft, 1984). Despite the overwhelming opposition of airline companies to deregulation and almost no initial support for deregulation, the Civil Aeronautics Board and the Congress deregulated air travel after 1978 (Brown, 1987). In fact, one study of interest groups shows several cases where smaller groups were able to triumph over larger groups in the policy process (Ornstein and Elder, 1978). Larger groups have more difficulty reaching consensus and often react too slowly to affect the policy process.

With the growth in policy complexity, information can be a valuable clientele resource. Interest groups who supply objective or alternative sources of information are valuable particularly to regulatory agencies since they permit a regulatory agency to avoid reliance on the regulated industry for information. Such information may permit an agency to develop greater autonomy. The value of information as a clientele resource is best illustrated by the rise in influence of public interest groups who have few traditional resources but often access to good information (J. M. Berry, 1977).

Clientele also vary in their geographical dispersion (Rourke, 1984). If a bureau's clientele are centered in only one part of the country, then other political elites may perceive that the bureau serves only a local interest. Politicians not from the area will be little concerned. The Bureau of Reclamation, for example, serves a western clientele;

the National Aeronautics and Space Administration's clientele are concentrated in Texas, Maryland, Florida, California, and Ohio. In contrast to these narrow bases, the Department of Defense engages in significant activity in most of the nation's congressional districts, and the Department of Labor's clientele is organized in most areas of the country. Some agencies exploit this, as the Navy did during the mid-1980s when it begin to disperse its fleet so that as many cities as possible could be home ports and thus gain the benefits of the Navy's presence (Weisskopf, 1985: 12).

The more cohesive a bureau's clientele is, the more value the clientele is in developing the bureau's power base (Rourke, 1984). A cohesive clientele is one that is organized, self-conscious (that is, recognizes that it has policy interests), and receives tangible benefits from the bureau. A small, well-organized, cohesive clientele is always better than a large, unorganized clientele because the former has the motivation and the ability to mobilize support for the bureau. As a result, producer interests *should* normally contribute more to the power base of a bureau than consumer groups or any other similar broad, but unorganized group.[6] Dissension among clientele groups weakens the agency because it can no longer claim that it is serving all its clientele.

Clientele groups vary by how intensely committed to a bureau they are, and this variation affects the bureau's political support. If an interest is intensely committed to a bureau, then it will be more loyal and more aggressive in advocating the bureau's interest. Ideally, loyalty and commitment can be best assumed if the clientele has only one bureau that can meet its demands. In such circumstances the interest is placed in a dependent position vis-à-vis the bureau. The railroads had this relationship with the Interstate Commerce Commission in the 1950s, as does the U.S. Merchant Marine with the Maritime Administration at the present time. With this commitment, the bureau can expect the clientele to strongly advocate and never criticize (assuming the bureau keeps the clientele reasonably happy).

Bureaus can augment their political support if the public in general and other political elites in particular hold the bureau's clientele in high esteem (Rourke, 1984). The impact of professional clientele such as physicians and scientists is impressive, especially when compared to such clientele as welfare recipients or prison inmates. Since professional groups also tend to be well organized, the impact of prestigious clientele is multiplied. High esteem is in the eye of the beholder, of course. Some political elites give great deference to environmental groups while others give similar deference to manufacturers. Bureaus lacking impressive clientele occasionally compensate by having well-known people support them. The agriculture community did this in 1985 when several actresses who had starred in films concerning farm problems testified before Congress in support of the farm bill.

Finally, the structure of a bureau's clientele effects its political support (Rourke, 1984). If a bureau's clientele is organized into a single group, the bureau probably depends on the clientele more than the clientele depend on the bureau. If the clientele

---

[6] In reality, the orientation of other political elites is crucial. If other political elites are proconsumer, then strong government support from producer clientele can be taken as an indicator of poor performance. Such a relationship has been found in insurance regulation (Meier, 1988) and could be found in other areas by reading congressional oversight hearings.

group withholds its support, the bureau is left with little specific public support. As a result the interest group can exercise a de facto veto power over bureau actions. Other political elites may perceive such a bureau as the captive of a narrow interest and deny it resources or autonomy. A bureau is more fortunate if its clientele are organized into several groups with no single dominant group. Multiple groups permit the bureau to be flexible, playing one interest's demands against another's.

The ideal clientele for a power-seeking bureau, therefore, is one that is dispersed geographically throughout the nation, well-organized, intensely committed to the organization, in possession of valuable policy information, valued in the eyes of the nation, and organized into several groups. The more a bureau is able to build and maintain a positive rather than a negative evaluation by such clientele, the greater the political support the bureau will have.

Bureaus are hardly passive pawns of their clientele. Many can choose which clientele to serve or what position to take relative to their clientele. The Food and Drug Administration can seek support from either pharmaceutical companies or the public interest groups that support stronger drug regulation (Quirk, 1980). The Federal Aviation Administration by determining how strict to set airline safety standards can seek to have either airlines or airline passengers as clientele. The Federal Reserve banks target major corporations as their clientele and appoint top executives from major corporations to their boards of directors in an effort to generate business support for the autonomy of the Federal Reserve (Havrilesky, 1986: 398). Such choices are important because the selection of certain clientele might violate the values of agency bureaucrats (e.g., the EPA and polluters) or might result in a loss of support from political elites who feel specific clientele should benefit (e.g., consumers versus industry in consumer protection policies).

Richard Fenno (1966) in his classic study of congressional budgeting has shown that clientele support is related to a bureau's ability to extract resources. Bureaus with strong public support were able to expand their resource base by receiving larger appropriations from Congress. Rubin (1985) also found that clientele support was the key variable in permitting some agencies to avoid major budget cuts in during the Reagan administration. Other studies of budgeting reveal a complex impact for clientele support. Meier and Copeland (1983) found that clientele support helped agriculture agencies avoid budget cuts in both the House and the Senate (it had no impact on budget growth) but that these impacts were eliminated by the conference committee. Copeland (1985) reexamined budgeting patterns after the conference committee was opened to the public (group concessions are easier to eliminate if the process is private) and found that interest group support did result in greater budget support for the supported agencies.

Other Political Elites

Other members of an issue network can have the same impact on resources and autonomy as traditional clientele. The support of journalists allowed individual members of the EPA to leak crucial documents, thus damaging the administration of Anne Burford and eventually leading to her ouster (Vig and Kraft, 1984). State agencies that enforce traffic safety laws have become a strong force for greater automobile safety. State program administrators for nutrition programs have developed strong links to Congress that are used to protect the Women, Infants, and Children nutrition program (Rauch, 1984: 2198). Even academics have been able to affect bureau power bases and policy actions; economists were critical in setting the intellectual environment favoring deregulation of the airlines, surface transportation, antitrust policy, and other areas (Derthick and Quirk, 1985; Eisner, 1991).

Perhaps the most important political elites are other policymakers, individuals in Congress and the executive branch. A long-held truism of politics is that a member of Congress is the best lobbyist an interest group or an agency can have. Members of Congress may be enticed to testify for a bureau if the members' constituents are served by the bureau. The Agricultural Research Service is very effective in getting members of Congress to advocate research programs that affect their districts (Hadwiger, 1982). One study of budget subcommittee actions found that budget decisions were highly responsive to requests by individual members of Congress, far more responsive than they were to requests from interest groups (Wanat, Burke, and Snodell, 1984: 396).

Separating out the difference between clientele support and support from individual members of Congress is sometimes difficult since they often overlap. In fact, such support may well be purposely linked because interest groups can generate support for an agency's programs by making campaign contributions. The popular literature contains numerous examples that show supporters of certain agencies (say, defense) receive larger campaign contributions from defense interest groups (Mapes, 1984: 1942). The more scholarly literature also shows an impact. Welch (1982) found that members of Congress who received contributions from milk producers were more likely to vote to raise milk price supports. In studies covering several areas, both Ginsberg and Green (1979) and Wright (1985: 411) also show a small but positive impact of campaign contributions on program support.

Support for a bureau among members of Congress is beneficial, but a bureau does not need political support from just any member of Congress. If the bureau can develop good relations with strategically placed members of Congress, then it should fare well at the hands of Congress. The leadership on the substantive committees that oversee the agency is important because these committees authorize bureau programs. Members of the appropriations subcommittee for the agency are vital since they have control over the agency's resources.

Since substantive committees are staffed according to the interests of member's constituencies, substantive committee support for a bureau is usually forthcoming (Ray, 1980; Fenno, 1966; McCool, 1989). Substantive committee members are usually bureau advocates. Welch and Peters (1983: 384), for example, found that every member of the House Agriculture Committee had a private financial interest in some phase of agriculture. Although agencies seek to cultivate these ties (Weisskopf, 1985), studies show that placing agency units in a congressional district can increase support for that individual program but not necessarily the entire agency (Ray, 1981).[7]

---

[7] McCool (1990: 280) argues that members of Congress do not actually need to benefit from committee assignments. If they perceive there are benefits, whether or not they actually materialize, this should be sufficient to seek substantive committee posts and support agency activities.

The appropriations subcommittees were traditionally viewed as the guardians of the public purse, and these subcommittee members treated agency claims with skepticism (Fenno, 1966). Under such norms if an agency could convince the appropriations subcommittee leadership that it was a well-meaning, efficient organization, then it could benefit many times over. Fenno (1966) found that legislative support for a bureau was translated into support for the bureau's budget; favored agencies were successful in avoiding cuts in their budget, that is, they received a higher percentage of the money that they requested. In recent years, however, the role of the appropriations committees has become less clear. With high inflation, executive budget cutting, and massive deficits, members of appropriations committees have become more supportive of spending (Kettl, 1989). Appropriations support is still important; the role the committee members play in the process, however, has become similar to the role played by substantive committee members.

Support for a bureau's programs can also be generated within the executive branch of government. Executive branch support resembles political support in general because executive branch support may be specific or diffuse. The best political support in the executive branch is presidential support (or gubernatorial support at the state level). In a study of eight agencies Shull (1978) found that presidential endorsement of an agency's position resulted in successful legislation 76 percent of the time. Thompson (1987) found support from the governor was a crucial factor in the ability of state agencies to get budget increases. The amount of specific, program-oriented support from the president or the governor, however, is limited. More often the president or the governor can give diffuse support to an agency by advocating general priorities that favor the agency's function as President Johnson did for poverty programs. In more recent times President Reagan's support for defense resulted in higher appropriations for all military programs. President Bush was able to bolster appropriations for drug abuse control. President Clinton, however, appeared to have little impact on appropriations.

More specific, program-oriented support must come from other members of the institutionalized presidency, specifically bureaucrats in the Office of Management and Budget (OMB). The OMB has developed into a first-rate power broker owing to presidential confidence and its strategic location. It acts as a budget and legislative clearing house; all bureau proposals for additional legislative authority must be cleared by the OMB. Of course, the OMB also compiles the budget and makes decisions on resources often with little presidential guidance. John Wanat (1974), a perceptive student of federal budgeting, found the OMB was the focus of key important budget decisions (see also Kamlet and Mowery, 1983: 640; Bromiley and Crecine, 1980; Pfiffner, 1979). OMB decisions define the base from which congressional decisions are made. Under the direction of David Stockman in the 1980s, the OMB increased its technological capacities and became one of the dominant policy actors in Washington. As a result, support from the OMB is a resource that all bureaus desire.

Executive branch support can also be generated among other government bureaus (see Rainey, 1991). For example, NASA could have increased its power base in the late 1960s if it had been more effective in gaining support from the Department of the Interior, the USDA, the Weather Bureau, and other agencies for its manned space program. These agencies' desire for cheaper unmanned satellites for the earth-resources and weather-prediction programs contributed to a lower priority for manned space. Not until the space shuttle program and the use of the shuttle to launch such satellites did NASA receive much support from these agencies. Lack of support can seriously limit an agency's actions. The Department of the Interior cannot set policies for national parks without considering the positions of the Forest Service and the Environmental Protection Agency. In perhaps the most extreme case, the Selective Service System, a powerful organization during the 1960s, essentially collapsed when its main clientele, the Defense Department, opted to support an all-volunteer army. Support among other executive agencies is especially important for bureaus whose clientele is defined as other federal agencies (for example, the General Services Administration or the Office of Personnel Management). Without support among government units these federal agencies have no power base at all.

In unique situations, agencies can even develop the equivalent of clientele support among the courts. At the state level, Hale (1979: 302) found that administrators perceived courts as another forum to resolve policy disputes. State agencies did not resist the efforts of federal courts to mandate expenditures by specific agencies (see also Harriman and Straussman, 1983).

In summary, the development of a bureau's clientele is necessary to augment bureau power and ensure organizational survival. Specific support is necessary to gain resources and autonomy in the use of those resources, the necessary components of bureau power. Diffuse support is valuable because it facilitates the acquisition of specific support. Since diffuse support is constantly changing, a rational bureau exploits diffuse support when it exists and at the same time seeks as much specific support as possible.

INTERNAL SOURCES OF BUREAU POWER

If organizational theory provides a lesson for the study of bureaucracy and politics, it is that organizations do not passively respond to their environment (see Perrow, 1972; Rainey, 1991). As an open system, a bureau not only responds to environmental pressures, the bureau interacts with the environment and shapes those pressures. This reasoning implies that the internal workings of a bureau can further the development of a positive bureau power setting. Three internal characteristics of a bureau affect the political power the bureau can exercise—knowledge, cohesion, and leadership.

Knowledge

Information is a source of power for bureaus simply because other political elites are concerned with making good public policy (Rourke, 1984). For this reason they cannot afford to press proposals against the advice of experts. Studies of utility regulation, for example, show that professional advice from career staff is a major determinant of utility regulation policy (Berry, 1984; 1979). Although knowledge usually results in greater bureau autonomy, if knowledge produces superior performance, it can also help an agency extract needed resources.

Bureaus have several natural advantages over other political institutions in developing superior policy information. First, a bureau's organizational size permits specialization beyond the capabilities of other political institutions; specialization in turn produces more detailed information about policy problems (Berry, 1984). Concomitant with specialization is a second factor, the ability of bureaucrats to concentrate their full time and energies on a single subject. Together concentration and specialization mean bureaus learn over time to develop better, more effective policies (Sabatier, 1988; Thompson, 1982a; Sabatier and Jenkins-Smith, 1993; Lebovic, 1995; Meier and Keiser, 1996). Such learning is enhanced as a policy weapon by the generalist nature of other political elites who cannot devote similar resources to the development of information. Fleishman's (1989: 343) study of Atlanta-area zoning decisions found that less than 15 percent of staff recommendations were reversed by elected officials. A study of state hazardous waste disposal policies found that state bureaucracies were especially dominant in states where the legislature was less professionalized (Lester, et al., 1983). Politicians in such situations lack an independent source of verification to determine the quality of bureaucratic information. Finally, the influx of professionals into bureaucracy adds the weight of scholarly reputation to bureaucratic advice. The federal government alone employs 150,000 engineers and architects, 10,000 physicians, 14,000 scientists (Plumlee, 1981b: 571), and 31,000 attorneys (*National Journal*, 1982: 1481). Federal laboratories employ one-sixth of all U.S. scientists and engineers (Kosterlitz, 1988: 73). Deference to professional advice is a longstanding American tradition. In combination, the above factors limit the control politicians can exercise over bureaucratic policymaking.

The task demands of public policy (Level 2, see Figure 3–1) provide a favorable soil for knowledge to develop into a bureau power source.[8] Complex policy problems can be solved only with technical expertise, giving an advantage to bureaus that possess technical knowledge. State governments cannot determine how to handle hazardous waste, for example, without the knowledge possessed by state pollution agencies and the Environmental Protection Agency. The nature of the bureaucratic function, implementation, also provides additional knowledge to bureaus. Day-to-day bureau operations provide administrators with insight into policy problems that cannot be gained from a casual inspection of program budgets once a year. This understanding places political elites at a relative disadvantage because they are unable to refute bureaucrats who can cite countless reasons why a proposed policy is not feasible.

Just as all clientele support is not equally beneficial in building a bureau's power base, neither is all knowledge. Knowledge gained from large numbers of professional employees is especially valuable. Every agency has some professionals—some lawyers, social scientists, planners, or natural scientists. The key, however, is the extent to which

---

[8] The variable under consideration is designated as knowledge rather than expertise, as Rourke (1984) terms it, to distinguish power as the result of professionalism and the ability to do a task well from power as information that others do not possess. J. Edgar Hoover's access to information about congressional leaders, for example, is knowledge but can hardly be characterized as expertise (Poveda, 1990). Few will contend such information did not augment the FBI's power. Similarly, the influence of David Stockman as budget director was a function of his knowledge of budget detail, a knowledge that others if willing to spend the time could also develop. Possession of information per se is the variable that affects bureau power. The possession of information as the result of specialization or professionalism is a special case.

the middle and upper levels of the organization are dominated by scientists, engineers, doctors, social scientists, and other professionals. The greater the penetration of professionals, the more likely that professional reasons will be presented to the outside world to justify the agency's decisions, justifications that are difficult to counter.

The incorporation of professionals into bureaus also incorporates their professional values. In 1973 the Antitrust Division of the Department of Justice began to hire economists and give them a role in selecting cases for prosecution. Over time economists were able to educate others in the organization to an economic view of antitrust policy. As a result, the Antitrust Division concentrated almost exclusively on price-fixing cases. Little attention was given to once-popular monopoly and merger cases (Eisner, 1991; but see Wood and Anderson, 1991). Similarly, Hodges and Durant (1989) found changes in management style among professional foresters that could be attributed to changes in professional norms.

A second aspect of knowledge that varies by bureau is whether the public holds the agency's specific profession in high esteem. Many agencies are dominated by professionals, but reaction to these professionals differs. While the nation and its political elites trust physicians and defer to natural scientists, lawyers and accountants are respected only as long as they remain in their specializations; and, except for economists, social scientists are rarely trusted. The more prestige a profession has both within and outside the government, the more members of that profession are allowed to regulate their own affairs. Many states have quasi-private professional organizations passing on the qualifications, ethics, and membership of the professions (Shimberg, Esser, and Kruger, 1973). The same relationship holds in the policy process; the more prestige a profession has, the more that profession is allowed to designate part of public policy as a professional matter and the more that profession is deferred to in that area. The argument that professionals should be allowed to regulate their own conduct has been translated into a justification for policymaking autonomy.

The third dimension of knowledge contributing to the power of professionals and experts is the possession of technical knowledge that a layperson cannot master. Open-heart surgery, high-tech weapons, environmental sciences, and other techniques impress the normal citizen with their complexity and requisite skills. In a survey of political elites' perceptions of the knowledge of policymakers in environmental protection, only one-third rated either legislators or environmental groups as knowledgeable, but 91 percent rated state water pollution agencies and 99 percent rated the federal EPA as knowledgeable (Zeigler, 1983: 125).

Not all professionals, however, are able to achieve autonomy with their knowledge. The scientists who conducted the drug research on cyclamates and saccharine were closely questioned. Not only were other scientists offering conflicting information, but the lay politician can understand injecting chemicals into rats even if he or she does not understand why it is done. Technical knowledge that the layperson cannot master is divisible into three categories. The bottom category includes all the tasks where the layperson can understand the entire process. In these cases, such as the processing of social security checks, the bureaucrat's autonomy is not enhanced. In the second category the layperson knows what the professional does but not how the task is performed; in the top category neither the process nor the professional's task is understood. Lawyers and bridge builders are examples of the middle category; the politician may not understand how the experts do these things but has a fair idea what they do. Professionals in the middle category have influence as long as the topic is within their area of expertise. Atomic scientists, research physicians, and weapons technologists fall into the top category. Since these professionals are removed from the everyday experiences of the politician, their expert advice, if unchallenged, will be accepted uncritically.

At times bureaus resort to secrecy to retain a knowledge edge over other policy-makers. Classification of documents or claims of confidentiality can serve as surrogates for technical knowledge. The Reagan administration with executive order 12356 in 1982 reversed a long-term trend toward less secrecy in government. In 1982 alone, the Department of Defense classified 291,000 documents and restricted another 13.7 million documents because they contained material similar to classified documents. According to Jones (1988: 245), in many cases information is classified to avoid accountability for agency actions rather than to protect national security.

The fourth dimension of knowledge contributing to bureau power is experience dealing with technical or even political problems. As noted above, over time bureaus learn how to approach problems and avoid mistakes (Sabatier, 1988). Often this learning is reflected in bureau standard operating procedures. Johnson (1990: 74) demonstrated that the Consumer Product Safety Commission was a weak policy-maker in the 1970s because, as a new agency, it had not developed the sophisticated standard operating procedures necessary for consumer product regulation. Experience also has a political side. Because agencies have fought numerous policy battles, they have extensive information about potential support or opposition and about tactics likely to succeed.

Finally, the position of bureaucrats and their knowledge is enhanced to the extent that the bureaucrats have credibility. Past actions that resulted in good policy generate acceptance and gain legitimacy for bureau policymaking (Maynard-Moody, 1989: 141). One study of information in the area of water pollution revealed that the information from state agencies was trusted by most participants in the process whereas the information of interest groups was not (Pierce and Lovrich, 1983: 629; see also Abney, 1988: 913). Credibility in turn is enhanced by performance, the production of tangible benefits. Mystery about the methods of science adds to bureau policymaking autonomy only if the mysterious actions produce something valued by others. As an example one only needs to note the rapid rise and fall of supply-side economics. If methods are mysterious and benefits lacking, the political elite is likely to believe mysterious behavior is one of the deleterious consequences of being an egghead. Something useful that the political elite can see, feel, or appreciate—for instance, a better economy, miracle drugs, or lessening of terrorist activity—must result from the process. Bureaucracy, in general, has produced such benefits; civil servants, for example, patent more than 1,500 inventions per year (Costle, 1980: 8). National Institutes of Health employees have won four Nobel Prizes and funded the research for 70 others (Kosterlitz, 1988: 71).

The best combination of knowledge variables for an agency desiring to build resources and autonomy includes a high percentage of experts in the bureau who belong to a highly esteemed profession, who use techniques that laypeople cannot understand,

and who produce tangible results. Under such conditions the contribution of knowledge to the power base of the agency is maximized.

Cohesion

The second internal bureau characteristic contributing to a bureau's power base is agency cohesion. Cohesion may be defined as the commitment of bureau members to the organization and its goals.[9] If an organization is dominated by members who believe in its goals, the bureau can more easily motivate its members (Wilson, 1973). People who strongly identify with an organization will see their job as more than a weekly paycheck and are quite willing to work long hours necessary to improve bureau performance. Problems of high turnover, which require the bureau to commit resources to recruitment and training rather than its prime function, are less severe in cohesive, vital organizations (Romzek, 1990: 377). Organizational involvement, thus, contributes to power in the policy process (Romzek, 1985: 282; Romzek and Hendricks, 1982).

The reason cohesion contributes to agency power is related to the task demands of public policy (see Figure 3–1). Public policy problems, as noted in Chapter 1, are complex and defy easy solutions. Public policy in such areas as drug abuse, health care, and defense require creativity, dedication, and long hours to produce solutions. Cohesion makes a bureau a more effective policymaker because it promotes better employee performance, and a reputation for effectiveness is an asset in power politics (Maynard-Moody, 1989).

Some agencies, the early Peace Corps and the Marine Corps being the best examples, clearly benefit from cohesion. If an agency performs a function that excites the general public or some portion of it, the agency can attract well-qualified people because it offers an identity as well as a job. Thousands of the best and brightest university products in the early 1960s turned down well-paying jobs to work in the Peace Corps. After a massive reorganization in 1969, the Federal Trade Commission became known as the place for talented consumer advocates; and many bright young attorneys joined the FTC. If an agency is stocked with zealous, talented people, it must only structure its tasks appropriately to take advantage of normally withheld energy. If the agency is organized creatively, it should be more effective on effort alone.

The key element in creating a cohesive organization are the values held by individual bureaucrats; cohesion is a direct product of shared values. Organizations in many ways consciously or unconsciously influence the values held by its members, especially those values relevant to agency policies (see Sabatier and Hunter, 1989). One study of federal bureaucrats found that agency of employment was a strong predictor of individual bureaucrat's values (Meier and Nigro, 1976; Sabatier and Zafronte, 1999). A study

---

[9] The reader should be aware that while cohesion is defined as commitment to the organization and that this commitment is a source of power, one cause of both is the performance of a function that excites the community. Commitment is the key variable, however, because agencies within limits can develop more or less commitment among their employees whereas the degree to which their function excites the general public is fixed.

of surface mine regulation found agency affiliation was the single best predictor of regulatory actions (Hedge, Menzel, and Williams, 1988: 331). Three major methods of instilling values are available to the agency—socialization of members, recruiting members who already hold the appropriate values, or establishing decision rules or procedures that incorporate certain values. Recruitment of individuals with the appropriate values may be intentional or may result unintentionally because individuals only apply for positions in agencies compatible with their personal values. Establishing standard operating procedures and decision rules is almost always intentional. Maynard-Moody (1989: 140) goes so far as to contend that administrative policy is shaped by "established definitions of problems and solutions that are enshrined in organizational rules, norms, and habits." Sometimes such procedures are imposed on the organization. Davis and Davis (1988: 7) found that after Congress required environmental impact statements for federal agency actions, the Bureau of Land Management had to hire environmental scientists who did not share traditional BLM values. As a result, BLM decisions began to reflect environmental concerns.

That values differ among bureaucrats should not be surprising. Individuals who seek government employment obviously have values different from those who do not. Several studies found that individuals pursuing a master of public administration degree and thus are likely candidates for public sector employment held predictably different values from individuals pursuing a master of business administration degree (Edwards, Nalbandian, and Wedel, 1981; Nalbandian and Edwards, 1983). Potential public sector employees were more likely to be empathetic to the plight of others, more innovative, more interested in the "public interest" (Nalbandian and Edwards, 1983), and more interested in public service (Rainey, 1982: 293; Perry and Wise, 1990: 371). They are more likely to be motivated by challenging work than by higher pay (Pearce and Perry, 1983: 318; see also DiIulio, 1994). In a comparison of engineers employed in the public and private sectors, Crewson (1997: 505) found that public sector engineers were more likely to support making contributions to society and helping others; because this study surveyed only engineers, the differences could not be attributed to differences in the types of professions employed in government. Crewson (1997: 512) also found that public sector employees had stronger organizational commitments than private sector employees did. Although not an attitude, public employees are also less likely to use illicit drugs than private sector employees (0.7 percent versus 14 percent, see GAO, 1990b; Rosenberg, 1990: 1).

In policy terms, civil servants are somewhat more liberal than the general population, although political ideology does vary by agency (Aberbach and Rockman, 1976; Lewis, 1990; Garand, Parkhurst, and Seoud, 1991a). In a study of state agencies, Uslaner and Weber (1983: 187) found agency heads were more liberal than legislators or party elites on seven of ten issues. Other studies reveal socialization; a study of social service bureaucrats found that certain task-related attitudes developed over time, a pattern consistent with agency socialization (Stone, 1977). The socialization/selection process of agencies has even been institutionalized as Miles' Law (1978), which states that "where you stand [on an issue] depends on where you sit."

Individual values, in turn, affect public policy whether these values are adopted from the agency, from professional training, or from personal experience (F. C. Mosher, 1982; Sabatier and Zafronte, 1999). Because most administrators have some discretion and are likely to exercise that discretion consistent with their personal values, several studies have demonstrated that bureaucratic values affect public policy. The initial policies of the EPA, for example, were determined in part because the first administrator, William Ruckelhaus, was an attorney and recruited several attorneys to top positions. As attorneys they implemented environmental laws using the technique they knew best, court suits against visible polluters (Marcus, 1980). A study of the Help through Industry Retraining and Employment (HIRE) jobs program demonstrated that it was changed from a program for veterans to a general jobs program because the latter was more consistent with the values of Department of Labor bureaucrats (de-Haven-Smith and Van Horn, 1984). Attainment of affirmative action goals has been related to the attitudes of personnel administrators toward affirmative action (Saltzstein, 1983). In housing policy, Bell (1985) found that when values are consistent with those favored by the organization, values affected policy; but when values were inconsistent with those of the organization, they had little impact. In a detailed study of land use decisions, Sabatier and others (1985) found that nearly 80 percent of decisions could be explained by knowing the values of the career bureaucrats. A study of legal services agencies found employee values affected the cases selected if the policy environment had a variety of interested groups (Kessler, 1987). Similar influences of values on public policy have been found for safety engineers in the Occupational Safety and Health Administration (Thompson, 1982a), for city planners (Vasu, 1979), and housing loan officials (Seldon, 1997).

Some agencies go so far in instilling values or recruiting individuals with the correct values that they create an organizational ideology (Romzek, 1990: 377). An organizational ideology serves as a perceptual screen on the outside world and ties the members closely to the organization and its goals. The Forest Service does this by rotating its personnel, stressing its goals of sustained product yields, and creating "saints" such as Gifford Pinchot (Kaufman, 1960). As a result, the Forest Service is a reluctant regulator; but when it responds, it regulates strictly. In contrast the National Parks Service, a competitor with the Forest Service, has socialized more ecological and preservationist values (see Allin, 1987). The U.S. Marines built an organizational ideology as the nation's elite military force. "The marines are looking for a few good men" is more than a recruiting slogan to the organization.

Nowhere is the impact of a bureau's function clearer than in shaping an organization's cohesion. Some organizations by their nature have difficulty in creating an organizational ideology. This prevents building agency power by announcing "the General Accounting Office is looking for a few good accountants" or "the few, the proud, the letter carriers." In all organizations some socialization is possible, but the development of a full-scale organizational ideology is limited by the agency's function.

Although cohesion is a difficult and elusive term to apply to agencies, some agencies have the ability to motivate their members with appeals to common goals. With this additional commitment, the agency can ask for and get better performance from its employees. Performance and the reputation for performance are invaluable assets to a power-seeking bureau.

Leadership

Leadership contributes to agency power both as a result of the organization of American government and the nature of politics (see Figure 3–1). The fragmentation resulting from the organization of government makes the bureau leader a politician in the classic sense. The bureau chief must build a coalition, seek resources to placate the coalition, and implement programs that please clientele, other political elites, and agency employees. The nature of politics makes leadership a factor because the sublimation of politics provides the leader with opportunities to aggrandize political power by making policy and allocating scarce societal resources.

Case studies indicate that leadership is a vital factor in augmenting agency power. One need only compare the differences in respect for the FBI when it was run by a power broker such as J. Edgar Hoover to its diminished respect under L. Patrick Gray (Poveda, 1990). Although individual bureau chiefs vary in their ability to build effective organizations, leadership is also situational. Casper Weinberger was perceived as the consummate bureaucratic politician when he remade the Federal Trade Commission in 1969 and consolidated power for the Office of Management and Budget shortly thereafter (earning the nickname Cap the Knife). Even from 1980 to 1984 with the Department of Defense, Weinberger was recognized as a strong leader; but when the diffuse support for more defense spending evaporated and delicate issues of control arose, Weinberger was perceived as less than able. The specter of expensive toilet seats, $7,000 coffee machines, weapons systems that did not work, and numerous examples of mismanagement destroyed Weinberger's reputation much faster than it was built.

Bureau leaders can build agency power by affecting both internal and external variables. Internally, a good leader can develop cohesion and expertise. The ability of William Ruckelshaus or Joan Claybrook to motivate agency personnel offers a sharp contrast to the impact that Anne Burford had on the morale of the Environmental Protection Agency (Vig and Kraft, 1984; Meier, 1985). Leaders of the Office of Surface Mining Regulation and Enforcement in the late 1970s adopted a vigorous enforcement policy as a way to instill cohesion in this new agency (Shover, Clelland, and Lynxwiler, 1986: 138; Hedge, Menzel, and Krause, 1989: 286). Jack Knott (1986: 206) found that successful chairs of the Federal Reserve Board were able to build a cohesive coalition of professional staff, members of the board, and heads of the regional banks. A bureau chief who loses the confidence of bureau personnel soon sees the agency's influence dissipate. In the mid-1970s IRS employees, who felt Commissioner Donald Alexander's leadership was not "nonpartisan" enough, leaked information damaging to the commissioner and undermined both Alexander and the status of the agency. Similarly the position of EPA chief Anne Burford was seriously weakened because unsympathetic members of Congress somehow gained access to internal agency documents (see Vig and Kraft, 1984).

A bureau chief can also increase a bureau's reputation for expertise either through the chief's own expertise or by developing research units within the agency (but see Wolf, 1997). The appointment of Eula Bingham, a well-known expert in occupational safety and health, was credited with improving the scientific competence of OSHA. Susan King was perceived as installing an economic analytic capacity in the Consumer Product Safety Commission for the first time, whereas her successor, Nancy H. Stoerts, was viewed as a person who did not listen to staff advice (*National Journal,* 1981: 1960).

Externally, the bureau chief may build power through a variety of strategies. The chief may cultivate congressional allies, as Bobby Inman, the deputy director of the CIA in the late 1970s, was able to do but Michael Pertschuk, the chair of the Federal Trade Commission at the same time, was not. For many years the Federal Aviation Administration and its leaders have had the ability to exploit accidents to augment the resources of the agency, but the Securities and Exchange Commission rarely was able to benefit from major securities' crises (Kemp, 1984). Frances Knight, former director of the State Department's passport office, had the reputation in Washington for developing strong congressional ties by doing favors for members despite the unexciting function of her bureau.

Fenno's (1966) study of the federal budget indicates congressional confidence in bureau leadership safeguards resources by allowing the bureau to avoid budget cuts. Bureau chiefs with strong ties to clientele groups can build an agency's power base by tying the beneficiaries closer to the agency. Mary Switzer, as head of the Rehabilitation Services Administration, had strong support from state agencies in vocational rehabilitation, but several of her successors were widely disliked by the same persons. Former Secretary of Health and Human Services Richard Schweiker lost support from that agency's clientele when he appeared to surrender control over the HHS budget to the OMB and failed to become an independent advocate (Demkovich, 1982: 848). Too much independence, however, can be fatal also as Margaret Heckler discovered in 1985 when President Reagan removed her from the HHS position.

Finally, leadership is important because an administrator's reputation for political skills is an aid that helps any agency. William Ruckelshaus was perceived as a good administrator, and his reappointment to the EPA revitalized the agency. David Stockman's reputation for mastery of detail enabled the OMB to become a dominant actor in the budgeting process. His replacement, James C. Miller III, lacked his political skills, and the reputation of the OMB dropped (Haas, 1987: 1690). Others who lack the reputation as good administrators detract from their agency's ability to win political battles. Don Noble, the head of the Synthetic Fuels Corporation, was perceived as a poor administrator who eventually destroyed the effectiveness of the agency's programs. Congress subsequently abolished the agency. Charles Z. Wick, an administrator with a reputation for cheerleading and little administrative ability, weakened the U.S. Information Agency's already marginal reputation (Madison, 1984).

The importance of leadership in bureaucratic politics is illustrated well by the role Paul Volcker, chair of the Federal Reserve, played in economic policy from 1978 to 1986 (Kettl, 1986). In 1979 Volcker began a campaign to lower inflation by manipulating reserve requirements, discount rates, and monetary policy. Volcker eventually was able to reduce inflation from double-digit range because he established a clear policy to combat inflation, built support for that policy among other political elites, and was sensitive in how far he could press unpopular policies (Kettl, 1986). Exercising such leadership, Volcker established effective policies that elected officials were unwilling to try on their own.

SUMMARY

The discussion of bureau power and its sources is not just a theoretical argument bolstered by a few case studies; it is an empirical theory that describes the actual process of building support for agencies. One study of 127 federal agencies that attempted to measure both the power of individual agencies (defined as autonomy and extraction of resources) and the independent variables—clientele support, knowledge, cohesion, and leadership found that each of these variables was related to bureau power (Meier, 1980). The results of this analysis are shown in Table 3–2. The table shows that the two stronger sources of bureau power are clientele support and agency cohesion while knowledge and leadership are somewhat weaker. The significant direct impacts illustrate that each force is a separate determinant of bureau power and that they are independent of each other. An examination of the separate dimensions of power (resources and autonomy) revealed that clientele support and expertise had a strong impact on autonomy but little impact on resource extraction (the latter might be expected given the mixed findings in the budgeting literature). Leadership and cohesion, on the other hand, had a major impact on resource extraction but did not affect the agency's autonomy.[10]

• TABLE 3–2 •

IMPACT OF CLIENTELE SUPPORT, EXPERTISE, COHESION, AND LEADERSHIP ON BUREAUCRATIC POWER

	IMPACT	
INDEPENDENT VARIABLES	TOTAL	DIRECT
Clientele	.40	.33*
Expertise	.31	.24
Cohesion	.33	.32
Leadership	.24	.18
	R = .60	

*Standardized regression coefficients; all are significant at .01 or less.

SOURCE: Meier, 1980: 369.

[10] The empirical example is shown for a specific reason even though the argument of the chapter does not require it. The study of public administration of which bureaucratic politics is a part at one time had a reputation as a methodological backwater. In part that reputation as well deserved, but much good quality research is now being done; and much of it is cited in this and other chapters. This research, however, is being ignored for the most part by texts on public administration, thus perpetuating the stereotype. Only by incorporating empirical research into the body of the chapter can attention be drawn to it.

Dennis Grady (1989) completed a similar study of bureaucratic power with state economic development agencies. He found a positive relationship between both agency expertise (knowledge) and clientele support and the ability to extract resources. Agency autonomy was linked to clientele support, gubernatorial support (another form of public support), and lack of partisan divisions in the legislature.

The growth of bureau power, therefore, is a function of both the characteristics of individual bureaus and the environment in which they operate. Bureaucracies in general become policymaking institutions in response to four environmental conditions. The nature of American politics defines many political questions as the responsibility of administrative agencies. The organization of government disperses political power, thus permitting bureaucracy to coalesce with others in an issue network. The task demands of public policy require an institution that can concentrate expertise on specific problems as the bureaucracy can. Finally, the bureaucratic function, implementation, has within it additional opportunities for discretion and power.

Individual bureaus, however, vary a great deal in political influence. One environmental factor and three internal factors permit individual bureaus to become powerful institutions. First, the political environment of the bureau provides specific and diffuse support for both the bureau and the programs it administers. Second, the bureau's ability to store and process information that other political elites do not have gives it a relative advantage in policymaking. Third, the organization's cohesion contributes to power by improving agency performance through motivation of agency personnel. Fourth, positive agency leadership is necessary to exploit environmental opportunities for building powerful bureaus. Powerful bureaus do not develop because bureaucrats conspire to bureaucratize American life. Powerful bureaucracies develop in response to environmental demands. Those agencies blessed with a favorable environment and the internal characteristics necessary to exploit that environment become power brokers of the first order.

CHAPTER 4

BUREAUCRACY AND PUBLIC POLICY

Public policy is a purposive course of action followed by an actor or set of actors (usually affiliated with the government) in dealing with a problem or matter of concern (Anderson, 1997; Jones, 1984). Policies adopted by the legislature or the political executive create an environment in which government agencies implement policy. Variations in this environment affect the actions individual bureaus can take and also affect the ability of bureaus to influence the policy process. Public policies have long been divided into three major types—regulatory, distributive, and redistributive. Regulatory policies are government limits on individual choice in order to restrict "unacceptable" behavior (Mitnik, 1980). Occupational Safety and Health Administration regulations concerning workplace safety standards are an example of regulatory policy. Distributive policies are government efforts to distribute benefits to some portion of the population and pay for those benefits from general tax revenues (rather than with user fees). Federal grants for urban development are an example of distributive policy. In redistributive policy the government taxes one group of people to provide benefits to another group; social security, for example, taxes workers to pay benefits to retired persons. Some policies do not fit into these three categories. Although some efforts have been made to provide more complex classifications for the remaining policies (see Ripley and Franklin, 1991), perhaps the most intuitive classification is Theodore Lowi's (1972). Lowi classifies the remaining policies as constituent policies because the prime constituent of these policies is either government or the nation as a whole. Included in this residual classification are defense policies, foreign affairs, and the housekeeping functions of government.

Examining the impact of bureaus on public policy within each policy type is useful for several reasons. Political elites have different policy goals in each policy area and, as a result, different expectations concerning bureaucratic performance. Each policy area targets somewhat different clusters of problems that require different skills and approaches. Correspondingly, agencies approach policy differently and use different bureaucratic tools depending on the policy area. This variation in bureau policymaking is the subject of this chapter.

Before proceeding with the analysis, one difficulty with the use of policy typologies must be noted. Several agencies implement policies in many different policy areas simultaneously (Mann, 1975). The Environmental Protection Agency, for example, was established as a regulatory agency to protect the nation's environment. The EPA, however, once acted as a distributive agency when it operated a large grant fund that allocated sewage treatment construction grants to local governments. In addition, when the EPA regulates pollution, it performs a redistributive function; it seeks to redistribute pollution costs from the general public to business and industry. The multifunctional nature of many government agencies means that the impact of bureaucracy on public policy is more complex than the following discussion reveals. Despite this difficulty, the four general policy types have some similarities that are helpful to understand bureaucracy and the policy process.

REGULATORY POLICY

Regulatory policy is government restrictions of individual choice to keep conduct from transcending acceptable bounds. People are prohibited from selling unsafe drugs, from competing unfairly in the marketplace, or from polluting the air and water. Bureaucratic regulation has been part of the federal government's policy repertoire since 1887 when the Interstate Commerce Commission (ICC) was created to regulate railroads. At the state level, in 1851 New Hampshire established the first state regulatory agency to regulate insurance. Although many government regulatory activities are conducted directly by legislatures or by law enforcement agencies, modern regulatory policy dates from these first attempts to protect the consumer from the pitfalls of modern capitalism.

As nineteenth-century laissez-faire capitalism matured in oligopoly, trusts, and monopoly, American consumers felt the impact of such monopolist practices as rate discrimination, exorbitant prices, and defective goods (Nadel, 1971). Charged with protecting the consumer from the practices of large corporations, a new form of bureaucracy, the independent regulatory commission was created. What began as a single attempt (the ICC) to regulate rail transportation spread to foods (the Food and Drug Administration), securities (the Securities and Exchange Commission), banks (the Federal Reserve and the Federal Deposit Insurance Corporation), and a host of other areas. At times regulatory agencies were created not in response to popular pressure but in response to industry demands for protection from the major hazard of market competition, failure. The Federal Communications Commission was created in response to broadcasters' demands; the Civil Aeronautics Board was established at the request of the airline companies (Sabatier, 1975; Brown, 1987).

State and local governments retain substantial regulatory authority. State agencies are responsible in all 50 states for regulating the insurance (an industry larger than any federally regulated ones) and the public utilities industries. Every state also has a bank regulator to regulate state financial institutions that do not use federal deposit insurance. State governments also regulate a variety of professions/occupations; although the specific professions vary from state to state, all states regulate the practice of medicine, law, and barbering among others. Local governments regulate local business, health-related matters, land use (through zoning), and some morality concerns (e.g., nude dancing).

The U.S. regulatory system does not follow a comprehensive plan; rather, it was built incrementally in response to individual problems without concern for overall regulatory policy. State and federal regulatory agencies frequently overlap each other and sometimes conflict. Despite the lack of planned development, however, American regulatory policies fall into four distinct patterns.

THE SCOPE OF REGULATORY POLICY

At the state and local level, one major form of regulation is legal restriction of criminal activity. Although our federal system generally delegates law enforcement functions to local government, several bureaus in the Department of Justice perform law enforcement functions at the federal level. The Federal Bureau of Investigation (FBI) serves as a national police force; the Immigration and Naturalization Service (INS) regulates the entry of persons into the United States; and the Drug Enforcement Administration (DEA) enforces narcotics laws. In the Treasury Department, the Customs Service regulates importation of goods while the Bureau of Alcohol, Tobacco, and Firearms regulates three of America's legal vices (Martinek, Meier, and Keiser 1998). Joint federal–state/local activities particularly for drug crimes or organized crime provide the federal government with a method of influencing the activities of local governments (Meier, 1994). In recent years, the federal government has aggressively declared a variety of crimes federal offenses; at the same time, however, most actual law enforcement is done at the local level.

A second set of federal agencies regulate American business to ensure that it is competitive and equitable. These agencies were established to regulate prices, check fraud, eliminate unfair practices, and prevent monopolistic actions in such areas as securities (SEC), raw food stocks (the Grain Inspection, Packers and Stockyards Administration), commodity exchanges (the Commodity Futures Trading Commission), and labor relations (the National Labor Relations Board). In recent years the federal government has deemphasized price regulation; the Civil Aeronautics Board was abolished in 1984, and significant portions of surface transportation, securities, telecommunications, and banking were deregulated. On the other hand, in an effort to control federal health care expenditures, the federal government has started to regulate health care costs through regulations governing the Medicaid and Medicare programs. Price regulation, however, is alive and well at the state level for some public utilities and, in some states, insurance companies. Local governments are also known to regulate prices; the most common area is taxi cab fares.

A third, more modern area of regulation is limiting access to public goods. The public, with government as its agent, can create a monopoly or permit a business to use a resource that belongs to the people in general. The nation's air, water, and communications spectrum are good examples of public goods where access must be regulated. If everyone who wanted to broadcast radio and television signals were permitted to do so, for example, the resulting interference would reduce all transmissions to mere noise and prevent coherent communications (see Krasnow, Longley, and Terry, 1982). Government regulation limits access to public goods in order to maximize possible benefits. A similar process occurs in pollution control: Public goods, clean air and water, are monitored by the Environmental Protection Agency and state environmental agencies.

The fourth area of regulation is public health and safety. Public concern raised by Upton Sinclair, Ida Tarbell, and other muckrakers mobilized the government in the early twentieth century to regulate the quality of food and drugs (Nadel, 1971). Since this early foray into health regulation, government has attempted public health and safety regulation in a wide variety of areas. Regulatory agencies monitor health and safety by inspecting food (the Food Safety and Inspection Service and the Food and Drug Administration), airlines (the Federal Aviation Administration), consumer products (the Consumer Product Safety Commission), and workplace conditions (the Occupational Safety and Health Administration). State and local governments inspect restaurants, morticians, and other businesses. They are also heavily involved in mandatory sanitation and vaccination programs.

Given the numerous areas of regulation, the size of the federal regulatory effort is not surprising. Nearly 185,000 employees work for 38 agencies spending about 5 percent of the federal budget to regulate the nation's businesses, its safety, its health, and its public goods. Little of a citizen's life is unaffected by regulation, either from the benefits of effective regulation or from compliance costs added to consumer goods.

Despite the scope of federal regulation, regulatory policy is an invisible process to most citizens. If the Federal Aviation Administration (FAA) increases airline safety and prevents airplane hijackings in the United States, the effort goes unnoticed. Only when the safety system fails does the FAA receive any public attention. The same can be said for the Food and Drug Administration, the Securities and Exchange Commission, and most other regulators. The regulation of savings and loans was virtually invisible before the major problems of the 1980s. Only in controversial areas such as environmental protection, worker safety regulation, and for a time transportation are agency actions visible; and in those cases usually only the people directly affected by regulation notice it.

REGULATORY BUREAU POLICYMAKING

Regulatory agencies affect policy through the normal mechanisms of policy implementation (see below). Another policymaker, in this case usually Congress, sets general guidelines on regulatory policy; and agencies expand these general guidelines into specific policy actions. Since most regulatory agencies are not known to be aggressive, they usually act within the broad parameters established by congressional policy. Because congressional policy is usually vague with language that instructs an agency to regulate some phenomenon in the "public interest, convenience, or necessity," regulatory agencies sometimes go beyond what Congress wants. Regulatory agencies affect policy via rulemaking, adjudication, and law enforcement. Occasionally a creative regulator will also influence policy through policy initiation.

Rulemaking

Rulemaking is a quasi-legislative process whereby an agency issues rules with the force of law that apply to all persons under the agency's jurisdiction. These rules specify more clearly the public policy that was announced by Congress. Rulemaking follows a legislative-like procedure as required by the Federal Administrative Procedures Act or other laws directed at the agency. Agencies, at a minimum, must give notice of possible rules to be issued, must allow interested parties to be heard, and must publish the final rules in the *Federal Register*. Some agencies such as the Federal Trade Commission and the Consumer Product Safety Commission have far more elaborate rulemaking procedures (West, 1985).

An excellent example of rulemaking and its political ramifications is the National Highway Traffic Safety Administration's (NHTSA) passive restraints policy. Shortly after its creation in 1966, NHTSA issued regulations that required all automobiles produced after 1968 to have seatbelts. In 1969 NHTSA proposed a rule to require the installation of airbags in all new vehicles and the following year issued a regulation that required passive restraints (either airbags or automatic seat belts) in passenger cars beginning in 1974. In 1971 President Nixon overruled NHTSA and delayed the rule's implementation for two more years (until 1976). In 1976 the Ford administration deferred the passive restraint rule until 1977. NHTSA then rescinded the rule and ordered a demonstration program with 500,000 airbag-equipped vehicles for 1980. After the election of Jimmy Carter in 1976, his NHTSA head, Joan Claybrook, abandoned the demonstration program and reopened rulemaking hearings to require passive restraints. Later in 1977 a rule was adopted requiring passive restraints starting in 1982 with a three-year phase-in period. After the 1980 election, however, NHTSA rescinded the passive restraint rule as part of President Reagan's efforts to aid the automobile industry. Several consumer groups and insurance companies sued NHTSA over this rescission, arguing that to withdraw a rule an agency had to go through the same rulemaking process as it did when rules were issued. In *Motor Vehicle Manufacturers Association* v. *State Farm Insurance*, the Supreme Court upheld this position. NHTSA responded with a new rule requiring passive restraints in 1990-model year cars unless states with two-thirds of the nation's population adopted mandatory seatbelt use laws by 1989 (see A. Cooper, 1985c; Meier, 1985). Many states balked at this attempt to avoid responsibility by the federal government. The end result was that passive restraints were required in all 1990-model year cars.

The passive restraint controversy is unique in that the same policy was decided several ways over a twenty-year period, but it illustrates how regulatory agencies affect policy via the rulemaking process. Other examples are numerous; the Consumer Product Safety Commission requires that baby cribs meet certain standards for safety. The Occupational Safety and Health Administration specifies that workers can be exposed to only a certain amount of cotton dust while working in textile plants. The Federal Trade Commission has issued rules that permit optometrists to advertise prices and engage in other competitive behaviors. State insurance commissions prohibit discrimination against blind people in the sale of life insurance. Other examples are far too numerous to mention.

Adjudication

Despite an estimated thirty thousand pages of federal rules issued by regulatory agencies (seventeen pages of rules for every one page of regulatory statutes), some critics contend that regulatory agencies eschew rulemaking for adjudication (Davis, 1965). Adjudication is a quasi-judicial process whereby each individual suspected of violating a law is charged and administratively tried to determine violations. Rules of procedure for adjudication are also quasi-judicial with requirements of notice, evidence, fairness, and so forth (see Heffron with McFeeley, 1983; P. J. Cooper, 1988). Unlike rulemaking, adjudication affects only the single case being adjudicated. Other persons who have committed similar violations must each be given the benefits of the adjudicatory process. Adjudication is generally preferred by regulated industries not only because it is slow and has procedural safeguards, but because it also permits the industry to present its case at length with frequent appeals to courts of law.

The National Highway Traffic Safety Administration uses an adjudicatory process to remove vehicles with safety defects from the roads. When NHTSA feels that a certain vehicle has a safety defect, it informs the manufacturer and holds a hearing. During the hearing process the manufacturer is usually able to negotiate with NHTSA concerning the content, scope, and wording of the recall (Tobin, 1983: 283). When recalls involve large numbers of vehicles, manufacturers are understandably hesitant to agree to a recall, and NHTSA must go to court to enforce its recall. One prominent example of this occurred in 1984 when NHTSA went to court to force General Motors to recall 1.1 million X-cars for defective braking systems. Adjudications are used by most regulatory agencies. Examples include the Food and Drug Administration hearings on withdrawing drugs from the market (Nadel, 1971), Consumer Product Safety Commission hearings on the safety of an individual product, Federal Reserve Board hearings about whether or not a bank holding company can sell insurance, and Federal Trade Commission adjudications concerning whether a specific advertisement is unfair. At the state level, the bulk of adjudications occur when occupational regulatory agencies seek to discipline their licensees (e.g., doctors or lawyers).

Law Enforcement

Policymaking through law enforcement means simply the selective application of laws; certain laws are vigorously enforced while others are virtually ignored. Local law enforcement agencies routinely ignore certain morality laws (e.g., laws prohibiting adultery). Some laws may be enforced against certain classes of people while others are unaffected. Several examples of the federal bureaucracy engaging in selective enforcement exist.

In a study of compliance with federal water pollution laws, Downing and Kimball (1982) found nonuniform enforcement was the norm. Over 80 percent of affected companies stated that they negotiated their pollution emissions levels with enforcement agencies; many were able to negotiate emissions levels far in excess of their current emissions (Downing and Kimball, 1982: 57). Bargaining and individual flexibility were the major mechanisms of enforcement. In another study one of every three companies was found to be in violation of air pollution laws that were enforced in much the same way (Downing, 1983).

In their study of the Internal Revenue Service (IRS), Scholz and Wood (1998) examined the variation in IRS enforcement of tax laws across the states. The ratio of corporate to individual audits changed when party control of government changed. Scholz and Wood (1998) also found the IRS adjusted their auditing to reflect their own concerns with effectiveness and efficiency.

Following the 1980 election, lack of enforcement of many regulatory laws seemed to be conscious policy. In 1981 OSHA reduced the number of inspectors by 26 percent, decreased citations for violations by 22 percent, citations for serious violations by 90 percent, and total fines 69 percent (Wines, 1983b: 2013). This drop in enforcement was attributed to OSHA head Thorne Auchter's philosophy of voluntary cooperation. Similar deregulation via selective enforcement was charged in environmental protection (Vig and Kraft, 1984), consumer protection (Pertschuk, 1982), and food and drug regulation (Claybrook, 1984; for a systematic analysis see Wood and Waterman, 1994). With the advent of the Bush and Clinton administrations, some of the regulatory vigor of the pre-1980s returned.

Policy Initiation

Although most bureaucratic regulatory policymaking is via the mechanisms of policy implementation, sometimes regulators can implement a law in such a way that radical new policies emerge. Until 1978 air transportation was highly regulated, with the Civil Aeronautics Board (CAB) setting prices, determining routes, and restricting competition. Under the leadership of first John Robson and then Alfred Kahn, the CAB began to deregulate by administrative action. The CAB liberally permitted airlines to set their own prices with various promotional programs and freely granted new routes. Air transportation had been deregulated administratively to such an extent that when Congress passed the Airline Deregulation Act of 1978, it essentially ratified a radical administrative change in policy; in fact, one portion of the law retroactively gave congressional blessing to the CAB's deregulatory action (Derthick and Quirk, 1985; Brown, 1987).

Regulatory agencies can also influence policy by stimulating the legislative agenda. At the federal level, bank regulators routinely identify policy problems and propose suggested solutions during congressional hearings (Meier, 1985). Federal bank regulators, for example, pointed out the "nonbank" loophole (a legal technicality that permitted financial institutions to receive deposit insurance but not be bound by banking regulations) to Congress in the early 1980s. At the state level many insurance regulators drafted proposed legislation to deal with the property and liability insurance crisis of 1986–1987 (Meier, 1988). These proposals were then submitted to state legislatures.

Sometimes agencies can go so far as to create a new agency. Before its demise in the 1980s, the Federal Home Loan Bank Board (FHLBB) was in charge of regulating the savings and loan industry. Faced with several insolvencies, the FHLBB needed to dispose of assets that were acquired when the FHLBB closed these institutions. Using its own discretion, the FHLBB chartered a private organization, the Federal Assets Disposition Association, and charged it with selling these assets to the private sector (Moe, 1987: 455).

THE STRUCTURE OF REGULATORY AGENCIES

Regulatory agencies come in three types: the independent regulatory commission, the department regulatory agency, and the department law enforcement agency. Since department law enforcement agencies such as the Federal Bureau of Investigation perform a special type of regulatory function, the normal policy decision when a regulatory agency is established is between creating an independent regulatory commission and a departmental regulatory agency. The Interstate Commerce Commission (abolished in 1995), the first major federal regulatory agency, was the first federal independent regulatory commission and set the pattern for many subsequent regulatory agencies.

Independent regulatory commissions are headed by a multimember commission composed of an odd number of bipartisan commissioners who establish regulatory policy. The independent regulatory commission is structurally independent; it is not in an executive department but rather reports directly to Congress. The department regulatory agency is headed by a single administrator and lodged within an executive department. The Agricultural Marketing Service (AMS), the Grain Inspection, Packers and Stockyards Administration, and the Animal and Plant Health Inspection Service (APHIS) within the Department of Agriculture are good examples of department regulatory agencies. Although some regulatory bodies are independent regulatory agencies as is the Environmental Protection Agency or department regulatory commissions as is the Federal Energy Regulatory Commission in the Department of Energy, the independent regulatory commission and the department regulatory agency are by far the most common forms. The congressional bias for these two forms is illustrated by the changes in the Commodity Exchange Authority (CEA), an agency within the Department of Agriculture that regulated commodity exchanges. In response to criticism of the CEA's regulation of commodity transactions, especially those prior to the 1973 Soviet grain purchases, Congress moved the CEA out of the Department of Agriculture and transformed it into the Commodity Futures Trading Commission, an independent regulatory commission. In general, then, regulatory bodies within executive departments are agencies headed by a single administrator, while regulatory bodies located outside the executive departments are usually headed by a commission. State regulatory agencies also use these two basic forms although there is greater variation among the states. One state might regulate medicine (or some other business) with a department regulatory agency that regulates several different businesses (e.g., California), but another will regulate the same function with an independent commission (e.g., Alabama).

The structural form of regulatory bodies is not without reason. Independent regulatory commissions are made independent because members of Congress recognized the ties between executive departments and organized interest groups (Renfrow, 1980). Congress, for example, considered creating the Consumer Product Safety Commission within the Department of Commerce as suggested by President Nixon, but rejected the proposal because it wanted the CPSC to be independent of business interests. The National Labor Relations Board was created as an independent agency so that it would not consistently favor either labor or business.

Many departments have strong clientele ties so that placing a regulatory agency in such a department will force it to come to an accommodation with these interests. The Department of Agriculture has strong ties to the major farm and commodity interest groups; the Department of Commerce considers big business its major clientele; the Department of Labor is tied closely to organized labor. The Occupational Safety and Health Administration was placed in the Department of Labor rather than the Department of Commerce by a Democratic Congress to make sure OSHA considered labor interests rather than business interests (Thompson, 1982a).

Independent status, however, does not guarantee political independence because some independent agencies are also created at the request of interest groups to serve the needs of those groups. The Civil Aeronautics Board, the Federal Communications Commission, and the Securities and Exchange Commission were created at the request of industries that they regulate (Sabatier, 1975). At the state level, virtually all agencies that regulate professions and occupations were created at the request of the regulated (Meier, 1985).

Although independent agencies may or may not be created to aid the regulated, most federal department regulatory agencies are. The Agriculture Marketing Service regulates agricultural markets with the goal of assisting farmers. Such agencies are placed within departments so that they will be responsive to the department's clientele.[1] Evidence from interest group testimony at House appropriations hearings supports this explanation. Nine department regulatory agencies had an average of seventeen clientele testifying for them over a three-year period while the independent regulatory commissions averaged less than two supporters each over the same time period.[2] Since department regulatory agencies are often encouraged to be more responsive to the needs of the regulated, their greater clientele support is expected.

---

[1] Not all department regulatory agencies are located in departments that have clientele interested in their actions. The National Highway Traffic Safety Administration is in the Department of Transportation, an agency with little attachment to the automobile industry. In addition, the Federal Aviation Administration, also in Transportation, has demonstrated a fair amount of independence from the airline industry. The FAA, in fact, predated the Department of Transportation. Another reasonably independent agency is the Food and Drug Administration located in Health and Human Services although its degree of independence is a matter of dispute (Quirk, 1980).

[2] The clientele measures were developed from a content analysis of all House Appropriations Committee Subcommittee hearings for the years 1974–1976. For a complete description of these measures, see Meier (1978).

For state level agencies the opposite is usually true. Independent regulatory agencies are generally assumed to serve the interests of the regulated. The creation of Departments of Regulation or Departments of Health Regulation to regulate doctors, nurses, chiropractors, pharmacists, and others is strongly resisted by the individual professions. Professions prefer to be regulated by small independent commissions who regulate only a single profession. The difference between the state and federal levels appears to be that interest groups do not dominate these state departments, as is the case with the national clientele departments (see Meier, 1985: Chapter 7).

A regulatory body's structure also reveals something about the agency's method of policymaking. Regulatory commissions are designed to operate as little legislatures with bipartisan members, an odd number of voters, and group deliberations. As a result, commissions should focus on the quasi-legislative process, rulemaking. Independent regulatory commissions, however, often lack political support (Downs, 1967; Bernstein, 1955). Regulation involves restricting behavior and, therefore, is not always welcomed by industry; in addition, public interest groups also demand to participate in rulemaking, thus making it a long and contentious process. This environment means that many independent regulatory commissions try not to offend any interests because the interests may appeal to Congress to reverse the commission's decision. Commissions often prefer adjudication to rulemaking, therefore, because adjudication provides greater opportunities for interests to object. The need for caution is exacerbated by procedural slowness caused by the commission's plural executive. Department regulatory agencies such as those in the Department of Agriculture, on the other hand, can often act faster and are usually not charged with functions hostile to their regulated clientele. As a result, department regulatory agencies are able to issue twice as many rules (an average of 1,400 pages per agency) as independent regulatory commissions (638), despite the legislative-like structure of the independent commission.[3]

THE ENVIRONMENT OF REGULATORY AGENCIES

The environment of regulatory agencies is significantly different from those of other agencies. As a result regulatory agencies also differ from other agencies in terms of clientele support, knowledge, cohesion, and leadership. Since regulatory agencies, with the exception of those designed to protect the regulated, do not deliver tangible benefits to the regulated, they generally have weak clientele support. Even the abolition of the Civil Aeronautics Board provoked only lukewarm opposition from the airline industry (Brown, 1987; Derthick and Quirk, 1985). The abolition of the Interstate Commerce Commission in 1995 went virtually unnoticed. Regulatory agencies have little to offer on a quid-pro-quo basis for the support of either consumer groups or the regulated industry. This lack of distributive benefits is illustrated by regulatory agencies' budget to personnel ratios; the average regulatory agency had a budget of only $86,400 per employee in 1991, barely enough to cover salaries and administrative costs. Table 4–1 demonstrates the resulting weak clientele support for regulatory agen-

---

[3] These data and others presented in this chapter on rules, laws, personnel and other variables are for 1985.

• **TABLE 4–1** •

A Statistical Summary of the Average Regulatory Agency

Number of Personnel	4,882
Size of 1985 Budget	$423 Million
Number of Clientele	7.1
Computers	Few
Pages of Rules Issued	765
Pages of Relevant Laws	67
Budget to Personnel Ratio	$86,400
Rules to Laws Ratio	17.0

$N = 37$ Federal Regulatory Agencies and Bureaus

cies; the average regulatory agency has fewer clientele groups supporting it than any other type of agency (see Tables 4–2, 4–3, 4–5). Regulatory agencies that enjoy a fair amount of public support (for example, the Environmental Protection Agency or the Federal Aviation Administration) also provide distributive benefits or operate in a salient political environment. Clientele support, therefore, is not normally a major factor in building a regulatory agency's power base. Not only are the clientele of most regulatory agencies small, but in many instances the agencies were created with the intent of regulating rather than serving the clientele. In such circumstances other political elites are likely to penalize a regulatory agency for close clientele ties.

Regulatory agencies normally do not gain political power as a function of knowledge either. According to Clarence and Barbara Davies (1975), regulatory agencies generally lack research units to counter industry claims about regulation's impact. Although many agencies without in-house research capabilities have the authority to contract with outside institutions for needed research, regulatory agencies rarely have this power. The few exceptions to this rule are fairly powerful. The EPA has its own highly regarded research unit. The Federal Reserve has some of the best economic research talent in the nation, and for a brief period of time in the late 1970s both OSHA and the CPSC had developed specialized research talents.

State-level regulatory agencies also vary on this dimension even for the same agencies in different states. Meier (1988) found extensive variation in the regulatory capacity of state insurance commissions. Some such as those in New York or California developed their own sources of policy expertise. In other, smaller states, insurance commissions were forced to rely on industry sources for policy-relevant information. Similar findings were revealed by Ringquist's (1993) study of state environmental regulation.

Before the massive influx of personal computers, a good indicator of a federal agency's technical expertise was the number of computers it uses to conduct its operations. Federal regulatory agencies in 1975 owned less than 3 percent of the federal government's computers. If the Federal Aviation Administration's massive computer system used for air traffic control was deleted from the total, the remaining regulatory agencies would have been somewhat backward technologically. Regulatory agencies with few exceptions (e.g., the Environmental Protection Agency, the FAA, and the Federal Reserve) cannot use technical knowledge as a source of agency power. Their best hope is to develop political knowledge as a substitute.

Lack of leadership and cohesion are also factors that weaken regulatory agencies in policymaking. At one time leadership was perceived as difficult to develop in regulatory commissions where a plural executive governs because any one person could easily be countered by the other commissioners. Such strong individuals as James Landis and Nicholas Johnson on the FCC were restrained by the commission form. This prevailing view has been effectively challenged by subsequent analysis (Welborn and Brown, 1980; Welborn, 1977). The experiences of regulatory executives under Presidents Carter and Reagan revealed strong leadership. Alfred Kahn persuaded a majority of the Civil Aeronautics Board to deregulate the airline industry; Paul Volcker had little trouble gathering support for his economic policies on the Federal Reserve Board. Strong regulatory leaders such as Elwood Quesada, who were thought of as exceptions in pre-1970s regulatory agencies, became the rule with individuals as diverse as Thorne Auchter, Joan Claybrook, Susan King, and William Baxter significantly influencing agency policy.

Similarly regulatory functions were once thought to be unexciting and thus the development of cohesion in regulatory agencies was perceived to be difficult. The Federal Trade Commission before 1969, for example, was criticized as a listless, ineffective regulator (Cox et al., 1969). Although economic regulation may well be a policy area that rarely excites with its focus on rates, routes, and prices all determined via technical calculations, social regulation does indeed attract zealous individuals.[4] The commitment of environmentalists to protecting the environment is as strong as commitments in other, nonregulatory agencies. The Federal Trade Commission attracted many young, consumer-oriented attorneys after its reorganization of 1969; and the Occupational Safety and Health Administration built some organizational cohesion around the values of safety engineers and industrial hygienists (Pertschuk, 1982; Meier, 1985). Under the correct leadership even economic regulatory agencies such as the old Civil Aeronautics Board can be cohesive (even though the policies in that case were designed to abolish the agency [Derthick and Quirk, 1985]).

Since many regulatory agencies lack strong clientele, technical knowledge, leadership, and cohesion, understanding why few regulatory agencies become powerful bureaus is not difficult. Regulatory agencies are often denied resources because their function is neither in high demand nor exciting, and Congress limits agency autonomy with extensive oversight (see Pertschuk, 1982). Effective regulatory agencies, in fact, sow the seeds of their own opposition as the regulated industry seeks political help to

---

[4]A reason why regulatory agencies lack cohesion may be the bipartisan requirement for commissioners. This ensures that partisan cleavages are always possible at high levels. On the other hand, Welborn (1977) found that commission chairs had little trouble exerting control, a finding similar to that of Derthick and Quirk (1985). At the professional level the oft-noticed conflict between economists and lawyers may handicap agency cohesion.

restrict the agency. The budget growth of regulatory agencies in the Carter years followed by major restrictions in the Reagan years illustrates how transitory the power of regulatory agencies can be (Claybrook, 1984). The impact of most regulatory agencies on public policy, therefore, is only in narrow specialized areas and then only with the acquiescence of the relevant congressional committees and interest groups. Those regulatory agencies with long-term impact (the EPA, the FAA, the Federal Reserve, and perhaps some of the Department of Agriculture bureaus) either have functions other than regulation that permit the development of a more permanent power base or have been able to develop political support within their issue network. Most regulatory agencies, however, are dominated by their environment rather than controlling their portion of the policymaking process. Changes in political forces greatly affect the policy actions of regulatory agencies (see Quirk, 1980; Derthick and Quirk, 1985).

REDISTRIBUTIVE POLICY

Redistributive policy taxes one group of people to provide benefits for a another group. Such direct taxation is also the reason why redistributive policies are among the most controversial in American politics. Redistributive issues such as health insurance reform, social security, and welfare reform are major legislative controversies that divide the public along party lines.

THE SCOPE OF REDISTRIBUTIVE POLICY

Because redistributive policy proposals are so controversial, few policy areas can be characterized as redistributive in the United States. Only five major areas of public policy are classified as redistributive—income stabilization, welfare, health care, housing, and income distribution.

Income stabilization policies are policies designed to smooth out major fluctuations in a person's income resulting from unemployment or retirement. Two major agencies, the Social Security Administration (SSA) and the Employment and Training Administration (ETA) in the Department of Labor (plus some retirement agencies such as the Railroad Retirement Board) operate the bulk of the income stabilization programs. The Social Security Administration, located in the Department of Health and Human Services (HHS) but in fact autonomous, administers not only the nation's social security program but also the supplemental income program that guarantees a minimum income to all persons over the age of 65 and the cash portions of the federal welfare effort. The Employment and Training Administration's contribution to income security is in the area of training and jobs. The largest part of the ETA's budget is the federal portion of unemployment insurance, a program designed to stabilize the incomes of the temporarily unemployed. For longer-term unemployment, the ETA operates the nation's public jobs programs, the apprenticeship and training programs, and the U.S. Employment Service. State and local government bureaucracies serve as the implementation agencies for many of these federal programs such as welfare and unemployment insurance. The worker's compensation program, a program designed to pay medical bills and compensate workers who are injured on the job, is completely run by state agencies.

Although welfare policy is dominated by state and local governments, some federal bureaus operate in these areas. The monetary welfare programs, those providing cash directly to the recipient, are housed in the Social Security Administration; and the service programs are lodged in the HHS's Office of Human Development Services and the USDA's Food and Nutrition Service (FNS). Human Development administers a series of programs delivering services to the aged, children (Head Start), and the disabled. The FNS administers the food stamp, school lunch, and other nutrition programs. Generally Human Development, the FNS, and the SSA engage in proxy administrations; they provide funds and guidelines to the state agencies that operate these programs.

The health care area completes those programs generally perceived as social welfare programs. The Health Care Finance Administration operates both Medicare (health insurance for the aged) and Medicaid (health insurance for the indigent). A 1977 reorganization joined these similar programs that were located in two different agencies. The reorganization was perceived by observers as an administrative step toward a full scale National Health Insurance. Such grand goals, however, were displaced by the rapidly increasing federal costs in health care. In an effort to limit these outlays, federal health care policy has become more regulatory, with efforts to limit capital expenditures, new construction, and reimbursement for specific treatments (Reagan, 1987). Even the more modest Clinton health care reform effort failed to change the general priorities in this area.

Federal redistributive housing programs are located in two executive departments, Housing and Urban Development (HUD) and Agriculture. Within HUD a group of agencies—the Federal Housing Administration, the Government National Mortgage Administration, and the Office of Fair Housing and Equal Opportunity—operate programs affecting the quantity and quality of housing by influencing mortgage rates and selling practices. HUD's programs for the poor most frequently make the news, but middle-class housing programs are far larger. The Farmers Home Administration (FmHA) in the Department of Agriculture is a much broader agency. The FmHA provides credit to rural areas not only for home purchases but also for farm ownership, farm operation, farm equipment, and other functions (Selden 1997).

The income distribution aspects of redistributive policy are housed in two agencies, the Internal Revenue Service (IRS) and the Bureau of Public Debt. The IRS, of course, administers the nation's tax system, with the exception of those portions administered by the Bureau of Alcohol, Tobacco, and Firearms and the Customs Service.[5] The myriad tax programs run 2,800 pages in the *U.S. Code* with another 11,000 pages of IRS regulations. In general the tax code becomes more redistributive when revenue needs are high such as during wars and less redistributive during times of

---

[5] The classification of the IRS as a redistributive agency is open to question. Since the IRS enforces the nation's tax laws, it could easily be classified as a regulatory agency.

peace (Witte, 1985). The Bureau of Public Debt handles the administrative matters related to financing the nation's $5 trillion public debt. The bureau's functions are generally administrative with little policy activity although decisions made can affect individual bondholders.

THE STRUCTURE OF REDISTRIBUTIVE BUREAUS

Unlike regulatory policy, redistributive policies follow a common pattern; and this commonality affects the bureaucratic structure needed to administer the policy. American redistributive policies at the federal level rarely provide services directly; they provide money either directly to an individual to procure services or to a public or private agency which in turn provides the services. Redistributive federal bureaus, therefore, are large (they average 20,361 people) transfer payment agencies; they are excellent examples of government by checkwriting. The Social Security Administration alone in fiscal year 1998 distributed $333 billion in benefits to 48 million individuals. As transfer payment agencies, redistributive bureaus are resource intensive despite their large size. Although only 7 percent of federal employees work in redistributive bureaus, these employees handle more than half the federal budget. Stating this relationship another way, in 1985 federal redistributive agencies spent $1.9 million for every person they employed, by far the highest ratio in the federal government (see Table 4–2).

Federal redistributive agencies have been termed *cybernetic* by political scientist Allen Schick (1971). A cybernetic agency is one that operates under legislation that anticipates environmental changes and automatically adjusts agency actions to the changes. The unemployment insurance program, for example, is tied to local economic conditions. If local unemployment is severe for a long period of time, benefits can be extended. Social security benefits also respond to this environment by increasing as the cost of living rises. Cybernetic agencies, in short, have enabling legislation that automatically adjusts the agency's programs to some environmental changes, thus depriving the agency of the discretion normally found in other agencies.

• **TABLE 4–2** •

A STATISTICAL SUMMARY OF THE AVERAGE REDISTRIBUTIVE BUREAU

Number of Personnel	20,361
Size of 1985 Budget	$38.4 Billion
Number of Clientele	14.7
Computers	Moderate
Pages of Rules Issued	271
Pages of Relevant Laws	51
Budget to Personnel Ratio	$1,887,824
Rules to Laws Ratio	6.8

N = 9 Federal Redistributive Agencies and Bureaus

State and local agencies that administer redistributive programs often have a great deal of discretion even though the federal government attempts to limit this discretion with regulations. Medicaid and other welfare benefits are determined either by state agencies or local government agencies. These agencies both issue regulations that govern eligibility and make the actual decision concerning whether or not an individual receives any benefits. Social security is the major exception to this pattern with both federal money and federal administration.

REDISTRIBUTIVE BUREAU POLICYMAKING

Despite attempts by Congress and the president to restrict redistributive bureau activities through detailed laws, redistributive bureaus can influence public policy in four ways—adjudication, program operations, policy initiations, and policy advice. Policymaking via law enforcement or rulemaking is not a frequent activity for redistributive agencies.[6] A version of rulemaking, however, is performed in those programs implemented by state agencies. Individual states set levels of unemployment insurance and welfare benefits even though some of the money for these programs are federal dollars. Such determinations are sometimes done via state legislatures who in this manner act as "rulemaking" agencies for the federal programs; in other programs state bureaucrats make these decisions (Schneider, Jacoby and Coggburn 1997).

Adjudication

Adjudication as practiced by redistributive agencies is somewhat different from adjudication in regulatory agencies. Redistributive agencies generally do not adjudicate cases under vague public interest standards. Because redistributive policy provides benefits to classes of people, adjudications determine whether or not individual X is a member of class Y. In many cases determining whether X is a member of Y is simple because the law states unambiguous standards. Is X over age sixty-five and, therefore, eligible for social security? Was X unemployed under certain conditions and, therefore, eligible for unemployment compensation? In such circumstances individual bureaucrats exercise little discretion (Goodsell, 1983). Although most redistributive agency adjudications concern such simple matters, some cases are more difficult. The Social Security Administration oversees the disability insurance program. Certifying a person as disabled is more difficult than determining if a person is over age sixty-five. In these more difficult cases agency discretion permits some policymaking. In the disability program such discretion became controversial when President Reagan tried to reduce the size of the program (see Mezey, 1986). Federal agency discretion even in these areas, however, is limited because many federal redistributive programs are administered by state agencies. Discretion is vested in state administrators, therefore, rather than in federal bureaucrats.

---

[6] On this dimension the IRS is definitely more like a regulatory agency than a redistributive agency. The impact of the IRS on the nation's tax policy is through rulemaking and law enforcement as well as on proposals for tax reform.

Program Operations

In areas where the legislative standards are not as precise as social security, federal bureaus can influence public policy via program operations. Implementing a program reveals countless instances where discretion must be exercised since, even in redistributive policies, Congress cannot anticipate all possible circumstances. The Federal Housing Administration's (FHA) implementation of housing standards noted in Chapter 1 is an excellent example of policymaking through program operations (Wolman, 1971; Boyer, 1973). Designed to upgrade housing standards, the agency applied conservative economic standards to transform the program. The practice of redlining poor areas (not guaranteeing mortgages in these areas) resulted in an efficient FHA program that provided greater access to middle-income and suburban-area homes through lower mortgage rates, but it also contributed to a general housing decline in poor neighborhoods because only more traditional, and more expensive, mortgages were available there.

Policy Initiation

Policy initiation, the process of proposing new policies and under certain conditions implementing them, is a long accepted method of bureaucratic policymaking. Redistributive bureaus can affect public policy either by implementing their own policy proposals or by commenting on the policy proposals of the president, Congress, interest groups or others. A good example of policy initiation by a redistributive bureau is an action taken by the Department of Health, Education, and Welfare (HEW, now Health and Human Services) in early 1976. Motivated by high costs in the Aid to Families with Dependent Children (AFDC, the welfare program at the time) program, HEW initiated a pilot program to counter one form of abuse. In many cases divorced fathers who were ordered by a court to support their children failed to make support payments and moved without leaving a forwarding address. If the mother could not support the children by herself, the children often became AFDC recipients. If fathers could be found and court orders enforced, AFDC costs could be reduced. Another HEW agency, the Social Security Administration, had information on the location of almost all workers, since social security earnings are reported to the SSA. HEW established a pilot program whereby it provided information from social security files that permitted AFDC administrators to find nonsupporting fathers and take legal action to enforce payment orders. Using social security accounts for nonsocial security purposes was a major, and potentially troublesome, policy innovation by the bureaucracy. The benefits in reduced costs, however, became apparent almost immediately. The program, with congressional support, expanded to become a major element of federal welfare policy (Keiser, 1996).

At the state level a study by Boyd (1991) has also documented the activities of redistributive agencies in policy initiation. Her study of proposed regulations in Arizona reveals that redistributive agencies were more likely than other agencies to use their own expertise to defend a rule (as opposed to stating that other actors required the rule). Redistributive agencies were also more likely to have their rules approved without change by the Governor's Regulatory Review Council.

Policy Advice

Federal redistributive bureaus also affect public policy through policy advice—either by writing new legislation or by commenting on the legislative proposals of others. This legislative comment function is more important for redistributive bureaus than for most other bureaus because redistributive legislation contains more specific policy directives than does legislation in other areas. President Carter's 1977 proposal for welfare reform, based on a negative income tax plus work incentives, provides a good example. The specific reform proposal was written by civil servants in the Departments of Labor and Health, Education, and Welfare and reflected the biases of those agencies (*National Journal*, 1977: 1928). HEW's reputed position was that only a negative income tax-based welfare reform would work; HEW's position was a function of the perceived weaknesses in state administered welfare programs and HEW's expertise in cash transfer programs. Although the initiative failed, bureaucrats did influence the policy's content. Bureaus such as HEW play an important role in policy formulation because a bureau's opposition can be fatal to a program if the bureau possesses sufficient expertise to convince Congress that a program will not work.[7] As an illustration, when President Reagan's new federalism proposed transferring welfare programs to the states, the initiative was so contrary to the way the federal bureaucracy had defined the problem that the proposal was considered infeasible by many political elites. Only after another fifteen years of development by state bureaucracies was the effort to move more control to the state level successful.

THE ENVIRONMENT OF REDISTRIBUTIVE AGENCIES

The environment of federal redistributive agencies is intensely political, reflecting the major divisions between the Democratic and Republican parties. This partisan atmosphere creates a unique environment that affects the clientele support, knowledge, leadership, and cohesion of redistributive bureaus. Congress tries to respond to the partisan atmosphere with policies that restrict agency opportunities to cultivate clientele; Congress perceives redistributive issues as so important that they should be resolved in the legislative branch rather than by bureaus in consort with their clientele (McCool, 1990: 284). The appropriations testimony figures demonstrate the lack of agency clientele activity (Table 4–2). The average redistributive agency had fifteen groups supporting it over a three-year period. A closer examination reveals that this figure is inflated by a few strong clientele agencies; four agencies—the Farmers Home Administration, the

---

[7] Note that in the welfare reform instance the structure of redistributive agencies affects the policy proposal. HHS supported negative income tax proposals probably because it could not handle a national welfare program that was service oriented. With the expertise of the Social Security Administration, however, a negative income tax would be feasible. A 1977 reorganization, in fact, moved the cash welfare programs of the national government from the now defunct Social and Rehabilitation Service to the Social Security Administration. The move probably reflected the department's preference for welfare reform in the form of transfer payments. Welfare policy was changed dramatically in the mid-1990s when time limits were established and states given more authority.

Federal Housing Administration, the Employment and Training Administration, and the vocational rehabilitation program—had 78 percent of all redistributive clientele. Each of these organizations had clientele support from the personnel who administer the program at the local level. Deleting these four bureaus from the figures in Table 4–2 would demonstrate that redistributive bureaus rival regulatory agencies for weak clientele. Even those redistributive bureaus with strong clientele support may not be able to capitalize on it because the salience of redistributive policy virtually guarantees that one of the major political parties will oppose any position advocated by the bureau's clientele.

Knowledge is a valuable asset to redistributive bureaus because U.S. redistributive programs are massive. Despite the average redistributive agency's access to computers, computer expertise for these bureaus is related to processing huge workloads not to research as it is in other agencies. As a result, redistributive agency knowledge relies heavily on social science knowledge, a much weaker form of professional knowledge than that based on physical science and technology. Despite such reliance, one study at the state level finds redistributive agency expertise positively linked to agency autonomy (Boyd, 1991).

The benefits of strong leadership and organizational cohesion can be developed in some redistributive agencies. The influential position of Wilbur Cohen in social security reform or Sargeant Shriver in the early poverty program demonstrates the role leadership can play in redistributive policymaking (Wolf, 1997). In general, redistributive bureaus also have political functions that excite people and motivate agency employees. Health care, providing for the nation's aged, and caring for the poor are functions that attract highly committed people. At the federal level, however, congressional policies generally prevent most federal bureaus from being action agencies. Federal bureaus must be content to fund state and local projects. As a result of these restrictions, the potential cohesion of federal redistribution agencies is lost in routine administrative procedures. At the state level cohesion is more frequent. Mashaw (1983: 216) describes the Social Security Administration as an exception to this rule. "SSA is a paramilitary organization. It has a band, a chorus, an anthem, and a flag. Many of its top-level administrators have worked nowhere else. Its headquarters on the outskirts of Baltimore constitutes almost a separate city. Three generations of families are sometimes employed there."

Although redistributive agencies fare better on the dimensions of bureau power than do regulatory agencies, they are not among the more powerful federal bureaus. Occasionally an Internal Revenue Service or a Social Security Administration may greatly influence policy because they possess policy knowledge and leadership, but generally these agencies are subject to strong congressional control. To be sure, redistributive agencies have access to vast resources; over one-half the federal budget is spent by redistributive bureaus. Unfortunately for these bureaus, however, the resources are usually transferred directly to citizens. Agency discretion, and therefore autonomy, is usually low. Although a bureau may occasionally develop autonomy as strong as the IRS did in 1973 when it refused John Dean's request for audits of President Nixon's "enemies," a redistributive agency rarely concentrates sufficient leadership and expertise to refuse a presidential request.

State-level redistributive agencies are another matter. With access to federal funds, state redistributive agencies have budget autonomy compared to other agencies. They can also develop higher levels of expertise and cohesion because they are action agencies, not just check writers. On a relative basis, therefore, state redistributive agencies may exercise far more power than their federal cohorts.

....

DISTRIBUTIVE POLICY

Distributive policymaking is the most common form of federal action to solve public problems. Government distributive policies use general tax revenue or other nonuser taxes to provide benefits directly to individuals. National parks, health research, crop insurance, and urban grants are all examples of federal distributive policy.

THE SCOPE OF DISTRIBUTIVE POLICY

A full listing of all federal government distributive programs is impossible; there are simply too many. Federal distributive policies may, however, be classified into five main types—the distribution of subsidies, the support of research, the collection and dissemination of information, the creation of distributive public goods, and the provision of insurance.

Distribution of Subsidies

The distribution of grants and subsidies is an accepted method of federal policy. The nation's agricultural system, for example, is frequently plagued with large surpluses. Rather than bear the consequences of lost production resulting from surplus-induced low prices, the government pays subsidies to farmers who voluntarily limit production when farm commodities are in oversupply. The federal government does not force farmers to limit production but rather grants them benefits such as cash or surplus grains if they agree to reduce production. Participation in such programs is voluntary (Anderson et al., 1984).[8] The lure of federal money is also used to encourage state and local governments to take specified actions. Mass transit grants, urban development grants, and education grants all seek to influence state and local government actors via the incentive of federal grants. In 1996 the federal government distributed $228 billion in grants to state and local governments. These distributive benefits are usually cash grants either with or without restrictions; rarely does the federal government provide

---

[8] In theory the 1996 Freedom to Farm Act was intended to wean farmers from subsidies and place the farm sector on the open market; I am skeptical that this policy will remain in effect permanently (Wrinkle and Meier 1998). In 1998 with the fall in farm prices and some serious weather problems, efforts were made to reinstate agricultural supports by President Clinton.

services directly to state and local governments.[9] Recipients who receive federal grants (including state and local governments) are subject to a wide variety of federal restrictions. Some relate directly to the grant; for example, states must limit welfare payments to two years. Other restrictions, such as nondiscrimination requirements or drug-free workplace requirements, are attached to federal funds that are not directly concerned with these problems.

Government-Sponsored Research

Distributive policy also includes government acting as the research arm of American industry. Government-supported research can be justified by the argument that many industries are too small and too fragmented to support the research necessary for improving productivity. Government, on the other hand, with its great resources can easily bear the costs of such research and distribute the results to industry. The public, in turn, benefits from the improved goods and services. As noted above, federal bureaucrats receive 1,500 patents per year; thousands more are obtained by private individuals working with federal research grants (Costle, 1980). Although the public, or more cynically industry, is normally perceived as the recipient of government research benefits, the most direct beneficiary is the researcher who could not support large-scale research without federal funds. Federal research efforts occur in numerous agencies, but most distributive research is located in six general areas.[10] The federal government's major research contributions are in agriculture (the Agriculture Research Service, the Cooperative State Research, Education, and Extension Service), environmental matters (the National Oceanic and Atmospheric Administration, the Environmental Protection Agency), health (the National Institutes of Health), education (the Department of Education), energy (the Department of Energy), and general science (the National Science Foundation).

Collection and Dissemination of Information

A distributive benefit related to government-sponsored research is government collection and distribution of information. Individuals and organizations often need to know the results of government and academic research or trends in the U.S. economy or demography. Although some private organizations distribute such information, in many areas only government disseminates this information. The agricultural research results of the Agriculture Research Service and the Cooperative State Research Service are

---

[9] The range of subsidy programs operated by the federal government covers a great many areas. Subsidies or grants are provided in agrulcture, law enforcement, Indian affairs, disease control, maritime shipping, mass transit, railroads, health care services and resources, education, veterans affairs, small business, and fine arts and humanities.

[10] Distributive research has research results that directly benefit industry. Nondistributive research is a major federal activity. Research on weapons systems or treasury policies are intended to directly benefit government rather than industry although industries do benefit by applying defense research to nondefense areas (for example, application of military aircraft research to civilian aircraft development).

transmitted to local farmers through the Agricultural Extension Service. The U.S. Geological Survey collects and distributes information on possible mineral deposits collected by its geological studies. The U.S. government does not restrict itself to distributing information to producer organizations; the U.S. Travel Service, for example, disseminates information about the United States to prospective tourists, thus benefitting the travel industry.

State and local governments also disseminate information. Consumer protection agencies frequently publish information about products; some insurance commissions provide information on the cost of insurance policies and the number of complaints about individual companies. Economic development agencies, although they sometimes offer tangible benefits such as tax breaks, primarily exist to offer business-related information to firms making location decisions.

Creation of Distributive Public Goods

All governments create public goods for their citizens. In some cases, such as national defense, these public goods are collective that a citizen has no choice about using them. All persons receive the benefits of collective public goods whether or not they desire them. Distributive public goods, on the other hand, are provided by government; but an individual citizen can decide if he or she will use them. National parks, recreation projects, federal highways, and conservation projects are examples of distributive public goods. Government can also create distributive public goods by permitting an individual to exploit a government-protected monopoly. Granting a patent, for example, rewards inventors by allowing them monopoly control over their invention.

Creating a distributive public good usually implies regulating public access to that good. Just as broadcasting frequencies can be destroyed by too many broadcasters, overuse and abuse of highways, parks, and patents also denigrates these public goods. As a result, agencies that create distributive public goods usually perform some regulatory functions.

A variety of distributive public policies are created by state and local governments. Agencies at this level also administer parks, highways, recreation areas, and even hospitals. Higher education is clearly a distributive public good at the state level. Because all states have compulsory school attendance laws, elementary and secondary education can be viewed as a collective public good.

Government Insurance

The final area of distributive policy is the provision of insurance benefits. In areas where private insurance is not feasible or profitable, the resources of government are sometimes used to provide the distributive benefits of insurance. Federal crop insurance and federal flood insurance are areas where private industry needs assistance in providing insurance protection. Offering deposit insurance to banks, savings associations, and credit unions has been used as a mechanism for extending regulation. All financial institutions that accept deposit insurance from the Federal Deposit Insurance Corporation must also accept federal government regulation of their activities. Insurance is a distributive benefit because it provides the benefits of protection that would not be available without government action. Distributive insurance benefits do not include what is termed "social insurance"—social security, unemployment compensation, etc. These are redistributive policies rather than distributive insurance benefits. The amount of federal insurance benefits is massive. In 1987 federal government insurance programs had a potential liability of $3.6 trillion (Thomas, 1987: 50).

THE STRUCTURE OF DISTRIBUTIVE BUREAUS

Similar to redistributive policy, the political environment of distributive policy affects the type of bureau that administers distributive policy. Distributive bureaus are small, averaging about 8,700 persons (see Table 4–3); this size is to be expected of agencies that distribute benefits to only a portion of the American people. The nature of distributive policy generates resources in addition to personnel. Since many distributive bureaus provide cash subsidies or grants rather than services, the ample budget to personnel ratio ($215,785 per employee) is not surprising.

The administration of distributive benefits usually entails a great deal of discretion. This discretion is reflected in two ways. First, the enabling legislation of distributive programs is brief (an average of less than fifty pages in the *U.S. Code*), permitting the agency some flexibility in meeting its clientele's needs. The National Institutes of Health, for example, operates a $14.9 billion budget under a law that runs less than twenty pages in the *U.S. Code*. Second, discretion is increased by the decentralized nature of distributive bureaus; most distributive agency employees are located in the field delivering services or monitoring programs rather than in Washington. The Departments of Agriculture and Interior, for example, two departments with many distributive bureaus, have fewer than one employee in seven stationed in the Washington, D.C. metropolitan area. As the distance from Washington increases, so does discretion.

Distributive bureaus are often able to translate the issue network involving the agency into an iron triangle composed of the bureau, the relevant congressional committees, and the affected interest groups. Subsystem government (see Chapter 3) is

---

• **TABLE 4–3** •

A STATISTICAL SUMMARY OF THE AVERAGE DISTRIBUTIVE AGENCY

Number of Personnel	8,666
Size of 1985 Budget	$1.87 Billion
Number of Clientele	58.1
Computers	Many
Pages of Rules Issued	205
Pages of Relevant Laws	49
Budget to Personnel Ratio	$215,785
Rules to Laws Ratio	7.2

$N = 58$ Federal Distributive Agencies and Bureaus

most prevalent in distributive policy areas (McCool, 1990). Since distributive bureaus provide benefits to only a portion of the American population, only small segments of Congress have any interest in the bureau; these members of Congress usually sit on the subcommittees that oversee the bureau (Freeman, 1965). Any group strong enough to persuade Congress to grant government benefits to it is likely to be highly organized; the environment of distributive bureaus, therefore, usually contains numerous powerful interest groups.

DISTRIBUTIVE BUREAU POLICYMAKING

The policymaking influence of distributive bureaus equals or exceeds that of most other federal bureaus. Although implementation is a distributive bureau's major means of affecting public policy, some bureaus have an impact through policy initiation and occasionally law enforcement. Adjudication and rulemaking, two major forms of policymaking for other bureaus, are not major activities in distributive policy. Because distributive bureaus are encouraged to deliver goods and services and because adjudication is the usual means of limiting access to benefits, these bureaus downplay their adjudicatory powers in preference for maximum benefit distribution.[11] Rulemaking varies greatly among distributive bureaus. Some agencies such as the Maritime Administration, the Department of Education, and the Department of Veterans Affairs issue extensive rules; but most distributive agencies eschew rulemaking (at the state level see Boyd, 1991).

Program Operations

Given the vague enabling legislation of most distributive bureaus, program implementation and program operations provide numerous opportunities for agencies to guide the direction of public policy. Every law must be translated into specific programs, and this translation involves agency discretion. Agricultural research provides a good example of policymaking through implementation. The agricultural research establishment composed of the Agricultural Research Service (the USDA's in-house research organization) and the Cooperative State Research Service with its affiliated college experiment stations has a simple mission. It is "to provide the necessary knowledge and technology so that farmers can produce efficiently, conserve the environment, and meet the food and fiber needs of the American people." By any standard the agricultural research establishment is remarkably successful in meeting its goals of providing food and fiber needs of the American people; the productivity of agriculture has tripled in the last 100 years (Hadwiger, 1982). The research establishment has been criticized, however, for its implementation of these goals (Hightower, 1972). According to critics, the research establishment has concentrated on high-technology processes that produce large surpluses of nutritionally questionable food through extensive use of pesticides and fertil-

---

[11] The Department of Veterans Affairs is an example of an agency that does use adjudicatory processes to determine if individuals are eligible for VA benefits. Unfortunately little is known about the impact of this agency's adjudications on veterans' policy.

izers (W. Berry, 1977). James Hightower (1972) contends that implementation of this policy is driving small farmers from the land because they cannot afford the capital investment necessary to compete in this high-technology agriculture system. A second-order consequence of this policy is the aggravation of existing urban problems by contributing to the flow of people to urban areas. From a more empirical perspective, the actions of the agricultural research establishment can easily be explained; they simply implemented congressional legislation by meeting the needs of the Department of Agriculture's prime clientele, the large, technologically advanced farmer (see Hadwiger, 1982; Baldwin, 1968; Wrinkle and Meier 1998). The resulting policy is different from what it would be if the agricultural research establishment implemented programs designed to benefit small farmers or more labor-intensive farmers.

Policy Initiation

Distributive bureaus and their clientele can become so powerful that they not only dominate policy implementation but also control the policy initiation stage. In 1964 wheat farmers rejected President Kennedy's effort to apply mandatory production controls to agriculture; President Johnson then called together leaders of the major agricultural interest groups and asked them to formulate a farm program (Lowi, 1969: 102–103). The resulting Wheat-Cotton Bill of 1964 was a product of the Department of Agriculture and the major farm interest groups. Congress accepted the Wheat-Cotton Bill, thus writing into law many of the bureaus' and interest groups' proposals. Until the 1973 food crisis, agricultural policy proposals without the support of the USDA bureaus and their clientele had little chance of passage. The continued decline of rural representation in Congress along with the rise of food as a salient issue after the Soviet grain sales has weakened the bureaus' influence in policy initiation (Barton, 1976; Peters, 1978). Agriculture subsystems, as a result, are more open to nonagriculture influences.

The National Institutes of Health research programs illustrate how a bureau can not only initiate a policy but also set the legislative agenda. Based on their own initiative, the NIH funded in-vitro fertilization research. The successful development of implantation techniques raised several policy issues in regard to surrogate parent contracts and whether fertilized embryos could be considered marital property. These issues were addressed by several state legislatures as they crafted policy in response to successful bureaucratic action (see Maynard-Moody, 1989). A similar process occurred in fetal research when NIH research attracted the attention of antiabortion interest groups and members of Congress (Maynard-Moody, 1995).

Law Enforcement

Although distributive agencies are rarely law enforcement agencies, occasionally they influence policy either by not enforcing a law or by selective law enforcement. The federal Reclamation Act of 1902 attempts to support the small farmer by limiting any one farmer to 160 acres of land irrigated by federal reclamation projects. The Bureau of Land Management in the Department of Interior, the agency that administered the law, never enforced the 160-acre provision, permitting some landowners to accumulate several thousand acres of reclamation-irrigated land. As a result of nonenforcement, a government policy designed to benefit small farmers was transformed into a policy congruent with the Department of Agriculture's preference for large farmers. Congress eventually modified the law to be consistent with the Bureau of Land Management's administration.

THE ENVIRONMENT OF DISTRIBUTIVE AGENCIES

Distributive agencies have the most favorable political environment of all federal bureaus. No agencies fit the powerful bureau described in Chapter 3 as well as distributive agencies because their environment is conducive to strong clientele, knowledge, leadership, and cohesion. Not only is a distributive bureau's environment full of strong clientele groups, but the agency is also encouraged by Congress to meet clientele needs. For the most part, distributive agencies were created in response to organized groups' needs; and, therefore, little conflict exists between congressional intent and clientele needs. Table 4–4 shows the top ten clientele agencies in the U.S. government ranked according to the number of interest groups testifying for them at appropriation hearings. All ten bureaus from the Army Corps of Engineers to the National Endowment for the Arts are distributive policy bureaus. Strong clientele support is characteristic of most distributive bureaus as reflected in the average of fifty-eight supporting clientele groups per bureau (see Table 4–3). This average is four times the support for any other type of bureau. Distributive politics is clearly clientele politics.

When strong clientele support for distributive bureaus can be combined with expert knowledge, bureaus are in enviable positions of power. Agencies with research functions (National Institutes of Health, the Agricultural Research Service, the Na-

• TABLE 4–4 •

TOP TEN CLIENTELE AGENCIES OF THE FEDERAL GOVERNMENT

AGENCY	NUMBER OF GROUPS*
1. Army Corps of Engineers (Defense)	1028
2. Bureau of Reclamation (Interior)	326
3. Forest Service (Agriculture)	275
4. National Institutes of Health (HHS)	223
5. Department of Education	156
6. Bureau of Indian Affairs (Interior)	153
7. National Parks Service (Interior)	96
8. Agricultural Research Service (Agriculture)	90
9. Soil Conservation Service (Agriculture)	85
10. National Endowment for the Arts	79

*Number of groups supporting the agency before the appropriate subcommittee of the House Appropriations Committee, 1974–1976.

tional Aeronautics and Space Administration) have a built-in advantage on the knowledge dimension. Although distributive agencies used two of every five federal government computers in the 1970s, the distribution of the computers, similar to the distribution of expert knowledge, was uneven. The bulk of distributive policy computers were located in the research agencies, especially the Department of Energy programs and the National Aeronautics and Space Administration. Most other distributive agencies rely on political expertise generated by familiarity with programs and clientele rather than technologically based expertise. Expert knowledge, therefore, is an asset only some distributive bureaus have.

Strong leadership in distributive bureaus is usually related to clientele support. Where bureau chiefs have strong clientele support and good congressional ties, agencies can be relatively autonomous vis-à-vis the president. Although in some cases, such as Agriculture Secretaries Earl Butz and John Block, department heads and bureau chiefs are recruited from the agency's clientele, the normal bureau chief-clientele ties are less obvious. Bureau chiefs develop strong clientele ties through long-term working arrangements with the bureau's clientele. The normal bureau chief may spend thirty or more years in the agency before assuming the top position. Much of this time is spent delivering services to the agency's clientele. During this time any rational future bureau chief realizes his/her agency's future is tied to clientele support; therefore, he/she cultivates clientele ties.

Since distributive agencies are charged with improving people's lives and since they are action agencies unlike redistributive bureaus, they can develop into cohesive organizations. The Forest Service uses personnel rotation plus heavy doses of socialization to instill organizational loyalty in its personnel (Kaufman, 1960). The dedication of NASA employees in the space program's early years was legendary. In some agencies cohesion is a function of professional commitment to scientific goals (e.g., the National Institutes of Health). Other agencies consciously use socialization techniques or personnel processes to increase their employees' commitment to organizational goals.

Despite the advantages of distributive agencies in regard to clientele support, expert knowledge, leadership, and cohesion, these agencies are still influenced by other portions of their environment. When a distributive agency's environment is quiescent, the political subsystem functions to protect the bureau and its clientele. Under these conditions distributive bureaus are among the most powerful in government. When the political environment is turbulent or politicized (that is, others are concerned about policy in the subsystem area), distributive bureaus may be overwhelmed by their environment (Harris, 1977; Baumgartner and Jones 1993). In 1973, for example, agricultural bureaus were overwhelmed by the public's reaction to high food prices forcing the bureaus to accept several policy changes (Barton, 1976). Only the strongest agencies can weather an all-out attack by the president, the Congress, and other interest groups.

In normal political times distributive agencies do well in aggrandizing resources. Without severe fiscal constraints, as might be imposed by recession or war, distributive agencies get average or better increases in resources every year. Although distributive agencies may not be among the fastest-growing agencies, their budget growth is stable. In tight fiscal times, however, such as the 1970s and 1980s, when inflation easily outruns agency budgets, distributive agencies take a backseat to uncontrollable programs.

Programs that have benefits written into law and tied to inflation rates or unemployment rates (for example, social security or unemployment insurance) have first claim on resources when revenues are scarce. Distributive agencies fare less well in these circumstances.

Distributive agencies are also highly autonomous when their scope of action is relatively narrow. When agency actions affect only the bureau's clientele directly, the bureau can usually operate without intervention by the president or Congress as long as no portion of the subsystem is unsatisfied. When issues outside the normal subsystem are concerned or when the environment is politicized, distributive bureaus become only one actor among many.

CONSTITUENT POLICY

The fourth type of policies are those intended to benefit government in general or the nation as a whole. Theodore Lowi (1972: 300) terms such policies "constituent" in that the nation is the constituency for the policies, but such policies are clearly a residual group that do not fit among the other three. In this section the term "constituent" policies will be used for convenience even though many of the policies have little in common.

THE SCOPE OF CONSTITUENT POLICY

Two types of bureaus exist in this policy area. National security-foreign affairs bureaus serve the nation by providing it with defense, diplomacy, intelligence, and propaganda. The Department of Defense and its major operating units—the Army, Navy, and Air Force—along with the support agencies (for example, the Defense Mapping Agency) provide one core of bureaus in the national security area. Attached to this core are the Selective Service System, now in mothballs, the intelligence community, and parts of the Coast Guard with defense-related functions. The second core of the national security bureaus are the diplomacy agencies with the Department of State at the center. A variety of agencies from other departments assist the State Department in its function—the foreign agricultural assistance units in Agriculture, the U.S. Information Agency, the international business divisions of the Department of Commerce, and so forth.

The government service bureaus—the second type of constituent bureau—perform a different role by providing services to government rather than to the nation. The Office of Personnel Management, for example, supplies the government with its personnel. The General Services Administration operates the physical resources of government, the supplies, the buildings, and other such needs. Several bureaus in the Treasury Department coin or print the nation's money and supervise the physical aspects of the government's money system. The Secret Service provides security for government officials as well as performing some regulatory functions. State and local governments all have similar agencies to perform these service functions.

STRUCTURE OF CONSTITUENT POLICY

Since constituent policy contains two types of institutions, any generalization about the structure of constituent bureaus must be qualified. Constituent policy bureaus, especially the national security bureaus, are massive government organizations. The average constituent policy bureau is twice the size of the average redistributive policy bureau, the next largest type of bureaucracy (see Table 4–5). Fully 65 percent of federal civilian employees are members of constituent policy bureaus. The large size and massive functions make constituent bureaus people intensive despite the large capital needs of the armed forces. The average constituent bureau spends $245,000 per employee, a figure only slightly larger than that for distributive agencies. Unlike redistributive bureaus, however, constituent bureaus deliver services rather than money to procure services.

As bureaus with the nation as their prime clientele, constituent policy bureaus are open to the environmental influences of government and politics. According to Harris's (1977) study of U.S.–China policy, the key variable in such circumstances is issue politicization—the degree to which the issue under consideration is subject to partisan debate. If an issue is not politicized (for example, U.S.–Paraguay relations), decisions are made at low levels in the bureaucracy. If issues are politicized as the issue of relations with China was during the 1950s and 1960s, then decisional authority moves upward with politicians resolving issues and imposing uniform behavior on the bureaucracy (Harris, 1977). In short, as issues become salient, bureaucrats lose influence to politicians.

CONSTITUENT BUREAU POLICYMAKING

Constituent policy bureaus influence government policy within their sphere of activity in a variety of ways. Implementation, policy initiation, and bureaucratic routines are the major methods of policy impact although rulemaking is important in some instances. Unlike other agencies, especially regulatory agencies, adjudication is not a major means of policymaking. To be sure, the Merit Systems Protection Board does

---

• TABLE 4–5 •

A STATISTICAL SUMMARY OF THE AVERAGE CONSTITUENT AGENCY

Number of Personnel	42,600
Size of 1985 Budget	$10.5 Billion
Number of Clientele	8.3
Computers	Many
Pages of Rules Issued	363
Pages of Relevant Laws	79
Budget to Personnel Ratio	$245,633
Rules to Laws Ratio	4.2

$N = 27$ Federal Constituent Agencies and Bureaus

adjudicate several thousand adverse actions against federal employees annually, and the Selective Service System at one time adjudicated draft deferments; but in general constituent policy bureaus have few opportunities for adjudication.

Implementation

Constituent policy bureaus, similar to other federal bureaus, affect public policy through implementation. Since legislation or executive orders establishing policy are often vague, bureaus must make policy more specific as they implement it. A good example of policymaking through implementation is the Civil Service Commission's (now Office of Personnel Management) implementation of equal employment policy for federal government employment (Rosenbloom, 1973). Before May 11, 1971, government policy on minority employment was one of nondiscrimination; government would not discriminate in hiring on the basis of race, color, religion, sex, or national origin. The commission's decision to alter this policy was forced by certain environmental events. First, the nondiscrimination policy was not successful in placing minorities in high-level positions in the federal bureaucracy; most minorities were located in low-level positions. Second, the commission was perceived as ineffective by other policymakers (Rosenbloom, 1973: 239). Two bills were introduced in Congress to move equal employment functions from the Civil Service Commission to the Equal Employment Opportunity Commission which had similar powers for private sector employment. To forestall this threat and gain back clientele support from minorities, the Civil Service Commission announced a new policy; federal agencies were to use goals for minority hiring and timetables for reaching those goals. Many observers believed that this change in policy marked the first use of quotas in federal government hiring policy (Rosenbloom, 1973: 230). The Commission's change from a policy of nondiscrimination to a policy of goals and timetables was accomplished administratively without altering the basic legislation covering the civil service. From a clientele standpoint, however, these changes came to naught when President Carter moved government equal employment programs from the Civil Service Commission to the Equal Employment Opportunity Commission in 1978.

Policymaking via implementation is also a major activity in national security bureaus. Chapter 1 provided several examples of national security agencies implementing policy during the Cuban missile crisis. In fact, the decision of the air force early in President Kennedy's term not to remove U.S. missiles in Turkey was a major factor in the Soviet decision to place missiles in Cuba (Allison, 1971; but see Bernstein, 1980).

Policy Initiation

Constituent bureaus may also alter and formulate policy through the process of policy initiation, by creating new policies and proposals to replace current policy. Although U.S. policy toward China is an area in which the president had been the dominant force during the 1970s and 1980s, the State Department was not without influence (Harris, 1977). Bureaucratic tactics focused on demonstrating that the "seamless web" position, which held that Americans should not tolerate *any* interaction with China, no longer dominated the perspectives of U.S. elites. Bureaucrats pursued alternative policies in the 1970s by isolating small components of China policy such as easing the trade embargo and encouraging the exchange of scholars and journalists. These incremental bureaucratic changes had a profound impact on U.S.-China policy by demonstrating the general ideological reaction to China was weakening, thus permitting additional steps toward normalization of relations (Harris, 1977).

A similar bureaucratic policy innovation resulted in the Fulbright Scholars program, a program that sends U.S. educators to other countries to teach and research. After World War II bureaucrats in the State Department noticed that the United States had a substantial amount of other countries' currencies that we did not want to convert to dollars for fear of destablizing these currencies. The solution was to send U.S. scholars to these countries and let them spend the currency there. State Department officials approached Senator J. William Fulbright, who agreed to sponsor a law authorizing the program (Hill, 1989a: 11).

Policymaking through policy initiation is also widespread in other constituent policy agencies. The Defense Department is usually the main initiator of new weapons systems with assistance from the defense industry. Other policymakers must often respond to Defense Department initiatives. In the government service area, the Civil Service Reform Act of 1978 was drafted and lobbied through Congress by Civil Service Commission Chair Alan K. Campbell. The resulting legislation, which has been termed the most significant change in federal personnel policy in a century, established the Senior Executive Service, divided the Commission into the Office of Personnel Management and the Merit Systems Protection Board, and established new procedures for labor relations (Ingraham and Ban, 1984)

Bureaucratic Routines

Constituent policy bureaus can also influence policy through bureaucratic routines— the standard operating procedures and organizational biases that most agencies possess. Since constituent policy bureaus are generally large organizations, they tend to be more bureaucratized than other federal bureaus and have set methods of handling problems that occur. Routines affect policy when a bureau must act in a manner that violates the bureau's perception of how the activity should be done. According to Adam Yarmolinsky (1971), the U.S. Army in the early 1960s perceived its function as fighting large massed land battles. When President Kennedy attempted to create a more flexible army through counterinsurgency training with the famed Green Berets, the innovation was strongly resisted by the regular army. The Green Berets soon were perceived as an unwanted assignment and were shunned by many of the Army's best officers, thus weakening the nation's counterinsurgency ability. After the end of the Vietnam War, the Department of Defense slashed budgets for counterinsurgency by 95 percent (Riley, 1986: 2566). The rigidities of constituent policy bureaus' routines, therefore, can affect policy decisions that others make either by preventing the selection of one policy or by handicapping the policy if the "wrong" alternative is selected. Routines and preferred methods of operation can explain much of defense policy including the navy's preference for large aircraft carriers, the marine corps' rejection of alternative combat roles, and the air force's unwillingness to be a support arm of the Army (Binkin, 1976: Bergerson, 1980). At the local level, Stein (1986) found that an autonomous civil service commission (as opposed to one controlled by the chief executive) reduced the level of minority employment. She concluded that the norms of professional bureaucrats resulted in resistance to affirmative action.

Rulemaking

Although most constituent policy bureaus use rulemaking as a strictly administrative function concerned with contract specifications and similar functions, some constituent bureaus establish public policy through the rulemaking process. The Office of Personnel Management, for example, has issued over four hundred pages of rules and regulations covering federal employment practices. The defense agencies issue a variety of rules on military procedures and practices, some with policy impact. In general though, constituent policy agencies, as illustrated by their low rules to laws ratio (see Table 4–5), are not rulemaking agencies.

THE ENVIRONMENT OF CONSTITUENT POLICY BUREAUS

The political environment of constituent bureaus conditions their ability to use clientele support, expert knowledge, leadership, and cohesion to strengthen a bureau's power base. Despite the well-established belief in the military-industrial complex, constituent bureaus are not strong clientele agencies. Since the prime recipient of a constituent bureau's services is government, few opportunities exist to develop potential clientele. Clientele support for constituent bureaus is, in fact, no stronger than is clientele support for regulatory agencies (Table 4–5). Although Defense Department operating bureaus average twice as many clientele as nondefense constituent bureaus do, they do not rival the clientele support of bureaus in distributive policy.[12] The primary clientele of constituent bureaus are other political elites in government. This lack of traditional clientele means that constituent policy agencies are extremely sensitive to their environment. When issues are highly politicized, as Harris (1977) notes, constituent bureaus are not strong policymaking actors. Constituent agencies, unlike distributive bureaus, lack the specific clientele support to withstand the pressure of unfavorable elite pressures. In fact, constituent bureaus may generate most of their clientele support from distributive policies they administer such as the location of local bases or offices. Despite the decline in military expenditures, for example, no U.S. military bases were closed from 1977 to 1988, and 13 new ones were opened (Morrison, 1988: 747). From 1988 to 1998, however, 42 of 97 targeted bases were closed. Support for bases, however, does not seem to be translated into support for more defense spending in general. As a result constituent bureaus must bend to the winds in the political environment. When issues are not politicized, however, bureaus have more influ-

---

[12] Defense bureaus may well receive no benefits from their clientele. With the exception of veterans organizations and former-officers associations, most defense clientele are defense contractors. Since defense contracting often is competitive at its early stages, most defense procurement policies will have groups on both sides of the issues. Clientele support for specific weapons systems may be difficult to translate into more diffuse support for the agency (see Ray, 1981).

ence because they are favored with expert knowledge, leadership, and cohesion (at the state level see Boyd, 1991).

A major factor permitting constituent bureaus to exercise policymaking power is a bureau's expert knowledge. Constituent bureaus are complex, technical agencies administering massive programs. Of the three major types of constituent policy agencies, only foreign policy agencies do not claim technical expertise. The intelligence bureaus, the defense bureaus, and the treasury bureaus all develop expert knowledge to accomplish their tasks. Cryptographers, linguists, physicists, and economists are only a few of the technical specialists in constituent bureaus. One good indicator of the technical capacity of these bureaus is that 56 percent of the U.S. government's computers in the 1970s were used in constituent policy agencies (see Table 4–5). With such expertise the absence of clientele support may be an advantage. In areas of "national interest" policy, clientele support may well be inappropriate since it indicates ties to special, nonnational interests. Bureaus can argue that their lack of clientele support makes them neutral, technical experts. Although other policymakers are less inclined to accept that argument than they were in the past, it is a more tenable position for constituent bureaus than it is for distributive bureaus with their strong clientele ties.

Leadership as a source of bureau power in constituent bureaus resembles leadership everywhere else; potential leadership exists. Unlike regulatory agencies headed by commissions, constituent bureaus are structured to permit leadership; that is, they are hierarchical organizations with norms of obedience. Given the importance of most constituent policy, many agency heads are usually either recruited from the outside with a reputation for leadership (Defense Secretary Robert McNamara, Office of Personnel Management Director Alan Campbell). Others develop expertise and leadership ability inside the agency (Admiral Elmo Zumwalt, Chairman of the Joint Chiefs of Staff Colin Powell).

Organizational cohesion is also easy to develop in some constituent bureaus. The importance of these bureaus' functions, supplemented by extensive socialization, make the defense and the intelligence bureaus among the most cohesive in the federal government (Janowitz, 1960). The ability of intelligence agencies to operate in secrecy so long is a testimony to their organizational cohesion. Where bureau tasks are less crucial, organizational cohesion is weaker. Foreign policy bureaus are at times marked by frequent internal squabbles. Government service bureaus appear to lack the exciting missions necessary to develop strong cohesive organizations.

The ability of constituent bureaus to aggrandize resources and develop autonomy is a function of the above environment. When the environment is politicized, bureaus must yield to the political pressures in the environment. Defense agencies, for example, did well in the late 1970s and early 1980s but found huge budget increases were not as easy to get after the mid-1980s. When the environment is not politicized, the bureaus can dominate portions of their environment if they possess expert knowledge, leadership, and cohesion. Although constituent bureaus, especially the defense bureaus, receive a large share of the government's resources, their ability to extract additional resources varies greatly over time. Because constituent policy is an area where expenditures are controllable, they are often the first to be sacrificed to the needs of uncontrollable programs. For approximately ten years after the peak of the Vietnam War, defense spending stood virtually still while inflation increased the budget of other agencies. Similar reductions began in 1990.

Constituent policy bureaus, especially the defense and intelligence bureaus, also have suffered a decline in policymaking autonomy. In the politicized environment of the Vietnam War, many people were quite willing to evaluate the performance of these bureaus and to evaluate them negatively. Where the results were not positive, as they were not in Vietnam or in Chile or in other areas of intelligence policy, bureau autonomy was gradually restricted. Even during the Reagan and Bush administrations, with the president backing the defense agencies and the successes of Grenada, *Achille Lauro*, and Iraq fresh in the minds of people, other political elites were quite willing to point out cost overruns and challenge the autonomy of the defense agencies.

Although these statements on the limits of constituent bureaus' resources and autonomy apply most directly to defense and intelligence bureaus, other constituent bureaus are much weaker. Treasury bureaus, government service bureaus, and foreign affairs bureaus lack the vital missions of defense and intelligence agencies. Although some of these constituent bureaus, under special circumstances, can develop into powerful bureaus, most must be satisfied with lesser goals.

SUMMARY

This chapter traced the policy implementation process in federal government bureaus. Because the myriad public policies are more different than similar, the U.S. policy process was divided into four types—regulatory policy, redistributive policy, distributive policy, and a residual category called constituent policy. The impact of government bureaucracy in each of these areas was examined. Bureaus have greater influence in distributive and constituent policies. In distributive policy, the area with the greatest bureaucratic impact, bureau policy influence is a function of strong clientele support and good leadership with an occasional assist from expert knowledge in the research agencies. Bureau influence in constituent policy is a function of knowledge, leadership, and organizational cohesion. Although both types of bureaus cannot resist the pressures of a hostile, mobilized political environment, distributive bureaus have more success because their strong specific clientele support can counter diffuse opposition. While distributive bureaus can influence policy more often, this power is limited by the narrower functions that distributive agencies perform. Regulatory agencies and redistributive agencies have less influence on public policy. Such bureaus become powerful policymakers only in special circumstances where they develop expert knowledge, display exceptional leadership, or are permitted to cultivate clientele support.

Bureau activities in the policymaking process also vary by policy area. Government bureaus influence public policy through rulemaking, adjudication, law enforcement, program implementation, policy initiation, comments on proposed policy changes, and bureaucratic routines. Bureaus in different policy areas engage in different policymaking activities with varying effectiveness. Not all government bureaus are power brokers in the policy process, and not all bureaus influence the process in the same manner.

CHAPTER 5

BUREAUCRACY AND THE PUBLIC'S EXPECTATIONS

Administrative power is a concern in a democracy because the exercise of administrative power differs little from the exercise of political power by other political institutions except that political power is usually more open to public view. Past scandals from Teapot Dome to Watergate to Abscam to HUD indicate that the people who occupy positions of power in American government are susceptible to corruption. We would be irrational to assume that the nation's bureaucrats are exempt from the same pressures that cause politicians to abuse the public trust.[1] Our expectations for bureaucrats are not low; we expect effectiveness, efficiency, loyalty, innovation, responsiveness, and countless other things; and the potential to abuse our trust is high because bureaucracy exercises a great deal of discretion over the allocation of scarce societal resources. The prospect that administrative power can be abused must be considered.

....

TWO STANDARDS FOR BUREAUCRACY

In general scholars seeking to control bureaucracy set two standards: responsiveness to public needs and competence in the performance of tasks.[2] Using responsiveness as a

---

[1] My impression is that bureaucrats are less likely to respond to these temptations. Given that bureaucrats substantially outnumber politicians in the country and given the relative balance of stories about political corruption, this appears to be a valid conclusion.

[2] The "public expectations" discussed in this chapter are those noted by scholars not by public opinion instruments. The responsiveness–competence distinction was first made to my knowledge by Carl Friedrich (1940) when he argued that bureaucracy ought to be subject to public opinion and the best scientific knowledge available. Other scholars suggest other values. Francis Rourke (1984) proposes openness and effectiveness as the key criteria; Robert Fried (1976) suggests liberalism, effectiveness, and responsiveness; William West (1983; 1984) argues for rationality and responsiveness. The present discussion tries to include all the suggestions of the other authors; Gilbert (1959), in fact, discusses twelve values that we expect bureaucracy to maximize. The concept of law which is Fried's definition of liberty should be noted since it seems not to fit within the analysis presented here. Law underlies all expectations of bureaucracy. We expect a bureaucracy to be responsive within the restraints of law and expect it to be competent also within those restraints (see West, 1995).

criterion for administrative behavior immediately raises many additional questions; the most basic is, to whom should the bureaucracy be responsive? Bureaucracy can be responsive to the general public, to organized groups with an interest in the bureau, to the public affected by the bureau's administration, to political institutions, and to the law. The first step in determining if a given bureaucratic action is responsive is defining the reference group.

Responsive administrative behavior may also be either passive or active. A bureau can be characterized as responsive if it responds to the demands of its environment, that is, passive responsiveness. Many times, however, waiting for environmental pressures, especially when the environment is not organized, is counterproductive. In such cases responsiveness requires active anticipation of public problems and innovative creative solutions even before demands have materialized.

Competence involves the bureau doing the best job that is technically feasible within the constraints placed on the organization. We expect the U.S. Postal Service to deliver all mail, not just the mail easiest to deliver. Competence also involves active and passive elements. We expect that a bureau will use not only the best available knowledge when presented with problems (passive), but that it will also use its expertise and knowledge to forecast problems and develop solutions while the problems are still small enough to be managed (active).

The expectations of competence and responsiveness may be jointly exhaustive, but they are not mutually exclusive. In practice the values of competence and responsiveness often conflict. The current problems facing the Postal Service illustrate this conflict. We, as citizens and policymakers, expect that the Postal Service should be responsive to the wants and needs of those it serves, the American public. Judging from the frequency of headlines devoted to rate increases and subsidies, the Postal Service is also assessed on the competence dimension, which for simplicity we will define as delivering mail as cheaply or efficiently as possible. If efficiency were the only value that the Postal Service should maximize, nothing would be more efficient than if all marginal post offices were closed or consolidated with large regional centers. Efficiency could also be enhanced by eliminating door-to-door delivery, substituting instead delivery to a central location in a neighborhood and having residents pick up their own mail at these centrally located boxes. Such ruthless efficiency would clearly conflict with the public's responsiveness and service desires even if the price of postage were cut by one-half. Responsiveness supports not only small nearby post offices but also door-to-door delivery six days a week.

Although the values of competence and responsiveness often conflict, we expect the bureaucracy to meet both.[3] Conflicting expectations may well lead to perceptions of administrative abuse when the bureaucracy is expected to maximize two inconsistent values. In short, much of what people cite as abuse of administrative power and much of what is cited in this chapter may well be the result of well-intentioned bureaucrats

---

[3] There has been a recent set of articles on value conflict in organizations and how they are managed; (see Meier, Wrinkle, and Polinard, 1998; Romzek and Ingraham, 1998). While multiple goals create problems for public agencies, many organizations are able to deal with more than one goal at a time as long as the general priorities among the goals is relatively stable.

attempting to maximize one dearly held public value that happens to conflict with another expectation of bureaucracy.

This chapter tries to specify with some precision what the American population and students of bureaucratic politics expect from administrative agencies. The goals of competence and responsiveness will be set within several contexts to illustrate the conflicting demands made on civil servants. Since our concern is with the exercise of administrative power in pursuit of these goals (competence and responsiveness), this chapter also notes by example various ways the bureaucracy can meet or fail to meet public expectations.

....

RESPONSIVENESS I: POLITICAL INSTITUTIONS, THE PUBLIC, LAW

In their policy role, bureaus should act as open systems, that is, they should be sensitive to the environment and the demands that the environment places on the organization. Immediately the question is raised, to whom should the bureau be responsive when making policy? That question is difficult to resolve. First, and least controversial, bureaus should be sensitive to other political institutions when making policy. Bureaucracy is not the sole nor even the dominant policymaking institution; bureaucrats should recognize this hierarchy of political institutions in our constitutional framework (see Burke, 1986; Wood and Waterman, 1994). Sensitivity to other political institutions requires that a bureau recognize the president's position as formal head of the bureaucracy. As the legitimate leader of the bureaucracy, presidential intentions should be treated as goals rather than as obstacles to circumvent. Responsiveness to Congress entails respect for Congress' role as policymaker. Since modern technology has required that Congress concentrate on general policy, responsiveness to Congress means that a bureau should comply with the intent of Congress rather than seeking loopholes. Given the close contact between Congress and the bureaucracy, congressional intent should not be difficult to discern. Finally, responsiveness to other political institutions includes recognition of the supremacy of law. The behavior of civil servants is subject to legal restraints. A public office does not bestow on its occupant any special status in regard to overriding the law. In fact, the possession of an office of public trust requires that actions should never violate criminal laws no matter what the reason (Rohr, 1989). Essentially, responsiveness to other political institutions requires that bureaucrats realize that bureaucracy was created as an institution designed to assist political institutions in performing their functions more adequately (Caiden, 1981: 150).

Examples of bureaucracies being unresponsive to political institutions and to law can be found. In the mid-1970s evidence that the Federal Bureau of Investigation (FBI) considered itself above the law in the previous decade came to light. The FBI not only wiretapped the conversation of civil rights leader Martin Luther King Jr., but it also sent a note to Dr. King implying that his only hope to retain respect was suicide (Poveda, 1990). In other activities the FBI attempted to provoke warfare between the Communist Party of the United States and the Mafia, exceeding by great lengths any reasonable definition of the agency's legal authority. With the FBI's more recent focus on white-collar and organized crime, some analysts feel that the FBI's use of sting operations violate constitutional restrictions on entrapment (Poveda, 1990). At times a lack of responsiveness to political officials is a function of policy disputes. In 1969 the Office for Civil Rights (OCR) defied President Nixon's request to slow down school desegregation efforts in the South, and the OCR cut off funds to several Southern school districts (Sickels, 1974). The OCR was strongly committed to immediate desegregation of public schools, a position endorsed by the U.S. Supreme Court; President Nixon preferred a much slower pace.

At times when bureaucracies are condemned for unresponsiveness to one set of political actors they may, in fact, be sensitive to other political actors. Few agencies were criticized as much as the Federal Trade Commission (FTC) in the late 1970s was for being overly aggressive in regulating business. The FTC, however, adopted this aggressive policy at the urging of members of Congress in the early 1970s (Pertschuk, 1982). As the composition of the oversight committees changed from very liberal to somewhat conservative, the FTC was essentially criticized because it had responded to the Commerce Committees as they existed in 1975; its major critics were the post-1976 Commerce Committees (Weingast and Moran, 1983).

A careful examination of government bureaucracies would reveal that they are generally responsive to political officials and that lack of responsiveness is rare and explainable (Wood and Waterman, 1994).[4] The federal institutions regulating banking including the Federal Deposit Insurance Corporation and the Federal Reserve often hold up policy initiatives to give Congress an opportunity to set policy. In 1982 several financial institutions found a loophole in the federal law that would allow a bank without commercial loans or checking deposits to engage in a variety of activities prohibited to banks such as interstate banking because technically such institutions were "nonbanks." Although the law appeared to permit such institutions, the federal regulators placed a moratorium on granting charters to nonbanks to give Congress time to act on the issue if it desired to do so (Meier, 1985).

Bureaucracies may, in fact, be too responsive to political institutions. The IRS in the past has been charged with being too responsive to the individual who occupies the presidency, by providing him with tax returns and audits, rather than being sensitive to the laws protecting an individual's right to privacy (Rowan, 1975). A systematic study of IRS audits found they responded to both partisan changes in Congress and changes in who was president (Scholz and Wood, 1998). Responsiveness to political institutions and law means that the bureau should be responsive to those institutions as insti-

---

[4] Many cases of resistance to political demands occur when political elites demand that government agencies fundamentally change their goals. The EPA, for example, was not especially responsive to President Reagan's efforts to downplay environmental protection (Vig and Kraft, 1984). EPA bureaucrats were placed in the position of not enforcing the existing law. Clearly an argument could be made that bureaus should not respond to political efforts to change policy via lack of law enforcement when such efforts come outside the normal political process for policymaking. When such instances occur and who is to judge the appropriate response are topics that are subject to debate.

tutions and to the Constitution and the law, rather than to the temporary occupants of the presidency and Congress (see Rohr, 1989).[5]

Bureau policymaking behavior should also be responsive to the needs and demands of the general public. Paul Schumaker (1975) argues that responsiveness can take five forms: (1) access, the willingness to hear concerns; (2) agenda, the consideration of the issues raised; (3) policy, the congruence of policy with public demands; (4) output, the actual implementation of the demand; and (5) impact, the degree to which the policy problem has been eliminated. Even if public demands on administrative behavior could be unambiguously defined, Schumaker's types of responsiveness reveal that the degree of responsiveness and its focus are controversial. A bureau, for example, might be responsive on access and agenda but conclude the public's demands are impractical and be unresponsive on policy.

Ideally administrative behavior should be responsive to the entire general public, but "the public" is an amorphous mass that never speaks with one voice and rarely make unambiguous demands on the bureaucracy. In fact, Leiserson and Marx (1959) feel that bureaus should not be responsive solely to the needs of interested parties but should contrast those interests, which are always present with the needs of the people who are not represented in the administrative policy process (see also Redford 1969). Bureaus, in fact, can be too responsive to narrow interests. Some analysts charge that the Department of Agriculture, for example, is responsive only to the prosperous farmer, the Federal Communications Commission responds only to broadcasters, and the former Interstate Commerce Commission listened only to a portion of the transportation industry (Salamon and Wamsley, 1975). This overresponsiveness to narrow interests often means a bureau and its clientele set policy without regard to the needs and preferences of the majority.

Administrative agencies, therefore, may abuse power both by being unresponsive to the needs of the public or by being too responsive to a narrow range of interests. At the practical level this means a charge of unresponsiveness may be a function of whose ox is being gored. The Occupational Safety and Health Administration under Eula Bingham (1977–1981) changed its priorities to focus on health dangers rather than the trivial safety violations that OSHA was previously famous for citing. OSHA was widely perceived as being unresponsive to business and the president's need to control regulatory costs (Yandle, 1982). When President Reagan replaced Bingham with Thorne Auchter, OSHA became more cooperative with business and the priorities of the president but was condemned for being unresponsive by organized labor and Democratic members of Congress.

Responsiveness to unorganized interests is difficult because such action can sow the seeds of agency destruction. After a massive reorganization in 1969, the Federal Trade Commission began seriously regulating several industries for the first time. Funeral directors, lawyers, physicians, oil companies, cereal manufacturers, television

---

[5] The reader will note that none of these prescriptions is easy to meet. Resisting the influence of the president is at times a blessing and at other times an abuse of power. A bureau without strong clientele support will have great difficulty resisting presidential and congressional requests that require unethical actions.

advertisers, insurance companies, and used car dealers were among the many industries that the FTC challenged on behalf of the consumer. These challenges generated a counterattack by the regulated interests, who persuaded Congress and then the president to greatly restrict the FTC (Pertschuk, 1982). Therein lies a dilemma for public bureaucracy, responsiveness to unorganized interests will likely bring the protests of organized interests. Without support from other political elites in such cases, bureaucracies will be forced to compromise their policies. Bureaucracies can be only as responsive to unorganized interests as other political institutions permit them to be.

RESPONSIVENESS II: FLEXIBILITY

When bureaus implement policy, responsiveness requires that a bureau be open to environmental pressures, but pressures much different from those in the policymaking process. In the implementation process bureaus must be flexible in dealing with problems. If the facts of a situation do not fit previously defined categories or if the citizen is an exception to normal rules, then the bureau should be flexible and make exceptions rather than rigidly, and possibly incorrectly, applying inappropriate rules. Another aspect of responsiveness in policy implementation is openness to criticism directed at the agency. The ideal agency admits its mistakes willingly and alters the questioned behavior.[6] Whether the source of criticism is other political elites, the public that interacts with the agency, or the agency's own employees, the criticism and possible changes should be considered.

Although bureaucracies are commonly perceived as rigid and rule bound, systematic studies fail to confirm bureaucracy's red-tape image. Charles Goodsell (1981) examined the behavior of welfare caseworkers in several jurisdictions and found that caseworkers usually tried to assist the client in attaining benefits. Deviations from neutrality were usually to the client's benefit. Similarly Regens and Rycroft (1981: 886) examined the highly criticized Federal Energy Administration (now Department of Energy) program of fuel allocation and price controls. They found that, by objective standards, the agency responded quickly to individual requests for regulatory relief. Under the Voting Rights Act of 1975, the Civil Rights Division of the Department of Justice required that in any locality where a minority made up a least 5 percent of the voting age population, the election ballot in that region must be printed in both English and the minority language. Elko County, Nevada, was initially required to print its election ballots in Paiute and Shoshone. Unfortunately for the state of Nevada neither language has a written alphabet. The Justice Department then exercised discretion and permitted oral voting in Elko county. In another example of flexibility, the Federal

---

[6] An agency will not necessarily admit mistakes out of altruism but as a rational process. My own observations indicate that to admit failure does more to quiet criticism and does less harm to the agency than to deny an accusation which is later revealed to be correct. A rational agency will attempt to cut its losses and regain support by admitting mistakes.

Trade Commission, which requires that every garment contain a label with washing instructions, was persuaded by the arguments of Stardust, Inc., manufacturers of string bikini panties, that the label, which would be nearly as large as the garment itself, would destroy the product's value. The FTC granted Stardust an exception.

Lack of flexibility and red tape should result in conservative organizations that will not take risks. Bozeman and Kingsley's (1998: 113) study of managers found no difference between public and private sector managers in terms of risk taking. The willingness to take risks was positively associated with organizations that had clear goals and an absence of restrictive rules (Bozeman and Kingsley, 1998: 115).

To be sure, red tape exists; but Rosenfeld (1984: 611) argues that inflexibility and red tape are often caused by factors outside the bureaucracy's control (see also Bozeman and Kingsley, 1998). Both he and Kaufman (1977: 36) argue that red tape results from demands that programs be responsive to legislative intent, the complexities of implementing federal programs with state agencies, the establishment of accountability mechanisms by Congress, and internal bureaucratic actions to make sure programs are efficient and effective. Red tape, according the this perspective, is imposed on the bureaucracy by its environment; red tape is not inherent in bureaucracy (see a similar argument by Chubb and Moe, 1990).

Openness also requires that bureaucracy keep citizens informed. Although government agencies are often criticized for operating in secret, they generally respond to demands for information. In 1983–1984, 88 percent of the public's Freedom of Information Act (FOIA) requests were fully granted (Relyea, 1986: 636). In 1988 FOIA requests totaled 394,914 (Moore, 1990a: 122). The development of Web sites in many cases improves this openness if those sites are used to provide information (e.g., the Office of Management and Budget) rather than for propaganda purposes (e.g., the Drug Enforcement Administration). The general responsiveness of many agencies, however, should not blind one to those agencies that strongly resist providing information.

Although agencies are normally responsive to clientele criticism because an unhappy clientele is a dangerous clientele, they are not as responsive to criticisms of their own employees. A. Ernest Fitzgerald, a Department of Defense cost analyst, repeatedly reported cost overruns on the Air Force C-5A cargo plane and offered corrective recommendations. When internal warnings went unheeded, Fitzgerald testified at a congressional hearing. Fitzgerald was rewarded for his criticism with a transfer to a bowling alley in Thailand and later dismissal from the agency. Only a long legal fight and substantial congressional pressure resulted in Fitzgerald's reinstatement to the department, where he continued as a "free lance" waste fighter (Nader, 1972). The Civil Service Reform Act of 1978 sought to protect individuals like Fitzgerald when it provided for specific legal protection for whistleblowers. An analysis of this law, however, was not optimistic (Jos et al., 1989). This study found that 62 percent of whistleblowers were fired by their agency. The Civil Service Reform Act protections were considered inadequate; the Merit Systems Protection Board closed 99 percent of all whistleblower complaints without taking any corrective action.

A detailed study of two whistleblowing cases found that openness to employee criticism could greatly benefit the organization (Johnson and Kraft, 1990). In both the

EPA and the Office for Civil Rights, whistleblowers were able to produce policy changes and correct problems in the organization. In both cases, however, the agency retaliated before other pressures produced support for the whistleblower.

The initial reaction of the Veterans Administration (VA, now the Department of Veterans Affairs) to Vietnam veterans provides an example of both inflexibility and the failure to consider criticism. When Vietnam veterans returned to the United States, the VA was faced with drug and rehabilitation problems of a magnitude never encountered before. The problems did not respond to traditional treatment available in VA hospitals. When veterans' groups began openly criticizing the agency, the VA responded by contending that no problem existed. Only after criticism became more vocal and some senators intervened did the VA leadership change; with the change the demands of the Vietnam veteran received more consideration. Problems related to "Gulf War syndrome," however, suggest the overall problem of openness has not been solved.

Although the flexibility and openness expectations concerning the responsiveness of bureaucracy appear simple, they may be most difficult to meet. Asking a bureau to be flexible is asking that the bureau take a public chance rather than playing it safe behind standard operating procedures. Asking a bureau to be open to criticism is asking the bureau to admit when it fails. Admission of failure, rightly or wrongly, is perceived as a fundamental weakening of a bureau's power position.

RESPONSIVENESS III: ETHICS

The public also expects individual bureaucrats to be responsive to acceptable standards of administrative behavior. In both behavior and appearance bureaucrats are expected to avoid misconduct; misconduct is defined as failing to obey restrictions of law in public actions. Since a position of public trust includes expectations far greater than the norms of behavior expected of private sector bureaucrats, the public bureaucrat must abstain not only from actual misconduct but from the appearance of misconduct.

Bureaucratic misconduct can have a major impact on the nation. Arthur Miller (1974) argued that political alienation and cynicism increased dramatically in the contemporary United States and that the increase was directly attributable to questionable government activities. If the nation's public servants are perceived as criminal or dishonest, the public's distrust of government increases. The position of former President Richard Nixon that occasionally the president may act outside the law if the action is in the public interest has no place in the administrative service.

Examples of unlawful behavior by federal civil servants are difficult to find because they are rarely reported, or more likely as Robert Fried (1976) argues, the United States federal civil service is fairly incorruptible (but see Heidenheimer, 1970). In a clear-cut case Charles R. McDonald, deputy director of the Federal Bureau of Drug Abuse Control for Baltimore, was convicted of conspiracy and distribution of heroin while a federal employee (*Houston Post*, December 4, 1975). This is not an unusual problem in drug enforcement (Meier, 1994). Because the economics of illicit drug markets are highly profitable, bribes are common; and some law enforcement officers yield to the temptation (Woodiwiss, 1988: 205–207). In 1978 an Urban Mass Transit Administration clerk was convicted of embezzling $857,577 in only three months (*Federal Times,* January 1, 1978: 5). In a well-publicized case in 1972, agents of the federal Drug Enforcement Agency were charged with illegally breaking into homes without warrants (into the wrong homes for that matter), harassing the occupants, and destroying property.[7] In 1989, thirty-two medical employees in Department of Veterans Affairs hospitals were disciplined for taking gratuities from drug companies that did business with the hospitals (Welch, 1989: 5).

A 1981 survey by the Merit System Protection Board found that civil servants perceived a fair amount of waste and fraud in government programs but did not report it because they feared retribution from their agencies (reported in Bowman, 1983). Perceptions of corruption in government led to the creation in 1976 of internal auditors called inspectors general in the major federal departments. President Reagan claimed that these inspectors general saved the taxpayers $5.8 billion that would have been lost to waste, fraud, or abuse in the six months ending in March 1982 (Lanouette, 1982: 1094). Close inspection of these claims by the General Accounting Office, however, revealed that illegal behavior was not nearly so prevalent; much was not clearly abuse, and the inspectors general were able to recover only $23.2 million. Federal bureaucrats, in fact, were not the individuals engaging in illegal behavior; most fraud, waste, and corruption was perpetrated by contractors or other private individuals against the federal government (Lanouette, 1982: 1094). Other highly publicized cases of fraud reveal similar culprits. The "Ill Wind" defense procurement probe produced thirty-eight criminal convictions by 1990, all private sector contractors or consultants (Howe, 1990: 31). The record of federal bureaucrats in terms of misconduct is clearly better than the people they serve.

Despite the detail of state and federal codes including the adoption of the federal Ethics in Government Act of 1978 (Bowman, 1981), laws are ambiguous. The responsiveness of individual bureaucrats to law includes a prohibition of actions that while not strictly illegal are of questionable propriety (i.e., unethical behavior). The most prominent example of such action is when an official makes a decision that he or she benefits from personally or appears to benefit personally. In the mid-1970s twenty-two Department of Defense officials who oversaw defense contracting were officially reprimanded for allowing Northrop Corporation, a large defense contractor, to entertain them at a Delaware hunting lodge. The twenty-two officials made decisions that affected the future profits of Northrop although they themselves had nothing to gain. In another instance Clarence D. Palmby, assistant secretary of agriculture for International Affairs and Commodity programs, in 1972 negotiated the generous credit terms that permitted the Soviet Union to purchase large quantities of grain from the United States. Three weeks later Palmby resigned to work for Continental Grain Company, a major grain exporter to the Soviets (Lanouette, 1977). Although Palmby did nothing

---

[7] The Bureau of Drug Abuse Control and the Drug Enforcement Administration are the same agency. Often, as Seidman and Gilmour (1986) point out, the names of bureaus are changed to give the impression that the bureau has changed and is pursuing new policies. The drug control programs of the Department of Justice underwent a series of name changes in their unsuccessful effort to combat the nation's drug problems.

illegal, his actions created the appearance that he placed the interests of Continental above those of the nation. Since the passage of the Ethics in Government Act in 1978, conflicts of interest are more difficult to hide because financial holdings must be reported. In general the law affects political appointees far more than it does career officials.

Bureaucrats can behave unethically not only for personal gain but also to build the agency's power base and, thus, make the bureaucrat's position more secure. FBI chief J. Edgar Hoover gathered files on the sex and drinking habits of members of Congress and their families. Hoover would then let the member know he had the information and would expect favorable treatment for the FBI. At his peak Hoover did not need to reveal he possessed any information; the thought that he might was sufficient for the FBI to benefit (Poveda, 1990).

The standards for ethical behavior of bureaucrats while general and often vague are clearly high. As citizens we believe that public officials were not placed in their positions for their own benefit but rather for our benefit. The decisions they make must, therefore, be responsive to legal rules and unwritten standards of conduct.

RESPONSIVENESS IV: FAIR AND IMPARTIAL

Interactions between bureaucrats and the public should be characterized by responsiveness to the American values of equity and procedural fairness. Bureaucrats should not show favoritism to any individual regardless of his or her political affiliation, political influence, wealth, friends, or relatives. All people appearing before the bureaucracy should receive equal treatment. Equal treatment, however, does not mean equally abusive treatment but rather treatment in accord with due process. Due process in administrative law requires at a minimum that an individual be given notice of a proceeding affecting him or her, the right to be heard before the agency, the right to hear and challenge any evidence against the individual, the right to a decision by an impartial arbitrator, and some limited right of appeal (Davis, 1965; P. J. Cooper, 1988; Heffron with McFeeley, 1983).[8] John Rohr (1989) suggests that bureaucrats should consciously go beyond these minimums to provide more elaborate due process.

If, in the best of all possible worlds, the bureaucracy treated all citizens in a spirit of equality and procedural fairness, criticism of bureaucrats' behavior by citizens would not cease. As Peter Blau and Marshall Meyer (1971) so effectively argue, people do not necessarily like impartial, albeit fair, treatment. Blau and Meyer contend that much of what is derogatorily referred to as red tape is, in fact, procedural safeguards and impartial treatment. People want their request acted on immediately; they do not especially want to wait their turn and then be treated like all other petitioners. On the other hand, simply because a bureaucracy should be impartial does not mean it cannot be humane. Bu-

---

[8] The due process required varies with the agency (West, 1995). Where the agency deals in denials of liberty, property, or life, the procedural rights should be all encompassing. When a question of general policy is considered that affects individuals only indirectly, the procedural limitations are substantially less.

reaucrats should facilitate public interaction by correcting a petitioner's mistakes and guiding the person through the maze of procedures. Evidence from welfare offices indicates that bureaucrats often assist individuals in this way (Goodsell, 1983).

Since procedural fairness and equality are often confused with red tape, clear examples of bureaucrats abusing administrative power by being unfair or partial are scarce. In 1975 the Civil Service Commission (now the Office of Personnel Management) accused the Small Business Administration (SBA) of partiality in its personnel policies. The SBA was charged with using political qualifications rather than merit in selecting at least four district managers. The SBA had aggressively replaced civil servants with Republican politicians (Watson, 1975). In a more substantive policy area, the *Washington Post* revealed that the Internal Revenue Service's tax audits varied a great deal in detail and severity. Among the more easily treated persons were members of Congress, including the chair of the House Ways and Means Committee, the committee that oversees the IRS. A more systematic analysis of IRS audits also found evidence of political influence (Scholz and Wood, 1998). For examples of administrative agencies violating procedural safeguards in administering policy, one need go no further than the loyalty and security cases of the 1950s. In a political climate fostered by Senator Joe McCarthy's attacks on communism, many federal employees were charged with disloyalty and fired. These persons were often discharged without hearing the evidence against them, being able to confront their accuser, or being granted any other procedural safeguards (Davis, 1965).

The problem with attempting to determine how well the American federal bureaucracy treats individuals is that one never knows if the reported cases are the full extent of the violations, the extent of the newsworthy cases, or the extent to which the bureaucracy is open to the news media (Fried, 1976). In a series of studies, Charles Goodsell (1983) found that the majority of citizens who contacted the bureaucracy reported that they achieved what they had sought, felt the bureaucrats had tried to help, and viewed the bureaucrats as courteous. Studies of several agencies revealed that more than two-thirds of citizens interacting with the bureaucracy report favorable experiences (Goodsell, 1983). Such a finding suggests that bureaucrats go out of their way to assist citizens even when operating a program according to set procedures.

COMPETENCE I: EFFECTIVENESS

Effectiveness is whether or not the bureau achieves the policy goals stated for it by other political decisionmakers. The concern is with the stated objectives of other political elites, preferably those objectives stated in law, not the objectives of the bureau. We are not concerned if the Food and Drug Administration is able to survive (the FDA's goal) but if it has promoted policies that create access to safe and effective pharmaceuticals. We are concerned not with the Department of Energy's ability to expand the range of its functions but rather its ability to make U.S. energy policy more rational. Because policy goals are often complex and each policy often has more than one goal,

Clarence Stone (1985) argues that bureaus should be evaluated on their ability to learn over time (see also Sabatier, 1988). Some evidence suggests that bureaucracies do learn (Lebovic, 1996). From 1973 to 1981 state implementing agencies were able to reduce "error" rates in the Aid to Families with Dependent Children program from 16.5 percent to 6.5 percent and errors in the Supplemental Security Income program from 11 percent to 5 percent (Young, 1983: 368). Between 1982 and 1991 state child support collections tripled (Keiser and Meier, 1996). From 1994 to 1997 the percentage of first-class mail delivered on the next day increased by 13 percent to 92 percent. Effectiveness, when viewed from this perspective, requires not only performance but also innovation, both in the formation of policy goals and in the methods used to achieve them. An agency cannot be considered effective if it efficiently pursues a goal no longer considered necessary. Agencies must adapt their goals to changing environments.

Ineffective administrative programs are usually considered major news stories. As part of former President Nixon's war on drug abuse, the Drug Enforcement Administration (DEA) was created to combat drug problems. Two years later in 1975 White House sources privately admitted that the DEA had failed. In an attempt to dry up the supply of heroin, the DEA purchased the entire Turkish opium crop, but other areas of the world quickly supplied the demand. In the United States the agency's tactic of arresting small dealers failed to reveal major suppliers, the program's objective (Woodiwiss, 1988).

In another recent example, the Defense Department in 1985 canceled the controversial Sgt. York air defense gun after spending $1.8 billion on development. The York gun was perceived in 1977 as a cheap, quick, and effective way to counter a Soviet air threat; but, according to Defense tests, it lacked both reliability and sufficient range. The shortcomings of the weapon were known as early as 1981, but the weapon system was not canceled until mid-1985 (Lerner with Barry, 1985: 23). Effectiveness can also concern agency goals. A Brookings Institution study of the U.S. Marine Corps argued that the corps' traditional role of amphibious assault was no longer a needed function in America's defense arsenal (Binkin, 1976). The Marine Corps had failed to innovate and change its goals with the changing needs of the nation's defense. The corps responded by ignoring the report.

These examples of ineffective programs should not lead one to conclude that most bureaucratic programs are failures. Failures are more likely to make news than successful programs. Given the vague goals established by Congress and the often impossible requirements, the bulk of government programs can be termed successes. The Consumer Product Safety Commission's requirement that all medicines contain child-proof caps is credited with eliminating 90 percent of infant deaths that result from ingesting medicines. Similarly the CPSC was able to reduce infant fatalities by requiring that all baby cribs have bars less than 2.375 inches apart so that babies could not strangle themselves by sliding through the bars (Greer, 1981: 441; Meier, 1985: 105). Numerous other cases of effectiveness could be cited from the Federal Aviation Administration's crackdown on skyjacking to the improvements in automobile and highway safety mandated by the National Highway Traffic Safety Administration.

Agency effectiveness might also be affected by constraints placed on the agency. Most agencies are not given sufficient resources to address their policy mandate; the Consumer Product Safety Commission, for example, tried to regulate more than 10,000 consumer products with a staff of 515 in 1999. Sometimes political factors intervene. The Public Health Service was prevented in 1989 from conducting a large survey of the sexual practices of Americans. This was opposed by vocal conservative groups even though the information was needed to design policies for the prevention of AIDS and other sexually transmitted diseases (Kosterlitz, 1989: 1699). In 1998 a proposal to provide addicts with clean hypodermic needles to prevent AIDS transmission was also shelved. The Internal Revenue Service's problems in data retrieval have been linked to high employee turnover resulting from low pay for clerical staff (Walsh, 1989: 33).

....

COMPETENCE II: TIMELINESS

When administering a policy, a bureau is expected to be timely in the disposition of cases; that is, it should act with all reasonable speed. One advantage of bureaucracy is that through specialization and routinization, it can deal with thousands of cases fairly quickly. The Social Security Administration distributes 48 million checks per month. In addition to the citizen's desire for speed, a bureau is well advised to process its cases quickly because timely action can contribute to a bureau's power base both by gaining pleased clientele support and by adding to its reputation for effectiveness.

A classic case of delay involves the Internal Revenue Service processing income tax returns in 1985. By the end of July the Philadelphia processing center alone had not responded to 845,000 tax returns (Sawyer, 1985: 6). Pressures to meet deadlines and the inadequacies of the new $103 million computer system led IRS workers to destroy 60,000 letters from taxpayers in the Fresno service center and 20,000 letters in the Austin center (Pressley, 1985: 33). Approximately 150,000 taxpayers in the Philadelphia region erroneously received dunning letters, including one to a Baltimore couple demanding $2,106,394.63 (Swardson, 1985: 32). Despite the huge scandal, the delay was not entirely the IRS's fault; Congress failed to give the IRS sufficient resources to process tax returns in a timely manner. From 1980 to 1985 the number of tax returns filed increased nationally from 41 million to 101 million while the number of IRS employees was reduced by 5,000 (Pressley, 1985: 33).

Because they handle large caseloads, few service agencies are immune from charges of delay. The Social Security Administration, normally a well-run agency, hears disability cases for persons who believe they qualify for disability pensions. At one time the agency took between 150 to 300 days to settle an average case and had a backlog of 105,000 cases. Congress' failure to authorize funds to update the massive SSA computer system resulted in greater delays in processing all types of claims (Schrage, 1985: 23).

....

COMPETENCE III: EFFICIENCY

When bureaucrats engage in policymaking, competence demands that their actions be efficient. Efficiency should not be confused with effectiveness since effectiveness concerns meeting goals and efficiency concerns program costs. Efficiency without regard for effectiveness, however, is a false economy. An efficient but ineffective program is still a waste of money. The objective is to achieve stated goals at the least possible cost. Since agencies must advocate their positions, the temptation not to consider efficiency is great. The Army Corps of Engineers was frequently accused of authorizing projects with high cost/benefit ratios (or adjusting the ratios) because those projects had local political support.

Although efficiency is frequently studied, many government organizations get little credit for efficiency gains. The Postal Service is frequently criticized as inefficient, but it improved its efficiency by 48.2 percent from 1970 to 1982, a gain that exceeded that of the private sector (Vittes, 1985: 508). In 1997 the Postal Service delivered 176.8 billion pieces of mail with only 764,000 employees. In addition, efficiency is often a function of factors outside the control of the agency. The Environmental Protection Agency administers the Toxic Substances Control Act, which requires that manufacturers get EPA approval before manufacturing new chemicals. EPA efficiency skyrocketed in this program because the number of new chemical proposals, something the EPA has no control over, quadrupled between 1980 and 1983 (Woodhouse, 1985: 498). Data from the Merit Systems Protection Board (MSPB) reveal that within 120 days it heard 82 percent of its cases in 1982, 17 percent in 1983, 77 percent in 1984, 95 percent in 1985, 99 percent in 1986, and 99.8 percent in 1987. The massive drop in efficiency in 1983 occurred because MSPB was swamped with appeals after the president fired all the striking air traffic controllers (Vaughn, 1988: 358). The MSPB's efficiency, therefore, was determined by factors outside the control of the agency.

Agencies seeking efficient policies may also be prevented from doing so for political reasons. For several years the National Highway Traffic Safety Administration required that automobile bumpers take a five-miles-per-hour impact without any damage to the vehicle. Several cost–benefit studies revealed that the five-miles-per-hour standard produced more benefits than costs. Under political pressure from the automobile industry, the Reagan administration commissioned new studies that "revealed" the standard was not cost effective, and the standard was reduced to 2.5 miles per hour (Meier, 1985: 99). In other cases Congress may have rejected the goal of efficiency. Langbein and Kerwin (1987) examine regulatory case processing and conclude that Congress often wants slower, less efficient procedures because policies are complex and many interests need to be consulted (see Golden, 1998). Stressing efficiency may also distort the policies of the organization. According to one study, the demand for efficiency caused the Internal Revenue Service to ignore complex cases and focus on easier cases of underpayment even though these priorities let many major tax violators escape (Crenshaw and Schatz, 1990: 20).

Even though efficiency is a difficult concept to apply to government agencies (see Chapter 1) and myriad forces restrict efforts to optimize, some reasonably clear-cut cases of inefficiency exist. In 1985 the *Washington Post* revealed that the Defense Department was still immunizing recruits for smallpox at an annual cost of $378,000 even though the disease had been eradicated. Side effects from the immunization, in fact, caused some harm to soldiers and medical personnel (Russell, 1985). The Defense Department has also produced some inefficiencies in contracting. At times weapons are purchased with no objectives in mind; the army began a helicopter procurement program that might have cost $87 billion without an estimate of what each helicopter cost; the navy spent $65 million and nine years on a communications system without defining what was required (Hiatt, 1985: 31). In 1985 a series of bizarre procurement stories made the news including $748 (later reduced to $90) for a pair of $7.61 pliers, a $7,000 coffee pot, and $600 toilet seats (Hiatt and Atkinson, 1985: 33). An internal air force audit in 1985 revealed that defense contractors were performing at efficiency rates between 73 and 13 percent (Gordon, 1985: 1285). Although in these cases the private sector was inefficient, the Defense Department's oversight was clearly inadequate.

That efficiency stories about the bureaucracy exist should not be surprising. All large-scale formal organizations, government agencies as well as private businesses, make mistakes (Goodsell, 1983). In large programs with complex objectives that are continually being redefined in a changing environment, some inefficiency is to be expected. Large social programs (Young, 1983: 363) and defense procurement are no different in this regard. Many defense procurement inefficiencies can be attributed to the unprecedented 1980s defense build-up when political pressures to spend money were great and incentives to control costs were not.

....

COMPETENCE IV: RELIABILITY

Competence when bureaucrats administer policy requires that bureaucrats be reliable; reliability includes three specific criteria. First, we expect that bureaucrats should be knowledgeable, that they should know what they are doing. Second, the civil servant should act consistently from case to case and from time to time on the same types of cases. Neither should a civil servant advise a citizen one thing will result if a given action is taken and then act differently when the action is taken. Third, bureaucratic behavior ought to be predictable. A citizen should know in advance that a bureau will decide a case in a specified way if certain conditions are met.

Since every component of reliability is somewhat distinct, the ways each may be abused will be discussed separately. Regarding knowledge, the Internal Revenue Service provides assistance to taxpayers filling out tax returns. Because IRS employees are trained specifically for this function, knowledge is not an extraordinary expectation. An IRS internal audit of its agents, however, revealed that agents made mistakes in 24 percent of the cases. Two studies using cases with more difficult and technical questions found errors 55 percent and 80 percent of the time. This lack of knowledge by IRS agents would not be problematic if the IRS were bound by an agent's advice, but unfortunately the individual taxpayer is liable for any mistakes made with IRS assistance (see also GAO, 1989).

The lack of confidence a citizen might have in an IRS agent's advice brings up the question of consistency. In a real case that was finally decided against the agency by the Supreme Court (*FCIC* v. *Merrill,* 332 U.S. 380), an Idaho farmer asked the Federal Crop Insurance Corporation if 400 acres of spring wheat reseeded on winter wheat could be insured by the corporation. The corporation agreed it could and insured the crop. When drought destroyed the crop, the farmer filed a claim. Checking its records, the corporation found that the crop had been reseeded; and since corporation regulations prevented recovery on reseeded crops, the claim was denied. The Supreme Court eventually reversed the agency's decision by denying the agency's claim that the farmer should have read the *Federal Register,* which contained the regulations, but the court has permitted agency inconsistency in other cases (see *Mosher* v. *United States,* 341 U.S. 41).

Predictability of agency action is important when people must make decisions now based on future agency decisions. Davis (1965) presents a hypothetical example based on several real cases concerning the Immigration and Naturalization Service (INS). An alien women enters the United States and is later engaged to an American citizen. At the time INS regulations required two years' foreign residency by the American citizen before they would admit the spouse to immigrate to the United States, although they waived this if it provided a hardship. Since the couple must plan their marriage, they must consider the possibility that the woman will not be granted immigrant status. The question is, will two years' residence in a foreign country with the loss of income it entails be a "hardship" permitting an exception to be made in this case? The INS, according to Davis, refused to give out information on the way they will decide this case or have decided similar cases in the past. The INS advised the couple to apply and take their chances. The lack of predictability offers the couple little certainty.

Except for the FCIC case, each of these cases was consistent with the law. The unfairness of the results, however, suggest that law cannot be the sole standard for administrative reliability. Laws can also be analyzed in terms of how well the make a process fair and reliable.

WHOSE FAULT IS IT? THE PROBLEM OF POLITICAL EXECUTIVES

Although the bureaucracy has a negative reputation for meeting the standards outlined in this chapter, in reality its performance has been reasonably good given the constraints on bureaucracy. One reason for the poor public image of the bureaucracy is that it is blamed for many problems that others create. Individuals appointed by the president to positions in the bureaucracy are politicians not bureaucrats, but their actions are often attributed to the bureaucracy. In a widely publicized foul-up in 1981 the Department of Agriculture announced that ketchup would be considered a vegetable in the school lunch program. After publicity generated by the Food Research Action Committee, the Department of Agriculture backed down. Although the ketchup caper was dismissed by many as bureaucratic bungling, in fact the decision was made by G. William Hoagland, a political appointee in charge of the Food and Nutrition

Service (*National Journal,* 1981: 2134; Claybrook, 1984). Several other examples suggest that such blame shifting is not an uncommon phenomenon. John D. Ward, a political appointee in charge of the Office of Surface Mining in the Department of the Interior, resigned in 1985 when congressional hearings revealed that the agency failed to collect millions of dollars in penalties for violating environmental regulations (*National Journal,* 1985: 875). Career civil servants in 1985 wanted to file criminal charges against the Eli Lilly company for failure to notify the Food and Drug Administration of deaths caused by its antiarthritic drug, Oraflex, but political appointees in the Justice Department overruled this decision (*New York Times,* October 25, 1985). In September 1985 a political appointee serving as a member of the Nuclear Regulatory Commission voted to approve a plant even though portions of the plant had been built by his former company while the person was employed by the company (*Madison Capital Times,* September 1, 1985).

The large number of problems with political executives suggests that the process of hiring political executives is inherently flawed. Hugh Heclo (1988) contends the political appointment system generates problems because appointees serve only short periods of time and thus do not learn enough to manage programs effectively. Because political appointees are often from the private sector, they might not be aware of the expectations of the public service. Patricia Ingraham (1987) argues the problems were especially severe during the Reagan presidency. Unlike other presidents, Reagan rarely appointed career personnel to political appointee positions. As a result he made more inexperienced political appointments than a president normally would.

Perhaps this inexperience could have been overcome if the Reagan administration provided greater moral leadership. Illegal and unethical behavior by high-level appointees was common. An independent counsel in 1989 concluded that former Attorney General Edwin Meese had violated federal conflict of interest laws and tax laws. One of Attorney General Richard Thornburgh's top assistants was convicted in 1991 of cocaine use and lying about such use on his security clearance (*National Journal,* 1991: 411). *National Journal* in 1984 listed 40 separate cases of unethical or illegal behavior on the part of Reagan political appointees (Riehle, 1984: 92–93).

No agency suffered as much as the Department of Housing and Urban Development. The department was used as a dumping ground for political appointees during the Reagan administration. Secretary Samuel Pierce Jr. was uninterested in management and left control to inexperienced political appointees such as Deborah Gore Dean. At the same time the career staff at HUD were reduced from 16,000 to 11,000. Contracts were awarded for political reasons, and fraud and corruption ran rampant (Kurtz, 1989: 31). Estimated loses ran as high as $8 billion (Martz, 1987: 16).

The problems of political appointees may have been most severe under President Reagan, but similar problems have marred other presidencies. Using the most recent example, Clinton cabinet appointees Mike Espy, Henry Cisneros, and Ron Brown were all implicated in major scandals. The universal nature of such problems suggests that the political appointment process is inherently flawed and needs reform.

This brief recapitulation of a few recent scandals suggests that a careful examination of examples of incompetence and unresponsiveness by the bureaucracy would reveal that many times political appointees rather than the career service are responsible for the failings. There have been no administrative equivalents of Watergate or Abscam. Although the standard of comparison might not be rigorous, the career civil service appears to provide more responsive and more competent service to the American public than the "political" branches of government do. Unfortunately according to Herbert Kaufman (1981: 7), this simple fact is not recognized; he states, "Bureaucrats have become convenient and credible scapegoats for politicians whose policies don't succeed and for journalists who can always find an instance of stupidity or injustice or incompetence to fill a story on a day without much news." The end result is a bureaucracy that becomes demoralized by constant criticism for results outside its control.

....

SUMMARY

Our expectations concerning the performance of American bureaucracy are not modest. No political institution in the world, and the U.S. bureaucracy is no exception, can meet all the expectations outlined in this chapter. In a small nation with strong political institutions, a well-trained civil service, and few government functions, the bureaucracy might be able to attain most of these goals; but in the United States where the bureaucracy must deal with thousands of problems daily each somewhat unique, the bureaucracy is doomed to fail occasionally.

One reason why the U.S. bureaucracy cannot meet all our expectations is that the expectations often conflict. Effectiveness sometimes conflicts with responsiveness to political institutions. The U.S. Army in Vietnam, for example, could have effectively "ended" the conflict in Vietnam if all the restrictions on the use of weapons and manpower were removed. Through a massive invasion of North Vietnam along with nuclear weapons, the army could have destroyed North Vietnam. This tactic, however, would have generated some political costs that the U.S. public and its elected officials did not wish to bear. In this situation responsiveness took precedence over one definition of effectiveness.

Romzek and Dubnick (1987) argue that the explosion of the space shuttle *Challenger* can be viewed in terms of conflicting expectations (see also Romzek and Ingraham, 1998). Effectiveness required that safety concerns be paramount in shuttle launches, yet efficiency demanded that launches not be delayed. Pressures for efficiency in this case led to negative safety consequences.

Bureaucratic procedures can also be consistent and predictable but not fair. The Immigration and Naturalization Service's procedures on resident aliens who leave the country and wish to return are consistent and predictable but sometimes not fair to the individuals involved. If a resident alien voluntarily leaves the United States, the INS can prevent the individual from reentering. The INS can deny entry without a hearing or informing the alien why entry is denied. The procedures are consistent, predictable, and well within the law; but occasionally an individual who resided peacefully in the United States for several years will be refused reentry without an opportunity to discover why (Davis, 1965).

Public administrators often feel the conflict between the goals of flexibility and timeliness. In the Social Security Administration's disability program, Congress publicly favors a quick response to disability claims. Unfortunately, the disability claimants also want the SSA to be flexible and to consider individual circumstances. If the SSA set up rigid uniform procedures for judging disabilities, decisions would be more timely but only at the cost of decreased flexibility.

Efficiency may also conflict with openness to criticism (Feinberg, 1986: 615). Efficient treatment in Veterans Administration hospitals might require the hospital adopt certain procedures that treat the patients as units to be processed rather than as individuals. Such a system would be more efficient if it were not open to criticism. If a patient processing system responded to criticism, its efficiency would suffer. As agencies respond to criticism, they must often take time away from their normal functions. If the criticisms do not indicate how to make agency procedures more efficient, then responsiveness to criticism will lead to decreased efficiency.

The above are only five of the possible conflicts among the expectations of bureaucracy. Clearly all responsiveness-competence expectations can conflict with each other under certain circumstances. In fact, some of the individual expectations contain items that are not always internally consistent. Effectiveness, for example, requires clear policy goals; but few bureaus are given precise legislative goals. Amtrak was established with goals of service, protection of workers jobs, and profitability; and the three goals often conflicted (Guess, 1984: 386). The savings and loan bailout of 1989 required efficiency but also that housing be offered to the poor, that minority contractors be used, and that real estate sales not disrupt local markets. Lerner and Wanat (1983) contend that establishing multiple goals for bureaucracy or what they call "fuzzy goals" is a frequent phenomenon in American politics. O'Toole (1989: 7) goes even further, contending that with all the crosscutting requirements for nondiscrimination, auditing, and participation that all programs have multiple goals (see also Denhardt, 1989: 188). Clearly the examples of conflicting expectations presented in this section only scratch the surface of possibilities.

Given conflict in expectations, an interesting question is how agencies resolve the conflicting demands (see Meier, Wrinkle, and Polinard, 1998). Although studies of bureaucracy have not addressed this question, we can hypothesize about the ways bureaus would resolve this conflict if we accept the assumption that bureaus are rational power-seeking organizations. Such bureaus would resolve the conflicting expectations by responding in a manner that would have the greatest impact on the bureau's power base. The Army Corps of Engineers, for example, is more than willing to sacrifice efficiency to congressional responsiveness. The Army Corps' major source of influence is its close congressional ties. Since the Army Corps' power base would be improved by building more dams and other projects rather than less, it would rationally emphasize responsiveness to other political institutions over efficiency, even if this strategy entailed building a few projects that were not justified on a cost–benefit basis.

Another agency might prefer efficiency rather than responsiveness. The Federal Reserve, for example, could be more responsive to banks and other financial institutions by borrowing money at interest rates higher than necessary. This tactic would be less than rational for the Federal Reserve, however, since its influence is based in part on its reputation for efficient operations. The Federal Reserve in this situation would likely maximize efficiency at the expense of responsiveness.

Knowing the power base of a bureau, then, will increase our ability to predict how a bureau will resolve conflicting expectations. From a normative perspective, however, bureaus should not be permitted to respond to some expectations and not to others, especially if the bureau can decide which expectations are important. The nation needs a bureaucracy, especially a bureaucracy exercising political power, to meet as many expectations as possible. To achieve such a bureaucracy, a system of checks and balances must be designed to generate the greatest possible responsiveness and competence. The following two chapters lay the foundation for such a system by analyzing the various means available to control bureaucracy.

CHAPTER 6

CONTROLLING THE BUREAUCRACY: EXTERNAL CHECKS BY POLITICAL INSTITUTIONS

The exercise of administrative power is a problem for American democracy because bureaucrats are not elected. Concomitant with the increased intervention of government into people's personal lives during the twentieth century, administrative power has also increased. Eliminating bureaucratic power is impractical; effective public policy is impossible without bureaus that possess autonomy and discretion. The question remains—can bureaucracy be controlled by the people it is meant to serve? Can bureaucracy be made responsive to public demands and desires? This chapter and the next examine the various methods proposed to control bureau power and evaluate each method's likelihood of success.

....

OVERHEAD DEMOCRACY

The most frequently proposed method of controlling bureaucracy is making bureaucrats subordinate to the will of elected public officials; a series of proposals described by Emmette Redford (1969) as overhead democracy. Overhead democracy was originally presented as a means of controlling bureaucracy by Woodrow Wilson (1887) twenty-five years before his election as president. Wilson and many later followers believed that government could be or should be divided into politics and administration. Politics concerned establishing public policy goals, and administration dealt with implementing policy decisions. Because the political branch of government (in Wilson's view of Congress) was in charge of politics and policymaking, the bureaucracy should limit its concerns to administration. The dichotomy between politics and administration quite naturally led to the prescription that bureaucracy should be subordinate to the will of politicians. Although most current students of bureaucracy reject the politics–administration dichotomy as a false description of reality (for an exception, see Devine, 1981), overhead democracy as a bureaucratic control has widespread support.

Overhead democracy as a bureaucratic control is divisible into two distinct stages.

The first stage requires popular control over elected officials through the sanction of elections. Voters must rationally select candidates who support the same policies that they do and must punish retroactively candidates who fail to satisfy the electorate or who act inconsistently with their campaign promises. The second stage, the main concern of this chapter, requires that elected officials control bureaucrats through one of several means they have at their disposal. Some people feel the most effective means of control is hierarchical control by the president; others favor congressional control over bureaucracy by budgets, casework, and oversight. Many people believe that supremacy of law and the right of disaffected persons to appeal administrative wrongs to the courts for redress is the major check on bureaucracy. Still others place little faith in current institutions and advocate the independent office of the ombudsman to prevent administrative abuse of power.

The first step in the overhead democracy model is popular control over public officials. Clearly this step is the *sine qua non* of overhead democracy. How well politicians exact compliance from the bureaucracy is an academic question if citizens are unable to control politicians. We can imagine the dangers if politicians controlled the bureaucracy but the people did not control elected officials.

Whether the public controls its elected officials and the role of elections is the subject of many books and extended discussions. Rather than examining the extensive literature, we will just assume that under conditions where candidates run on issues, people have the means to control the actions of elected officials. We can also assume that politicians act consistently with the promises they make to gain office. We must now examine the ways elected officials can control the actions of bureaucrats. The remainder of this chapter examines the control of bureaucratic power via six avenues of overhead democracy: the legislature, the judiciary, the executive, federalism, the ombudsman, and direct democracy.

....

LEGISLATIVE CONTROLS ON BUREAUCRATIC POWER

Congressional control of bureaucracy was one of the first proposals for checking bureaucratic power. Since Congress was created as the nation's representative institution, congressional controls were a means to ensure that the bureaucracy was responsive to the American people. Although this section will focus mostly on Congress, the discussion also applies to state legislatures. The legislature can serve as a check on administrative actions (Key, 1959). First, it can pass legislation defining the extent of governmental activities, setting limits on bureau actions, describing procedures, and delimiting tasks and responsibility. Second, legislatures have control over fiscal and personnel resources through the appropriations process. Although an agency can spend less than it is appropriated, the agency will find it difficult to operate without resources if the legislature decides to deny them. Legislatures, in some instances, have gone so far as to deny all funds to an agency, thus eliminating it. The Subversive Activities Control Board and the Area Redevelopment Administration were both abolished because Congress refused to fund them (Ripley and Franklin, 1991: 15). Third, even though some forms of legislative veto were declared unconstitutional at the federal level, Congress still uses a form of the consultation process from the veto to influence administrative action. Under the legislative veto, Congress authorized an agency to set policy in a given area. All regulations issued or decisions were then submitted to Congress for approval.

The first three methods of controlling bureaucracy all contain sanctions that can be invoked against the bureaucracy. The final two methods are used to gather information, but they are backed by the possibility that the legislature will use one of the three sanctions. The fourth way the legislature can check on bureaucracy is through its oversight function. Legislatures can review bureaucratic actions, uncovering in the process information useful to the lawmaking or appropriations process. Finally, informal means exist that allow a legislator to exert some influence over the bureaucracy. Constituents frequently request legislative assistance in dealing with the bureaucracy; this casework is the primary way a legislator informally intervenes in the administrative process.

LEGISLATION

The use of legislation to control administrative action has received much theoretical attention but little systematic empirical analysis on its effectiveness as a bureaucratic check. To be sure many, though by no means all, agencies have their origins in legislation and their duties delimited by law.[1] In addition, no agency can continue to operate without congressional approval. Congressional legislation forms broad boundaries beyond which bureaus, in theory, cannot go. Although bureaus can influence the size and direction of their programs, whether or not to have such a program rests with Congress. In principle such authority is absolute. In the Airline Deregulation Act of 1978 Congress went so far as to abolish the Civil Aeronautics Board. In 1986 Congress also abolished the health care planning program, which required states to issue certificates of need before new health care facilities could be built (Mueller, 1988: 724). In 1995 Congress terminated the Interstate Commerce Commission.

Legislation has been used to guide administrative policy and reverse bureaucratic decisions. In an effort to encourage the Federal Trade Commission's efforts to be an aggressive consumer protection agency, the Magnuson-Moss Act of 1974 authorized agency rulemaking and gave the agency substantial new powers (West, 1985). The FTC responded to this grant of authority with a series of proposed rules, court suits, and regulations. As the composition of the Commerce Committees in Congress changed and the support for the consumer movement waned, Congress restricted FTC

---

[1] Kaufman (1976) discovered in his analysis of agency deaths that statutory origin was less frequent now than in the past. Agencies can be created by executive order of the president or by departmental order. Congress ratifies these creations by appropriating funds to them.

activities with legislation called the Federal Trade Commission Improvements Act. The act addressed FTC actions in great detail; it ended the FTC's study of the insurance industry, limited the use of federal funds to pay consumer groups to testify before the FTC, restricted the scope of the FTC's children's television study, required the FTC to use cost-benefit analysis, prohibited the FTC from petitioning another agency to remove the protection of a trademark, and subjected FTC rules to a legislative veto (Pertschuk, 1982; Meier, 1985: 110; Yandle, 1986: 524). In a period of only six years Congress, by legislation, urged the FTC to be an aggressive consumer protection advocate and then restricted the FTC's advocacy.

The number of examples demonstrating the successful use of legislation to control bureaucracy is virtually limitless. In 1984 Congress required that child support agencies assist custodial parents who were not on welfare (Keiser and Meier, 1996; the agencies were originally established to recoup welfare payments). At the local level, Chaney and Saltzstein (1998) found that city councils were able to change police behavior on domestic assaults via mandatory arrest laws (see also Haider-Markel, 1998). Agencies in all states responded with greater efforts to assist these parents. In 1972 the Consumer Product Safety Act required that the Consumer Product Safety Commission (CPSC) use a bizarre rulemaking process that essentially required the agency to contract out its rulemaking functions. Later, frustrated by the slow pace of CPSC rulemaking, Congress wrote and adopted a regulation for cellulose home insulation by law (Johnson, 1990: 75). Congress often specifies what are essentially regulations. The federal Surface Mining Control and Reclamation Act included 115 specific environmental performance standards for regulatory enforcement (Shover, Clelland, and Lynxwiler, 1986: 130).

Using legislation to establish procedures that benefit one set of interests or another has received a great deal of theoretical attention (McCubbins, Noll, and Weingast, 1989). By establishing procedures that generate predictable results, Congress can control the bureaucracy without having to monitor it. While this idea is logical in theory, Congress rarely gives procedural questions much attention. In addition two attempts to study congressional structuring empirically both failed to confirm Congress' ability to control the bureaucracy in this way (Balla 1998; Robinson 1998).

Not all legislative attempts to control the bureaucracy via substantive legislation (as opposed to changing procedures) are successful. Joseph Harris (1964) provides a case study of Congress' attempt to limit the number of permanent employees during the Korean War to prevent bureaucratic expansion. The Whitten Amendment set personnel ceilings and allowed promotions only after a person had spent at least one year in grade. Bureaus affected by the amendment appealed to their friends in Congress to exempt them from the requirement. Agencies that were denied exemptions demonstrated a great deal of ingenuity in following the letter but not the spirit of the law. Harris concluded that the Whitten Amendment did not prevent bureaucratic expansion. Even had the amendment been successful, Harris contended that program administration would have been hampered by limiting agency flexibility and thus preventing agencies from attracting qualified personnel.

Although the case studies demonstrate several instances of success and an instance of failure for legislation as a control on bureaucracy, legislation in practice is not necessarily a panacea for several reasons. First, legislation is often devoid of detail or fails to express clear policy goals. Even the *United States Tax Code*, at 2,800 pages, possibly the most detailed law the nation has, is so vague that the Internal Revenue Service must issue an additional 11,000 pages of regulations that interpret the law.[2] McFarlane's (1989) study of family planning statutes found that laws with specific and ranked goals, a valid causal theory (about policy problems), integration of the program with the agency hierarchy, and several other factors provided more congressional control over administrative implementation (see also Meier and McFarlane, 1996; Keiser and Meier, 1996). In short, clear and detailed laws enhance legislative control. Unfortunately, most laws do the meet this standard.

Second, laws can be blunt instruments. While Congress would like more influence in the administrative process, too much interference can hamper effective administration. The Magnuson-Moss Act of 1974, for example, specified such extensive procedures for rulemaking that rules took three times as long to issue after the act as before (West, 1985; Breyer, 1982: 347). Similarly the offer or process of rulemaking for the Consumer Product Safety Commission was so cumbersome that Congress eventually repealed it. To avoid these problems, Congress often relies on nonstatutory means of control such as suggesting changes in policy during hearings, putting recommendations in committee reports, and urging action in conference reports (Kirst, 1969).

Third, legislation may be more effective in preventing action than in initiating a policy. Positive actions provide more opportunities for bureaus to influence policy because they usually require nonspecific, discretionary changes in agency behavior. Prohibitions, on the other hand, can often name the specific behavior that is prohibited. In 1987, for example, Congress ended a loophole in the surface mining law by prohibiting strip mines from subdividing themselves so that individual mines were too small to come under the federal law (Harris, 1989: 74).

Fourth, specific laws and rigid requirements can backfire if the needed knowledge base does not exist. One of the leading examples of statutory control is the environmental laws of the 1970s that specified goals and timetables for reaching the goals. The Nuclear Waste Policy Act of 1982 followed this pattern, establishing short deadlines for evaluation and selection of nuclear waste disposal sites despite the arguments of the Environmental Protection Agency, the Nuclear Regulatory Commission, and the U.S. Geological Service that the technical information to make these decisions did not exist. As it became clear during implementation that the scientific base necessary to make these decisions did not exist, the policy process broke down and was stalemated by political pressures (Clary and Kraft, 1988: 108).

Fifth, a lack of controls may reflect a rational policymaking strategy on the part of Congress. Bawn (1995) contends that Congress sets up many agencies with the idea that the agency will balance the competing interests and make decisions about policy

---

[2] The IRS also writes much of the tax code initially. When Congress feels it necessary to write detailed legislation, it must rely on bureaucratic expertise to draft the legislation. This dependence dampens the impact of law as a check.

choices. Congress then can claim credit for positive results and can intervene if results are negative. This minimizes some of the political risks to Congress.

Finally, a problem related to all four previous limitations is the size of Congress. Congress is not too small or too unspecialized to effectively control the bureaucracy via legislation if legislation were Congress' only function. Because Congress is also interested in casework, constituency service, and other nonlegislative actions, it may be too small and too unspecialized to do these things and also to control the bureaucracy via legislation. Legislation clearly can be an effective check on bureaucratic discretion if Congress gives it a high priority.

BUDGETING

An objective scholar interested in maintaining political control over administration would probably design a process similar to the appropriations process. In the appropriations process elected officials have a clear sanction to apply against administrators who disregard congressional intent; they can withdraw the resources that administrators need to operate programs. Budgeting can also be used to reward agencies that perform as the legislature intends. Budgeting's advantage over legislation is periodicity; Congress is required to scrutinize administrative budgets annually. The decision to use the sanction, therefore, occurs at frequent intervals and is an accepted means of exercising control.

The initial empirical analyses of budgeting revealed that the budget was not as potent a weapon as it had appeared to be. Most early studies of congressional budgeting found that the budgetary process did not examine policy issues but proceeded incrementally (Fenno, 1966; Davis, Dempster, and Wildavsky, 1966; Thomas and Hanberg, 1974). In an incremental system past budget decisions are considered final. An agency, therefore, asks for a given percentage more than it received last year; and the appropriations committee examines only the difference between this year's budget and last year's budget. Although some agencies raise congressional ire and find their entire budget reevaluated, most can assume that last year's base is safe.

The incremental nature of budgeting has recently been challenged by several scholars. Almost everyone agrees that the *process* of budgeting is incremental, that budgeteers make decisions by looking at small changes from year to year (Bailey and O'Connor, 1975). An incremental process, however, does not guarantee incremental results; some agencies may get larger or smaller increments than other agencies, and such variations have policy implications. Kemp's (1982: 650) study of budgeting for regulatory agencies found that budgets exceeded incremental ranges (10 percent or more) as much as 50 percent of the time. Taggart (1985: 710) discovered that over one-half the budget changes in state air quality control expenditures over time revealed similar nonincremental changes in agency budgets.

If incremental, nonpolicy changes were once the norm in budgeting, they no longer are. Changes in the political environment have changed budgeting so that it no longer produces incremental results. Much of the federal government's budget had been protected from the annual budget cycle by making automatic appropriations for such programs as social security, food stamps, and unemployment compensation (Kettl, 1989: 233). Such programs are entitlements; any individual qualified is entitled to the benefits; total expenditures, therefore, are uncontrollable via the appropriations process. Many entitlement programs also have benefits that increase as the cost of living increases. During the rampant inflation of the 1970s the cost of entitlements grew faster than federal revenues (Berry and Lowery, 1990: 696). When President Reagan began his defense buildup, the expansion of defense expenditures and the growth of entitlements exceeded the increment that could be generated from tax revenues. Under such circumstances an agency's budget base was no longer sacred and was reexamined every year for possible cuts. With ballooning deficits in the 1980s not even the increment for entitlements was safe (Bozeman and Straussman, 1982: 511; Caiden, 1984: 109; Kettl, 1989: 237).

Closer examination of individual budgets found policy controls via budgeting. Arnold Kanter (1972) determined that defense subcommittees were not so much concerned with increments but rather with research and development projects and procurement decisions. Such a focus permitted Congress to affect defense policy. Although these subcommittees were often more interested in rewarding the services and thwarting the secretary of defense, the decisions influenced defense policy (see also Fox, 1971). At times the detail of the effort was impressive; in 1984 Congress changed nearly 1,200 of 1,860 line items in the defense budget (*Washington Post*, August 12, 1985: 7). Robert Art (1985) found a similar magnitude of changes when he examined fiscal and program management actions rather than overall defense policy (see also Mayer, 1993).

Even though microbudget decisions might not be as policy oriented as possible, this does not mean that budgets do not control agency actions by setting priorities. Several studies suggest the attempt to control by linking budget outcomes to partisan distributions in Congress. Auten, Bozeman, and Cline (1984) linked Democratic strength in the House to larger budgets for health, education, and welfare programs and more Senate Democrats to larger appropriations for agriculture and labor. Bozeman (1977: 124) found partisanship affected individual agency budgets for forty-two agencies between 1950 and 1971. Similarly Kiewiet and McCubbins (1985) tied high appropriations for domestic agencies to Democratic party strength (see also Hill and Plumlee, 1984). Some examples of specific budget actions taken to "persuade" agencies also exist. In 1946 Senator Pat McCarran cut the U.S. Grazing Service's appropriations and personnel allocation in retaliation for attempting to raise public grazing feels (Davis and Davis, 1988: 6). A similar case involving soil conservation occurred in 1987 (Sinclair, 1987: 33). Farnham's (1995) study of the Forest Service found budgeting changes when accompanied by legislative changes had a significant impact on agency priorities.

The same environmental trends that have made budgeting less incremental and increased the potential for agency control have also resulted in other budgeting behaviors that have reduced control efforts. Budgeting has become so complex and so partisan that Congress rarely passes appropriations bills by the start of the fiscal year. In such circumstances, Congress funds federal agencies via a continuing resolution that sets agency budgets at last year's level or some level passed by one house of Congress. Continuing resolutions are incremental budgeting of the highest order in that the entire budget of last year is simply extended to this year (Caiden, 1984: 115; Pitsvada and Draper, 1984: 404). The use of entitlements and the pressures to cut these programs also results in more programs running out of money before the end of the year. In such circumstances Congress must grant supplemental appropriations (95 percent of supplemental requests are granted); excessive supplementals indicate that budgets are not being used even as a fiscal control. Although the volume of supplementals varies from year to year, in 1977 supplementals totaled 13.7 percent of the total budget (Congressional Budgeting Office, 1981: 8).

Efforts to control bureaus via budgets can take forms other than cuts or increases in the budget. An appropriation is a piece of legislation, and often attached to appropriations are specific instructions known as appropriations' riders. The 1981 budget, for example, contained an appropriations rider that granted states the option of adopting mandatory workfare programs for AFDC recipients (Gueron and Nathan, 1985: 417). Similarly Congress used an appropriations rider in 1984 to prevent the FTC from filing antitrust suits against cities for one year. State governments such as Wisconsin's often use the budget bill as their major policy effort and include major legislative changes in the budget.

Bureaucratic control is not the only objective of congressional budgeting, budgets are also a battleground between Congress and the president for control over policy. With the executive budget and the flow of political power from the Congress to the president, congressional budgeting has become less influential. The Congressional Budget and Impoundment Control Act of 1974 was a serious attempt by Congress to reestablish control over the budget process. At a minimum the act increased the analytical capacity of Congress by establishing the Congressional Budget Office. Because the act focused on relationships with the president, it did not greatly restrict the bureaucracy. The need to deal with massive federal deficits in the 1990s led to another redefinition of budget roles; with exclusive focus on the deficit, efforts to control bureaus were sometimes lost. In the budgetary struggles between Congress and the president over the deficit or over funding priorities, Congress often sees bureaus as willing allies in its war with the president. Congress can provide a sympathetic ear to the National Institutes of Health, the Environmental Protection Agency, and other agencies whose funds the president cuts. Until 1995 the congressional budget process, in many cases, had become an appeals process whereby Congress acted to restore presidential budget cuts rather than focusing on controlling the bureaucracy. Earlier roles of rigorous examination of agency budgets have been modified (Malachowski, Bookheimer, and Lowery, 1987: 336). In 1995 the Republican majority severed some of the long-standing budget ties between Congress and the bureaus. With the budget finally in balance in 1998, the future use of budget controls is an unexplored territory.

Two other factors limit the congressional budget as a control device. The budget is no longer integrated; many programs have been moved "off budget" and out of the control of the budget process (Caiden, 1981: 1219). Caiden (1981) identified nine agencies with a budget total of $18 billion that were not in the congressional budget; these figures do not count the massive number of government guaranteed loans that only appear in the budget when loans are defaulted (see Ippolito, 1984). Also missing are tax expenditures. Kettl (1989: 236) estimated that tax expenditures (deductions or tax offsets for specific activities, e.g., home mortgages) totaled $315 billion. Second, despite its complexity, the budget still permits a great deal of discretion. Agency heads can reprogram funds within the agency to change policies without congressional approval. In 1982, for example, the administrator of the Agency for International Development reprogrammed funds so that budget cuts would not harm the Peace Corps (Reeves, 1988). In sum, the budget process clearly has the potential to control the bureaucracy, it is sometimes successful in doing so, but it is not being used extensively by Congress for that purpose.

LEGISLATIVE VETO AND CONSULTATIONS

For a time the legislative veto was a favorite congressional tool used to assert some control over the bureaucracy. Under the procedures of the legislative veto, Congress authorized a bureau to take certain actions (such as allocating oil supplies in an emergency). When the bureau exercised its authority under this legislative grant, it was required to inform Congress and send the proposed action to Congress. Congress, then, within a specified period of time could veto the administrative action. Twenty-two states also have legislative veto provisions (Renfrow and Houston, 1987: 659). In 1983 the Supreme Court declared that one-house legislative vetoes, those that permitted a single house to veto an action, were unconstitutional (*Immigration and Naturalization Service v. Chadha*). This single Supreme Court decision called into question hundreds of federal laws (Craig, 1983). Since 1932, Congress has passed approximately 500 veto provisions; three-fourths of those were passed after 1970 (J. Cooper, 1985: 368). Although the court decision dealt only with one-house vetoes, the decision's logic appeared to include all veto provisions.[3]

The veto is of crucial concern to Congress because it is a weapon not only for controlling the bureaucracy but also for checking the president. The veto is in such important legislation as the War Powers Act and the impoundment sections of the Budget and Impoundment Control Act as well as in minor legislation such as the General Services Administration's control over presidential papers and the Department of Education's authority over sex discrimination. The use of the veto has focused far more on presidential–congressional relations than bureaucratic control. Congress considered 1,180 veto proposals before mid-1985; 226 were adopted, but only 19 nullified agency rules (Labaton, 1985: 10). A study of North Carolina legislative vetoes found even more modest use; only 60 rules out of 6,450 were challenged, or about 1.6 per year (Miller, 1987: 638).

---

[3] The legislative veto can come in a variety of forms. It may either be positive, so that Congress must act to veto an action, or negative, so that if Congress does not act, the action is void. The time period for veto can vary substantially. Before the Supreme Court decision, who could exercise the veto also varied. In some instances only one house could veto the action and in special circumstances committees of either house could veto the action (see J. Cooper, 1956; 1985).

The importance of the veto to Congress is illustrated by Congress' reaction to the Supreme Court ruling. Congress made a concerted effort to establish alternative forms of the veto. Congressional scholar Louis Fisher (1984; 1985) found that within two years of the *Chadha* decision Congress enacted 53 additional laws that contained legislative veto provisions. These new vetoes take a wide variety of forms, but all attempt to distinguish themselves from the veto provisions that were declared unconstitutional (J. Cooper, 1986: 60). One common form of the new veto required a joint resolution passed by both houses of Congress, a form that is still clearly constitutional (Fisher, 1987).

According to legislative veto advocate Joseph Cooper (1985; 1956; West and Cooper, 1983), the veto is designed primarily as a method of gaining executive branch (i.e., the president) control, but it also has some advantages as a bureaucratic control. Having a veto allows Congress to reassert power in areas where it has previously lost it, such as the power to declare war or the power to budget funds without impoundment. The veto also encourages Congress to delegate authority to agencies that can apply their expertise; without the check of the veto, Congress might hesitate to grant agencies broad discretion. Finally, the veto also allows for more precise oversight by focusing Congress' attention on executive actions (West and Cooper, 1983: 299).

West and Cooper (1989) contend that restrictions on the legislative veto can harm the legislative process. Without the ability to review administrative rules, West and Cooper feel, Congress will pass laws that grant less discretion to administrative agencies. To retain control of the policy process, Congress might enact highly detailed restrictions on administrators; as an example they note a legislative provision that specified a cross-ownership rule (owning more than one form of media) for the Federal Communications Commission (West and Cooper, 1989: 605). Similar legislation covering what are clearly administrative rules can be found. The 1986 Antidrug Abuse Control Act, for example, required the Environmental Protection Agency to study the use of cyanide and specified new procedures for the Interstate Commerce Commission to license interstate bus and truck drivers.

Despite Cooper's optimism concerning the legislative veto, some serious limitations exist. The continued adoption of veto provisions, especially after a Supreme Court decision, may well be an admission by Congress that it has lost control of the policymaking process. If so, the veto may be an inappropriate solution for several reasons. First, the veto relegates Congress to a negative role in checking administrative policymaking. Congress in a sense admits that it cannot positively command action through legislation, so it must ask others to initiate policy and respond to those initiatives. A negative role reduces the options that Congress has to control bureau policymaking because it is restricted to reacting to the policies that the bureaucracy proposes. To see the relative disadvantage of the veto, one need only compare the impact Congress has had on environmental policy, where it frequently exercises its lawmaking powers, to its impact on consumer protection via the veto on the Federal Trade Commission (see below).

Second, increased use of the legislative veto sanctions the decay of the legislative process. Theodore Lowi (1969) argues that legislation has ceased to be legislation and has become instead broad grants of authority to administrators. With the legislative veto Congress can be even more vague, assured that it can intervene in administrative matters at its leisure. Increased use of the veto causes congressional policy to lose its coherence because vetoes narrow Congress' perspective to the single question involved rather than focusing on broader policy issues. As a result congressional vetoes may well hinder effective policymaking by preventing an agency from issuing rules, as they did for the first Federal Elections Commission.

Third, recent vetoes of administrative rules have provided opportunities for vested interests to defeat more diffuse interests after administrative agencies have taken proconsumer stands. In 1982 Congress, responding to the campaign contributions and pleas of automobile dealers, vetoed the Federal Trade Commission's famed used-car rule, which required that dealers report known defects to customers. Although the rule was hardly a burden on honest dealers, Congress willingly provided a mechanism to reverse the FTC's proconsumer decision. The mere existence of a veto provision may well discourage agencies from making correct, yet unpopular, decisions (see Cooper, 1985: 380). An excellent example of the bias generated by the presence of a veto process is revealed in Ethridge's (1981: 489) study of state environmental protection laws. Ethridge found that states with veto provisions had adopted less comprehensive and more lenient pollution laws than states without veto provisions. In a separate study Ethridge (1984) found the legislative veto was associated with less stringent regulation of professions, an area notorious for favoring the interests of the profession rather than the interests of consumers (but see J. Cooper, 1985; West and Cooper, 1989).

Fourth, heavy reliance on the veto would result in congressional overload. With veto provisions in numerous laws and with agencies adopting an estimated 7,000 regulations per year, Congress could easily devote all its time to veto reviews. Such a flood of regulations, even if given a cursory review, could overload Congress and reduce its performance in other areas.

OVERSIGHT

Investigation/oversight is a congressional information-gathering function. The Legislative Reorganization Act of 1946 requires that the House and Senate Government Operations Committees oversee all government activities, reorganizations, and intergovernmental relationships. Other congressional committees also perform oversight during legislative and appropriations hearings. In 1972 and 1973, for example, oversight hearings revealed that agencies were not complying with the Freedom of Information Act. These oversight hearings led to legislation limiting agency cost charges and permitting more general information requests (Feinberg, 1986: 617). The potential volume of congressional oversight is massive; Aberbach (1990: 35) estimates that one in four congressional hearings is concerned with oversight.

The oversight process is fairly simple; a congressional committee investigates a bureau or a policy by holding hearings, conducting staff evaluations, or requesting audits by the General Accounting Office. The General Accounting Office has established a good reputation as a program evaluator to complement its role as a financial auditor (F. Mosher, 1979). GAO completes between 50 and 100 studies a month for Congress.

Although oversight can be the initial step in legislation, budgeting, or the legislative veto, oversight itself may be a sanction. Oversight hearings by the environmental committees of Congress were used to demonstrate EPA's shortcomings under Anne Burford in the early 1980s. The extent of oversight can be massive; the Department of Defense claimed that between January 1982 and August 1985 Secretary Casper Weinberger spent 147 hours in 54 separate appearances before Congress; other DoD witnesses devoted 1,453 hours of testimony before 91 different committees and subcommittees (*Washington Post*, August 12, 1985: 16). Such careful records, however, are rare; most oversight blends into legislation, budgeting, or veto processes so that it cannot be easily distinguished as oversight (see Aberbach, 1990, for a discussion of how to define oversight).

Numerous case studies of oversight exist. In the early 1950s a Republican Congress, dissatisfied with the prounion policies of the National Labor Relations Board (NLRB), held a series of hearings detailing areas where they felt the NLRB had failed to be neutral (Scher, 1960). The hearings created pressure on President Dwight Eisenhower to appoint more conservative, business-oriented members to the NLRB. With these appointments the NLRB began supporting business interests rather than union interests.

Perhaps the best-known case of oversight was the series of congressional hearings conducted on environmental policy during the early 1980s. Responding to leaks about lax environmental regulation, Congress conducted more than 70 hearings between October 1981 and July 1982. The hearings were used as a forum to criticize EPA administrator Anne Burford on a variety of issues including enforcement credibility, management effectiveness, support for state agencies, openness to public access, and relationships with industry. Revelations concerning the hazardous waste program led to the forced resignation of Burford, the appointment of William Ruckelshaus, and a less controversial administration of environmental policy (Meier, 1985). In the mid-1980s Congress also used oversight hearings to support the Equal Employment Opportunity Commission's effort to become a more vigorous regulator (Wood, 1990: 525).

Not all cases of oversight, however, are congressional successes. Examining the investigation of the National Aeronautics and Space Administration's (NASA) decision to use liquid fuel rather than solid fuel rockets, Kerr (1965) found that despite continued congressional pressure on NASA to consider solid fuel rockets, NASA was able to resist by relying on arguments based on expertise. When the scientific arguments failed, NASA conducted a token analysis to placate the committee but did not change its policies.

In some cases agencies actually seek congressional oversight, preferring that Congress resolve certain policy questions. Bradley (1980) determined that bureaucrats administering the Medicare program used the oversight process to get congressional decisions on policy questions and also to get congressional approval of administrative actions. Banking regulators, in their frequent oversight hearings, often provide Congress with a list of policy decisions they would like resolved (and include suggestions about how they should be resolved). Such issues as interest bearing checking accounts, the chartering of nonbanks, and the powers of thrift institutions were presented to the Banking Committees for review and decision (Meier, 1985: 68–70).

One method of legislative oversight that has been used extensively at the state level is sunset legislation (only a small number of federal sunset cases exist). Under a sunset law, an agency is given a fixed term of existence (say ten years). Unless the legislature acts to recreate the agency, it must be shut down when the term expires. The logic behind sunset laws is to place the forces of inertia in favor of eliminating agencies rather than keeping them. It requires a full oversight review to keep an agency. First passed by Colorado in 1976, thirty-six states adopted sunset laws by 1981 (Kearney, 1990: 50). Sunset's performance, however, has been less than its promise. Some small, weak agencies were eliminated, but most survived and prospered (Slaughter, 1986: 242; Kearney, 1990: 52). Perhaps the best assessment of sunset is that eleven states have repealed their sunset laws or allowed them to atrophy (Kearney, 1990: 50).

Although a definitive, empirical analysis of oversight's impact has not been done, most students of oversight believe that the successes are less common than the failures (Huitt, 1966; Bibby, 1966; Ripley and Franklin, 1991; Ogul, 1976; Del Sesto, 1980). Several logical reasons support this view. First, oversight is less than universally successful because it does not fall within most members of Congress' perception of the role of Congress. The function of Congress is legislation, and through legislation members of Congress establish their institutional reputations. The rewards of legislation and casework far exceed those in oversight (Ripley and Franklin, 1991: 193–195). To be sure, some members of Congress, such as Representative Les Aspin, regarding the Department of Defense, or Senator William Proxmire, regarding the National Science Foundation, concentrated on oversight, but these were exceptional cases. This generally critical view of oversight has been challenged by Aberbach (1990: 34); he contends that oversight tripled from 1961 to 1983 both in number of hearings and percentage of hearings devoted to oversight. Aberbach finds that oversight, however, is generally favorable to the programs under review. As a result, the increase in oversight might not reflect increased efforts to control bureaucracy.

Second, staffing problems also limit the quantity and quality of oversight given the massive task of overseeing the entire federal bureaucracy. Oversight is essentially an extra function, peripheral to budgeting and legislation. The time pressures to complete these tasks often drive out opportunities for oversight. Congress, for example, held only one oversight hearing between 1934 and 1976 on the Federal Communications Commission's regulation of telephones (Wilsford, 1984: 434). Congress often does not have the staff to legislate, appropriate, and also oversee bureau operations.

A third and perhaps most important reason why oversight does not occur more frequently is that members of Congress lack the motivation for oversight (Ripley and Franklin, 1991: 193). Oversight places the member of Congress and the bureau in an adversarial position. A member of Congress who expects his or her constituents to benefit from agency programs may jeopardize those benefits with overzealous oversight. Only in regulatory policy do the interests of the member and the constituents coincide in opposition to the bureau's interests; the anticonsumer protection oversight of the

Commerce Committees in the late 1970s was such a case. With few exceptions, therefore, oversight does not help a member's standing either in Congress or with his or her constituency. As a result, few members will spend much time in oversight.

Oversight at the state level has many of the same problems that congressional oversight has. Miller's (1987) study of North Carolina concludes little real oversight was done in that state. Wohlstetter's (1989) study of oversight in six states found that it was used for credit claiming but not for bureaucratic control. She concluded, "legislators may not be interested, at least not primarily, in controlling implementors. Oversight, therefore, may not really be effective as an accountability tool" (Wohlstetter, 1989: 65).

Oversight, much like budgeting and legislation, is potentially an effective way to control bureaucracy. Most students of oversight, however, agree that it is not used more frequently because Congress lacks the motivation to oversee the bureaucracy more effectively.

INFORMAL CONTACTS

The final legislative mechanism available to control administrative agencies is the legislator's informal contacts with bureaucrats. These contacts can be used to advise on policy or to point out errors that the bureau might have made. The major reason why a member of Congress contacts a bureaucrat is that one of the members' constituents requested assistance. William Gwyn (1968) estimated that Congress received more than 200,000 constituent requests a year for assistance with the bureaucracy. In 1982 members of Congress received an average of 102.5 casework requests per week, but the distribution of requests varied greatly from 4 to 800 for individual members (Johannes and McAdams, 1987: 538). Even at the state level, Elling (1980: 331) found legislators had approximately five contacts per week.

Although McCubbins and Schwartz (1984) argue that informal contacts are an essential method of obtaining information that can then be used in the oversight process, they present no data to support this claim. Dean Mann (1968) did a detailed study of three California legislators' casework. Mann found the informal contact process was used infrequently; the three legislators handled 81 cases in a three-month period, an average of nine cases per month (but see Elling, 1980). The cases came generally from middle-class constituents and dealt with minor matters, the most frequent concerning automobile registration. Not once in all the cases, according to Mann (1968), did an agency change its policy in response to a legislative contact.

Complaints registered with legislators are not only minor, but they also usually request special favors that the administrative process does not permit. The most common casework at the federal level involves social security checks and veterans benefits (Cain, Ferejohn, and Fiorina, 1984: 115). Congressional pressure on administrators means special treatment for the few with access to a member of Congress, not more effective public policy. The Department of Defense alone gets 2,500 phone calls and 400 written inquiries from Congress every day (Liedl, 1990: 24). Because most agencies require that congressional requests be processed within forty-eight to seventy-two hours, a congressional request interrupts normal work procedures and moves a case to the top of the stack for processing (Johannes, 1984: 59; Davis, 1965; Elling, 1980: 334). Casework thus introduces an element of political bias that administration with its neutral procedures was originally designed to eliminate. Not even personnel processes are exempt; in 1990 House Judiciary Committee Chair Jack Brooks intervened in the Immigration and Naturalization Service to rescind the transfer of a manager from Houston to St. Paul (*National Journal,* 1990: 1598). Even Johannes's (1984: 60) generally favorable analysis of casework notes that midlevel administrators, those who actually implement policies, were more likely to see casework as disrupting agency actions (see also Abney and Lauth, 1982a: 449, at the local level).

Casework, in addition to distorting the administrative process, also has the potential to foster corruption. In 1990–1991 the U.S. Senate was shaken by the "Keating Five" scandal when five senators used informal contacts to pressure federal regulators to ease up on savings and loans owned by Charles Keating (Leidl, 1990: 24). In 1989 Speaker of the House Jim Wright and Democratic House leader Tony Coelho resigned after similar scandals involving thrift regulation. Some people blamed the Department of Housing and Urban Development corruption scandals of the 1980s on congressional committees more interested in getting favors from HUD than in overseeing the department (Leidl, 1990: 24).

CONGRESSIONAL CONTROLS: SUMMARY

If the sole function of Congress were to control the bureaucracy, Congress would not be credited with a good performance. Because Congress has directed its attention to major policymaking issues and presidential activities, bureaucracy receives relatively less scrutiny. Still if the process worked as designed, budgeting, oversight, legislation, and the legislative veto in combination could provide the tools necessary to check administrative power. Casework would counter the benefits of the other mechanisms. In some cases, Congress is fairly effective at influencing the policy decisions of the bureaucracy. Cohen (1985a) examined the policy outputs of the Interstate Commerce Commission, the Securities and Exchange Commission, the National Labor Relations Board, the Federal Trade Commission, and the Federal Communications Commission and found strong correlations with many congressional variables over time (see also Moe, 1985). Hansen's (1990) study of the International Trade Commission revealed that the commission was responsive to pressures from members of key committees. Yantek and Gartrell (1988) found that as Congress became more conservative, the FTC and the Antitrust Division of the Department of Justice were more willing to permit corporate mergers. Scholz and Wei (1986: 1261) found greater enforcement of Occupational Safety and Health Administration regulations in states that had prolabor congressional delegations. Hedge and Jallow (1990: 795) found surface mining enforcement increased in states that were represented on the oversight committees. At the state level, Brudney and Hebert (1987: 199) found legislators had greater control over the bureaucracy when agencies received less federal funds, when political parties were competitive, and when the legislature was professionalized (more staff, higher salaries, etc.).

In general, Congress uses its control mechanisms less than it could because it lacks the necessary information and resources. In other cases Congress may not want to restrict the bureaucracy. During the Reagan administration when the president was viewed as the enemy of the House of Representatives, the bureaucracy was often perceived as a friend. In such circumstances, control of the bureaucracy is not a high congressional priority.

JUDICIAL CONTROLS ON BUREAUCRATIC POWER

The courts have a few simple mechanisms designed to limit bureaucratic power. Under the separation of powers, the judiciary's role is to interpret laws and declare executive/bureaucratic actions void if they fail to meet Constitutional or statutory requirements. The courts have two standards they generally apply to administrative action. First, is the action consistent with legislative intent? Overstepping legislative intent is grounds for overruling an administrative agency as the Supreme Court did to the Occupational Safety and Heath Administration in the famed benzene case (*Industrial Union Department, AFL–CIO* v. *American Petroleum Institute*). Similarly, a Department of Health and Human Services rule requiring that the parents of all minors receiving contraceptive information be notified was voided in 1983 for overstepping legislative intent (Hult, 1988: 318). Second, courts will overrule an administrative agency if it has violated proper procedures including not only legislatively established procedures but also general Constitutional principles of due process (P. J. Cooper, 1988).

Courts can limit administrative actions either prior to any decisions through declaratory judgments and injunctions or after the fact through damage awards against the bureaucracy. The administrative problems that courts are designed to prevent, however, are limited. Courts are generally more concerned with procedural fairness than with substantive issues of responsiveness (but see Shapiro, 1988). Courts want to know if the correct procedures were followed not if the policy is responsive or beneficial. Despite these limits, many students of bureaucratic power believe, as William Robson (1964: 31) does, that "the strongest safeguard against maladministration in the US appears to be the Courts of Law."

COURT IMPACT

Court relationships with the bureaucracy have evolved over time. Initially courts, using the doctrine of substantive due process, were hostile to administrative agencies and frequently voided agency actions. Gradually the principle that courts should defer to administrative expertise took hold, and courts accepted most agency decisions. The 1960s and 1970s saw less deference to agency decisions as such administrative law principles as exhaustion, ripeness, standing and intervention, estoppel, and official immunity have been weakened (P. J. Cooper, 1988; Wenner, 1983: 671). Thompson (1982a: 206), for example, blames court activism for the willingness of business and labor to litigate almost every occupational safety and health regulation. Since the mid-1980s, the court remains skeptical of bureaucratic action but is more deferential than in the 1970s.

The number of successful court interventions in administrative activities has increased dramatically in recent years. Federal courts have been especially harsh on state and local agencies. Federal courts in conjunction with the attorney general exercise control over state and local election procedures to ensure they are not discriminatory under the Voting Rights Acts (Binion, 1979). The U.S. Supreme Court has restricted the actions of local governments by establishing the equivalent of strict liability standards in regard to constitutional violations (Spurrier, 1983: 199; P. J. Cooper, 1984: 269). Courts have taken over the administration of local school districts (Stewart and Bullock, 1981) and state prisons and even mandated state expenditures. Harriman and Straussman (1983: 346) looked at fourteen states with prison systems under court order and found court-mandated increased capital expenditures in twelve of them (see also Straussman, 1986). In a survey of state administrators, 31 percent stated that court decisions had caused a reallocation of funds in such areas as mental health, hospitals, education, and corrections (Hale, 1979: 363).

Courts have also become fairly active in certain areas of federal policy. Plant and Thompson (1983: 9) concluded that courts had done more to define institutional discrimination and shift the burden of proof in employment discrimination cases than the Equal Employment Opportunity Commission; in a sense the courts set policy beyond what the EEOC could (see also Thompson, 1984). In 1989, however, the Supreme Court rejected its own line of precedent in employment discrimination and established more rigorous tests to demonstrate discrimination (see *Ward's Cove* v. *Antonio*, subsequently overturned by the Civil Rights Act of 1991). A successful lawsuit requesting equal time to respond to cigarette ads fundamentally changed the Federal Communications Commission's regulation of such fairness doctrine issues (Goldoff, 1984: 421). Sometimes, however, in protecting individual rights, the court restricts agencies and impairs their performance. The courts required that the Office for Civil Rights respond to all complaints within a specified period of time. The decision required the agency to spend all its time processing complaints rather than addressing itself to major policy priorities (Bullock and Stewart, 1984: 409).

One major success story for advocates of judicial controls is the Environmental Protection Agency (Melnick, 1983). Two aspects of the EPA are unique, so that legal mechanisms not only work but often work to the benefit of nonindustry interest groups. First, the National Environmental Policy Act (NEPA) puts the benefits of delay on the side of the environmentalists. Under this law agencies must file environmental impact statements for major construction projects; environmental groups were able to affect federal projects by delaying them with suits to force compliance with NEPA. In its first five years, more than 400 environmental impact suits were filed (Caldwell, 1982). Second, most environmental laws set a variety of deadlines for the promulgation of regulations and specify conditions when certain actions must be taken

(Vig and Kraft, 1984). Such legislation means that individuals can go to court in an effort to force the agency to set policy, a situation that differs from that of most other agencies, and can merely plead they are exercising discretion.

One aspect of litigation that may have promise is *qui tam* suits against fraud. Several federal laws contain a *qui tam* clause, which permits individual citizens to sue corporations who defraud the federal government. If the citizen wins, he or she receives a percentage of the settlement. By 1990, 274 *qui tam* suits resulted in recovering a total of $70 million (Moore, 1990b: 2006). Although such suits cannot be used as a general control over bureaucracy, they can address questions of corruption.

LIMITS ON COURTS

Despite the promise of judicial controls on administration, they have several serious limitations. Kenneth Culp Davis (1965) argued that relying on judicial controls has judicialized the administrative process, a current deficiency of American regulatory policy. Since regulatory agencies are concerned that their decisions will be reversed by the courts, these agencies have established elaborate procedural safeguards. Some regulatory agencies have ceased using their more general rulemaking powers relying instead on case-by-case adjudication procedures similar to courtroom procedures.[4] Adjudication requires that each case be tried on its merits rather than applying a general principle to all cases. The reliance on adjudication means that the public lacks clear guidelines about how a regulatory agency will act before it rules on a specific case, that regulatory agencies will be slow, and that often a regulatory agency will ignore policy for procedure. A study of the West Virginia Human Rights Commission confirmed the slowness of judicialized procedures. Employment discrimination cases took an average of 3.5 years to resolve; recent procedures were even slower; no case filed in 1979 had been resolved by 1984 (Hawley and Witt, 1986: 20). West (1988) compared federal rulemaking in the Environmental Protection Agency, the Food and Drug Administration, the Federal Communications Commission, and the Federal Aviation Administration in 1986 and 15–20 years earlier. He found rules took four times as long to issue and the amount of supporting material had tripled.

The logic used by the courts might also limit their effectiveness as a bureaucratic check. Courts often announce general principles and then determine if the specific case in question meets the criteria of the general principle. At times courts announce general principles that appear to restrict bureaucracy but at the same time rule in favor of the agency in the case under consideration. P. J. Cooper (1986b), for example, noted that in Freedom of Information Act cases, the court had consistently endorsed a liberal "free flow of information" approach. In seventeen of nineteen Supreme Court cases, however, the court permitted the agency to withhold the requested information.

---

[4] Whether or not Davis's assertion is still true is open to question. Regulatory agencies today frequently issue rules; the agencies in social regulation in particular rely heavily on rulemaking and less on adjudication. Even after the Reagan restrictions on regulation, 57,000 pages were published in the *Federal Register* in 1983. In addition, some rulemaking processes such as that used by the Federal Trade Commission are also heavily judicialized (West, 1985).

Theodore Lowi (1969) argues that despite their vigilance, courts have been ineffective in controlling administrative action. According to Lowi, the courts have been an active partner in permitting the legislative branch of government to delegate its political power to bureaucratic agencies without legislative guidelines for its use. Since the first New Deal measures were voided in the *Panama* and *Schecter* decisions, the courts have rarely prevented Congress from granting vague powers to an agency. Courts of law in the United States, Lowi concludes, have willingly sanctioned the congressional abdication of power to the bureaucracy.

Courts are also a limited check on bureaucracy because suing an agency in court may not guarantee a citizen any relief. Agencies have developed impressive legal expertise concerning administrative law. A series of studies have revealed that agencies are fairly difficult to defeat in courts of law (Pritchett, 1948; Tannenhaus, 1961; Canon and Giles, 1972; Handberg, 1979; Crowley, 1987; Clinton, 1989; Sheehan, 1990). Although the time periods and the agencies varied, each study showed that agencies won approximately 70–75 percent of their cases before the Supreme Court. In the most recent study, economic regulatory agencies won 73 percent of their cases, and social regulatory agencies won 75 percent (Sheehan, 1990: 878). Agencies winning more than 90 percent of their cases included the Interstate Commerce Commission (since abolished), the Nuclear Regulatory Commission, the Environmental Protection Agency, and the Food and Drug Administration (Crowley, 1985: 9). For regulatory agencies, the Court of Appeals for the District of Columbia hears all the initial appeals from agency decisions. Willison (1986) found agency winning percentages for the D.C. Circuit similar to those for the Supreme Court, even though the D.C. Circuit had an antiregulatory reputation.

Generally when agencies lose a case in court, they are fairly responsive to court demands. Spriggs (1997: 1137) examined 229 Supreme Court cases from 1953 to 1990 and found agencies implemented policy changes in 92.7 percent of the cases (see also Jones and Taylor, 1995, for a similar study of the Forest Service).

Despite the general responsiveness to courts, agencies sometimes ignore court rulings. The Social Security Administration (SSA) during the 1980s practiced what Mezey (1986) calls "nonacquiescence." When an SSA decision was reversed by a court, the SSA would apply the court case to the individual who brought suit, but would not apply it to other individuals in similar circumstances. Neither would SSA inform its administrative law judges (the individuals who hear cases for the agency) of these cases (Mezey, 1986: 346).

The high cost of litigation is an additional reason why judicial controls on bureaucracy are ineffective. Krislov (1965) notes that the average race relations case cost the National Association for the Advancement of Colored People (NAACP) between $50,000 and $100,000 to take to the Supreme Court; the classic *Brown* v. *Board of Education* school desegregation case cost $200,000 in the preinflation 1950s. With lawyers' fees of $300 per hour plus expenses in many metropolitan areas (more for a good lawyer versed in administrative law), an injunction in federal court that requires any research at all will cost several thousand dollars. With the costs of research, briefs, transcripts, and lawyer's time, judicial appeals are beyond the financial means of most citizens. We often do not recognize this limit because our perceptions of the courts as forums for the disadvantaged were shaped excessively by the experiences of the NAACP in racial discrimination cases (Olson, 1990). In general, however, courts are not a means for redress for citizens with few resources.

Legal remedies to bureaucratic harms are also characterized by excessive delay. Agencies, rather than courts, are established to administer programs because agencies are able to operate with greater dispatch. Crowded dockets mean that several months often pass before a case can be heard in federal district court. Krislov (1965) estimated that traveling the road to the Supreme Court requires from two to five years. An extreme example, the classic Ohio Bell Telephone case, was before the courts for seventeen years before it was finally resolved. In a case that would have eclipsed the Ohio Bell standard, the antitrust case against IBM had been going on at the *trial* level for thirteen years before it was dropped in 1982 by the government who admitted it lacked merit. A federal land claim filed in 1930 on behalf of the Seminole nation was not resolved until 1988 and then only through legislation (*National Journal,* 1990: 1398). With the flood of drug-related criminal cases taking more court time, the delays for civil suits against agencies have increased. Unless a citizen can demonstrate a pressing emergency, judicial remedies are available only long after the deleterious action has occurred.

Courts, despite their function in dispute resolution, are not designed to be bureaucratic monitors. O'Laughlin (1990: 276) contends that any means of bureaucratic accountability must have effective communication with the bureaucracy. The legislature and the chief executive have regularized methods of communication that lets each of them monitor the bureaucracy. Courts only interact with bureaucracies on specific cases or controversies. As a result, courts do not receive communication of the full range of bureau policy but rather only on the litigated issue. Information received by the courts, therefore, is more likely to be distorted or present only a partial view.

Courts are also not designed to be a policymaking institution but rather to decide disputes on a case-by-case basis. While sometimes this process results in a set of consistent guidelines, in many cases it does not. David Rosenbloom (1994), the foremost scholar of law and public administration, strongly criticized the U.S. Supreme Court for issuing several cases in October 1993 term that were inconsistent with one another and sometimes internally inconsistent. Wise and O'Leary (1997) similarly criticize the courts for providing conflicting signals to the agencies involved in environmental protection.

One barrier to being an effective policymaking institution is the general lack of expertise of courts. Law is a profession and judges a job category that resists specialization. Judges are expected to deal with criminal cases, immigration cases, administrative procedures, and civil cases even though the specific laws and the procedures vary dramatically. In other countries and in some areas such as bankruptcy, tax law, patents and trade disputes there are specialized courts that only handle one type of case so that judges can develop expertise. In such situations, courts are less likely to defer to administrative actions (see Hansen, Johnson, and Unah, 1995).

A final criticism of judicial controls is that agencies can use the judicial process for their own ends. Agencies can coerce citizens by withholding benefits and pointing to the courts as a remedy if they are wrong. The Internal Revenue Service, for example, can disallow tax exemptions, forcing the taxpayer to sue the IRS to regain the tax payments. In effect, the agency forces people to undertake a long, costly court fight if they decide to challenge the agency.

Courts of law can provide one of many checks on the bureaucracy in the American political system. As the sole or even major control on bureaucracy, the courts have fundamental weaknesses that prevent them from adequately checking bureaucratic power. For those with the resources and the patience to work the system, results may be forthcoming. For the normal citizen the courts, in most cases, are not a viable option.

....

PRESIDENTIAL CONTROLS ON BUREAUCRATIC POWER

The American contribution to the control of bureaucracy is the elected chief executive. Early scholars of administration, such as Woodrow Wilson and Frank Goodnow, treated the president and the bureaucracy as one, a situation that today is inconsistent with reality in the United States. The bureaucracy owes little loyalty to the president and may see the president more as an outsider than as a fellow bureaucrat. The president knows or should know that he does not completely control the bureaucracy even though the president is hierarchically superior to the bureaucracy (Seidman and Gilmour, 1986).

The president cannot be ignored as a possible control over administrative power. The president, no less than a member of Congress, is a politician responsible to the people for actions taken while in office. In fact, since the president is more visible to the public than is Congress, the probability of popular control through the president may be greater. The Constitution underscores the importance of the presidency by granting it "executive power," the powers of commander-in-chief, and the responsibility that the laws be faithfully executed (Fried, 1976). These provide a constitutional imperative that the president control the bureaucracy.

The president's relationship with bureaucracy, however, is not as clear cut as the Constitution presents it. Modern presidents are handicapped by being strangers to bureaucracy. Many recent presidents (for example, Truman, Kennedy, Johnson, Nixon, and Ford) were trained in Congress, where contact with the bureaucracy is more cooperative than hierarchical. Others were trained as governors in states where they faced smaller and less powerful bureaucracies (e.g., Carter, Reagan, Clinton). This problem was never more evident than when President Richard Nixon, a former vice president, expressed surprise during his first term that some of his policy initiatives were delayed by the bureaucracy (Seidman and Gilmour, 1986).

Despite the presidential–bureaucratic estrangement, many students of bureaucracy see executive control as potentially the most effective (Daley, 1984: 23; Sabatier and Mazmanian, 1981: 229; Abney and Lauth, 1982b: 136). Given congressional ties to more specialized interests, Powell and Parker (1963) argue for a bureaucracy responsible to the president rather than one responsible to Congress. Arthur Maass and Lawrence Radway (1959) contend that the bureaucracy should be directly responsible to the president and that all other means of controlling the bureaucracy should be exercised through the president.

Presidents have numerous tools for controlling bureaucratic behavior. Presidential powers may be divided into organizational powers, budgetary powers, powers of command, and leadership. Although these powers are more effective in making bureaucracy responsive than in ensuring competence, they can have impacts in both areas. Each presidential power will be examined separately.

ORGANIZATIONAL POWERS

Appointments

Organizational powers of the president include the president's appointment of line officials, his ability to use staff personnel, and his power to reorganize the federal government. The president appoints all cabinet officers and most bureau chiefs in the federal government. Although this power once extended even to minor clerical posts, the growth of the merit system has restricted presidential appointments to about 2,900 positions (Ingraham, 1991: 182). Of these about 600 are policymaking positions—cabinet posts, subcabinet positions, and bureau chiefs. Another 1,400 are subordinate positions (schedule C) meant to provide the president with a source of patronage and a source of information within the bureaucracy. The remaining positions are professional and technical ones the president may fill but usually go by default to career civil servants. Under the Civil Service Reform Act of 1978 the president through his appointees can reassign members of the Senior Executive Service after the first 120 days of a new term.

A president can influence bureau behavior by appointing an administrator in tune with the president's political philosophy and by granting that administrator ample presidential support in any and all disputes. Perhaps the best example of presidential control of the bureaucracy through appointments is President Ronald Reagan's effort in regard to regulation. Under President Jimmy Carter a series of proregulation advocates were appointed to key regulatory positions, and many of these individuals were aggressive regulators. Consistent with his campaign pledges, Reagan stressed easing the regulatory burden on business and appointed individuals who were not regulatory advocates. Raymond Peck replaced Joan Claybrook at NHTSA, Thorne Auchter replaced Eula Bingham at OSHA, Anne Burford replaced Douglas Costle at the EPA, James Miller replaced Michael Pertschuk at the FTC, and Nancy Stoerts replaced Susan King at the CPSC. The president backed these appointees by requiring that all regulations be subjected to cost-benefit analysis (Executive Order 12291) and by appointing a task force on regulatory relief headed by Vice President George Bush (Fuchs, 1988). The impact on regulatory policy was impressive. NHTSA repealed twenty-four rules to assist the automobile industry; OSHA emphasized voluntary compliance with the law; the EPA became a battleground between political appointees and career civil servants; the FTC became a free market advocate; and the CPSC virtually disappeared (Meier, 1985). Statistical evidence supported these impressions (see Wood and Waterman 1994); only one species was added to the endangered species list in the first fourteen months of the Reagan administration, compared to 150 during Carter's term (L. Mosher, 1982: 722). Of the 182 major rules under consideration during the last year of the Carter administration, only 93 remained under consideration the following year (*National Journal*, 1981: 1304). The head of the Justice Department's hazardous waste prosecution team resigned in early 1982 because the EPA had sent no cases over to be prosecuted for a year (*National Journal*, 1982: 40). For the entire year of 1981, 5,648 regulations were published in the *Federal Register*, compared with 7,192 the previous year (*National Journal*, 1982: 781), and many of those were less stringent.

President Reagan's effort to redirect regulatory policy was not without precedent (see also Schmidt, 1995 on the NLRB). David Stanley (1965) analyzed six agencies during the Kennedy transition and found that if the political appointee had clear goals regarding the agency's programs and took immediate action (sometimes even before taking office), bureaucratic activities could be affected. Joseph Zentner's (1972) study of presidential transitions argued bureaucrats will respond to political pressures if the pressures are strong and consistent and if they feel the pressures have presidential support.

James Pfiffner's (1982; 1984; 1987a; 1987b; 1988) excellent studies of the Reagan transition, however, reveal that the elements contributing to the Reagan success were somewhat different from those of previous transitions (see also MacKenzie, 1981). First, personnel recruitment was given a high priority in Reagan's administration as a series of checks were established to make sure appointees had acceptable political beliefs. Cabinet secretaries were given less discretion than normal, with subcabinet appointments made in the White House; regular cabinet meetings were held so that the secretaries knew what the party line was (Pfiffner, 1982: 19–20). Appointments reflected this effort—an attorney who represented management in civil rights cases was appointed to be in charge of the Office of Federal Contract Compliance (*National Journal*, 1981: 1082), oil-state citizens were appointed to the Federal Energy Regulatory Commission (*National Journal*, 1982: 1071), and a construction executive was appointed to regulate workplace safety.

Second, strategic subcabinet and bureau chief positions were left vacant; four months into Reagan's term only 45 percent of the top 400 positions had designated appointees (Newland, 1983: 4). Normally such a slow appointment process would inhibit presidential control over the bureaucracy, but in this case it worked to the president's advantage. When Reagan announced his fiscal year 1982 budget cuts early in 1981, key positions that normally would have been the focal point for opposition were vacant. As a result, there were no individuals to organize political opposition to the large budget cuts. Similarly the EEOC was unable to file any discrimination law suits for 107 days in 1981 because a quorum had not been appointed (Plant and Thompson, 1983: 16).

Third, the president was able to take full advantage of the flexibility of the Civil Service Reform Act of 1978. Reagan reassigned 520 Senior Executive Service members in his first year (which was actually fewer than Carter had reassigned the previous year [Newland, (1983: 18]). An additional 11,000 civil servants were terminated in the first year as the result of reductions in force. More important was the more subtle effort to restrict the policymaking authority of civil servants because they were not trusted by the Reagan administration appointees. The end result was massive resignations from the career staff and a precipitous drop in morale (Bann and Johnson, 1984: 65; Ingraham and Colby, 1982; Stanley, 1984: 261).

The hostility of the Reagan administration toward civil servants was not unusual since most incoming administrations distrust the career bureaucracy (Aberbach and Rockman, 1976; Cole and Caputo, 1979). Such a distrust, however, is unwarranted unless the new administration plans actions that border on illegality (e.g., the EPA). Pfiffner (1988) argues that career civil servants are not hostile to the goals of Republican administrations and that they look forward to being able to change some policies that they disagree with personally (see also Stehr, 1997). Evidence to support Pfiffner's view exists; Reagan's initial job freeze was rewritten by a career civil servant so that it would not also freeze political appointments (Pfiffner, 1984: 12). Reagan was able to abolish the Community Services Administration, the last vestige of the war on poverty, using civil servants (Newland, 1983: 13). Three case studies of agencies under Reagan found that civil servants willingly assisted political appointees in implementing the Reagan agenda (Ingraham, 1991: 190). One observer of six presidential transitions concluded that civil servants wanted to work with politicians to establish their programs (Rosen, 1981: 204).[5]

The president's ability to control the bureaucracy via appointments is not absolute; it is limited by the Senate's power to confirm many appointments. Although confirmations were once thought to be routine, Congress refused to consider many of President Reagan's appointments or held up action on some of the appointments to get concessions on other appointments (Gordon, 1984: 1917; *National Journal,* 1982: 346, 1317; 1983: 2498; A. Cooper, 1985: 734). In the first two years of the Reagan administration, the Senate refused to consider eighteen appointees; and Reagan withdrew twenty-six other nominations that would probably not have been confirmed (Bryner, 1987). Opposition to appointments on policy grounds was also evident during the Clinton administration.

The president's appointment powers may also be limited by the appointees themselves. Appointees can be persuaded by their subordinates or by their own expertise to change their policy views. Perhaps the best example is President Reagan's surgeon gen-

---

[5] A final innovation in appointment control over the bureaucracy by the Reagan administration can be termed control via incompetence. If a president disagrees with the fundamental goals of an agency, one way to make sure the agency has little impact is to appoint an individual with few political or managerial skills. President Reagan replaced Eleanor Holmes Norton, perhaps the first competent head of the EEOC, with Clarence Thomas. The number of enforcement lawsuits dropped from 368 in 1980 to 24 in 1981, and the EEOC became an invisible regulator (Plant and Thompson, 1983: 29). The Office for Civil Rights ceased to be an advocate for civil rights after the appointment of Clarence Pendelton. Similar other appointees had detrimental impacts on their agencies; Don Nobel was credited with destroying the Synthetic Fuels Corporation; Food and Nutrition Service head G. William Hoagland proposed that ketchup be considered a vegetable in school lunch programs. One Education Department appointee resigned after expressing her view that a person's physical handicaps reflected his or her spiritual development. The Department of Housing and Urban Development was practically destroyed by the hands-off management of Samuel Pearce. Lynn's (1984: 369) examination of five Reagan political appointees also concludes that Reagan would have had more long-run impact on government if his appointees had been more capable. Numerous other examples of corruption and illegal activities were discussed in Chapter 5.

eral, Charles E. Koop. Originally viewed as an archconservative, Koop became a forceful advocate of more research for AIDS and an advocate of safe sex rather than abstinence (Boodman, 1988: 6).

Staff Control

Creative staffing is another presidential approach to controlling bureaucracy. One problem that concerns many presidents is the tendency of political appointees to "go native"; they yield to the pressure from other members of their bureau to advocate the bureau's interests (Heclo, 1977; Seidman and Gilmour, 1986). The president's appointee who was sent out to control a bureau in this way ends up being coopted by the bureau's civil servants. One solution to this problem, used by Presidents Eisenhower and Nixon, was to vest control over programs in the White House staff, people with loyalties to no one other than the president (Nathan, 1983). Nixon attempted to control the bureaucracy and also to coordinate domestic policy by creating the Domestic Council under John Ehrlichman. The Domestic Council was to be a domestic National Security Council that monitored all aspects of domestic policy. Unfortunately for any evaluation of the Domestic Council, Watergate distracted President Nixon from his goal of controlling bureau policymaking (Nathan, 1983).

Perhaps the major success of staff control was President Reagan's regulatory effort (see Fuchs, 1988). Executive order 12291 required cost-benefit analysis for all major regulations and staff review by the Office of Management and Budget (OMB). The OMB used this power to change regulations that were contrary to the president's deregulation objectives. In 1981, 12.7 percent of submitted rules were changed; by 1985 this figure had grown to 29.3 percent (Cooper and West, 1988: 875). These changes are only the tip of the iceberg. Cooper and West (1988) feel the major impact of this staff review process was invisible because agencies changed regulations in anticipation of OMB review. Social regulatory agencies such as the Environmental Protection Agency were affected most by the process. The success of this staff review process was increased by President Reagan's ability to appoint supporters to line positions in the regulatory agencies. West and Cooper (1989), however, argued the OMB program had less impact than it could have had, because the OMB simply rejected rules that it did not like rather than attempt to provide consistent policy.

The staffing approach to control has limitations not present in the line administrators' approach. Because the federal bureaucracy is so large and diverse, controlling bureaucracy via staffing requires a large White House staff. Under this approach the cure for bureaucracy becomes more bureaucracy. Because bureaus are perceived as biased, the White House staff often rejects all bureau-generated information, denying themselves their most important sources of information and making their task difficult if not impossible. Chris DeMuth (1984: 29), for example, stated that as the OMB's regulatory czar he rejected a Department of Agriculture cost-benefit analysis without reading it because he felt it came to the wrong conclusion concerning marketing orders. In such circumstances the White House staff must establish duplicate information sources. Finally, presidential staffers who act in the name of the president often develop power bases independent of the president. Since the president cannot monitor all staff activities, responsive bureaus may well become responsive to a staff member rather than to the president.

Reorganization

Former Budget Bureau official Harold Seidman (Seidman and Gilmour, 1986) believes that reorganization can be an effective tool to check bureaucratic power (but see Thomas, 1993). A major theme of Chapter 3 was that bureaus are influenced by their environment (see also Rainey, 1991); reorganization can be used to shape the environment of an agency by creating a climate hostile to or receptive to agency programs (see Hult and Walcott, 1989; 1990). The president can stress a program by granting an agency organizational autonomy. To emphasize President Nixon's commitment to cancer research, for example, the National Cancer Institute was granted substantial independence and privileges not given to other bureaus in the National Institutes of Health. Reorganization can also handicap a program. If pesticide regulation were transferred back to the Department of Agriculture from the Environmental Protection Agency, pesticide users would have a more sympathetic ear than would environmentalists. USDA administrators are more sensitive to farmer needs than to environmentalists' concerns. Since the actual pesticide program is administered at the state level, a second phenomenon occurs. Many states have assigned this program to their agriculture agencies, thus blunting the EPA's impact (Reagan, 1987).

Creative placement of programs and careful reorganizations can create climates of opinion favorable to the president's policies. A president hostile to the regulations of the Occupational Safety and Health Administration could place OSHA in the Department of Commerce. The probusiness biases of the Commerce Department would stifle many OSHA policies. Affecting organizational performance by manipulating the organization's environment has the advantage of not requiring constant monitoring by the president or his staff. With reorganization environmental biases can be made to work for the president.

A variety of successful reorganizations have been documented. Cohen (1991) demonstrated that a reorganization of the National Transportation Safety Board resulted in a greater concern for safety; a reorganization of the Consumer Product Safety Commission in 1981 resulted in an emphasis on voluntary regulation and produced more probusiness decisions. A 1960s reorganization of the federal Department of Housing and Urban Development changed the department's orientation from building buildings to social welfare (Hult, 1987). A study of federal drug law enforcement found that reorganizations consolidating the federal drug efforts resulted in major increases in the level of law enforcement (Meier, 1991). Berkowitz and Fox (1989) demonstrated that placement of the federal disability programs in the Social Security Administration (SSA) over time produced a program that stressed transfer payments (SSA's expertise) and downplayed rehabilitation. A 1981 reorganization of the Office of Surface Mining stripped field personnel of some enforcement authority, reducing the overall level of enforcement (Wood and Waterman, 1991).

State level studies have also documented the use of reorganizations as a bureaucratic control; reorganization has altered power relationships, strengthened the position of the chief executive (Brudney and Hebert, 1987: 199; Herbert, Brudney, and Wright, 1983: 253), and increased the governor's appointment power (Conant, 1988: 895). For city governments, Saltzstein (1986a; 1986b) demonstrated that placing responsibility for affirmative action in the office of the mayor increased the hiring of women and minorities.

The use of reorganization is not without limitations. Even though the Nuclear Regulatory Commission was split off from the Atomic Energy Commission (now the Department of Energy) so that regulators would not be affected by the prodevelopment biases of the AEC, the NRC was still criticized for its proindustry bias (Temples, 1982). To use organizational strategies effectively, according to Seidman and Gilmour (1986), presidents must have a conscious organizational strategy, and the last president to have one was Franklin Roosevelt. To use reorganization to control the bureaucracy, Seidman and Gilmour believe, policymakers must first reject the orthodox belief that the goal of reorganization is economy and efficiency. Even if this occurs, Thomas (1993) contends that the multiple goals for public sector organization make it difficult to use reorganization as a control technique. Chief executives must consciously use reorganization to exploit organizational biases for reorganization to lead to greater policy control over the bureaucracy. The final limit on reorganization is that major changes must also be approved by Congress.

BUDGET POWERS

After 150 years of experimentation with legislative budgeting, Congress in 1921 authorized the president to prepare the budget and present it to Congress for review. The president, as a result of the executive budget and later reforms, can withhold resources from an unresponsive agency at both ends of the budget process. Initially, the Office of Management and Budget can deny an agency funds for a program; if the OMB denies a request, agencies are not permitted to request those funds from Congress. After funds are appropriated by Congress, the president can, if he deems necessary, impound funds subject to legislative veto. Since 1974 Congress has generally allowed the president to defer expenditures (put them off for one year) but except for 1979 through 1982 has generally rejected rescissions (permanent impoundments, see Ornstein et al., 1990: 169–170). The president can also veto appropriations. Concomitant with the president's budget powers are the powers of legislative clearance. Any agency request for additional legislation, whether or not it requires funding, must be certified by the OMB as consistent with the president's program.

In combination, the budget and legislative clearance powers are formidable (for empirical studies see Kiewiet and McCubbins, 1988; Stewart, Anderson and Taylor, 1982; and Lowery, Bookheimer, and Malachowski, 1985). President Johnson used these powers to restrict domestic programs and free funds for the Vietnam War. Johnson used these powers so enthusiastically that he actually submitted a balanced budget for fiscal year 1969 (the nation's last balanced budget until 1998). President Reagan exercised perhaps the greatest control over programs ever via the budget as he reallocated funds to support a massive buildup in military expenditures while restricting those social programs that were not entitlement programs (Kamlet, Mowery and Su, 1988). In fiscal year 1982, for example, Reagan was able to use budget cuts to reduce enforcement of the Clean Air Act by 69 percent (Wood, 1988: 226). Federal low income housing assistance programs dropped from $17.4 billion to $8.4 billion in Reagan's fiscal year 1983 budget (Hays, 1990: 860).

The Congressional Budget Reform and Impoundment Control Act gave the president two additional budget weapons. President Reagan in 1981 used the reconciliation process, whereby Congress adjusts overall appropriations to be consistent with spending ceilings. Through reconciliation Reagan forced extensive cuts in the proposed Carter budget for FY 1982. The act also legalized the longstanding practice of impoundment whereby the president may refuse to spend funds or delay spending funds appropriated by Congress. President Kennedy used this power to prevent the armed services from building a new manned bomber. President Nixon impounded funds for policy purposes in a wide variety of programs ranging from social services to pollution grants (Fisher, 1975). The broadest use of impoundments occurred in 1981 when Reagan deferred $7 billion and rescinded another $14 billion, the latter figure more than double all rescissions in the history of the 1974 law.

The use of budget powers to control bureaucracy is enhanced by the professionalism of the Office of Management and Budget and the OMB's ability to serve presidents of different political philosophies with equal enthusiasm. The budget process is a powerful tool because it creates an environment of expectations; if a bureau responds in certain sanctioned ways, it will be rewarded in the executive budget (Carpenter, 1996). The power is not without limits, however. The president is not the final step in the budget process; agencies can and do appeal successfully to Congress for more funds. President Reagan's effort to eliminate the Small Business Administration through the budget failed because Congress rejected his budget proposal (Rauch, 1985a: 1845). In several budgets during the 1980s, Reagan asked for nothing or almost nothing for low income housing, but Congress never appropriated less than $7.6 billion (Hays, 1990: 860).

Presidential budget powers are especially effective in personnel intensive agencies that process cases. Shull and Garland (1995) found the president exercises strong control over the volume of civil rights cases though the budget. Meier (1994) found budget control of drug abuse agencies so strong that he termed the control similar to a water faucet as a regulator.

At the same time budgets can prevent a president from attaining his policy goals. Durant (1993) found severe budget cuts presented the Bureau of Land Management for implementing policy changes under President Reagan. Similarly between 1992 and 1996 federal inspectors general (units that monitor agencies for fraud and abuse) were drastically cut back at the same time that demands for greater oversight were made (Newcomer, 1998: 131).

The budget cannot be used with maximum effectiveness as a control device without an OMB director of David Stockman's ability (President Reagan's first budget director) because the budget is too large, detailed, and difficult to understand for almost any set of individuals. Even the OMB approaches the budget incrementally with an emphasis on only a few priorities in most years because this is the only way the budget can be made simple enough to be passed in a single year. The president's budget powers are also restricted by uncontrollable expenditures. Certain portions of the budget are committed in advance to contractors or pledged without limit to American citizens who qualify (for example, social security, welfare, and unemployment compensation). These funds are beyond the president's control in the short run unless he can force Congress to change the basic legislation. Estimates of uncontrollable expenditures in the federal budget range as high as 75 percent (Kettl, 1989: 233). Waterman (1989: 179), in fact, concludes that Reagan's fiscal 1982 budget successes reflected highly favorable conditions that are not likely to recur.

At the state level, many governors have stronger budget powers than the president. Thompson's (1987: 761) study of state budgeting concluded that governors could control agencies via budgeting but legislatures could not. In more than forty states the governor has not only a budget veto but also a line item veto (Abney and Lauth, 1985a). The line item veto permits the governor to veto specific appropriations in a large budget bill without vetoing the entire bill. Perhaps the most creative use of the line item veto occurs in Wisconsin, where governors have been known to veto individual words in the budget bill, radically changing appropriations (Gosling, 1986).

THE POWERS OF COMMANDER-IN-CHIEF

The president is the commander-in-chief of the armed forces, with precedent generalizing this power to all domestic policy, theoretically making all bureaus subordinate to the president. Presidents are not shy about exercising this power; they issued more than 14,700 executive orders by 1999 and 6,000 proclamations that have the force of law (P. J. Cooper, 1986a: 234; 1998, 530). As a result of his hierarchical position, the president in many cases can reverse administrative decisions, as President Ford did once when he revoked a decision that prohibited schools from sponsoring father-son or mother-daughter events because they were sexually discriminatory. P. J. Cooper (1998) provides numerous other examples of these powers.

Richard Neustadt (1960) analyzed the powers of the president in great detail, with emphasis on three presidential decisions—Harry S. Truman's firing of General Douglas MacArthur, Truman's seizure of the steel mills during the Korean War, and Dwight Eisenhower's decision to send troops to Little Rock to desegregate the schools (see also the application by Waterman, 1989). Neustadt (1960: 19) argues that the president can issue an order and expect obedience only when five conditions are met. First, the president's involvement must be unambiguous; the other actors must be certain that the president is concerned with the administrative actions. Second, the president's orders must be clear and unambiguous so that the recipient of the order knows precisely what is expected. Third, the orders must be accompanied by widespread publicity so that disobedience will attract the attention of the media and, thus, be relayed back to the oval office. Fourth, the recipient of the order must have the resources necessary to carry out the president's intent. Fifth, the actors must have no doubt that the president has the authority to direct the actions ordered.

Neustadt's detailed analysis of these case studies convinces him that the real power of the president is the power to persuade. Instances when the president can issue a direct order and have it obeyed are few and far between. The small range of presidential command is further limited by resistance to presidential orders after they are issued. The resistance may be covert as was the air force's delay removing offensive missiles from Turkey in 1962 (Allison, 1971; but see Bernstein, 1980), or the resistance may be overt. In a classic case of overt resistance to presidential directives, 2,000 education executives and professionals in 1970 petitioned then-HEW Secretary Robert Finch to defend the administration's weak position on civil rights. When a spokesman for the secretary responded to criticism at a meeting, he was loudly booed (Sickels, 1974: 72). Despite President Nixon's order to ease the pressure on southern schools to desegregate, Office for Civil Rights (an agency then in HEW) bureaucrats vigorously pursued pre-Nixon policies (Sickels, 1974: 73). Nixon eventually triumphed on this issue, however, when he eliminated the OCR's authority to cut off federal funds (Bullock and Stewart, 1984: 392).

Neustadt's analysis should not lead us to underestimate the long-term influence of the president. In certain policy areas, the president can reshape public policy. President Reagan, for example, had a major impact on the space program. In addition to his advocacy of the "Star Wars" space defense system, his support for the NASA space station saved it from the scrap pile (Lambright and Rahm, 1989: 517). Stressing military uses of space, the Reagan presidency permitted the Department of the Air Force's space budget to grow to be twice as large as NASA's (Lambright and Rahm, 1989: 523).

LEADERSHIP

A president attempting to control the bureaucracy must face two facts. First, the president and his staff do not have the resources, time, or the need to control every detail of bureaucratic policymaking. Second, criticizing bureaucrats for lack of cooperation will only alienate them and make the problem worse. If a bureaucrat is resistant to presidential direction for reasonable technical reasons, denouncing the official only makes future cooperation less likely.

One alternative open to the president is to set goals or an image for his administration (Sullivan, 1970). All presidents have general policy directions that set the priorities for their administration. Lyndon Johnson wanted his administration to be known for helping the unfortunate. Ronald Reagan wanted to be known for putting a check on big federal government. President Bush referred to himself as the environmental president. To control bureaucracy, the president must set and communicate a consistent theme and then motivate bureaucrats to respond.

The essence of presidential leadership is the motivation of other policymakers. Leadership requires that the president provide positive reinforcement for performance in accord with the president's program. It requires the creative use of symbols: presidential visits, promotions, and the status of the office. Presidents vary in how successfully they are able to influence the bureaucracy through leadership. Lyndon Johnson achieved some significant successes, but Richard Nixon met with continual frustration.

Ronald Reagan had several early successes but later met resistance. The difference may be that Johnson, as an advocate of big government, was leading the bureaucracy in the direction it wanted to go. Reagan and Nixon wanted to reduce the influence of the federal bureaucracy, and negative reinforcement of bureaucrats who believe in the programs they administer will only harden resistance. A president's ability to use leadership and motivation to control bureaucracy, as a result, may be a function of the political goals of the president.

In an excellent assessment of presidential leadership, Waterman (1989) contends that presidents should follow Neustadt's (1960) advice. They should bargain with bureaucrats and other political institutions to establish control over the bureaucracy. Successful presidential controls require the acquiescence of Congress, interest groups, the courts, and bureaucrats. The president must persuade these groups to accept his bureaucratic policy goals. Unilateral efforts to control the bureaucracy, according to Waterman (1989), will succeed only in the short run.

RESTRAINTS ON PRESIDENTIAL CONTROLS

In recent years several excellent empirical studies have demonstrated the president's ability to affect bureaucratic policymaking. Terry Moe (1982; 1985), in studies of the National Labor Relations Board, the Federal Trade Commission, and the Securities and Exchange Commission, found that bureau policy outputs varied systematically and predictably with presidential administrations. Cohen (1985b) found a strong presidential impact on the Federal Communications Commission; Beck (1984) demonstrated similar impacts on monetary policy of the Federal Reserve Board; Scholz and Wei (1986) showed the reduction in OSHA enforcement under Reagan; and Randall (1979) revealed President Nixon's influence on welfare policy implementation. Wood (1988) has demonstrated President Reagan's ability to influence environmental enforcement through budgets and appointments; he also demonstrated significant impacts of both Carter and Reagan on the Equal Employment Opportunity Commission (Wood, 1990). In a study of seven federal regulatory agencies, Wood and Waterman (1991) found that for five agencies outputs shifted immediately after the appointment of a new agency head. In four cases (NRC, EEOC, FTC, and FDA), this shift occurred at the start of the president's term (see also Wood and Waterman, 1994).

Despite this series of convincing studies, presidential controls on the bureaucracy are not without limits. The president's control is limited both by the time he can devote to bureaucracy and by the large size of the bureaucracy (the federal government currently spends $1.7 trillion annually). Presidents also find their time dominated by the press of foreign affairs. As the result of size and presidential preoccupation with foreign policy, communication of goals to bureaucracy is sometimes garbled (if the president has goals for the bureaucracy, see Waterman, 1989). The result is less control even though many bureaucrats attempt to anticipate what the chief executive wants (Pfiffner, 1984: 8; Johnson and O'Connor, 1979). A second time limitation on the president is the limited term he serves. A presidency lasts for at most eight years; permanent bureaucrats can wait out a president. As Walcott and Hult (1987: 116) argue, bureaucracies act more independently as the term of the president progresses.

The quality and quantity of information available to the president also limit his ability to control the bureaucracy. To be sure, the president receives an excess of communications; but because communications to the president are so massive, they cannot be analyzed to provide timely information. Public inputs in the form of letters, for example, can be a valuable assessment of bureau performance; but the *Washington Post* estimates that the president receives as many as 300,000 letters in a single day.

Efforts at presidential control can also cancel out the effects of each other. Durant (1987; 1993) found that the Reagan budget cuts for the Bureau of Land Management were so severe that the agency lacked the resources to make the policy changes advocated by the president (increased production on public lands). Budget control in this case limited hierarchical control.

Presidential control can also be limited because the president misperceives the viewpoints or skills of his appointees. George Anikis, a Carter administration appointee to the National Highway Traffic Safety Administration, was perceived as a vigorous regulator. Anikis, however, was indecisive, so enforcement activities actually dropped during his tenure and rose after he left (Wood and Waterman, 1991). Just as presidents at times appoint Supreme Court justices who surprise them, the same is true with political appointees to the bureaucracy.

Presidential control over the bureaucracy is also restricted by the relationship between Congress and the bureaucracy. If the bureaucracy and Congress can cooperate, they can effectively stalemate the president; Congress can supply the bureaucracy with the resources necessary to resist presidential commands. Nothing prevents Congress from appropriating more funds than the president requests, and Congress often does. Nowhere is Congress' ability to stalemate more pronounced than in executive reorganization. Congress has consistently resisted presidential efforts to reorganize bureaus that are congressional favorites; the congressional efforts to protect the Army Corps of Engineers and the Department of Interior are legendary. One reason why President Reagan's early efforts to control bureau policymaking succeeded was that his party controlled the Senate, thus limiting the ability of agencies to appeal to Congress.

Finally, the policy preferences of the bureaucracy restrict presidential control somewhat. When presidential direction is lacking or when the presidential monitoring slackens, a bureau will generally make decisions consistent with its own biases. In anticipation of the Reagan inauguration, for example, the Environmental Protection Agency dramatically increased clean air enforcement in late 1980 (Wood, 1988). Although bureaucrats are willing to follow policy directives that are different from their own goals (see Stehr, 1997), control of the bureaucracy is easier if control objectives are consistent with bureaucratic values. A classic example involves antitrust policy under Reagan. Appointees to the Justice Department found an Antitrust Division not only willing to follow a free-market antitrust policy, but in many cases had already implemented one (Eisner, 1991). The resistance occasioned by bureaucratic values might be more subtle than these illustrations suggest. Bureaucrats can limit presidential control by resigning, thus leaving the bureaucracy with less capacity to respond to presidential directives (Lowery and Rusbult, 1986: 71).

Based on their study of several federal agencies, Wood and Waterman (1994) argue that certain agencies are more likely to be controlled by the president. They find that executive agencies are more responsive to presidential direction than are independent regulatory commissions. The president also has greater control when programs are not highly visible, when agencies have less constituency support, and when Congress is not as concerned (Wood and Waterman, 1994).

FEDERALISM AS A CHECK ON BUREAUCRACY

Few public policies are solely the responsibility of the federal government or solely the responsibility of state and local governments. At the federal level many programs such as welfare, disability insurance, and unemployment compensation rely on state and local government agencies to implement the programs. Traditionally state policies for education, public health, and land use are in turn affected by federal government agencies that provide funds and issue regulations that directly or indirectly influence the operation of state and local government bureaucracies. In the past several years, many of the checks and balances of federalism have become more visible as agencies and political institutions at one level seek to influence those that work at another.

STATE AGENCIES AS A CHECK ON FEDERAL AGENCIES

State governments and their bureaucracies have at least five ways to influence the policy actions of federal bureaucracy: (1) establishing implementation rules, (2) enforcing federal laws, (3) running parallel programs, (4) providing an alternative source of policy values, and (5) directly challenging federal programs. Since states vary in their use of local government agencies to implement programs (Berman and Martin, 1988), the actual check on federal actions might well be a local bureaucracy.

Implementation Rules

Under proxy administration the ability of state agencies to serve as a check on federal programs has become more prominent. By relying on state and local agencies to implement their programs, federal agencies must yield some discretion to these agencies for the same reasons that federal agencies gain discretion from political institutions. Along with this discretion, state and local agencies use their own political power bases to respond to demands in their environment. As a result they can shape policy in directions different from those intended by federal agencies and thus provide a check on the bureaucratic power of the federal bureaucracy. Perhaps the most prominent example, the state of California adopted more stringent air pollution controls for automobiles than the federal government. The 1991 amendments to the federal Clean Air Act recognized this state leadership by adopting California standards nationwide.

Harris (1989) documented a second case involving federal surface mine regulation. States were allowed to implement federal law; in some states state regulators permitted surface mines to subdivide themselves to be less than two acres and thus be exempt from the federal surface mine regulations. Also related to surface mining, Hedge, Menzel, and Krause (1989) found that the federal Office of Surface Mining

Regulation and Enforcement began in the late 1970s as a vigorous and strict regulator. Those states that were authorized to implement the federal program took a bargaining approach rather than a policing approach and were more flexible and less strict in regulating surface mining. States, thus, provided an alternative to strict federal regulation.

The federal government's intrusion into the previous state domain of welfare policy has left state agencies as the prime implementation agencies. Proxy administration in this case has created limits on the authority of the federal government. In recent years, the Department of Health and Human Services as well as federal political institutions have made a concerted effort to control health care costs paid by the federal government. In one program, Medicaid, the rules for eligibility and program implementation are written at the state level. Schneider (1988; see also Schneider, Jacoby, and Coggborn, 1997) found that federal efforts to restrict costs in this area were undercut by state governments that aggressively sought out potential recipients and provided more lenient eligibility regulations. For social security disability claims, Mezey (1986) found that state agencies resisted the effort of the federal Social Security Administration to eliminate individuals from the roles. As noted earlier in this chapter, the SSA removed a large number of recipients from the disability roles and, when overturned in court, practiced nonacquiescence, that is, it accepted the court case but applied it only to the person who filed suit. The status of all other persons was not affected by the court ruling. State agencies tempered these federal actions, according to Mezey (1986: 35), by applying the federal court's standards in cases that they resolved.

Federalism is often a two-step implementation process with federal programs passing through the state level on their way to local governments for implementation. Variations in the autonomy of local implementation agencies can also result in policy variation. Albritton and Brown (1986) examined Aid to Families with Dependent Children and general assistance policies in the states. They found that in states without an overall state agency in charge (i.e., more autonomy for local government agencies) there was much more variation in policies than in states with a single state-level organization.

Enforcing Federal Policy

Although many federal agencies enforce their own regulations, some rely heavily on state and local bureaucracies for enforcement. Such a pattern is particularly the case in environmental regulation, workplace safety regulation, traffic safety regulation, and surface mining regulation. In many cases states act to check the actions of the federal bureaucracy because they feel that the federal government is too passive in enforcement (Crotty, 1988). As noted earlier in this chapter, the election of Ronald Reagan resulted in a major reduction in enforcement of occupational safety and health laws. Some twenty states, however, have the authority to implement workplace safety regulations subject to federal oversight. Scholz and Wei (1986: 1258) found that these states continued to enforce the federal law during the Reagan presidency at the same rate as before, thus limiting the president's effort to control the Occupational Safety and Health Administration. A second OSHA example concerns the efforts during the Carter administration to change the policy emphasis from occupational safety (workplace injuries) to occupational health (exposure to harmful chemicals). During the Carter administration, state-run programs lagged behind the federal government in occupational health regulation. With the Reagan administration, seventeen of the twenty-one state-run programs increased occupational health regulation at the same time that the federal government was decreasing it (Thompson and Scicchitano, 1987: 105). A similar pattern occurred in environmental regulation. During the Reagan efforts to reduce federal enforcement levels, state government enforcement efforts continued without interruption (Wood, 1992) and generated cleaner air in those states (Ringquist, 1995).

Running Parallel Programs

In some cases, federal and state agencies both run programs in the same policy area. Consumer protection, antitrust law, law enforcement, and business regulation are areas of overlapping federal and state policies. Antitrust policy provides a good illustration of how state agencies can check federal bureaucracies. As noted above, federal antitrust regulators have focused primarily on price-fixing cases and ignoring other areas of antitrust law. State attorneys general stepped into this void and filed a variety of suits concerning the restraint of trade. The Supreme Court recognized this effort in *California* v. *American Stores* (1990), permitting the California attorney general to require changes in a merger even after the merger was approved by federal antitrust regulators.

Consumer protection is a second area where aggressive state regulators have stepped into a void created by a passive federal regulator. State consumer protection agencies have filed deceptive-advertising suits against a variety of businesses that were not challenged by federal regulators (Moore, 1990d: 1220–1221). Local prosecutors have also used state laws to fill the void left by federal regulators. By filing criminal cases for endangering workers, local prosecutors have taken over part of the function of the federal Occupational Safety and Health Administration (Moore, 1990c: 964). Individual states also enforce their own environmental liability laws; one prominent case involves the state of Alaska and the 1989 *Exxon Valdez* oil spill (Moore, 1990e: 1758). Perhaps the most notable case of state activity recently was the series of lawsuits against tobacco companies in the late 1990s. Even after a federal effort at greater tobacco regulation failed, these suits continued at the state level, resulting in billions of dollars in payments.

Establishing Alternative Values

Hedge, Menzel, and Krause (1989: 286) argue that state agencies create a check on federal agencies by providing an alternative set of organizational values. Using the case of surface mining regulation, these authors argue that state bureaucracies socialize their employees just as federal bureaucracies do. In many cases these values might be more supportive (or less supportive) of the program than the values held by federal bureaucrats. The differences in values then lead to differences in policy. Keiser and Soss (1998), for example, find that federal child support policies are adapted by state and local bureaucracies to be more consistent with local political pressures and circumstances.

Directly Challenging Federal Agencies and Policy

The above four federalism checks on federal bureaucracies are part of the subtle interplay between federal and state agencies. The final method state agencies use to check federal government bureaucracies is not subtle at all; state bureaucracies can directly challenge federal agencies by lobbying Congress and the president or by filing suit against federal agencies. In short, state bureaucracies can attempt to invoke federal political controls against an agency operating in a manner that state implementing agencies disapprove.

Clary and Kraft (1988) document the federal bureaucracy's effort to find a site for the disposal of nuclear waste. This effort was stymied by three states that went to court to challenge the legality of the disposal site designation process. A similar case involves the 1982 Department of Health and Human Services regulation that required that the parents of adolescents be notified if the adolescents received birth control information. Many states do not implement federal family planning policies directly but rely on private organizations such as Planned Parenthood to do so. In this case Planned Parenthood filed suit in federal court and got the regulation struck down as overstepping legislative intent (Hult, 1988).

Slightly more subtle, but still a direct challenge, states can ignore federal mandates. Federal law delegates responsibility to the states to regulate commercially generated low level radioactive wastes, a responsibility the states did not seek. Rather than directly refuse to comply, states simply delayed implementation in hopes the law would eventually be changed (Hill and Weissert, 1995).

FEDERAL CHECKS ON STATE BUREAUCRACIES

The notion of federal bureaucracies or political institutions serving as a check on state agencies is more visible than the state actions that limit federal policy. Perhaps the most documented cases of federal bureaucratic and political action to check state agencies are the effort to provide voting rights to black citizens and the parallel effort to require that local schools desegregate (see Bullock and Lamb, 1984). The federal government has numerous ways of limiting the activities of state and local bureaucracies, but only four will be discussed here: (1) preemption or partial preemption, (2) reductions in funding, (3) varying federal activities, and (4) varying the degree of oversight.

Preemption

In policy areas where the federal government shares authority with state governments, the federal government can decide to preempt state authority by declaring that federal law takes precedence over all state laws. Many federal regulatory statutes substitute federal regulation for state regulation (Reagan, 1987). In some cases, state agencies implement these preemptive statutes; in other cases federal agencies do. Since 1789 Congress has enacted 350 federal laws that preempt state statutes; fully one-half of these laws have been adopted since 1970 (Moore, 1990e: 1759). Even when federal laws do not specifically preempt state action, federal courts have been known to rule that federal law supersedes state legislation. At times federal legislation can target specific state regulations. In the case of state surface mine regulation, where state agencies permitted mines to subdivide to become too small to be covered by federal requirements (see above), Congress eventually eliminated this exemption by federal legislation (Harris, 1989: 74).

Reductions in Funding

The widespread use of proxy administration means that federal government actors can limit state bureaucracies by reducing federal funds for joint programs. The Environmental Protection Agency encouraged local governments to improve wastewater treatment by supplying 75 percent of the cost of such projects. When the federal share was reduced to 55 percent in the early 1980s, local governments had to cut back their efforts (Moore, 1986: 2370). In many other cases federal requirements are placed on states without federal funds to pay for such requirements. The Advisory Council on Intergovernmental Relations in 1984 found that such requirements cost the states $200 billion per year. One survey of state administrators found that perceived federal influence dropped as federal grant funds declined (Yoo and Wright, 1993).

Varying Federal Activities

In policy areas where both the federal and the state governments operate programs, the federal government can act as a check on state bureaucracy by varying its output. If the state operates an effective program, the federal officials might do less. If state programs are inadequate, federal efforts could increase. Hedge and Jallow (1990: 797) found this pattern in surface mining regulation; states who had previously done little to regulate surface mining received the largest amount of federal enforcement.

Varying Federal Oversight

Federal agencies are usually charged with monitoring state agencies that implement their programs. Concerns about food stamp and Medicare error rates at the federal level were part of a response to increase federal oversight of state agencies. Scicchitano, Hedge, and Metz (1989), in their study of surface mining, found that federal agency heads systematically increased or decreased the amount of state oversight that they did reflecting their policy preferences. They found that oversight of western state programs declined under Secretary of Interior James Watt but increased after his departure from the office.

FEDERALISM AS A CHECK

The full implications of federalism as a check on bureaucracy remains to be assessed. What is clear from the above discussion is that state and local government agencies serve as a check on federal bureaucracies under some conditions. Federal agencies, in turn, limit the bureaucratic discretion available to state and local government agencies (see Hedge and Scicchitano, 1994).

....

THE OMBUDSMAN

Since controlling bureaucracy via other political institutions does not guarantee beneficent administration, some students of bureaucracy have shown interest in foreign and domestic applications of the ombudsman (see Hill, 1976). The ombudsman is a Scandinavian invention designed to check administrative abuse of power. An aggrieved citizen complains directly to the ombudsman, usually an official with high public recognition and esteem. The ombudsman investigates the complaint and tries to work out an agreement between the citizen and the bureau. If the ombudsman fails to resolve the problem, his only sanction is to publicize poor administrative behavior and pressure the administrator to change his/her ways.

Five states—Alaska, Arizona, Hawaii, Iowa, and Nebraska—have created an independent office of the ombudsman (Hill, 1998). According to a recent survey some forty states list officials as ombudsmen, although in many cases these work for an individual agency rather than the entire jurisdiction (Hill, 1998). Several federal agencies, including the Environmental Protection Agency and the Internal Revenue Service, also operate ombudsman-like offices.

The ombudsman's function is controlling small bureaucratic abuses similar to the courts; it does not concern itself with broad questions of policy and public control. American analyses of the ombudsman are usually glittering reviews of the institution's effectiveness in other political systems (Anderson, 1968; Gwyn, 1973). This evaluation addresses two issues, the extent of the ombudsman's coverage and the ombudsman's limitations.

Caiden's (1983) review of several ombudsmen concludes that ombudsmen are little known, receive few complaints, have limited jurisdictions, perform only superficial investigations, and lack political clout. In Finland, Rowat (1968) found the ombudsman received 1,200 complaints annually with about 5 percent requiring remedial action. The Swedish ombudsman received 1,400 complaints annually and took remedial action on 15 to 20. In the first year of the New Zealand ombudsman, the ombudsman received 799 complaints and acted on 56. In the United States, the city of Buffalo, New York, experimented with an ombudsman funded by the federal poverty program for 71 weeks; 1,224 complaints were processed, most concerning social services, public housing, and demolition (Tibbles and Holland, 1970). Larry Hill's (1982) survey of both executive ombudsmen and classical ombudsmen (see below) found that they processed an annual mean of 7,035 and 2,328 complaints respectively; most were concerned with denials of service rather than administrative malfeasance.

Several conclusions are possible. Considering the foreign examples first, ombudsmen receive few complaints and actually seek redress on only a minute portion of those received. Clearly the ombudsman cannot be a comprehensive control over administrative action if 15 complaints a year are addressed in a nation the size of Sweden. Second, the American experience reveals that the problems considered are not of earth-shaking importance. In most cases they concern services the citizen wants, not some administrative abuse he or she has suffered.

Larry Hill's (1982) survey of ombudsmen in several American cities and states reveals that American governments have adapted the institution to make it more effective. The major change is the movement away from the classical independent ombudsman to the executive ombudsman, who is under the hierarchical authority of the chief executive. American executive ombudsmen processed an average of 7,035 cases per year (Hill, 1982: 410). These numbers probably reflect the outreach programs of the ombudsman in the United States. Many have branch offices and toll-free phone lines, and accept complaints over the telephone. Although most complaints remain in the category of inefficient or absent services, a fair percentage concern complaints about administration. In a study of the Hawaiian ombudsman, Hill (1983) found 335 cases of administrative reform over a fourteen-year period; a detailed analysis of 49 reforms revealed that about one-half had a major impact on administrative agencies' policies and procedures. The extended work of Hill (1998) suggest that the success of an ombudsman relies heavily on the political and managerial skills of the person holding the office.

Despite the adaptation of the American ombudsman and the positive results of at least one such ombudsman, the institution has some inherent limitations. First, the ombudsman often handles only minor matters. The American experience shows that executive ombudsmen are often just a place to complain about services denied rather than administrative malfeasance. Second, Miewald and Comer's (1986) study of the Nebraska ombudsman found that the ombudsman's clientele are those who need little additional help in bureaucratic encounters, that is, the middle-class, better-educated citizen with experience in dealing with the bureaucracy (an exception to this rule might have been in Buffalo, where field offices were specifically placed in low income areas). Third, the ombudsman has never been implemented for a government the size of the U.S. federal government. Although most ombudsmen have very small staffs, they also serve small governments. A federal ombudsman would likely require a bureaucracy as large as many of the bureaus it would investigate. Establishing an ombudsman is clearly a positive step, but it is unlikely to counter maladministration if current administration is not already generally responsive and competent.

....

DIRECT DEMOCRATIC CONTROL: NONCOMPLIANCE

For those who feel that citizens do not control elected officials via elections, a final overhead democracy check exists. Citizens can control bureaucratic policymaking directly by refusing to comply with public policy. If the costs of noncompliance with a policy including any potential costs of punishment are less than the costs of compliance with a policy, citizens will rationally refuse to comply with public policy (Stover and

Brown, 1975).[6] Federal efforts to establish prohibition were effectively stymied by public violations of the law. Broad noncompliance with marijuana laws prompted some communities to recognize that compliance determines policy, and they decriminalized possession of small amounts. Black resistance to Jim Crow laws in the South via lunch counter sit-ins and other forms of noncompliance triggered efforts to eliminate *de jure* segregation.

Recent studies have revealed numerous situations where policy was redefined by noncompliance. Perhaps the classic example was the public's refusal to drive 55 miles per hour despite extensive publicity, increased enforcement, and federal threats; in many western states, the public redefined an acceptable speed limit as approximately 65 mph (Meier and Morgan, 1982). Eventually the federal government changed the law. In the area of school desegregation, noncompliance effectively delayed policy implementation for fifteen years (Rodgers and Bullock, 1976). When formal desegregation occurred, withdrawal of students from public schools limited the policy's impact (Gatlin, Giles, and Cataldo, 1978; Giles and Gatlin, 1980). School districts often failed to comply with the spirit of desegregation; ability grouping, tracking, and discipline were used to separate minority students from their white classmates (Meier, Stewart, and England, 1989).

Nieman (1989) found that efforts to conserve energy though home energy conservation programs were limited by homeowners' unwillingness to make changes in their energy consumption. Brudney's (1990a; 1990b) work on agency volunteers suggests another aspect of noncompliance for some agencies. Brudney found that more than one-half of all cities larger than 4,500 residents use volunteers to deliver at least one service. Because agencies have less control over volunteers than over regular employees, noncompliance by volunteers (or unwillingness to volunteer) can virtually eliminate these programs.

Noncompliance may also be a check used by other bureaucracies. Johnson and Bond (1982) found that many hospitals that disagreed with the Supreme Court's *Roe* v. *Wade* abortion decision refused to perform abortions. Studies of environmental protection reveal that actual policy in the field is heavily influenced by the degree of voluntary compliance (Downing and Kimball, 1982; Downing, 1983). Similarly, surface mining policy was significantly changed in the late 1970s when some state agencies resisted federal regulations (Menzel, 1981: 217).

Because the level of compliance with most government policies is fairly high, cases of noncompliance indicate serious citizen objections to public policy. No government agency is ever given sufficient resources to force universal compliance; the cost would simply be too high. The Reagan-Bush drug war is a perfect illustration. In 1990 the federal government alone spent $11 billion on drug abuse; nationwide 1.3 million persons were arrested for sale or possession of drugs. Despite evidence that casual use of drugs had been declining since 1979, addictive use of drugs appeared to be resistant to law enforcement. Noncompliance by a small percentage of the population left the goal

---

[6] I am indebted to Anderson (1990) for raising this issue in regard to public policy. Recognizing that citizens can check bureaucratic power via noncompliance is separate from endorsing specific uses. Bureaus must consider such resistance when exercising their political power.

of a drug-free environment far from realization (see Meier, 1991). In a nontotalitarian state, therefore, citizens can directly check bureaucratic policy by refusing to comply with such policies.

....

SUMMARY

Overhead democracy is the traditional method of controlling the bureaucracy. Congress has sanctions it can apply to unresponsive bureaus through the legislative process, through the budget process, and through the legislative veto. Gathering information to support actions in these three areas is a function of oversight and informal contacts. Other than weaknesses of size and resources, Congress has some limitations in each of these areas. Legislation has become too vague to be more than a general boundary on bureaucratic action. The budgeting process has become focused on relationships between Congress and the president. The legislative veto reduces Congress to responding to bureaucratic initiatives. Oversight offers too few rewards to Congress, and casework introduces harmful favoritism in the administrative process.

Although many individuals favor using the courts to check administrative abuse of power, courts are less likely to be effective than Congress. Some agencies are difficult to defeat in courts of law; legal recourse, therefore, offers little chance of success. Low success is coupled with the high cost and long periods of time necessary to pursue legal redress of administrative errors. Using the courts to check bureaucracy, in fact, may be harmful because the process leads to the judicialization of administrative procedures and thus eliminates one relative advantage of bureaus, speed.

The president has a variety of tools to control administrative action; he may use the powers of command, his ability to appoint bureau heads and reorganize bureaus, his budget powers, and his leadership abilities. Although powers of command may be nothing more than the power to persuade, the president's organizational powers may be the most effective control on bureaucracy if used correctly. Leadership, reorganization, appointments, and budgets can control administrative action if the president focuses his attention on the bureaucracy.

Federalism has become a strong institutional check on bureaucratic power. State and local government agencies implement many federal policies; in the process they temper the influence of the federal bureaucracy. Federal bureaucrats, in turn, through regulations, funding, and oversight limit the power of state and local agencies.

Because the traditional institutions of American government do not offer any guaranteed method of controlling bureaucracy, some scholars support the establishment of an ombudsman. Although the ombudsman has much to recommend it, it is designed to rectify minor administrative ills in a system that is generally competent and responsive. The ombudsman has never been tested successfully in a bureaucracy the size of the American federal bureaucracy.

For those who feel people do not control political elites, direct control over bureaucracy via noncompliance is possible. Citizens can check bureaucratic power by refusing to obey bureaucratic edicts. If sufficient numbers do not comply, the policy is void. Although such circumstances of massive noncompliance are rare, they do exist.

This chapter has presented a large volume of research that generally concludes that elected officials can control the bureaucracy if they desire to do so. Individual agencies vary in their ability to resist controls, and political institutions vary in their use of individual controls, but determined politicians can usually produce changes in bureaucratic outputs. The changes may take some time, and they may not be all the politicians want, but the changes are generally forthcoming.

Overhead democracy works best when the political institutions are unified in their attempts to control the bureaucracy. If bureaucracy can appeal to one of the political institutions for support, then overhead democracy controls will be weaker. As Waterman (1989) contends, a lack of control over the bureaucracy usually reflects a lack of political consensus on the goals for bureaucracy.

CHAPTER 7

CONTROLLING BUREAUCRACY: ETHICS AND PARTICIPATION

Many students of bureaucracy believe that overhead democracy is not an effective check on administrative power. The essence of overhead democracy is the accountability of a bureaucrat to another person for his or her behavior. Even with multiple checks administration always involves discretion, and discretion opens the administrator to temptations that may be contrary to the public's best interest. External means of controlling administrative action and limiting these temptations can be only partially effective because they operate retroactively and then only infrequently. The initial control on a person's behavior must be the person's values.[1]

Scholars who criticize overhead democracy generally advocate two different approaches to controlling bureaucratic power—establishing ethics for administrators and allowing individual citizens to determine directly what administrative policy will be. Between these two polar approaches at least six methods of controlling democracy have been proposed: the Administrative Platonist, the scientific administrator, the new public administration, representative bureaucracy, participative administration, and public choice. This chapter discusses each of these approaches.

....

THE ADMINISTRATIVE PLATONIST

The driving force behind the school of thought advocating high ethical standards for administrators was Paul H. Appleby, once dean of the Maxwell School of Citizenship and Public Affairs and a high-level administrator for Franklin Roosevelt. Appleby (1965; 1952) used a content approach to ethics and described at length the characteristics that an ethical administrator should possess. The administrator must be willing to

---

[1] The argument here can be related to the principal–agent model. That model assumes goal conflict between bureaucrats and elected officials. The approaches in this chapter probe the ways that conflict can be reduced rather than the monitoring activities of most principal–agent models.

assume responsibility, be able to deal with people, have a sense of urgency, be a good listener, be effective with people, recruit the ablest of people, use institutional resources effectively, avoid using power for its own sake, be self-confident, welcome troublesome problems before they get out of hand, be a team worker, and be an initiator (Appleby, 1952: 342). Administration, according to Appleby, has a moral quality when it conforms to the process of political freedom, leaves itself open to public modification, and responds to public needs; and the pursuit of the public interest ties it all together.

Stephen K. Bailey (1966: 24), also a former dean of the Maxwell School, continued the Appleby tradition through his interpretations of Appleby's writings. Bailey's ethical administrator would recognize moral ambiguity; that is, administrative cases are neither black nor white, only various shades of gray. The administrator would perceive that contextual forces condition moral priorities in the public service so that what is moral depends on the situation. Bailey's administrator would also recognize the paradox of procedures—that procedures established to treat all people equally inevitably discriminate against those who are ill-equipped to deal with bureaucracy. Bailey also believed that three moral qualities are needed—optimism, courage, and fairness tempered by charity—to be an ethical administrator. Both Bailey and Appleby felt that a public administrator has a moral responsibility to "the highest ethical and moral principles of the state and society in which he lives" (Powell and Parker, 1963: 353).

The ethics advocated by Bailey and Appleby show some similarities to those adopted by the American Society for Public Administration (ASPA). After extended study ASPA, the professional association of many public administrators, proposed a code of ethics. Among the admonitions of the ASPA code are avoiding conflicts of interest, supporting affirmative action, exercising discretion in the public interest, striving for professional excellence, and supporting open communications (see Table 7–1). ASPA, however, has done a poor job of publicizing its code; Bowman (1990: 348) found that only 57 percent of ASPA members in administrative positions were familiar with the ASPA code of ethics.

Broad ethical statements as those of Appleby, Bailey, and ASPA have been criticized for using ambiguous concepts (moral ambiguity, courage, optimism, etc.) that defy definition. Because everyone could define these terms differently, an administrator can never be sure if a specific action is or is not ethical. To Oliver North, working to trade arms to Iran in exchange for aid to Contras in Nicaragua conformed to the highest ethical principles. To his critics, North put personal policy preferences over Congress' role in the constitutional system. Appleby, Bailey, and ASPA provide us with ambiguous solutions to this and other administrative dilemmas.

Several other scholars have attempted to provide more specific guidelines for ethical action (for a good bibliography see Gunn, 1981). John Rohr (1989), in a provocative argument, contends that bureaucrats should use regime values as guidelines for acceptable behavior. In the United States these regime values are embodied in the Constitution and can be determined by studying Supreme Court decisions. Rohr is arguing for what Huddleston (1981: 69) calls polity-based ethics in that ethics are defined by the broader polity that the administrator serves. Rohr's arguments, therefore, apply to the United States only.

• TABLE 7–1 •

AMERICAN SOCIETY FOR PUBLIC ADMINISTRATION CODE OF ETHICS AND IMPLEMENTATION GUIDELINES

The American Society for Public Administration (ASPA) exists to advance the science, processes, and art of public administration. The Society affirms its responsibility to develop the spirit of professionalism within its membership, and to increase public awareness of ethical principles in public service by its example. To this end, we, the members of the Society, commit ourselves to the following principles:

I   Serve the Public Interest

Serve the public, beyond serving oneself. ASPA members are committed to:

1. Exercise discretionary authority to promote the public interest.
2. Oppose all forms of discrimination and harassment, and promote affirmative action.
3. Recognize and support the public's right to know the public's business.
4. Involve citizens in policy decisionmaking.
5. Exercise compassion, benevolence, fairness and optimism.
6. Respond to the public in ways that are complete, clear, and easy to understand.
7. Assist citizens in their dealings with government.
8. Be prepared to make decisions that may not be popular.

II   Respect the Constitution and the Law

Respect, support, and study government constitutions and laws that define responsibilities of public agencies, employees, and all citizens. ASPA members are committed to:

1. Understand and apply legislation and regulations relevant to their professional role.
2. Work to improve and change laws and policies that are counter-productive or obsolete.
3. Eliminate unlawful discrimination.
4. Prevent all forms of mismanagement of public funds by establishing and maintaining strong fiscal and management controls, and by supporting audits and investigative activities.
5. Respect and protect privileged information.
6. Encourage and facilitate legitimate dissent activities in government and protect the whistleblowing rights of public employees.
7. Promote constitutional principles of equality, fairness, representativeness, responsiveness and due process in protecting citizens' rights.

III   Demonstrate Personal Integrity

Demonstrate the highest standards in all activities to inspire public confidence and trust in public service. ASPA members are committed to:

1. Maintain truthfulness and honesty and to not compromise them for advancement, honor, or personal gain.

· TABLE 7–1 ·

AMERICAN SOCIETY FOR PUBLIC ADMINISTRATION CODE OF ETHICS AND IMPLEMENTATION GUIDELINES (CONTINUED)

2. Ensure that others receive credit for their work and contributions.

3. Zealously guard against conflict of interest or its appearance: e.g., nepotism, improper outside employment, misuse of public resources or the acceptance of gifts.

4. Respect superiors, subordinates, colleagues and the public.

5. Take responsibility for their own errors.

6. Conduct official acts without partisanship.

IV   Promote Ethical Organizations

Strengthen organizational capabilities to apply ethics, efficiency and effectiveness in serving the public. ASPA members are committed to:

1. Enhance organizational capacity for open communication, creativity, and dedication.

2. Subordinate institutional loyalties to the public good.

3. Establish procedures that promote ethical behavior and hold individuals and organizations accountable for their conduct.

4. Provide organization members with an administrative means for dissent, assurance of due process and safeguards against reprisal.

5. Promote merit principles that protect against arbitrary and capricious actions.

6. Promote organizational accountability through appropriate controls and procedures.

7. Encourage organizations to adopt, distribute, and periodically review a code of ethics as a living document.

V   Strive for Professional Excellence

Strengthen individual capabilities and encourage the professional development of others. ASPA members are committed to:

1. Provide support and encouragement to upgrade competence.

2. Accept as a personal duty the responsibility to keep up to date on emerging issues and potential problems.

3. Encourage others, throughout their careers, to participate in professional activities and associations.

4. Allocate time to meet with students and provide a bridge between classroom studies and the realities of public service.

A careful reading of Rohr (1989) reveals that he emphasizes the process of constitutional reasoning as much as he does the content of court decisions. Such a stress permits Rohr to skip over or deemphasize court opinions that support sterilization of the retarded (*Buck* v. *Bell*), the execution of juveniles (*Stanford* v. *Kentucky*), the voiding of child labor laws (*Lochner* v. *New York*), and the absence of an alert, competent jury

(*Tanner* v. *U.S.*). Even with these omissions, Rohr's position is troublesome. Burke (1989) contends the Supreme Court is rarely consistent enough to provide an unambiguous guide to action (see also Rosenbloom 1994; Wise and O'Leary, 1997). One could also contend that legal reasoning with its emphasis on technicalities and hairsplitting is poor way to train administrators in ethics; public reaction to President Bill Clinton's narrow legal defense of his affair with Monica Lewinsky was overwhelmingly negative. Nor are judges especially good ethical models, since they have little training in ethics and the legal profession in general is rarely held up as an ethical ideal (Plumlee, 1981a; Kemp, 1986).

Several other approaches to make ethics more specific exist. A traditional public administration view is that public administrators should deliver neutral service to elected officials (Lovrich, 1981: 69; Devine, 1981) even though the recognition that administrative techniques are not neutral is what caused Appleby to make his proposals. Burke (1986) presents an extended argument that administrators need to refer ethical issues to elected officials who should serve as the arbiter of what is ethical. Burke strongly endorses political supremacy. His ethical administrator only makes ethical choices when political institutions decide that such choices are to be delegated to administrators. Others might criticize Burke for placing excessive faith in the ethical judgements of politicians. Getting politicians to make tough ethical decisions is also quite difficult (Meier, 1997).

A second approach is to instill ethics in organizational arrangements so that individuals cannot but act ethically in their duties (Boling and Dempsey, 1981: 13; Bowman, 1981: 60). By establishing standard operating procedures, using ethical training, and creating ethical consultants, these authors argue that organizational arrangements can foster higher ethics in public service. Few organizations actually do this. Denhardt (1988) is highly critical of the ethics of most contemporary organizations; she sees organizations as the source of many ethical problems. If someone wants to structure an organization to produce ethical decisions, the process to do so is not especially clear. Denhardt (1988) places more faith in participatory decision making, contending that hierarchical decisions lead to ethical compromises. This approach assumes that overt consideration of ethics along with widespread participation will generate ethical decisions.

A third approach is the one adopted by the U.S. government in 1978 in the Ethics in Government Act. That act defines unethical behavior as conflicts of interest, a very limited view of ethics (Plant and Gortner, 1981: 6). Because we are often concerned with actions that are legal but not ethical, the conflict of interest approach cannot provide administrators with much guidance on such issues. Conflict-of-interest approaches at best establish no more than the minimum requirements for ethics.

Fourth, Terry (1990), in an argument reminiscent of Burke's, stresses the need to restrain administrative advocacy. Bureaucracies are established for legitimate policy reasons; and many such institutions, he contends, are performing fairly well. He argues for what he calls "administrative conservatorship," a bureaucratic charge to preserve an agency's special capabilities, its proficiency, and its ability to perform a desired social function. In Terry's view bureaucracy's major contribution to the policy process is its stability. Bureaucrats need to conserve administrative skills so that bureaucracy can play an effective role in the policy process.

Fifth, Terry Cooper (1987) shares Denhardt's (1988) perspective that ethical problems have organizational origins. Specifically, he feels that hierarchy places demands on employees to satisfy their superiors rather than the American people. Ethics, according to Cooper, requires that bureaucrats have some understanding of employment by the public rather than by a specific agency. Cooper refers to what he calls the "internal goods of public administration," the values public administrators should seek—the public interest, accountability, social justice, liberty, etc. These, Cooper feels, must be emphasized to counter the external goods of the organization (pay, security, etc.), and thus, to avoid ethical problems.

The difficulty in specifying the precise content of ethical values, especially when divorced from specific situations, has led Denhardt (1988; 1989) to advocate a process approach to ethics.[2] Her objective is to design a process that produces ethical results. Denhardt (1989) argues that administrators perform a political role just as politicians do; administrative discretion, therefore, should be encouraged. The ethical process urged by Denhardt (1988) involves examining the values that underlie administrative decisions while recognizing the changing nature of such values and permitting administrators to be advocates. The process approach to ethics, while likely to encourage administrators to focus on ethics, still leaves the administrator without specific guidelines when making decisions.

In addition to the problem of determining if an individual act is ethical, several other limitations of ethical approaches to control exist. One major criticism is that reliance on ethics sets up ethical guardians (hence the term *Administrative Platonist*). If ethics rather than overhead democracy is used as a control, bureaucrats will be responsive to no one other than their own self-conception of morality (Fox and Cochrane, 1990). Kaufman (1969) argued that precisely this attitude caused New York City civil servants to see themselves as protectors of their clientele against the evil city politicians. As a result they resisted political control and gave the city uninnovative and unresponsive administration.

How ethics are instilled in public servants and why they will engage in ethical behavior are also not clear. Presumably ethics will result from an administrator's training (F. Mosher, 1982); but in the United States, unlike many other countries, administrative training is not uniform. In fact, most high-level administrators in the federal government were trained as technical specialists rather than as administrators. Even high-level administrators trained in administration were usually trained in techniques of administration rather than ethics. At the Maxwell School, home of the Administrative Platonist, MPA candidates often eschewed occasional "ethics and the public service" courses for budgeting, personnel, and public policy courses. Even if education for the public service did instill ethics, Downs (1967: 86) argues that the pressures of

---

[2] Denhardt contends that her approach to ethics is both process and content. My reading of her work, however, reveals a great deal of concern with process and little attention to content. Perhaps the best illustration of this is the final chapter in her book, a case study where the process for decision is discussed but none of the ethical questions are resolved. This criticism should not be taken to imply that Denhardt's approach lacks merit; in many situations a process approach to ethics would be helpful in defining possible actions.

everyday administration would force the bureaucrat to be an agency advocate rather than Applebian statesman.

Finally, the question of training uniformity raises an additional question. To what extent do administrators hold the values espoused by Paul Appleby and others? If public bureaucrats, especially those at high levels, have personal ethics like those of Paul Appleby, then the citizen can sleep soundly knowing that bureaucratic power will rarely be abused. Unfortunately, we must plead ignorance on this question. To date the systematic studies of the impact of ethics training on public employees, while positive, are few in number (Menzel, 1997). Administrators are quite willing to argue that their ethics are higher than those of politicians (see Bowman, 1990: 347), but this is not an especially high standard. Attempts to determine the level of ethics have been disappointing (see Bowman, 1981), and we do not have a good assessment of the ethics held by the nation's public servants. Until this question is resolved, those who rely on ethics as the major check on bureaucracy must place a great deal of faith in administrators.

THE FELLOWSHIP OF SCIENCE

A second proposal for an inner check on administrative action developed from the influx of scientists and professionals into national government. Demand for sophisticated military technology, space hardware, and advanced health care made the national government the nation's largest employer of professionals. Soon professionals were not subordinate to political masters but were actively participating in policy decisions because policy decisions such as developing a supersonic transport, determining the effectiveness of weapons and assessing the dangers of recombinant DNA research require expertise that only scientists can provide. Not only were professionals making policy, they were making policy in terms incomprehensible to lay politicians.

Friedrich (1940) argued that the situation posed new problems for politicians; however, the need was not to restrict professional discretion but to motivate professionals to anticipate public needs. Public policy decisions, according to Friedrich, should be accountable to both public sentiment and technical knowledge. The former could be achieved by inputs from elected officials, the latter through a fellowship of science where other scientists interpreted and challenged the results of scientists in government. Friedrich's solution to the problem of scientists in government was to add more scientists. These scientists, by advocating both sides of a policy issue, would give elected officials the information necessary to decide complex issues. Although Friedrich's proposal was controversial, it gathered a great deal of support from other students of science and government. C. P. Snow (1961), Don K. Price (1965), and Frederick Mosher (1982) echoed both Friedrich's fears and his solution, emphasizing the need for both professional decisionmaking and competing scientists. The most recent, and perhaps most optimistic, view of the fellowship of science is presented by Kearney and Sinha (1988). They argue the advantages of professionals in government far outweigh the costs; accordingly, a larger fellowship of science in the bureaucracy is to be preferred. Although these arguments also hold that administrative behavior must respond to public sentiment, the major concern of the fellowship of science advocates is competence rather than responsiveness.

The fellowship of science idea has also gathered support in policymaking areas where expertise is present. Both the president and Congress responded to the growth of bureaucratic power by developing their own bureaucracies staffed by experts (see Chapter 2). In an effort to equalize the competition between consumer and business advocates, the Magnuson–Moss Act of 1974 allowed the Federal Trade Commission to fund individuals, including some experts, to represent alternative policy views (the program has since been eliminated). Public interest groups including both environmental groups and the Nader organizations have developed expertise to compete with the expertise of the agencies (J. Berry, 1977). At the state level, Gormley (1983) documented the use of proxy advocates (public employees in other agencies) to counter the technical claims of utilities in utility regulation. The importance of expert consultants in equalizing the state battle over environmental protection is also evident (Zeigler, 1983: 125).

Although Friedrich's government by scientists and fellowship of science covers only a portion, albeit a growing portion, of public policymaking, the major shortcomings must be noted. Only recently are we beginning to learn about the impact of professional norms on administrative behavior. A great deal of academic training is actually a socialization process whereby young professionals accept the norms of their profession (Mitroff, 1974). The microeconomist, for example, is trained to perceive that the solution to most government problems is greater reliance on the market system (Lowery, 1998). Lawyers are trained to use the adversarial process to resolve disputes (Plumlee, 1981a). City planners hold a variety of beliefs about land use consistency and the correct goals for zoning (Sabatier et al., 1985; Vasu, 1979). Many occupational health and safety policies reflect a professional consensus among industrial safety engineers (Thompson, 1982a). Although not all professionals in a given specialty share identical norms, the greater the consensus on norms, the more difficult controlling professionals will be. Friedrich's proposal requires professional conflict and competition. If these factors are absent because scientists are professionally socialized to similar views, then one group of scientists cannot serve as a check on another.

A recent illustration of professions protecting themselves involves the North Chicago Veterans Hospital. Designed as a long-term care facility, the hospital began performing more surgical procedures to attract more physicians to the hospital. The results were disastrous; the General Accounting Office documented numerous misdiagnoses, poor supervision, excessive use of drugs, and many patient deaths. Despite these problems, a medical team of VA physicians brought in to review the hospital gave it a clean bill of health. Only the insistence of Secretary of Veterans Affairs Edward Derwinski prevented this collusion among the fellowship of science. He sent a second review team to detail corrective procedures (Abramowitz, 1991: 24).

The problems of controlling scientists are not just public policy problems. Some excellent studies of scientists and the difficulties in controlling them concern private sector organizations (Hall, 1967). Unfortunately this literature is fairly pessimistic about the ability of generalists (which most politicians are) to direct scientists in directions that they do not wish to proceed. Using their technical superiority, scientists can limit the alternatives considered to those acceptable to the scientists. If a generalist–administrator cannot understand the scientific issues in a given area of public policy, then that administrator is at the mercy of his or her scientists.

Because the relationship between technical responsibility and public sentiment has not been fully explored, the internal consistency of the fellowship of science is open to question. To what extent are those two goals incompatible? Public opinion, as expressed through elected officials, has generally favored more applied science to produce immediate benefits for mankind. To accomplish this end, a division of the National Science Foundation, Applied Science and Research Applications (ASRA), was established. With ASRA a great deal of scientific resistance to applied science surfaced. While public policy demands applied research, the rewards within a profession are geared more to basic research that deals with theoretically important scientific issues (Lambright, 1976). In some cases, therefore, technical responsibility opposes public sentiment.

Another limitation of the fellowship of science approach is that disagreement among scientists does not always solve the problem. In debates over the regulation of occupational safety and health, several scientific studies found that regulation had no positive benefits while others found significant benefits (see Greer, 1981, for a summary). West's (1988) study of rulemaking in four federal agencies also found that some disputes over rules could be traced to different technical specializations. Estimates of the cost of the 1991 Clear Air Act amendments ranged from $104 billion per year to $14 billion per year depending on which expert made the estimate (Starobin, 1990: 1212). Science, especially social science, is not so exact that it consistently produces uniform advice, especially when it deals with social problems. When scientists disagree on occupational safety or environmental hazards, politicians have no objective means of resolving the disagreement. Competing scientists may well be no guide to policy decisions at all especially if a politician selects the "wrong" position. The famed "star wars" missile defense system, for example, was rejected by the overwhelming majority of scientists as unworkable, yet an expensive program was started.

A final limitation of the fellowship of science, according to Finer (1941), is that relying on a fellowship of science to check scientific decisionmaking may be an abdication of public power to private groups. Simply because a group of people are scientists who possess technical knowledge does not mean that they do not also have policy preferences. The American Medical Association (AMA) was a vocal opponent of government interference in health care. If the AMA were the fellowship of science on Medicare, National Health Insurance, or hospital cost containment, effective public policy would be hampered (Kessel, 1970). All professionals have policy goals including the economic security of fellow professionals (Stigler, 1971). Whenever professionals advise on their own professions, therefore, the advice becomes less reliable.

....

THE NEW PUBLIC ADMINISTRATION

In the late 1960s and early 1970s the American Society for Public Administration and practicing public administrators were rocked by a group of insurgents advocating a philosophy that became known as the new public administration (Marini, 1971; Waldo,

1971). Under the auspices of the Maxwell School, the young turks of the discipline attempted to reformulate the "values of public administration" at the Minnowbrook conference center. Advocates of the new public administration charged that administrators were to blame for many of the injustices of modern society. The professed neutrality of administration was not neutrality at all. The "bias-free" procedures used by modern administrators were nothing more than procedures designed to allow the white middle class to interact favorably with the bureaucracy and to shut the poor and minorities out of the process. Procedures such as impersonality, written forms, and a long series of steps to receive some benefits were acceptable to the middle class but were obstacles for the poor (but see Goodsell, 1981).

Administrators, according to the new public administration, had long created inequities in power, influence, income, and services. If administrators were responsible for injustices, then administration must be reformed. The new public administration would actively foster conditions to further social equity.

Unlike other proponents of the inner check to control bureaucracy, the new public administration had specific policies and programs to achieve their ends. Bureaus should be decentralized and designed so that the people affected by the programs had more control over them. Through organizational development techniques, administrators should be made sensitive to the needs of the people they serve. Because bureaucrats often become committed to agencies and obsolete programs, organizations should be temporary, set up to achieve a single task and disbanded after task completion. To further prevent harmful bureau loyalties, the new public administration strongly supported contracting out services, perhaps to the service recipients so that they could provide their own services. Incremental policymaking with its emphasis on the status quo should be rejected; goals must constantly be reexamined to determine if progress is being made. The new public administration even advocated confrontation as an administrative tactic; disrupting normal bureaucratic services served to focus attention on problems that were not being solved.

Although the new public administration caught the imagination of the profession, it was not really new. Much of the new public administration with its emphasis on values is similar to Paul Appleby's writings on administrative ethics with advocacy added. Fifteen years before the new public administration, Arthur Maass and Lawrence Radway (1959) argued that the task of administrators was to equalize the differences between organized and unorganized interests. Such equalization implies that an administrator would either advocate the interests of the disadvantaged or discount the interests of the better represented.

The new public administration is concerned with the responsiveness of both policy and administration; competence is not usually a goal sought by the movement. In attaining this goal, the new public administration faces a major obstacle. The norm of technical neutrality is so ingrained in administrative mythology and political culture that moving to a role of administrative advocacy would be almost impossible. Dennis Daley (1984) found that political elites endorsed almost every means of controlling the bureaucracy except those relating to administrative advocacy. A survey of administrators found that they too rejected notions of administrative advocacy (Evans, 1981).

Shortly after becoming director of the Office of Personnel Management, Donald Devine (1981) vehemently denounced the new public administration.

The strength of the technical neutrality norm has been verified by the recent literature on urban services delivery. Following the innovative research leadership of Kenneth Mladenka, several scholars have examined urban services to see if they are biased against minorities and the poor. Mladenka and Hill (1978) found police services were better in lower-class neighborhoods in Houston as the result of bureaucratic decision rules. Similarly no upper-class biases in service distribution were found in parks, education, fire protection, and garbage collection in Chicago (Mladenka, 1980; 1981); in seven policy areas in New York (Boyle and Jacobs, 1982); in response to citizen complaints in Dallas (Vedlitz and Dyer, 1984); and in housing inspection in Boston (Nivola, 1978). Before concluding that no biases in service distribution exist; however, two factors should be noted. First, some studies do show some class bias even though the upper-class neighborhoods are not always favored (Jones, 1987; Jones et al, 1978; Cingranelli, 1981; Bolotin and Cingranelli, 1983). Second, the services observed and the measures used are often those that permit little discretion; police officers have to respond to calls, fire departments must respond to fires. What would be more interesting would be an analysis of areas with a great deal of discretion, for example treatment of individuals after an arrest, educational policies that further segregation (Stewart and Bullock, 1981), or hiring practices of local governments (Eisinger, 1982). In one good study of such problems Goodsell (1981) found that case workers were somewhat biased in favor of clientele at least in terms of making sure that procedures did not prevent the allocation of needed benefits. Meier, Stewart, and England (1989) and Meier and Stewart (1991) found educational systems were biased against minority students and poor students, but these biases were overcome when districts hired more minority teachers.

In addition to the obstacle of neutrality, two weaknesses limit the argument of the new public administration. First, the solutions advocated by the new public administration—decentralization, confrontation, organizational development, and nonincrementalism—do not logically result in greater social equity. New public administrators make a leap of faith from the reforms they advocate to the results they wish to achieve. The U.S. Department of Agriculture, for example, has long used decentralized programs and participation by farmers to run their programs. The USDA techniques, however, have been condemned for benefitting only the large, progressive farmer rather than the disadvantaged farmer (Baldwin, 1968). In the Department of Agriculture, some critics would contend that new public administration techniques were used to foster social inequity. Confrontations, for another example, are an excellent means to focus attention on bureaucratic problems; but continued use of confrontation in administration becomes counterproductive. Confrontations may well disrupt service delivery to all clients including the disadvantaged rather than reallocate benefits to the disadvantaged.

A second problem plaguing the new public administration is the ambiguity of goals. Although "social equity" is an admirable goal, what social equity means is difficult to discern. Usually the goal is expressed in terms of providing everyone with equal opportunities, but in many cases equality of opportunity results in outcomes much like the current state of affairs because people lack the necessary skills and education. In such cases social equity requires ameliorative or reverse discrimination. Exactly which cases require ameliorative discrimination, however, is not clear. The new public administration faces a problem similar to Appleby's Administrative Platonist, the administrator is never sure when a given action is acceptable. If consensus is lacking on the goals of administration, the new public administrators run the risk of becoming ethical guardians.

Despite such problems, the new public administration has made somewhat of a comeback recently (Frederickson, 1990). Twenty years after the first Minnowbrook conference, a second one was held. Commenting on the results of that conference, Guy (1989: 219) concluded that social equity is now an accepted goal, at least among academic public administrators. Guy, however, feels shortcomings continue to exist among its advocates including an unwillingness to address technological issues and an unwillingness to look at the political changes necessary to achieve social equity. The movement, in short, is warm and fuzzy.

Three recent scholars have staked a claim to the new public administration mantle: Wamsley and colleagues (1987) with "The Blacksburg Manifesto"; George Frederickson (1996a) with *The Spirit of Public Administration*; and Robert Behn (1998). Several faculty members at Virginia Tech argue that public administration should and does have a constitutional role in American politics just like Congress, the presidency, or the courts. "The Blacksburg Manifesto" argues for citizen participation, advocacy administration, a robust (confrontational?) policy dialogue, and treating public administration as a "calling." The authors boldly state, with a variety of religious metaphors, public administration's contribution to governance. As a result, they conclude, "It is not appropriate, therefore, for public administration to cower before a sovereign legislative assembly or a sovereign elected executive. Our tradition and our Constitution know no such sovereign" (Wamsley et al., 1987: 312; see also Long, 1993). "The Blacksburg Manifesto," in short, seeks a new politics administration dichotomy where administration is equal to, not subordinant to, politics.

George Frederickson's (1996a) approach is to establish the values base of public administration. He defends administrative discretion and in fact contends that effective governance in a democracy requires the energetic exercise of bureaucratic discretion. *The Spirit of Public Administration* is a wide-ranging essay and call for action that puts public administration at the core of all collective action (not just at the core of government action). Organizations should be managed to enhance the prospects for "change, responsiveness and citizen involvement." Equity and fairness are as important as efficiency and effectiveness. The public administrator is ultimately responsible to the citizens, and this responsibility takes precedence over other demands for responsiveness.

Robert Behn (1998) focuses on the need for public managers to be leaders, which includes a role as advocates. He notes that political institutions all have potential failures, including democratic failures. Without an active role for bureaucrats, other political institutions will not be pushed to overcome their own limitations in governance. Behn's manager might be characterized as a pragmatic version of Appleby or a somewhat more active version of the Terry's conserving administrator.

....

REPRESENTATIVE BUREAUCRACY

To meet the demands for both increased administrative discretion and more responsive bureaucratic power, Long (1952), Van Riper (1958), Kingsley (1946) and others suggest making the bureaucracy more representative demographically. If policymaking bureaucrats hold attitudes similar to the attitudes and values of the general population, the proponents of representative bureaucracy feel, then that policy will be more responsive to the needs of the public. They assume that when making a policy decision, a bureaucrat will attempt to maximize his or her own personal policy values. If the values of the bureaucrats and the citizens are similar, then policy made by the bureaucracy should be responsive to the desires of the public. How might these similar attitudes be achieved? If the socialization experiences of the bureaucrats are similar to those of the general public, attitudes should be similar since attitudes are a product of the socialization process. How can policymakers ensure that socialization experiences are similar? If the bureaucracy is recruited from a wide range of people, then the socialization experiences of the bureaucracy and the people should be similar. If, therefore, the social origins of the civil service mirror the social origins of the general population, then we can be sure that socialization experiences are similar, attitudes are similar, and policy is responsive to public needs.[3]

Notwithstanding the theoretical justification for representative bureaucracy as a check on bureaucratic power, some reasons suggest that a representative bureaucracy may not be a responsive bureaucracy. First, similar social origins do not necessarily lead to similar socialization experiences. To be sure the family, education, and social status do have an impact on values, but that impact is far less than total. Detailed political biographies have shown that individuals with such diverse backgrounds as Richard Nixon and Herbert Hoover had similar socialization experiences (Barber, 1972). The determinants of a person's attitudes and values are often so idiosyncratic that social origins are only a rough indicator of a person's socialization experiences.

Second, the linkage between social origins and values is not strong. Socialization, as a learning process, continues throughout the lifetime of an individual. Continuous socialization limits the ability of a personnel officer to predict a person's values from that person's social origins in two ways. Agencies take advantage of the socialization process; they create roles for adult bureaucrats and socialize them to advocate agency interests no matter what their own background (Downs, 1967; Selden 1997). For those values important to the agency, agency socialization impacts have been found in such divergent agencies as pollution control agencies (Wenner, 1973; Goetze, 1981) and social welfare agencies (Stone, 1977). Continuous socialization means that a group of civil servants must of necessity differ from a population with the same social origins. Civil servants will not only be more in favor of agency programs, but the simple fact that they are civil servants means their experiences are different from the general public's. Becoming a civil servant also generally means an increase in social status; James A.

---

[3] Although the idea of a representative bureaucracy was first presented in 1942, it has been recently revived to support policies of affirmative action. For an excellent discussion of representative bureaucracy see Saltzstein (1979).

Barber (1970) has demonstrated that upwardly mobile people hold values different from the values of nonmobiles with the same social origins. Upwardly mobile civil servants, therefore, would likely hold different values than their childhood counterparts especially on policy-relevant issues.

Third, the proponents of representative democracy may be focusing on the wrong level of bureaucracy. They consistently stress the representativeness of the bureaucracy as a whole; but, as earlier chapters have argued, decisions are not made at department or entire bureaucracy levels but rather at the bureau and division levels. For bureaucracy to be representative then, every bureau must be representative of the American people or decisions made at the bureau level must be appealable to a more representative bureaucracy.

These three criticisms of representative bureaucracy indicate that a representative bureaucracy may not be responsive to the desires of the American people. A more direct way to evaluate representative bureaucracy as a means of bureaucratic control is to examine the social origins and attitudes of the higher civil service. Table 7–2 shows the social origins on selected variables of the higher civil service (now the senior executive service), the upper-management levels of the civil service. Clearly the higher civil service is unrepresentative of the American people; compared to the population, civil servants tend to be white, male, urban, highly educated professionals from upper-middle-class backgrounds. As noted earlier whether or not the entire higher civil service is representative is an academic question because the entire bureaucracy does not make any policy decisions. Decisions are made at the bureau level; for the bureaucracy to be representative, each bureau must be representative. In general, studies have shown that bureaus tend to recruit from their clientele (Meier and Nigro, 1976). The Department of Agriculture recruits heavily from big farm interests and state land-grant universities. The Department of Housing and Urban Development recruits more from urban dwellers and minorities. No bureau is totally homogeneous in social origins, but bureaus generally are less representative than the higher civil service as a whole.

State and local bureaucracies have not been examined on as wide a range of demographic factors as the federal government. Most studies assess representativeness in terms of race, ethnicity, or sex because these variables must be collected to satisfy federal affirmative action regulations. The findings come to a consistent conclusion. Minorities and women are overrepresented at lower levels of the hierarchy and underrepresented at management and policymaking levels (Preston, 1977; Cayer and Sigelman, 1980; Hall and Saltzstein, 1977; Dometrius and Sigelman, 1984).

Comparing the attitudes of the higher civil service and the American people shows different results from the comparison of social origins. In general, the higher civil service holds attitudes that are similar to the attitudes of the population (see Table 7–3). The higher civil service is slightly more liberal than is the population (see Table 7–4). In a more recent study comparing the attitudes of all government employees to the general public, Lewis (1990) also found a general attitude congruence. Government employees are somewhat less likely to support the regulation of private behavior, more likely to support the First Amendment, less likely to support law and order approaches to crime, and less likely to be fundamentalist Christians. Differences increase as one ascends the bureaucratic hierarchy, but the differences remain modest. In a similar study

• **TABLE 7–2** •

SOCIAL ORIGINS OF THE HIGHER CIVIL SERVICE AND THE AMERICAN POPULATION, 1974

	PERCENTAGE OF GENERAL POPULATION	PERCENTAGE OF CIVIL SERVANTS
Father's occupation		
Blue Collar	48%	27%
Farmer	25%	18%
Clerk/Sales	7%	7%
Business	13%	31%
Professional	8%	17%
Education		
Less than High School	18%	0%
Some High School	18%	0%
High School Graduate	33%	1%
Some College	18%	3%
College Graduate	13%	96%
Race		
White	87%	96%
Nonwhite	13%	4%
Sex		
Male	47%	98%
Female	53%	2%
Birthplace		
Rural	49%	24%
Urban	51%	76%
Region		
South	31%	22%
East	28%	39%
Midwest	32%	31%
West	8%	8%

SOURCE: Meier, 1975.

based on 1982, 1984, and 1986 surveys, Garand, Parkhurst and Seoud (1991a: 190) found public employees were consistently more liberal than the general public but the differences were not dramatic.

State and local government bureaucrats, in turn, are more liberal than federal bureaucrats (Garand, Parkhurst, and Seoud, 1991b). The reason for this difference may be linked to agency socialization. The largest employer of federal bureaucrats is the Defense Department, a conservative organization. The largest employers of state and local bureaucrats are the local school systems, organizations likely to favor a larger government role.

• TABLE 7-3 •

PUBLIC OPINION AND ADMINISTRATIVE ELITE ATTITUDES: PERCENT SUPPORTING MORE EXPENDITURES*

Policy Area	Percentage of Civil Servants	Percentage of Population
Space	13	8
Environment	54	59
Health care	62	64
Urban problems	55	50
Crime control	52	67
Drug abuse	44	60
Education	46	50
Minorities	33	31
Defense	6	17
Foreign aid	11	3
Welfare	12	22

*The question permits the respondent to advocate more spending, less spending or the same amount of spending

SOURCE: Meier, 1975.

The reason why two groups with such diverse backgrounds can have such similar attitudes is because social origins are weak predictors of policy attitudes. What then does predict the attitudes of bureaucrats on policy issues? According to one study, the agency affiliation of the bureaucrats has three to five times more influence on policy attitudes than the bureaucrat's social origins do (Meier and Nigro, 1976). Agencies are apparently successful in socializing their personnel to agency prescribed roles (Selden, 1997). A study of California state executives confirms this view. Rehfuss (1986) found that women and minorities adopted a "management ideology" as they became top level

• TABLE 7-4 •

THE IDEOLOGY OF THE HIGHER CIVIL SERVICE AND THE AMERICAN POPULATION, 1974

	Very Liberal	Liberal	Moderate	Very Conservative	Conservative
Civil Servants	30%	27%	14%	22%	10%
Population	23%	29%	17%	15%	9%

SOURCE: Meier, 1975.

managers. Such findings mean that while the higher civil service may be representative in terms of attitudes, the top management contingent in individual bureaus will likely be much less representative.

The theory of representative bureaucracy cannot be completely discounted, however. Not all social origins are equally effective in determining attitudes, and not all policy positions are equally relevant to each bureaucrat. Some studies have shown significant support for representative bureaucracy by linking social origins with policy outputs (see Saltzstein, 1979). Saltzstein (1983) finds that individual attitudes of personnel managers affect the employment of women in the bureaucracy (see also Saltzstein, 1989). Winn (1989) contends that black managers are more likely to advocate the interests of blacks if they have contact with black organizations. In a study more specifically linked to representative bureaucracy, Meier, Stewart, and England (1989) found that school districts with more black teachers established policies that were less detrimental to the development of black students. Similar results were also found for Latino students (Meier and Stewart, 1991). Hindera (1993a, 1993b) revealed that the racial composition of the regional offices of the Equal Employment Opportunity Commission influenced the racial composition of the cases processed by the regional offices (see also Hindera and Young, 1998). Representative bureaucracy matters in situations where the social origin in question is highly salient, such as race, and the policy output is directly linked to the social origin (for example, educational discrimination; see also Hindera and Young, 1998; Selden, 1997). Selden (1997) finds that adopting the role of being a representative of a group is more important than being a member of the group; that is, role orientation is more important than even salient demographics such as race.[4] In many other instances, the overwhelming impact of agency socialization and the lack of linkage between social origins and policy limits the impact of representative bureaucracy.

In sum, representative bureaucracy is a check on administrative power only in highly specific circumstances. The U.S. higher civil service is not representative at the bureau level in terms of social origins and probably not representative in terms of attitudes. Certainly no other industrialized nation has a civil service as representative of its people as the American civil service, but our civil service still has a long way to go to be fully representative. Even if a representative bureaucracy were achieved in the United States, the pressures on administrators to advocate the mission of their agencies and the other constraints on administrative discretion would likely destroy much of the potential responsiveness (Romzek and Hendricks, 1982). This does not mean a representative bureaucracy should not be sought. The symbolic nature of representation is valuable, there are some instances where representation matters a great deal, and recently some research argues that representative bureaucracies are more effective (Meier, Wrinkle and Polinard, 1999b; Thielemann and Stewart, 1996).

---

[4] Recent work on representative bureaucracy has focused on the conditions and types of impact of representation. Meier, Wrinkle, and Polinard (1999b) present evidence that representative bureaucracy is non-zero sum, that is, minority gains do not come at the expense of majorities. They present the provocative argument that representative bureaucracies are simply more competent than nonrepresentative bureaucracies (see also Thielemann and Steward, 1996). Other work suggests that the relationship is nonlinear, that minorities must attain a critical mass to have an impact (Meier, 1993; Hindera and Young, 1998).

PARTICIPATIVE ADMINISTRATION

Individual participation and pressure groups participation have been proposed as a means of making bureaucracy more responsive. In the past four decades, the federal government at times has strongly endorsed citizen participation, placing participation requirements in 155 programs, including one-third of all grant programs (Langdon, 1981: 371). Most of these federal programs rely on state implementation, and states have adopted a variety of additional mechanisms for increasing citizen participation in policymaking (Schutz, 1983).

Because the participative administration model has a solid grounding in pluralist political science, the model makes many of the same assumptions as pluralism. The participation model assumes that each individual is the best judge of his or her own self-interest. As the best judge, each individual decides the ends he or she wishes to achieve and the means (including organizing into groups) to achieve them. The perceptions of administrative elites about any individual's interests should be discounted. The model makes several other assumptions that, if true, guarantee the responsiveness of political and administrative elites to the general population.

The participation/pressure groups model assumes all interests and opinions are expressed. Citizen demands that are not expressed cannot be considered salient to either the people or to government because these demands are not important enough to motivate people to express them. The model assumes that each individual will join others holding similar interests to form a pressure group; the objective of the group is to pursue the members' common interests. Since each individual is interested in many aspects of the positive state, everyone will join a variety of groups. Each pressure group, therefore, is composed of people who hold memberships in several groups. A close analysis of pressure group theorists reveals that the proponents feel that real interests in a society number in the hundreds rather than the millions so that aggregating all interests is physically possible (Truman, 1951). People who have common interests but are not organized are a latent group. Since people are assumed to be rational, the cost of organizing a latent group probably exceeds the benefits the group would gain by being organized; or the group would organize and enter the political process.

The group participation model ensures responsiveness by having groups take individual interests, aggregate them, and articulate the interests to policymakers. The groups influence political and administrative elites by offering rewards (support in battles with other elites or information that facilitates job performance) or by threatening punishments (withholding support or actual expressed opposition). Interest groups, because they represent valid interests and have political resources, have access to a wide variety of administrative policymakers (Zeigler and Peak, 1972).

If all interests concerned with an issue are represented, then all positions on a policy issue will be presented to the decisionmaker. The decisionmaker seeks to ensure his or her continuation in a position of power and influence by satisfying the demands of as many groups as possible. This statement applies to bureaucrats as well as to politicians because bureaucrats need support to gain legislative authority, budgets, and other resources (see Chapter 3). If a decisionmaker cannot satisfy a group's preferences, then the disaffected group can shift its support to another bureau (or political elite) that, if there is a great deal of group dissatisfaction, may be able to capture control over the program. The result should be the representation of all interests in policy decisions and, therefore, a general satisfaction of citizen demands.

A major concern of this model is the linkage between the group members and group leaders. What is to prevent group leaders from conspiring against group members or nonparticipants for their own benefit? First, each group is prevented from taking extreme actions that infringe on the rights of other groups because each citizen has multiple group memberships. Taking extreme actions would alienate some of the pressure group's membership and, therefore, weaken the group's claim to represent a large number of people; this weakened legitimacy would cause a decline in the group's power base. Second, the model also predicts that participants in the process cannot exploit nonparticipants because latent groups exist. A latent group, if threatened with a denial of its interests, would soon find that organizing and participating would cost less than foregoing the organizational costs and continuing to suffer the exploitation. Third, the assumption that competing elites will cater to unmet demands of the masses prevents any elite or set of elites from long ignoring the demands of any group. If one political or administrative official ignores a group, then another one eager for more political resources will adapt his or her policy to appeal to that group.

Interest groups and political participation are generally seen as a means to achieve a responsive bureaucracy. Only if the participants have relevant policy knowledge will participation affect bureaucratic competence.

Because the group participation check on administrative power is theoretically different from many of the others, the evaluation of this model will progress in two parts, the first dealing with the linkage between individuals and the group participants and the second considering the linkage between group members and administrative and political elites. Too often students of administrative power assume the first linkage is sound and proceed to discuss only the second. This procedure, in fact, artificially inflates the perceived effectiveness of participation as a check.

INDIVIDUAL–GROUP LINKAGE

Concerning the individual–group linkage, four questions must be examined. What is the extent of individual participation in groups, and is it common or fairly infrequent? What types of people belong to pressure groups, and are they different from nonparticipants? Do people in fact belong to multiple groups so that individual groups are restrained in their demands? Can individual participation be substituted for group participation to overcome the limitations of group participation?

The Extent of Participation

The pressure group check on administrative power assumes that group participation is a universal characteristic of American society. Similar to Alexis de Tocqueville, the pluralists see America as a nation of joiners. If participation is not universal, the probability increases that significant interests in society are left out of the process. We cannot assume that a citizen who does not participate is satisfied with the status quo so that nonparticipants can be ignored. Studies have shown that nonparticipation is associated with alienation and cynicism about the political process rather than satisfaction (Miller, 1974). A more logical inference about nonparticipation, then, is that certain policy demands are not being met. Participation must be widespread for the model to work.

The extent of American participation in the group process was examined by Almond and Verba (1965) in their five-nation analysis of political culture. They found that only 57 percent of the U.S. population belonged to one or more organizations remotely related to politics. Since Almond and Verba defined groups very broadly to include unions, business and professional associations, farm organizations, social groups, charitable, religious, civic, cooperative, veterans, and fraternal organizations, the extent of participation in political pressure groups was not staggering. Fully two of every five individuals did not belong to any groups at all. The inclusion of social and fraternal organizations (the fourth and third largest categories) in the analysis means that participation in *political pressure groups* is much smaller.

A more recent survey by Baumgartner and Walker (1988) confirms these earlier findings. Only 33 percent of the population affiliated with a group that tried to influence public policy. The authors concluded, "most people do not affiliate with groups in order to pursue overtly political ends" (Baumgartner and Walker, 1988: 922). They reconciled this lack of participation with the dramatic increase in interest groups (see below) by noting that technological developments (television, computers, high-speed printers) have allowed a small number of people with ample financial backing to make a great deal of noise. They contend, "Many groups are little more than figments of public relations" (Baumgartner and Walker, 1988: 908).

Are Participants Representative?

The lack of widespread group participation brings up the second question—how do the participants differ from the nonparticipants? If, on the one hand, the group participants are a microcosm of the nonparticipants, the possibility still exists that all interests in the nation are represented. If, on the other hand, the participants are distinctly different from the nonparticipants, the assumption of representativeness must be challenged.

Group participation has often been characterized as so unrepresentative that as Schattschneider (1960) has suggested, the flaw in the pluralist heaven is that the heavenly chorus sings with an upper-class accent. Verba and Nie (1972) found Schattschneider's colorful prose to be accurate. Community activists were better educated, from higher income groups, male, middle-aged, white, Protestant, and from suburban or small towns. Peterson's (1986; 1988) studies of older Americans who contact bureaucracy found they are more interested, better educated, and less needy than those who do not contact the bureaucracy. Other studies reveal similar distributions (Huckfeldt, 1979: 589; Giles and Dantico, 1982: 146). The policy interests of such people are likely to be different from those of the poor, the unemployed, the rural, the old, the young, and countless others. The nonparticipation by society's disadvantaged groups, then, is a direct challenge to the contention that pressure group politics is an effective means of making bureaucracy more responsive to all the people.

Multiple Group Memberships

If every individual belongs to several groups, then any single group is restricted in the actions it can take by the possibility of losing the support of its membership to other groups. If the individual participants do not belong to multiple groups, then their control over group leaders is diminished; their only alternatives to nonresponsive group leaders are to withdraw or to form an alternative group. Both options are less likely to succeed than the multiple groups reaction. If a member of the Teamsters Union, for example, believes the union's political alliance with the Republican Party contributes to policies detrimental to the rank and file, the teamster's probability of forming a successful countergroup within the union is marginal at best.

Almond and Verba (1972) revealed that multiple group memberships were restricted to 32 percent of the population. Even with their liberal definition of groups, only 9 percent of the population belonged to at least four groups. This number by itself is hardly sufficient to ensure that extreme actions taken by one group will alienate some of the group's supporters who are active in countergroups.[5] The 9 percent figure indicates that Schattschneider may be correct when he stated that possibly 90 percent of the population is shut out of the pressure group process.

Individual Participation

A fourth question the model raises is that of individual participation. Although individual participation is not as effective as group participation, individual participation to some extent can be substituted for group participation in keeping administrators responsive.[6] The intent of the community action programs in the 1960s war on poverty, for example, was to ensure responsive administration by having individual clientele directly participate in decisions and administration.

The extent of individual participation, however, was not impressive. A comprehensive study of American political activities classified 12 acts of political participation ranging from voting in presidential elections to membership in a political organization. Even without discounting overstated reports of participation, Verba and Nie (1972: 34) found 31 percent of the population performed no political acts and an additional 22 percent performed only one act (usually voting for president). When the acts were classified by difficulty, fully 77 percent of the population participated in one or fewer political activities, hardly the massive participation needed to ensure responsiveness.

The studies of participation in federal programs provide some evidence more closely related to the administrative process. The community action programs were designed to fight poverty by having the poor organize themselves and participate in administering the programs. When compared to the number of eligible participants,

---

[5] Most overlapping groups probably have consistent policy interests so that few stands would alienate members. Finding someone who belongs to such diverse groups as the American Civil Liberties Union, the National Rifle Association, Common Cause, and the American Soybean Producers would be difficult.

[6] I assume group participation is more effective because groups have more resources to reward or punish policymakers than do individuals. This does not mean that individuals occasionally cannot have more influence on public policy than groups, only that this is unlikely.

however, only a small percentage actually participated in any part of the program (Reidel, 1972). Similar low levels of participation were found in water pollution policy (Plumlee, Starling, and Kramer, 1984). In addition to the low level of individual participation, most participation was by members of the community with higher socioeconomic status (Sharp, 1982: 110; Thomas, 1982: 510; but see Jones et al., 1977).

GROUP–ADMINISTRATIVE ELITE LINKAGE

The second linkage in the pressure groups/participation model is the link between the pressure group and both group leaders and administrative elites. As Redford (1969: 14) argues, "the attainment of the democratic ideal in the world of administration depends much less on majority votes than on the inclusiveness of the representation of interests in the interaction process among decision leaders." If, as Redford contends, all relevant interests are represented in the process and political or administrative elites are held responsible for meeting the demands of the interests through some type of sanction, then the policy outputs of such a process will, in general, be responsive to the American people.

The effectiveness of pressure groups or direct participation in checking administrative power is dependent on three conditions. First, the linkage between the interest group's members and its leaders must be fairly strong; the leadership must be cognizant of membership desires and seek to further those desires. Second, all interests must be represented in the process or the policy will reflect the consensus of the participating interests rather than all interests. Third, relationships between elites must be characterized by competition rather than cooptation. Administrative and political elites must compete for support from the interests, and interests must compete for favorable public policies.

The Representativeness of Interest Group Leaders

The first necessary condition for interest groups to act as an effective check on administrative power is that the interest group leaders represent members' interests not their own interests. The union leader who negotiates a sweetheart contract with a manufacturer does not represent the best interests of the rank and file. Most students of interest groups assume that leaders do, in fact, represent the members effectively, assuming that if they did not the members would leave the group. But continued membership cannot be taken as implicit acceptance of leadership actions because people join groups for many reasons other than policy objectives (Wilson, 1973; Hayes, 1981; Moe, 1981; Cook, 1984; Hansen, 1985). A small farmer may remain in the Farm Bureau because the bureau provides low-cost crop insurance. A welder may retain his affiliation with his union to avoid the social stigma of being scab labor. The manufacturer may continue membership in a trade association because the national convention provides a tax-deductible vacation. Many interest group resources are devoted to providing non-policy benefits to members; clearly some members remain for these benefits even if they disagree with the group's policy goals (Browne, 1977).

If we assume leaders are not devious and they advocate the interests they perceive the members hold, the question remains, do interest group leaders perceive the world in the same way that members do? A study of the Oregon Educational Association found that leaders held positions on important educational issues that were substantially different from the rank and file (Luttbeg and Zeigler, 1966). Although the leadership knew the members' opinions were different from their own, they actually misperceived membership positions as being more like their own than they actually were. Franke and Dobson (1985) found similar leader–member differences in the American Association of Retired Persons and the National Retired Teachers Associations. Sabatier and McLaughlin's (1988; 1990) studies of local environmental issues found that leaders of both environmental and developmental groups took positions more extreme than their members. These differences between members and leaders grew larger as issues became more conflictual. In the only study to compare group leaders, group members, and latent group members, Sabatier (1991) found mixed results. For his environmental group, leaders were more extreme than members and members were more extreme than potential members. For his business group, there were no differences between members and nonmembers; leaders, however, held more extreme attitudes than members. A consistent pattern in the linkage between interest group members and leaders is that the leaders perceive member's positions on issues to be more like their own than they actually are. Elites consistently hold less centrist positions than do the rank and file.

The evidence presented here seriously questions how well group leaders represent members' interests. The representation process breaks down when leaders do not accurately perceive the interests and desires of the people who represent. Why this occurs is that interest groups are also organizations; and, as voluntary organizations, they can exist only if members receive more from the organization than they contribute (Wilson, 1973). To maintain such a positive balance, many organizations provide other incentives for joining (e.g., insurance, magazines, social interaction). This strategy permits the leadership to lobby on policy issues without the burden of representing members' interests. This strategy has been taken so far as to create interest groups without members; in the food policy area, interest groups who speak on behalf of the poor and the hungry are usually supported by foundation grants and charitable contributions rather than by membership dues (J. Berry, 1977; see also Colarulli and Berg, 1983).

Are All Interests Represented?

To be an effective check on administrative power, all interests must be represented in the process so that all views are presented to policymakers. Although no one has systematically examined the American political process to determine if all interests are represented when policy decisions are made, evidence suggests that all interests are not usually present. At the general level, the rise of public interest groups like the Nader organizations and Common Cause, and the growth of environmental groups such as the Sierra Club and the National Wildlife Federation, have given the impression that interest groups are broadly representative of American society. Recent scholarship, however, reveals that this impression is incorrect. Scholzman (1984: 1012), in a classification of 7,000 groups located in Washington, D.C., found that 45.7 percent of these groups were corporations, another 17.9 percent were trade associations, 6.5 percent were foreign corporations, and 6.9 percent were professional associations. Only 5 percent were organizations that represented people who had few political resources (Scholzman, 1984: 1013). In fact, this study found that the proportion of groups representing business increased from 57 percent in 1960 to 72 percent in 1980. In a separate study, Salisbury (1984: 75) found a similar dominance of favored institutions among the lobbyist population.

The dominance of business organizations among interest groups is furthered by bureaucratic and legislative decision rules. In 1977, Priest, Sylves, and Scudder (1984) found that almost one-half of the 50 largest financial and 150 largest nonfinancial corporations were represented on federal government advisory boards. An extensive review of the health planning literature revealed that participation was high among physicians and health care planners but not among health care consumers (Checkoway, O'Rourke, and Bull, 1984: 300).

In an excellent study of interest group participation in eight rulemaking processes for three agencies, Golden (1998: 252) found business interests dominated the participation and comment process. In no case did citizen group participation exceed 11 percent of the total. Who participated, however, did not translate into who benefited. Agencies changed rules only when opposition to a rule was virtually unanimous. Overall such changes were on peripheral issues rather than on central issues (Golden 1998: 259). Golden concluded that agencies were most responsive to voices that support the agency's position. In short, what mattered most was agency values, not the extent of participation.

The case study literature similarly documents the biases in the interest group process. Theodore Lowi (1976) documented several instances of public policy where all interests were not represented. In fact Lowi believes that cooptation and one-agency–one-interest politics is the dominant form of politics in the United States. Seidman and Gilmour (1986) in their analysis of bureaucratic politics also contend that important interests are excluded from the policy process. They feel the exclusion results from interest participation in subsystem politics; if participation could be limited to large agencies or to the entire Congress, the process would benefit more people.

This general bias does not mean that consumer and public interest advocates always lose in the policy process; they do not (J. Berry, 1977; Ornstein and Elder, 1978; Meier, 1988; Golden, 1998). In many cases broader public interests are able to defeat better-organized producer interests as the result of intervention by political elites or as the result of external events. In general, however, the interest group process represents only those groups with narrow interests who benefit greatly from organization.

Do Interest Groups Compete?

If interests are not competitive, bureaucrats will be under no pressure to respond to all groups but could respond to one interest and ignore the rest. The fact that all interests are not represented lessens the need to compete for political support. Competition among interest groups is also hindered by the fragmented nature of American politics. Some scholars believe that the dominant form of policymaking in regulatory and distributive policy is subsystem politics (Ripley and Franklin, 1991; Lowi, 1976). Interest groups, congressional committees, and bureaucracies form a triumvirate to extract resources from the environment. Interest groups receive services, bureaus receive resources, and committee members receive clientele support. Subsystem politics, as conceived by many, does not permit competition.

Maintaining a noncompetitive subsystem is more difficult than the literature contends, however. A subsystem is permitted autonomy only to the extent that the subsystem does not impose significant costs on the political system, that is, to the extent that subsystem issues are not salient. At the federal level in recent years, maintaining a noncompetitive subsystem has become difficult for several reasons. First, the budget crisis resulting from both massive deficits and efforts to redistribute federal funds has created a zero-sum game in which no subsystem can increase its resources without taking funds from other subsystems. Second, the inflation of the late 1970s increased the demands of all subsystems so that one subsystem often looked enviously at the resources of other subsystems. Third, numerous political elites became entrepreneurs and advocated the interests of nonsubsystem members against the interests of the subsystem. Major changes, particularly in regulatory policy, resulted as new legislation or new policies were established for banking, consumer protection, airlines, telecommunications, surface transportation, and securities trading (Meier, 1985; Derthick and Quirk, 1985).

Two other trends, however, increased subsystem politics (McCool, 1989). The increased decentralization of Congress has led to smaller and narrower policy spheres, so that many more interests now have their own subsystem. The increased stress on logrolling and accommodation has led outsiders to acquiesce in the decisions of other subsystems in exchange for autonomy in their own subsystem (McCool, 1989: 267).

Whether these events represent a change in interest group politics whereby elites come to dominate interest groups is not yet clear. At the state level Abney (1988: 912) has found evidence that agencies mediate interest group disputes before the legislature is involved. At the federal level with the end of the regulatory reform movement in 1981 and balanced budget of 1998, subsystem politics may well reassert itself as strongly as it did during the 1950s (see McCool, 1988; 1989). If it does, the practice of interest groups not competing will become more common; and the use of competing interest groups as a check on administrative policy will decline.

In recent years the general studies of subsystem politics have been supplemented by two specific studies on interest groups and their coalitions. Browne's (1990; 1988: 247) studies of agricultural interest groups found that groups specialized in very narrow issue areas. Most agriculture interest groups "avoid issues that bring them either cooperation or conflict with one another. The give and take so critical to the pluralist assumption is surprisingly absent" (Browne, 1990: 492). A study of interest groups in agriculture, health, labor, and energy also found little interaction among groups, the competitive component was clearly missing (Heinz et al., 1990). Golden (1998) comes to a similar conclusion.

Are Interest Groups a Check?

If all the assumptions of the pressure groups/participation model of controlling the bureaucracy held, it might be a way that bureaucratic power could be checked. Examining the individual linkages and assumptions, however, leads one to conclude that the ideal theory does not resemble the actual process of American politics. The weaknesses of the theoretical model of interest groups and participation does not mean the mechanism cannot work at times to make bureaucratic policy more responsive.

The literature contains numerous examples of successes. Studies of state utility regulation reveal that pricing policies are more favorable to consumers in those states with active consumer groups or with proxy advocates who designate themselves as consumer representatives (Gormley, 1983; Berry, 1979). In federal communications policy citizen groups, once they achieved standing to sue, were able to negotiate changes in policy with local broadcasters particularly in the areas of minority content and minority hiring (Longley, Terry, and Krasnow, 1983: 259). Studies of California Coastal Zone Commission decisions revealed that these decisions were highly sensitive to public participation at hearings (Mazmanian and Sabatier, 1980; Rosener, 1982: 342). Federal transportation regulations required significant changes in accessibility for handicapped persons after handicapped individuals were allowed to participate in the regulation drafting process (Poister, 1982: 7; Percy, 1989). Cities that held public hearings on potential projects to be paid for with revenue sharing funds made different expenditure decisions than cities that did not, although this relationship changed after all cities were required to hold hearings (Cole and Caputo, 1984). Studies of zoning decisions in metropolitan Atlanta found zoning proposals were more likely to be rejected if citizens appeared and objected to the proposal (Fleischman, 1989; Fleischman and Pierannunzi, 1990).

Other studies reveal that participation makes no difference in public policy decisions. Plumlee, Starling, and Kramer (1984: 461) could find no substantive policy changes as the result of extensive participation requirements for water quality planning. A survey of urban administrators by Abney and Lauth (1985b: 150) found that interest groups were minor participants in the policy process. Browne's (1985: 466) four-state study of aging policy found that interest group influence was dwarfed by other political and social forces (see also Golden, 1998). What is evident from this range of studies is that the exact impact of participation by either interest groups or individuals on bureaucratic policy is unclear.

PUBLIC CHOICE

Perhaps the most radical proposed check on bureaucratic policymaking is that proposed by the public choice advocates (Ostrom, 1973; Niskanen, 1976; Tullock, 1965). Arguing that the norms of democracy require that the preferences of the public be given the greatest weight in determining public policy outcomes, public choice advocates press for policy mechanisms that allow public policy to be determined by individual citizen choices rather than bureaucratic choices. Accepting bureaucratic views as to the appropriate policies desired by citizens, according to this view, is paternalistic.

The implications of public choice are market oriented. Because market mechanisms are based on voluntary transactions and because voluntary transactions enhance utility for both parties to the transaction (or no transaction would be made), public choice theorists often advocate private sector solutions for public policy problems. High-quality schools, they contend, can be achieved by giving citizens vouchers and letting them select their own schools (Chubb and Moe, 1990). Individual schools would then have to compete to offer the best education and attract students to survive. More responsiveness to citizen wishes can be achieved via coproduction, allowing citizens to participate in the production of government services. Contracting out government services to private corporations can improve competence because private corporations must produce superior services or they will cease to attract business. Voluntary organizations can be used to replace government organizations and thus produce allocational efficiency, since citizens would not volunteer unless the benefits they received exceeded the costs.

Public choice is a radical approach to controlling bureaucracy because its solution to bureaucratic power is to eliminate bureaucrats. Vouchers, coproduction, contracting out, and volunteerism essentially bypass government bureaucracies that have vested interests in current programs. The citizen in this model becomes sovereign in the same sense that the consumer becomes sovereign in the marketplace. The public choice approach is well represented in the current Reinventing Government movement; this movement seeks to use market-like and private sector approaches to reform government.

In many cases government has used public choice–style systems to deliver public policy. One program seeks to expand employment by giving corporations tax credits for hiring disadvantaged individuals; deHaven-Smith's (1983: 728) analysis of this program, however, found that it suffered from many of the same problems as other jobs programs. Other examples of public choice mechanisms at the federal level include Medicare, Medicaid, food stamps, and the GI Bill for education (Crompton, 1983: 537). At the local level, public choice mechanisms, particularly volunteerism, are found frequently in cultural arts, recreation programs, senior citizen programs, and public safety (crossing guards, neighborhood watch groups, etc.; see Brudney, 1990a; Ferris, 1984: 328). School choice systems have operated through either vouchers, magnet schools, or charter schools (Smith 1999). In fact, some programs such as drug abuse prevention, family planning, and nutrition programs require citizen participation to be effective (Rich, 1981: 61). Lowery (1982a; 1982b) even found that some cities in Michigan contracted with private organizations for tax assessments. He found that while the cost of the service declined when contracted so did the quality.

Public choice proposals are highly controversial in public administration with liberals generally opposing such mechanisms and conservatives advocating them (see Golembiewski, 1977). Existing evidence suggests that public choice approaches must be carefully designed to avoid some of the documented problems of privatization. First, efforts to privatize public services have been marked with extensive corruption (see Moe, 1987). The largest scandal of the Reagan administration, the Department of

Housing and Urban Development scandal, involved private contractors stealing government funds that were allocated to housing (Waldman, 1989; Steinbach, 1989). The Small Business Administration was embarrassed by the Wedtech Corporation scandal. A private organization with $250 million in federal contracts, Wedtech pleaded guilty to charges of bribery and fraud (Matlack, 1987). Grocery store owners are frequently indicted for food stamp fraud. Privately owned vocational schools sometimes appear to be no more than fronts to collect student loan money (McAllister, 1989: 32). Defense contractors periodically are found to bill the U.S. government for private swimming pools and other nondefense goods; in 1988 alone the Department of Defense recovered $280 million in contract fraud cases. Perry and Wise (1990) provide an explanation for the corruption in public choice delivery systems. Privatization, they argue, undercuts the public service ethic; motivations other than financial ones are eliminated. As a result, corruption is common.

Second, public choice advocates believe that the private sector will both be more competent and more responsive to citizens. Responsiveness, however, is predicated on competition. If privatization simply substitutes a private sector monopoly for one in the public sector, there is no reason to think that the private bureaucracy will be any more responsive (Wise, 1989; Durant, Legge, and Moussios, 1998; Seidenstat, 1996). In a perceptive assessment Lowery (1998) found that market-like solutions also failed for many of the same reasons that markets themselves failed (lack of adequate information, lack of supply, inadequate competition). Goodsell (1983) compared a wide variety of public and private sector organizations and concluded that neither was definitely superior to the other.

Third, contracting out can rob government of needed expertise. O'Toole (1989) examined public and private wastewater treatment programs. Public agencies developed expertise over time and provided useful skills both in water treatment and in other areas. The result was that government treatment facilities were more innovative, had better minority hiring records, and were more accountable to complaints (see also Frederickson, 1996b). On the competence side of public choice, Kobrak (1996) criticizes the reinvention movement because it has a narrow view of competence. By defining competence as efficiency, the movement overlooks the broader competencies (e.g., effectiveness, proaction, fairness) involved in the governance of public programs. Theobald (1997) further argues that there is a fundamental conflict between a market-driven philosophy and public organizations' goals of openness and accountability.

Fourth, citizens may be less willing to cooperate with private organizations that deliver services. Public organizations have the advantage of the legitimacy attached to government organizations. Nieman (1989) examined the California home energy conservation program. Administered through utility companies, this program did little to reduce the actual level of energy consumption.

Fifth, public choice may well be hostile to the idea of democracy in some situations. Smith (1994) notes that Chubb and Moe (1990) lay many of the problems of education at the feet of democracy and its procedures. Smith's (1994) implication is that public choice cannot necessarily be accepted as a democratic control since it tries to set up institutions buffered from democratic processes. Frederickson (1996b), while discussing the reinvention form of public choice suggests that short-run gains in efficiency could produce long-term losses in administrative capacity and social equity.

Sixth, private bureaucracies are still bureaucracies with many of the same sources of power and problems. Private bureaucracies are probably just as likely if not more likely to adapt a program to its own goals. Morris's (1997) study of privatization in water quality regulation, for example, found that private implementation significantly altered the patterns of resource distribution and was less likely to meet national program objectives.

Finally, public choice assumptions about citizens and how they respond to government and incentives might be wrong. Although they do not address directly questions of efficiency and competence, Lyons, Lowery, and DeHoog (1992) have empirical evidence that citizens do not respond as public choice theory suggests they should (see also Lyons and Lowery, 1989). The implication of this study is that public choice approaches to bureaucracy will produce far less benefits than their advocates claim. Given the costs of public choice in terms of corruption, elimination of public sector expertise, and ability to gain citizen compliance, public choice proposals to eliminate government bureaucracies should be evaluated with skepticism.

SUMMARY

This chapter evaluated six proposals to ensure bureaucratic responsiveness and competence: the Administrative Platonist, the scientific administrator, the new public administration, representative bureaucracy, participative administration, and public choice. The Administrative Platonist position advocates instilling ethics in civil servants. Unfortunately the proponents are vague about what values they wish to instill, about how they will instill them, and about why their proposals will not create a cadre of uncontrolled ethical guardians. At the same time ethics are a vital element of public agencies and their programs.

The scientific administrator approach generates competent administration by recruiting scientists to government service so that scientists can check other scientists. The professional norms of scientists that blind them to certain options, however, may be so strong that additional, competing scientists cannot overcome them. Competing scientists offer a solution to bureaucratic power only when policymakers can make rational choices among the competing scientists.

The new public administration takes the values of the Administrative Platonist and adds advocacy so that administrators pursue social equity. The new public administration has many of the same problems that the Administrative Platonist has. In addition, the new public administration also has vague goals and methods that do not necessarily lead to social equity.

Representative bureaucracy seeks to control bureaucratic power by recruiting a microcosm of the American population to the civil service. The theory assumes these individuals will hold the same values as the rest of the American public so that as they pursue their own self-interest they will further the ends of the American people. Unfortunately for this theory, representative bureaucracy appears to work only in those situations where social origins produce lasting values and the public policy issues are directly related to such values. In many cases, as a result of upward mobility and agency socialization, this does not occur.

The pressure groups approach to administrative responsibility requires that representative groups press the demands of the general public. Pressure politics does not ensure administrative responsibility, however, because interest group leaders are not closely linked to their members and because interest groups represent only some segments of society and ignore others.

The public choice approach offers a unique method of making bureaucracy more responsive and competent, eliminating as much of the bureaucracy as possible. By contracting out for services, by encouraging coproduction, by fostering volunteerism, by using vouchers and other market mechanisms, public choice seeks to use market place incentives to deliver needed government services. Such an approach is highly controversial and lacks consistent empirical support.

CHAPTER 8

REFORMING THE BUREAUCRACY

This chapter outlines several political reforms designed to produce a more competent and responsive bureaucracy. Because both competence and responsiveness are difficult to define unambiguously (see Chapter 5), none of these reforms will please everyone. The basic underlying assumption is that the American people have both the capacity and the desire to control elected officials. If they do not, then any reform must rest on the good will of the bureaucracy. Before discussing the proposed reforms, the major themes of this book will be reviewed to illustrate why reforms to control the bureaucracy will be necessary.

Bureaucracies are political institutions of the first order. The American polity and many others no longer authoritatively allocate scarce societal values only through legislative and executive processes. Bureaucracy in the United States has developed political power through access to resources and discretion in the use of those resources. Although bureaucracy may not be the dominant political institution in all aspects of public life; in regulation, in taxation, in health care, in national defense, and in a variety of other areas, bureaucracy is a coequal power with the legislative and chief executive.

Bureaucracy did not become a major political institution because a select group of bureaucrats with evil intentions conspired to make it so. Rather, bureaucracy gained power because people demanded that the government perform certain functions and only bureaucracy could perform them. Public policy is nothing if not complex; the task demands of public policy forced policymakers to turn to bureaucracy with its access to expertise. The organization of government in the United States, with its checks and counterchecks, stalemated the major political institutions; where action was required, bureaucracy became the logical choice. The nature of American politics, with its glorification of technology and administration and its denigration of politics, forced additional public policy problems into the bureaucracy. Even the intended function of bureaucracy, implementation, required discretion for policy to be successful.

Although the nation's political institutions with the acquiescence of the American public granted great discretionary powers to public bureaucracy under the assumption that administration is different from politics, the problems of bureaucratic power are no different from the problems of political power. The Founding Fathers correctly believed that any unchecked exercise of political power was dangerous. Watergate, Abscam, the HUD scandal, and the White House intern scandal are grim reminders that political officials still succumb to the temptations of power. If American politicians have weaknesses, we should bear in mind that bureaucrats are neither more nor less culpable than the rest of the nation's citizens.

....

HOW MUCH CONTROL IS NEEDED?

Determining the needed amount of external and internal controls on bureaucracy is not an easy task. Clearly the absence of any controls would produce *government by bureaucracy*, resulting in government much like the muckraking journal *Washington Monthly* portrays it to be. Bureaucracy in such a system would have a life of its own with little direction from Congress or the president. Responsiveness to anything other than internal norms of correct rules and procedures would not exist. Citizens would be treated as objects to be administered rather than sovereigns to be served.

Controls on bureaucracy can also be excessive. Perhaps the most responsive bureaucracies known in American politics are those that existed in the great urban political machines. By relying on patronage appointments, frequent turnover, and direct administration by elected officials, bureaucracy was rendered an appendage of the urban machine. Corruption flourished and competence suffered, but the bureaucracy was responsive.

Clearly the extent of control needed is relative. Controls should be strong enough to guarantee the responsiveness of bureaucratic policymaking to the policy directives of the people yet not be so strong as to stifle bureaucratic initiative. Advocacy of reforms in controlling bureaucracy normally is based on perceptions of the current performance of American bureaucracy. If the bureaucracy is perceived as unresponsive, then greater external controls are urged. If the bureaucracy is perceived as lacking in competence, the greater internal checks are advocated. Each of the control processes discussed in Chapters 6 and 7 addresses some but not all of the expectations of bureaucracy.

Congressional controls are designed primarily to make bureaus more responsive to the public. Legislation, budgets, the legislative veto, and informal contacts attempt to persuade bureaucrats that they must respond to the people and to the people's institution, Congress. Of all the congressional controls, only oversight considers competence a goal to be maximized; in many cases of oversight, however, responsiveness to legislative intent is given greater attention than the technical competence of administration.

Presidential controls are also designed to deal with responsiveness rather than competence. Presidential checks are intended to make bureau behavior responsive to the public through the elected office of the president. Budgeting, reorganization, powers of command, leadership, and so forth all attempt to subordinate the bureaucracy to the president's will or to motivate the bureaucracy to pursue that will. Although such reforms as cost–benefit analysis or rationalized budgeting systems are often sold as techniques to improve bureaucratic competence, their actual impact is to increase presidential control. Competence is only a presidential concern when competence prevents responsiveness because public policies are ineffective.

The courts' standards for bureaucracy are in a state of flux. Only a few years ago one could claim that courts were primarily concerned with competence and that they defined competence in terms of procedures. Fairness, impartiality, and consistency were the guidelines the courts used to judge a bureaucracy's competence. Present-day courts have moved directly into areas of responsiveness. Under decisions advocating responsiveness to law or to the Constitution, courts have mandated administrative actions and taken a greater role in the *policy* process of the bureaucracy.

Federalism controls seek both responsiveness and competence. Because state and local governments also face bureaucratic power, they can be a force for responsiveness. State agencies are also sources of policy expertise and therefore can improve bureaucratic competence as well.

Direct citizen action regarding public policies is primarily concerned with responsiveness. Citizens do not refuse to comply with public policy because the policy is not competently made. An incompetent policy may well be ineffective and of little bother to the citizen. The noncompliant citizen is more likely to be motivated by concerns of responsiveness. Noncompliance can be taken as an indicator that policy is unresponsive to the individuals who fail to comply.

The participation and ethics approaches to controlling the bureaucracy have different expectations. The Administrative Platonist and the scientific administrator, while both concerned with responsiveness, feel that the key issue is competence. They are concerned with skills and performance, particularly effectiveness, innovation, and knowledge. Public choice also raises issues of competence with its stress on efficiency in the provision of public services. Given the antigovernment tenor of most public choice writings, however, responsiveness must also be a concern.

The other ethical approaches center firmly on responsiveness. The new public administration and its followers rarely speak of competence as a goal (but see Frederickson, 1996a; Behn, 1998). They reject the goals of economy and efficiency for the broader goal of social equity in administration. Bureaucracy, in a new public administration world, responds to the needs of those excluded from normal political processes. Representative bureaucracy is nothing more than a passive form of the new public administration with the same goals. Finally, the participation model concerns only responsiveness in attempting to make the administrative process as representative of the American people and their interests as possible.

THE PERFORMANCE OF AMERICAN BUREAUCRACY

Since proposed reforms are a function of the reformer's perception of the specific shortcomings of bureaucracy, the biases of the author should be noted. Under most circumstances, the federal bureaucracy is remarkably responsive institution. Universal responsiveness, however, is limited by one important factor. Top-level bureaucrats, similar to successful people in other organizations, believe in what they are doing. Few career administrators in the Environmental Protection Agency are not committed to protecting the environment. Bureaucrats in the Defense Department are committed to strong national defense. They are no different from employees of IBM or Mary Kay Cosmetics in this regard. What is unique about the public service is that, as a result of the electoral process, policy priorities can change radically. In any organization that relies on normative attachments to motivate personnel, changes in policy are bound to create resistance. Imagine the resistance if Mary Kay Cosmetics was taken over by a conglomerate that decided that henceforth all products would only be sold through department stores. The resistance of the EPA to Anne Burford would be mild compared to the resistance of the Mary Kay sales staff.

Despite the commitment of federal bureaucrats to the programs they administer, there is ample evidence that bureaucrats are responsive to policy changes. The Civil Aeronautics Board administered a policy that abolished the board with an attitude that bordered on enthusiasm (Brown, 1987). Regulators in the Occupational Safety and Health Administration made the transition from a by-the-book enforcer of safety rules to an agency emphasizing occupational health issues in the late 1970s (Thompson, 1982a). The Federal Trade Commission responded to at least two major shifts in congressional priorities in the last twenty-five years (Yandle, 1986). Numerous other examples could be cited (see Wood and Waterman, 1994). Resistance occurs in those cases where policy is changed without going through normal political procedures (Pfiffner, 1987a: 62). President Nixon met resistance with his desegregation policy because he wanted less strict enforcement of laws with no effort made to change those laws. President Reagan met resistance in the environmental area because many of the policies of James Watt and Anne Burford were direct reversals of previous policies that had been established by Congress. President Reagan's automobile safety regulators, in contrast, had less resistance from the bureaucracy as policy shifted to be more concerned with the costs of safety.

The danger in the twenty-first century may well be the insistence that bureaucracy be hyper-responsive to all political institutions even though those institutions cannot approach a policy consensus. The demands of hyper-responsiveness have clearly had an adverse effect on bureaucratic competence. "Bureaucrat bashing," the common reaction of presidents to perceived lack of immediate compliance by the bureaucracy, has seriously damaged the prestige of the federal service. Bureaucrat bashing, now often termed "reinventing government," always seems to be accompanied by job freezes and cutbacks in the financial incentives to become or to remain a public servant. Add to that basic distrust as illustrated by random drug tests, and the result is a drop in morale. Bureaucrat bashing by politicians has likely persuaded many bright, young public servants to avoid Washington. Although this is paying dividends in Albany, Austin, and Helena, it has undermined the federal bureaucracy. Our concerns in controlling bureaucracy, therefore, should focus more on cultivating competence in all its dimensions rather than in forcing even greater responsiveness. Accordingly, most of my reforms will seek to provide an environment conducive to greater competence.

....

REDUNDANCY: THE IMPACT OF DUPLICATION

One reason why some individuals advocate greater controls is that each individual control is rarely ever completely effective. What such critics fail to realize, however, is the system of controls affecting bureaucracy has an impact that is greater than the impact of each of the individual controls. Although a system of controls greater than the sum of its parts sounds impossible, the process of creating such a system is relatively simple. Such problems rely on the concept of redundancy.

Political control systems are designed in a redundant manner (Landau, 1969; Heimann, 1993; Bendor, 1995). The U.S. Constitution, for example, contains several redundancies. In the nation's original constitutional framework, any significant policy change required the approval of the president (selected by a group of local elites), the House of Representatives (elected by the voters), the Senate (representing the state legislatures), and the courts (representing older political coalitions through the appointment process). The Founding Fathers designed a system with independent constituencies so that if a group harboring evil intentions was strong enough to seize control of one branch of government, the other branches, because they must agree to policy changes, could prevent rash actions. Although the major institutions of American government are no longer designed to represent the same groups that the Founding Fathers envisioned, the major institutions still operate in sequence so that policy changes can be challenged at a variety of points by other political actors.

If duplication and redundancy are characteristics that provide for political control in government, does not the same principle apply to bureaucracy? Even though the intent of policymakers was not to design such a system, the current controls on bureaucracy form a redundant system. A series of semi-effective checks on bureaucracy combine into a redundant control system that exerts great influence over bureaucracy (Sherwood and Breyer, 1987).

Redundancy means control can be increased simply by adding additional checks on bureaucracy. Assume for the sake of argument that Congress with its myriad checks on bureaucracy were able to eliminate 60 percent of the mistakes that bureaucracy would normally make. While 60 percent is not spectacular, it might be sufficient in combination with other political institutions. If the president and the courts were similarly 60 percent effective, and the institutions overlapped (as they do), then in combination the system could be 93.6 percent effective.[1] If Congress created an ombudsman and the ombudsman were also 60 percent effective, then the percentage for

---

[1] The 93.6 percent figure is reached by the following calculations: Congress by being 60 percent effective is able to prevent 60 percent of the cases of administrative abuse. The president is 60 percent effective for the 40 percent that Congress lets slip through, adding another 24 percent. The courts are 60 percent effective on the 16 percent missed by both other institutions, adding another 9.6 percent, for a total of 93.6. These calculations assume, of course, total overlap. The percentage of effectiveness figures are arbitrary and are used only to illustrate the argument. Given the varied expectations of bureaucracy, calculating such precise figures is impossible.

the entire control system would be 97.4. The addition of a single control mechanism would reduce the amount of abuse, even in a basically responsive system, by more than one-half.

The ability to improve a system of checks by increasing redundancy depends on two crucial assumptions. First, we assume that no institution is so ineffective (or effective) in checking the bureaucracy that its addition actually restricts bureaucratic action more than is beneficial. Excessive restrictions may indeed occur when various political institutions pull the bureaucracy in dramatically different directions. In this way partially effective controls may in combination be detrimental to good policymaking by stressing responsiveness (as most overhead democracy controls do) to the exclusion of competence. Second, we assumed that each institution totally overlapped the others so that one institution's oversights would be caught by another institution. In fact, not only is each political institution capable of preventing certain abuses better than others, but each political institution also defines abuses in different ways. An Environmental Protection Agency responsive to the president may well be one that Congress thinks is abusing its position of power. As a result, redundant control systems should be augmented only with great care; new controls should be added only if they increase performance on some neglected performance criterion or if they eliminate some of the ill effects of current controls. These criteria will be kept in mind in the following proposals for bureaucratic reforms.

STRENGTHENING POLITICAL INSTITUTIONS

Those who seek a responsive, competent, and effective bureaucracy by weakening the power of bureaucracy misperceive the problem. The U.S. government cannot effectively perform its functions and meet the demands of the people without a bureaucracy that has access to political resources and is quasi-autonomous.

A wide variety of research has documented that strong bureaucracies are a prerequisite for effective public policy. An extended analysis of natural resources agencies concludes that those with power (e.g., the Forest Service, the Army Corps of Engineers) are more effective than those without (e.g., the Bureau of Reclamation, the Bureau of Land Management; see Clarke and McCool, 1985). The performance of the federal reserve system has been linked directly to its autonomy (Harrison, 1988). Declines in the performance of the Food and Drug Administration, the Social Security Administration, and the Internal Revenue Service have been linked to major reductions in personnel (Williams, 1990: 26). During the 1980s the Food and Drug Administration was given major new powers to regulate generic drugs and to approve medical devices, increasing workloads by one-third. At the same time personnel were cut from 8,100 to 7,000. At the state level, economic development policies are more likely to work if the implementing bureaucracy has a well-developed capacity (Lowery and Gray, 1990). Similar results have been found for Medicaid policy (Barrilleaux and Miller, 1988) and in treatment of alcoholism (Meier and Johnson, 1990).

The solution is not to weaken bureaucracy via creating job insecurities and continual budget crises but rather to strengthen other political institutions in a manner that they can structure and guide the power of bureaucracy. Only a strong president and a strong Congress that understand the need for and the problem of bureaucratic power can provide an effective counterweight to a powerful bureaucracy. This section proposes several means of reforming these political institutions with the goal of improving bureaucratic performance.

THE PRESIDENT

The key to presidential control over the bureaucracy is holding the president responsible for all bureaucratic actions that take place during his administration. The American people should treat presidential attacks on bureaucratic resistance and inefficiency as confessions of failure. Although contemporary presidents are clearly not responsible for all bureaucratic actions taken, until presidents are held responsible, they will continue to "bash bureaucrats" with little effort at reform.

The president currently has all the tools and resources needed to control the bureaucracy. No student of public policy could observe the Carter and Reagan presidencies and still argue that the president can not influence the bureaucracy (see Wood and Waterman, 1994). President Carter had a significant impact on several areas of the bureaucracy. He began the massive defense buildup that continued under Reagan. Carter had perhaps his greatest impact on regulatory policy in a two-pronged impact. First, during his term many industries that were regulated in terms of prices and other economic restrictions were deregulated. Financial institutions, trucking, railroads, airlines, securities dealers, and energy producers were all significantly deregulated. At the same time health and safety regulation was improved dramatically. OSHA became more rational in its enforcement policy, the CPSC targeted its scarce resources more effectively, and the EPA considered several incentives-based reforms of environmental policy.

President Reagan was even more successful than President Carter in bending the bureaucracy to his will. The focus on the "Star Wars" defense policy and the definition of disarmament in terms of bargaining chips will influence defense policy for many decades. In regulatory policy, health and safety regulation were relaxed so that industries rarely complained with the frequency they did during the 1970s. Both Reagan and Carter influenced the bureaucracy the easiest way possible; they appointed agency heads who shared their political philosophy and supported the policy decisions made by those individuals. Reagan coupled his appointments with vigorous use of his budget powers. So effective was his assertion of control that such gimmicks as reorganization, a rationalized budgeting system, or greater legislative grants of power to the president were not needed.

One mechanism that permitted greater control for President Reagan and may have for President Carter, if he had more time to use it, was the Civil Service Reform Act of 1978. Presidents can transfer recalcitrant civil servants after 120 days, and political appointees can control the rewards given to civil servants by giving them negative performance ratings. If anything the Civil Service Reform Act goes too far. A perceptive observer of the Carter–Reagan transition, James Pfiffner (1988; 1987a) argues that civil servants were generally cooperative with the Reagan transition. In such cases, trusting the career of a civil servant to political appointees with little government experience is an irrational personnel process. The Civil Service Reform Act should be amended so that performance evaluations of civil servants are completed by individuals with sufficient experience in government to know good performance from bad performance. If such protections were established, then the practice of transferring provides all the control a political appointee needs to discipline the occasional problem bureaucrat.

A second reform of presidential control involves the appointment process. Political appointments by the president are the most effective method of changing policy priorities. Yet even in the area of political appointments, less could be more. Low-level patronage appointments (schedule C) play little role in controlling the bureaucracy and could be eliminated. Intermixing careerists with political appointees in the senior executive service no longer makes much sense. The SES should be limited to merit-based appointments, that is, they need not be career civil servants in the federal system, but those not recruited from federal career ranks should be selected solely on merit criteria. By limiting political appointees to the 600 policymaking positions, political control could be enhanced (for an opposite view see Maranto, 1998). Recruiting and coordinating 600 talented appointees is clearly easier than recruiting 3,000.[2]

Presidents should also reevaluate the recent "reinventing government" policies that have reduced federal employment by 400,000 persons. Most changes simply moved the jobs to the private sector rather than actually reducing government commitments. Quite clearly political institutions will have less control over these private organizations than they do over government agencies. The reinventing reforms, as a result, will hinder future efforts at control. In addition to these responsiveness problems, reinventing may also reduce competence since it reduces the overall capacity of government to deal with policy problems.

By structuring the way presidents control bureaucracy, perhaps some of the problems of presidential control can be avoided. Clearly some ways to control the bureaucracy are harmful to effective government. The continual adoption of budget reforms so that budgeting is always in a state of confusion does little to improve government performance. Similarly excessive use of reorganization to the point that agencies spend their time moving rather than implementing policy destroys the confidence of the public in government. Perhaps the most dangerous way to control the bureaucracy that is available to the president who does not favor an agency's goals is to appoint individuals with little political or managerial ability. Control via inept political appointees is doubly dangerous. It results in bad public policy, and it further increases the public's cynicism about government.

---

[2] Over time I have changed my position on patronage appointments. While I still feel the restrictive court cases of the 1980s are incorrect in terms of law and policy, patronage involves more costs than benefits.

CONGRESS

Strengthening Congress is more difficult than strengthening the president because Congress' problems are more motivational than procedural. The expansion of the budget process so that it fills almost the entire congressional year and the rise of the errand boy member of Congress who specializes in casework have effectively destroyed any rational congressional controls over bureaucracy. Even though Congress as a representative institution cannot be expected to control bureaucracy as well as the presidency, a hierarchical institution, several improvements in congressional procedures and emphasis can be suggested. All these reforms have a common theme, that Congress needs to reassert its role as a policymaking institution.

First, Congress needs to continue its efforts to acquire policy information equal to that of the president. The General Accounting Office has developed into a competent program evaluator in addition to its previous role as a financial auditor. More improvements are needed; often bureaucrats relate to one another how they used their superior expertise to fool the GAO. The GAO needs to be given a general authorization to evaluate the effectiveness of all federal programs (based on some reasonable schedule) and report the results of these evaluations to Congress. To implement such a grand goal, the GAO needs to be able to contract out for studies and other needed expertise and to be granted substantial autonomy.

Congress also needs to use its other information sources more effectively. The Congressional Research Service of the Library of Congress provides high-quality information on more general policy problems. The Congressional Budget Office has developed a reputation for the most objective budget and economic analysis in Washington. While the Office of Technology Assessment did not live up to the expectation that it would provide timely policy advice to Congress, abolishing the organization in 1995 was a mistake. Other specialized information units could be attached to committees so that the Education and Labor Committee, for example, might have the staff to do independent evaluations of educational programs.

Second, nothing prevents Congress from focusing on questions of policy and priority more than its current emphasis on casework. Casework is perceived by many as the way to be reelected continually. Giving casework a high priority means that members of Congress and their staffs have less time for other roles, including legislation. Casework also introduces an element of favoritism and bias into administration that bureaucracy was designed to eliminate. Congress needs a way to perform the casework role yet allow members of Congress to focus on other matters.

Congress should establish a congressional ombudsman office to handle all casework. Such an office would differ significantly from a classical ombudsman in that it would have a dual role of facilitator and monitor of abuses. Essentially, members of Congress would still receive individual requests for constituent assistance. These requests would be routed immediately to the ombudsman, who would contact the bureaucracy concerning the problem. The ombudsman would negotiate with the agency to resolve the complaint. If the agency failed to respond in a manner that the ombudsman felt was appropriate, the ombudsman could inform the member of Congress, who could apply additional pressure. After a resolution, the citizen would be informed via a letter sent over the member's signature. In this way, the member could take credit for constituency service yet not be forced to devote scarce resources to the task. The ombudsman would also be responsible for monitoring the type of complaints to determine if patterns exist; and if the patterns suggest abuse, to propose corrective legislation to Congress.

Given the power of the ombudsman and the potential to abuse that power, the ombudsman and its staff must be isolated from temptation. Civil servants employed by the ombudsman must be perceived as above temptation. The ombudsman's personnel must have an intense loyalty to the function they perform, similar to the personnel in the General Accounting Office. To guarantee loyalty and performance, the proposed ombudsman should have a separate career system with entry based on rigorous exams covering administrative law and procedure. The high prestige and separate career system for ombudsmen should be balanced by a ban on accepting employment with any other federal agency after leaving office so that ombudsmen do not make decisions with future careers in mind.

Third, Congress should recognize the futility of the legislative veto in terms of setting policy priorities. The veto encourages broad general grants of authority and reduces Congress to a negative role of nitpicking administrative action. Although such a role might be appropriate in regard to the president, it is inappropriate for relationships with a bureaucracy that looks to Congress for policy guidance. Congress should reassert its legislative role and concentrate on passing specific legislation.

Finally, Congress should assist other actors in controlling bureaucracy by simplifying the federal Freedom of Information Act. Government that operates in secrecy is government that is able to abuse its citizens. If all operations of the federal government except those that require secrecy for defense reasons are open to public view, bureaucrats are less likely to make decisions that benefit a few individuals at the expense of the general public. Specifically placed under this law should be all contacts between regulators and individuals affected by the regulation. Even contacts between agencies such as those between the OMB and the regulatory agencies it oversees should be open to public view.

The purpose of the suggested congressional reforms is to reestablish Congress as an institution as the major determinant of administrative priorities. Congress cannot control the detail of administration nor should it. Congress can make a better contribution to a responsive and competent bureaucracy by focusing on specific policy legislation. Many agencies perceive that Congress is the legitimate forum to resolve political disputes; Congress needs to perform that role.

THE COURTS

Courts of law in the United States will never be an effective check on the abuse of bureaucratic power. Currently the courts are too costly for most Americans. Even if the cost of using the court system could be lowered by legislation or good management, the result would be increased court caseloads, slower court action on review of administrative actions, and the judicialization of more administrative procedures. Administrative agencies are the preferred means of implementing policy because bureaus can operate quickly and uniformly with simple procedures on a wide scale. Court intervention that produces court-like procedures for agencies defeats the purpose of using bureaus to implement public policy.

A more fundamental objection to court control over administrative can be lodged. Courts are essentially undemocratic institutions with few political restrictions on the actions of judges. Although no one can argue with the courts' previous role in protecting civil liberties, court intervention in administrative action is no longer predictable. At one time courts were concerned solely with procedure so that as long as procedures were fair, administrative determinations were acceptable. At the current time, different courts have established widely varying positions on administrative action with little coherence (see Shapiro, 1988; Rosenbloom, 1994). Courts have become the forum of last resort in the regulatory process so that rules almost automatically get appealed to the courts by one or both sides in a controversy. How the public benefits from an Occupational Safety and Health Administration rule being delayed four years pending court appeals is unclear. When the courts perceived their role as protectors of civil rights and civil liberties, such actions had some overall benefit. Without such a role, court delays provide little value.

INTEREST GROUPS

American politics is pressure group politics, but pressure group politics has the normative limitation of unrepresentativeness, thus, preventing all possible viewpoints from influencing public policy. If all interests on a given policy were organized and if government responded to those organized interests, then interest groups would be an effective means to responsive public bureaucracy. The only problem is that all interests are not represented.

Government has played a major role in forming and developing interest groups in all policy areas. The American Farm Bureau developed in the early twentieth century under the auspices of the Department of Agriculture; the National Farmers Union rose to prominence under the depression-era Farm Security Administration (Baldwin, 1968). The National Rifle Association grew to be a powerful lobby as the result of government assistance in the form of surplus weapons, ammunition, and government-sponsored target ranges; assistance that started with the Spanish–American War. After the Wagner Act in 1935, the federal government became an advocate of labor unions.

For a period of time the federal government sponsored the representation of interests that were normally unrepresented. For the Federal Trade Commission, Congress authorized the use of federal funds to pay interveners, individuals who represented interests not otherwise represented in the political process. This emphasis on representation reached its acme in 1976 when both houses of Congress passed legislation to create an Agency for Consumer Advocacy; President Ford vetoed this legislation.

Under pressure from business interests that opposed the representation of consumers, Congress then began restricting such efforts. In 1978 the Agency for Consumer Advocacy was defeated in Congress, marking what many observers call the end of the contemporary era of consumer protection. The Federal Trade Commission has also been prohibited from funding interveners by subsequent legislation.

Government organizations are the most promising means to represent individuals who are unrepresented in the process (Seldon, 1997). Unfortunately, little effort is being made to do so. Congress has greatly restricted agencies' efforts to provide alternative forms of representation. Government sponsorship of procedures that increase the representativeness of the administrative process could be a major improvement in the responsiveness and probably the competence of the administrative process. Such an effort at the federal level, however, is unlikely.

One surprising development in this area is the rise of state governments as advocates for interests that are normally unrepresented. Because many federal programs are implemented by state agencies and because many states have a more progressive tradition than the federal government, state agencies have become proxy advocates for the public in a variety of policy areas (see Gormley, 1983). State agencies may well be among the strongest advocates of otherwise unrepresented interests.

CREATING A BETTER MERIT SYSTEM

The nation's merit personnel processes have a major impact on the competence and responsiveness of the bureaucracy. The merit system was designed as an attempt to maximize the goal of competence and to counter the perceived ill-effects of responsiveness. Evaluated by the standard of competence, the civil service system has made great strides since the Arthur administration (1883), but something is still amiss.

Every year two types of students descend on schools of public administration and public affairs. One group is the freshly scrubbed college graduates seeking the master of public administration degree. These students are young, enthusiastic idealists eager to join government and fight for the public interest. In sharp contrast to the new college graduates are the midcareer people, who have spent ten years or so in a bureau and are returning to school for a master's degree or some training judged essential for their career advancement. The midcareers are pessimistic, disillusioned, and cynical; they listen to their idealistic counterparts, shake their heads, and mutter that the idealists just do not understand.

Ten years before these same cynics were also idealists off to Washington, Albany, Springfield, and Pierre to seek the public interest. They blame their own transition on the merit system, which they denigrate as a demerit system. The cynics have long since lost any belief that the merit entrance exams measure anything remotely related to job performance except for literacy, a bare minimum requirement. Once in the civil service, promotions occur on a more or less regular schedule unless the employee does something disastrous or the employee reaches the agency's upper ranks, where he or she must wait for others to retire or die. The system does not reward merit, according to the cynics, but rather punishes "lack of merit," thus stifling initiative.[3]

A prestigious national commission has characterized the current status of the federal civil service as in a state of crisis (Volcker, 1989). Years of bureaucrat bashing are seen as draining the civil service of its talent. Fully 52 percent of the original senior executive service had retired by 1985 after only six years in the service (Ingraham, 1987: 431). Over 40 percent of presidential management interns, a prestigious fast-track recruiting system, leave the federal government without making a career in the federal service (Newcomer et al., 1989: 374). Lewis (1991: 151) found that federal employees had higher exit rates in 1988–1989 than they did in 1978–1979 for comparable positions. Experienced employees were the most likely to leave. Only 24 percent of federal managers said they would encourage young people to seek a career in the federal service, compared to 66 percent of city managers who would (Schmidt and Posner, 1987: 408). A series of General Accounting Office (1990d; 1990e; 1990f) reports have documented problems of recruitment and retention. Clearly the merit system is in trouble.

REFORM ENTRANCE PROCEDURES AND EDUCATIONAL TRAINING

The goal of public service training and entrance examinations is to train and select the best possible people as civil servants. For the minority of positions, the process of designing job-relevant tests so that the tests measure tasks similar to those performed on the job is relatively easy. In lower level positions and technical fields, tests can be designed that accurately tap ability to perform job tasks.

For management and higher level positions, the reform of entry procedures is more difficult. To counter the cynicism about the relationship between the performance and rewards, all noncompetitive entry procedures should be eliminated. One-half of the current higher civil service originally entered the civil service through noncompetitive entry procedures either because they had specified occupations or because the agency specifically requested them from a list of applicants.[4] Of the 1,600 midcareer (GS9 to GS12) personnel hired by the federal government each year from outside government, fully 80 percent are requests for specific individuals, and the remainder are selected by the "normal" competitive entry process (Pincus, 1976).

If tests could be designed to tap all the needed dimensions for middle and high-level managers, an effective merit system could be created. Although performance-related tests are nonexistent, some skills necessary to be an effective government

---

[3] The midcareers and most upper-level personnel do not feel that the bureaucratic superstars are not rewarded. Truly exceptional people are able to make the system work for them if they are not overly eccentric. The problem lies with the remainder of the civil service, the bright, competent but not exceptional civil servants whose contributions are not singled out either because the less competent receive the same rewards or because they are denied rewards granted to more skillful organizational politicians.

[4] Lawyers are the most prominent exception to normal entry procedures. Civil service laws prevent the Office of Personnel Management and the agencies from examining, via tests, the qualifications of lawyers. As a result, lawyers are hired by interview and noncompetitive procedures.

manager—reasoning, problem-solving ability, and organizational ability—can be measured. The civil service needs procedures that measure performance on these criteria, but do not discriminate on the basis of irrelevant characteristics such as race, sex, religion, region, or national origin.

The procedure for establishing a performance-based exam is relatively simple. The new exams should contain a series of administrative problems. Staffing organizations, deciding organizational programs given a specified set of objectives, knowledge of government operations, quantitative aids to administration, and the results of organizational theory research are all possible topics. To make sure that this exam is not discriminatory, some core knowledge must be offered by the schools that train potential civil servants. The National Association of Schools of Public Administration and Affairs (NASPAA), an association of schools that train many management-level civil servants, has already set standards for member schools. Although these standards tend to focus on structural questions rather than quality of education, they could be redefined to focus on a common core of administrative knowledge, especially if federal entrance exams were based on that core.

To guarantee that admissions to NASPAA schools are not discriminatory (so that civil service entry procedures become nondiscriminatory), and to provide incentives for schools of public administration to cooperate with the OPM, Congress needs to establish a large public service fellowship program. Through a series of regional competitions based on undergraduate performance, work experience, and other factors, people would be selected to receive a public service fellowship. If the fellowship was usable at any accredited NASPAA institution, the institution would have an incentive to reform the curriculum because a significant number of public service fellowships could solve both tuition and placement problems. To have an impact on the public service, the program would need to be massive, with perhaps 10,000 fellowships a year at an estimated annual cost of $150 million; but $150 million is a small price to pay to see the entry procedures of the civil service rationalized.

A second-order benefit of the fellowship system is that it could be used to recruit individuals from disadvantaged groups. Studies of representative bureaucracy show that where educational backgrounds are relatively equal, minorities compete quite favorably with whites for government jobs (see Chapter 7). Regional competitions plus extensive recruiting could be used to make sure that fellowship recipients were broadly representative of the American people. Since each fellow would receive a similar education, they would have a relatively equal chance to pass the entrance exams. The result should be a more representative civil service; representation, though not often a means to responsive bureaucratic policy, has some other positive benefits. By employing people from similar backgrounds as those receiving services, representative bureaucracy enhances the competence of the bureaucracy. This representation permits more open communications and a better understanding of clientele needs. A representative bureaucracy also enhances competence because discrimination wastes personnel resources by limiting jobs to only one type of person (see Meier, Wrinkle, and Polinard, 1999b).

When the examination system is fully developed, the Office of Personnel Management should offer the results of the exam to state governments so that they can also staff their bureaus with people who pass the national exam. At this point the exam will become much like the proposed national bar exam advocated by the Educational Testing Service.

A critic of uniform exams might challenge this proposed system by arguing that a single exam encourages a uniform curriculum; and thus, a single exam would limit creativity and innovation in public service education. A good counterexample to this criticism is the nation's law schools. Although each state gives a single bar exam and the topics covered on the exam do not vary greatly from state to state, law schools have not become carbon copies of each other. Law schools, while offering a basic core of courses, provide a great number of approaches to legal education. Even within the core courses, the emphasis varies from school to school. Schools of public administration, anxious to guard their reputations for excellence, will probably offer different programs to attract the best public service fellows.

RAISE THE PRESTIGE OF THE CIVIL SERVICE

Given the public's image of the federal bureaucracy, the quality of the civil service is surprisingly high (see Goodsell, 1983). The senior executive service probably has no peer group in the nation. Unfortunately, the public perceives civil servants as lazy, overly secure, and uncreative; as a result, many talented people never consider a career in the public service. Only 25 percent of the Kennedy School of Government's master of public policy graduates, for example, entered the federal service (Karp and Benesch, 1986: 31). To guarantee the best possible people to fill positions in the higher civil service, conscious efforts must be made to raise the prestige of the civil service. Two such efforts are included here.

First, in a nation that accepts almost without question the teachings of Adam Smith, the worth of an individual is often measured, however, inappropriately, by that person's income. Because Congress has established salary ceilings for high-level positions far below those for equivalent positions in the private sector, the lower salaries reflect negatively on the civil servant's image. Congress also has refused to budget sufficient funds for the salaries authorized for upper-level civil servants and has restricted the use of bonuses under the Civil Service Reform Act. As a result a GS14 can be paid approximately the same salary as a member of the senior executive service. Salary rewards for higher civil servants, therefore, are virtually nonexistent. Although the civil service is competitive with private industry at entry levels, it is at a relative disadvantage at the top management level. The official comparison of federal government salaries with those in the private sector revealed that public sector salaries were 25 percent lower (GAO, 1990d: 36). An executive paid less than $75,000 who makes decisions worth millions of dollars would be rare to find in the private sector but very common in Washington. The pay ceiling needs to be lifted so that upper level civil servants receive an income commensurate with their responsibilities. Overall levels of pay should be brought in line with private sector salaries.

Second, the visibility of the civil service should be increased. The popular perception of the civil servant as a pencil pusher or a paper shuffler does not correspond to the actual situation. Every year numerous public servants win prestigious prizes or patent valuable inventions, yet such information is reported only as filler in a few newspapers. Congress needs to upgrade the merit awards given to public servants so that they are accompanied by publicity. Civil servants receiving awards should be given recognition both within and outside Washington so that the image of the civil service is also improved.

INCREASED EXECUTIVE MOBILITY

A major problem with bureaucracy is the narrow perspective harbored by some bureaucrats. The oft-quoted bureaucratic saying, where one stands on an issue depends on where one sits, is too often true (Miles, 1978). Narrow perspectives are a function of both the agency socialization process and the self-selection process whereby civil servants agree to work only for those agencies with goals compatible to their own. To broaden bureaucratic perceptions, a bureaucrat must be exposed to more and different experiences. Past attempts to encourage broader perspectives by increasing executive mobility have met with little success because civil servants are reluctant to leave their bureaus for extended periods of time. This reluctance is related to the belief that during a person's absence other bureaucratic politicians will divide up the missing person's sphere of influence. Even the attempt to create a more mobile senior executive service has failed to increase upper level executive mobility. Similar problems affect state government personnel systems (Sherwood and Breyer, 1987).

Congress should amend the civil service laws so that every federal executive over the rank of GS12 would be required to spend one year out of every seven in another federal agency, a private organization, a university, a state agency, or in an educational program. If these experiences are made mandatory and prerequisites for promotion, the executives have a greater probability of achieving broader bureaucratic perspectives. The program can be used as an exchange program so that for every executive sent to an organization, the organization would send one of its executives to Washington for a year.

An exchange program not only increases executive mobility and breaks down narrow viewpoints, but it also serves as an ideal recruitment mechanism. After watching a state executive for a year, an agency may decide it would benefit by keeping the employee. If lateral entry into an agency at management levels can be increased this way, then agencies will be able to revitalize themselves by constantly adding people with new perspectives.

AWAKENING THE AMERICAN PEOPLE

A country normally has an administrative apparatus no worse than it deserves. In the United States we are fortunate because the federal bureaucracy is much better than we deserve. Combining the value dimensions of responsiveness and competence, the

American federal bureaucracy is clearly the best in the world.[5] No other national bureaucracy has won as many Nobel prizes, and no other bureaucracy responds to as wide an array of interests. The benefits of bureaucracy have come despite numerous obstacles posed by the American people. According to Powell and Parker (1962: 362):

> In a country where the "politician" is a symbol of corruption and dishonesty, if not dishonor, where a large majority of parents, as reported by the Gallup Poll, prefer not to have their children enter the public service, where the bureaucracy is regarded as a legitimate object of ridicule and even revulsion and the term "bureaucrat" is a nasty name, how can one expect high standards of public service and responsibility? The wonder is not that we have not achieved a competent, devoted, and responsible bureaucracy, but that we have come so close to doing so.

Adequate service in the past, however, is no reason to assume the bureaucracy will always be beneficent. To guarantee effective performance, a variety of beliefs and behaviors of the American citizenry must be changed.

INCREASE PUBLIC AWARENESS OF POLITICS AND PARTICIPATION

Chapters 6 and 7 demonstrated a variety of ways to influence politics and control bureaucracy. Many political controls, however, are underused. The American public needs to exercise the options it has to influence government through the ballot box, through interest groups, through noncompliance with public policy, and through other forms of participation. If ordinary people do not control their elected leaders, then eventually bureaucracy will be responsive to an unscrupulous politician; and the worst fears about bureaucracy will be realized.

INCREASE PUBLIC AWARENESS OF BUREAU POLICYMAKING

Much bureaucratic power results from the secrecy of the bureaucratic policymaking process. If the public has no knowledge of decisions being made, then bureaucratic decisions are presented as a *fait accompli*. The media bear a heavy burden to present the actual process of government and its subsystem politics at work. Few college students today know about subsystem politics and its impact on public policy, and even fewer high school graduates have this knowledge. Until the nation's students, and by osmosis the majority of the voting public, learn about the nature of subsystem politics and the role of bureaucracy in them, the public will remain for the most part at the mercy of the bureaucracy.

---

[5] The contention that the U.S. bureaucracy is the best in the world is the author's opinion. Few bureaucracies in other countries surpass the U.S. bureaucracy on the competence dimensions. Those that may (for example, France, England, and Germany) are not nearly as responsive to as wide a variety of interests as the American bureaucracy is.

ELIMINATE THE STEREOTYPES OF BUREAUCRACY

If a large group of reasonably intelligent students is informed about the quantity and quality of expertise in the federal bureaucracy—the discoveries of sonar, dextran, synthetic lubricants, wash-and-wear fabrics, and disease research contributed by these bureaucrats—the student's reaction is one of disbelief and shock. The image of the federal service is that they are lazy, unambitious, and less than competent.

The negative image of the federal service must be changed for two reasons. First, the negative image dissuades some of the best individuals from considering a career in government at a time when government needs them more than ever. Second, the negative image means that bureaucrats are consistently underestimated by the population. Underestimating bureaucrats is dangerous because, when the bureaucracy does exercise power, it comes as a surprise, thus weakening the opposition to bureaucratic influence. Most people then react by denouncing bureaucracy rather than attempting to understand it; understanding it is a prerequisite for changing and controlling bureaucracy.

END PASSIVE ACCEPTANCE OF DELAY

Although the general performance of bureaucracy is positive and humane (Goodsell, 1983), every member of the American public has at one time in his or her life tolerated bureaucratic delays, arbitrariness, and rudeness. Although such behavior may be logical for a bureau that believes most petitioners are bending the truth and believes that a little delay separates the deserving from the undeserving, the behavior is unacceptable from a systemic viewpoint. Bureaus can refuse benefits or assess costs without being rude, arbitrary, and slow. The system must be redesigned so that the public can provide feedback to the bureau chief or to his superior on the type of service they receive. Such feedback can be generated via polls, complaints, or evaluation forms. Bureaucrats with poor public service records should be sent to training seminars to correct the problem. Bureaucrats who show no improvement after the training seminars should be transferred to jobs where contact with the public is not necessary.

LOWER PEOPLE'S EXPECTATIONS OF GOVERNMENT

For people in a nation established on the principle that big government is the quickest way to tyranny, we expect far too much from government today. The social security system is constantly criticized because benefits do not permit one to live adequately despite the fact the system was never designed to provide for full support. When the St. Louis police struck the city in 1975, the city's mayor immediately appealed to the federal government to do something. When Chrysler Corporation (now Daimler-Chrysler) ran heavily into debt as the result of poor marketing and management, the corporation appealed to the federal government to bail it out.

These are not just three isolated examples; government increasingly has been asked to intervene in the lives of its citizens. We should not be surprised that when welcomed to intervene, government does so. Responsiveness is a trait of government as well as of bureaucracy. As more and more tasks are shifted to the public sector in response to people's demands, the scope of government becomes too large. When government operates massive programs too complex for the private sector, it is bound to fail; when it fails, people become cynical about government.

More harmful than cynicism, however, is the effect on individuals who rely on bureaucracy. When a mayor appeals to Washington to solve a city problem or when a business executive appeals to Washington to solve a business problem, it means that these people lack the creativity and skills to handle the problems themselves. As a citizenry we have become so dependent on bureaucracy that we have lost the ability to function without it.

Lessening our expectations of government bureaucracy does not mean that we should transfer those expectations to private section bureaucracy. Microsoft is clearly no better as a *deus ex machina* than is the Social Security Administration. In fact, Microsoft is likely much worse because it is a private organization and does not have the formal mechanisms for public control that the public sector has.

New government policy must persuade citizens to depend on themselves and force other units of government and corporations to do likewise. This policy will permit the federal government to concentrate on the tasks only it can perform and will prevent major drains on federal resources that restrict effective policymaking. The days of laissez-faire, if they ever existed, are truly gone forever; but between the poles of laissez-faire and government by bureaucracy, there is ample room for a government policy that forces people to influence their own futures.

A HOBSON'S CHOICE

This chapter has proposed some sweeping changes in American politics and, at times, has ignored political reality to do so; but realities are alterable conditions. The American people, either directly or through their leaders, must learn to channel bureaucratic discretion in responsive and competent ways. We can harbor no expectations that bureaucracy can become completely responsive and competent overnight. Like most public policy problems, reforming the bureaucracy must be done a piece at a time, a frustrating and trying experience; but there are no other alternatives.

BIBLIOGRAPHY

Aberbach, Joel D. 1990. *Keeping Watchful Eye: The Politics of Congressional Oversight.* Washington, D.C.: The Brookings Institution.

Aberbach, Joel D., and Bert A. Rockman. 1995. "The Political Views of U.S. Senior Federal Executives, 1970–1992." *Journal of Politics* 57 (August): 838–852.

———. 1978. "Bureaucrats and Clientele Groups: A View from Capitol Hill." *American Journal of Political Science* 22 (November): 818–832.

———. 1976. "Clashing Beliefs Within the Executive Branch." *American Political Science Review* 70 (June): 456–468.

Abney, Glenn. 1988. "Lobbying by the Insiders: Parallels of State Agencies and Interest Groups." *Public Administration Review* 48 (September/October): 911–917.

Abney, Glenn, and Thomas P. Lauth. 1985a. "The Line-Item Veto in the States: An Instrument for Fiscal Restraint or an Instrument of Partisanship?" *Public Administration Review* 45 (May/June): 372–377.

———. 1985b. "Interest Group Influence in City Policymaking." *Western Political Quarterly* 38 (March): 148–161.

———. 1982a. "Councilmanic Intervention in Municipal Administration." *Administration and Society* 13 (February): 434–456.

———. 1982b. "Influence of the Chief Executive on City Line Agencies." *Public Administration Review* 42 (March/April): 135–143.

Abramowitz, Michael. 1991. "A Veterans Hospital's Critical Condition." *Washington Post National Weekly Edition* (May 27): 37.

Albritton, Robert B., and Robert D. Brown. 1986. "Intergovernmental Impacts on Policy Variations Within States." *Policy Studies Review* 5 (February): 529–535.

Allin, Craig W. 1987. "Park Service v. Forest Service: Exploring the Differences in Wilderness Management." *Policy Studies Review* 7 (Winter): 385–394.

Allison, Graham. 1971. *Essence of Decision.* Boston: Little, Brown.

Almond, Gabriel, and Sidney Verba. 1965. *The Civic Culture.* Boston: Little, Brown.

Anderson, Charles W. 1990. *Pragmatic Liberalism.* Chicago: University of Chicago Press.

Anderson, James E. 1997. *Public Policymaking: An Introduction.* Boston: Houghton Mifflin.

Anderson, James E., David W. Brady, Charles S. Bullock, and Joseph Stewart. 1984. *Public Policy and Politics in America.* Monterey, Calif.: Brooks/Cole.

Anderson, Stanley V. 1968. *Ombudsman for American Government?* Englewood Cliffs, N.J.: Prentice-Hall.

Appleby, Paul H. 1965. "Public Administration and Democracy." In *Public Administration and Democracy,* ed. Roscoe C. Martin, 333–348. Syracuse, N.Y.: Syracuse University Press.

———. 1952. *Morality and Administration in Democratic Government.* Baton Rouge: Louisiana State University Press.

————. 1949. *Policy and Administration.* Tuscaloosa: University of Alabama Press.

Art, Robert J. 1985. "Congress and the Defense Budget: Enhancing Policy Oversight." *Political Science Quarterly* 100 (Summer): 227–247.

Auten, Gerald, Barry Bozeman, and Robert Cline. 1984. "A Sequential Model of Congressional Appropriations." *American Journal of Political Science* 28 (August): 503–523.

Bacharach, Samuel B., and J. Lawrence French. 1981. "Role-Allocation Processes in Public Bureaucracies." *Administration and Society* 12 (February): 399–426.

Bailey, John J., and Robert O'Connor. 1975. "Operationalizing Incrementalism: Measuring the Muddles." *Public Administration Review* 35 (January/February): 60–66.

Bailey, Stephen K. 1966. "Ethics in the Public Service." In *Public Administration,* ed. Robert Golembiewski, Frank Gibson, and Geoffrey Y. Cornog, 22–32. Chicago: Rand-McNally.

Baldwin, Sidney. 1968. *Politics and Poverty.* Chapel Hill: University of North Carolina Press.

Balla, Steven J. 1998. "Administrative Procedures and Political Control of the Bureaucracy." *American Political Science Review* 92 (September): 663–673.

Ban, Carolyn. 1984. "Implementing Civil Service Reform: Structure and Strategy." In *Legislating Bureaucratic Change,* ed. Patricia W. Ingraham and Carolyn Ban, 42–62. Albany: State University of New York Press.

Ban, Carolyn, and Patricia W. Ingraham. 1990. "Short-Timers: Political Appointee Mobility and Its Impact on Political-Career Relations in the Reagan Administration." *Administration and Society* 22 (May): 106–124.

————. 1988. "Retaining Quality Federal Employees: Life After PACE." *Public Administration Review* 48 (May/June): 708–718.

Ban, Carolyn, and Toni Marzotto. 1984. "Delegations of Examining Objectives and Implementation." In *Legislating Bureau-cratic Change,* ed. Patricia W. Ingraham and Carolyn Ban, 148–160. Albany: State University of New York Press.

Bann, Charles, and Jerald Johnson. 1984. "Federal Employee Attitudes Toward Reform." In *Legislating Bureaucratic Change,* ed. Patricia W. Ingraham and Carolyn Ban, 65–86. Albany: State University of New York Press.

Barber, James David. 1972. *The Presidential Character.* Englewood Cliffs, N.J.: Prentice-Hall.

Barber, James A. 1970. *Social Mobility and Voting Behavior.* Chicago: Rand-McNally.

Barrilleaux, Charles J., and Mark E. Miller. 1988. "The Political Economy of State Medicaid Policy." *American Political Science Review* 82 (December): 1089–1107.

Barringer, Felicity. 1981. "Overregulation: Public Finds Agencies Not Guilty." *Washington Post* (November 10), A17.

Barton, Weldon V. 1976. "Coalition Building in the United States House of Representatives." In *Cases in Public Policymaking,* ed. James E. Anderson, 141–162. New York: Praeger.

Baumgartner, Frank R., and Bryan D. Jones. 1993. *Agendas and Instability in American Politics.* Chicago: University of Chicago Press.

Baumgartner, Frank R., and Jack L. Walker. 1988. "Survey Research and Membership in Voluntary Organizations." *American Journal of Political Science* 32 (November): 908–928.

Baumol, J. 1967. "Macroeconomics and Unbalanced Growth: The Anatomy of the Urban Crisis." *American Economic Review* 57 (June): 415–426.

Bawn, Kathleen. 1995. "Political Control Versus Expertise: Congressional Choices about Administrative Procedures." *American Political Science Review* 89 (March): 62–73.

Beck, Nathaniel. 1984. "Domestic Political Sources of American Monetary Policy: 1955–1982." *Journal of Politics* 46 (August): 786–817.

Behn, Robert D. 1998. "What Right Do Public Managers Have to Lead." *Public Administration Review* 58 (May/June): 209–224.

Bell, Robert. 1985. "Professional Values and Organizational Decision Making." *Administration and Society* 17 (May): 21–60.

Bendor, Jonathan. 1995. "A Model of Muddling Through." *American Political Science Review* 89 (December): 819–840.

Bergerson, Frederic A. 1980. *The Army Gets an Air Force*. Baltimore, Md.: Johns Hopkins University Press.

Berkowitz, Edward, and Daniel M. Fox. 1989. "The Politics of Social Security Expansion: Social Security Disability Insurance, 1935–1986." *Journal of Policy History* 1 (Number 3): 233–261.

Berman, David R., and Lawrence L. Martin. 1988. "State-Local Relations: An Examination of Local Discretion." *Public Administration Review* 48 (March/April): 637–641.

Bernstein, Barton J. 1980. "The Cuban Missile Crisis: Trading Jupiters in Turkey?" *Political Science Quarterly* 95 (Spring): 97–125.

Bernstein, Marver. 1955. *Regulating Business Through Independent Commission*. Princeton, N.J.: Princeton University Press.

Berry, Jeffrey M. 1977. *Lobbying for the People*. Princeton, N.J.: Princeton University Press.

Berry, William D. 1984. "An Alternative to the Capture Theory of Regulation." *American Journal of Political Science* 28 (August): 524–558.

———. 1979. "Utility Regulation in the States: The Policy Effects of Professionalism and Salience to the Consumer." *American Journal of Political Science* 23 (May): 263–277.

Berry, William D., and David Lowery. 1990. "An Alternative Approach to Understanding Budgetary Tradeoffs." *American Journal of Political Science* 34 (August): 671–705.

———. 1987. "Explaining the Size of the Public Sector: Responsiveness and Excessive Government Interpretations." *Journal of Politics* 49 (May): 401–440.

———. 1984a. "The Growing Cost of Government: A Test of Two Explanations." *Social Science Quarterly* 65 (September): 735–749.

———. 1984b. "The Measurement of Government Size: Implications for the Study of Government Growth." *Journal of Politics* 46 (November): 1193–1206.

Berry, Wendell. 1977. *The Unsettling of America*. San Francisco: Sierra Club Books.

Best, Samuel, Paul Teske, and Michael Mintrom. 1997. "Terminating the Oldest Living Regulator." *International Journal of Public Administration* 20 (Number 12): 2067–2096.

Bibby, John F. 1966. "Committee Characteristics and Legislative Oversight of Administration." *Midwest Journal of Political Science* 10 (February): 78–98.

Bickers, Kenneth N., and Robert M. Stein. 1994. "A Portfolio Theory of Policy Subsystems." *Administration and Society* 26(2): 158–184.

Binion, Gayle. 1979. "The Implementation of Title 5 of the Voting Rights Act." *Western Political Quarterly* 32 (June): 154–173.

Binkin, Martin. 1976. *Where Does the Marine Corps Go From Here?* Washington, D.C.: The Brookings Institution.

Blau, Peter M., and Marshall W. Meyer. 1971. *Bureaucracy in Modern Society*. New York: Random House.

Boling, T. Edwin, and John Dempsey. 1981. "Ethical Dilemmas in Government." *Public Personnel Management* 10 (1): 11–19.

Bolotin, Fredric N., and David L. Cingranelli. 1983. "Equity and Urban Policy: The Underclass Hypothesis Revisited." *Journal of Politics* 45 (February): 209–219.

Boodman, Sandra G. 1988. "Chick Koop, Unpredictable Surgeon General." *Washington Post National Weekly Edition* (January 11): 6–7.

Bowman, James S. 1990. "Ethics in Government: A National Survey of Public Administrators." *Public Administration Review* 50 (May/June): 345–353.

———. 1983. "Whistle Blowing: Literature and Resource Materials." *Public Administration Review* 43 (May/June): 271–276.

———. 1981. "The Management of Ethics: Codes of Conduct in Organizations." *Public Personnel Management* 10 (1): 59–66.

Boyd, Kathy J. 1991. "Regulatory Review as Constituent Policy." Paper presented at the annual meeting of the Southwest Political Science Association, San Antonio.

Boyer, Brian D. 1973. *Cities Destroyed for Cash.* Chicago: Follett Publishing Co.

Boyle, John, and David Jacobs. 1982. "Intracity Distribution of Services." *American Political Science Review* 76 (June): 371–379.

Boyne, George A. 1998. "Bureaucratic Theory Meets Reality: Public Choice and Service Contracting in U.S. Local Government." *Public Administration Review* 58 (November/December): 474–484.

Bozeman, Barry. 1977. "The Effective of Economic and Partisan Change on Federal Appropriations." *Western Political Quarterly* 30 (March): 112–124.

Bozeman, Barry, and Gordon Kingsley. 1998. "Risk Culture in Public and Private Organizations." *Public Administration Review* 58 (March/April): 109–118.

Bozeman, Barry, and Jeffrey D. Straussman. 1982. "Shrinking Budgets and the Shrinkage of Budget Theory." *Public Administration Review* 42 (November/December): 509–515.

Bradley, John P. 1968. "Party Platforms and Party Performances Concerning Social Security." *Polity* 1 (Spring): 335–358.

Bradley, John P. 1980. "Shaping Administrative Policy with the Aid of Congressional Oversight." *Western Political Quarterly* 33 (December): 492–501.

Breyer, Stephen. 1982. *Regulation and Its Reform.* Cambridge, Mass.: Harvard University Press.

Broder, David S. 1990. "Getting the Government Its Due." *Washington Post National Weekly Edition* (February 26): 4.

Bromiley, Philip, and John P. Crecine. 1980. "Budget Development in OMB: Aggregate Influences of Problem and Information Environment." *Journal of Politics* 42 (November):1031–1064.

Brown, Anthony E. 1987. *The Politics of Airline Deregulation.* Knoxville: University of Tennessee Press.

Brown, Clyde. 1989. "Explanations of Interest Group Membership over Time: The Farm Bureau in Five Midwestern States." *American Politics Quarterly* 17 (January): 32–53.

Browne, William P. 1990. "Organized Interests and Their Issue Niches." *Journal of Politics* 52 (May): 477–509.

———. 1988. *Private Interests, Public Policy, and American Agriculture.* Lawrence: University Press of Kansas.

———. 1985. "Variations in the Behavior and Style of State Lobbyists and Interest Groups." *Journal of Politics* 47 (May): 450–469.

———. 1977. "Organizational Maintenance: The Internal Operation of Interest Groups." *Public Administration Review* 37 (January/February): 48–57.

Brudney, Jeffrey L. 1990a. *Fostering Volunteer Programs in the Public Sector.* San Francisco: Jossey-Bass.

———. 1990b. "The Availability of Volunteers: Implications for Local Governments." *Administration and Society* 21 (February): 413–424.

Brudney, Jeffrey L., and F. Ted Hebert. 1987. "State Agencies and Their Environments: Examining the Influence of Important External Actors." *Journal of Politics* 47 (February): 186–206.

Bryner, Gary C. 1987. *Bureaucratic Discretion: Law and Policy in Federal Regulatory Agencies.* New York: Pergamon Press.

Buchanan, James M., and Gordon Tullock. 1977. "The Expanding Public Sector: Wagner Squared." *Public Choice* 3 (Fall): 147–151.

Budge, Ian, and Richard I. Hofferbert. 1990. "Mandates and Policy Outputs: U.S. Party Platforms and Federal Expenditures." *American Political Science Review* 84 (March): 111–131.

Bullock, Charles S., and Charles M. Lamb. 1984. *Implementation Civil Rights Policy.* Monterey, Calif.: Brooks/Cole.

Bullock, Charles S., and Joseph Stewart. 1984. "New Programs in 'Old' Agencies: Lessons in Organizational Change from the Office for Civil Rights." *Administration and Society* 15 (February): 387–412.

Burke, John P. 1989. "Reconciling Public Administration and Democracy: The Role of the Responsible Administrator." *Public Administration Review* 49 (March/April): 180–185.

———. 1986. *Bureaucratic Responsibility.* Baltimore, Md.: Johns Hopkins University Press.

Caiden, Gerald W. 1983. *Organizational Handbook of the Ombudsman.* Westport, Conn.: Greenwood Press.

———. 1981. "Ethics in the Public Service: Codification Misses the Real Target." *Public Personnel Management* 10(1): 146–152.

Caiden, Naomi. 1984. "The New Rules of the Federal Budget Game." *Public Administration Review* 44 (March/April): 109–118.

———. 1981. "Dilemmas of Budget Reform." *Policy Studies Review* 9 (4): 1215–1227.

Cain, Bruce E., John A. Ferejohn, and Morris P. Fiorina. 1984. "The Constituency Service Basis of the Personal Vote for U.S. Representatives and British Members of Parliament." *American Political Science Review* 78 (March): 110–125.

Caldwell, Lynton. 1982. *Science and the National Environmental Policy Act.* Tuscaloosa: University of Alabama Press.

Canon, Bradley, and Micheal Giles. 1972. "Recurring Litigants: Federal Agencies Before the Supreme Court." *Western Political Quarterly* 25 (June): 183–191.

Carmines, Edward G., and James A. Stimson. 1980. "Two Faces of Issue Voting." *American Political Science Review* 74 (March): 78–91.

Carpenter, Daniel P. 1996. "Adaptive Signal Processing, Hierarchy, and Budget Control in Federal Agencies." *American Political Science Review* 90 (June): 283–302.

Cater, Douglas. 1964. *Power in Washington.* New York: Random House.

Cayer, N. Joseph, and Lee Sigelman. 1980. "Minorities and Women in State and Local Government: 1973–1975." *Public Administration Review* 40 (September–October): 443–450.

Chaney, Carole Kennedy, and Grace Hall Saltstein. 1998. "Democratic Control and Bureaucratic Responsiveness: The Police and Domestic Violence." *American Journal of Political Science* 42 (July): 745–769.

Checkoway, Barry, Thomas W. O'Rourke, and David Bull. 1984. "Correlates of Consumer Participation in Health Planning Agencies." *Policy Studies Review* 3 (February): 296–310.

Chubb, John, and Terry Moe. 1990. *Politics, Markets and America's Schools.* Washington, D.C.: The Brookings Institution.

Cingranelli, David L. 1981. "Race, Politics, and Elites: Testing Alternative Models of Municipal Service Distribution." *American Journal of Political Science* 25 (November): 664–692.

Clarke, Jeanne Nienaber, and Daniel McCool. 1985. *Staking Out the Terrain: Power Differentials Among National Resource Management Agencies.* Albany: State University of New York Press.

Clarkson, Kenneth W., and Timothy J. Muris. 1981. *The Federal Trade Commission Since 1970.* Cambridge, England: Cambridge University Press.

Clary, Bruce B., and Michael E. Kraft. 1988. "Impact Assessment and Policy Failure: The Nuclear Waste Policy Act of 1982." *Policy Studies Review* 8 (Autumn): 105–115.

Claybrook, Joan. 1984. *Retreat From Safety.* New York: Pantheon.

Clinton, Robert L. 1989. "Federal Court Involvement in the Application of Surface Mining Law." *Policy Studies Review* 9 (Autumn); 88–97.

Cohen, Jeffrey E. 1991. "The Policy Implications of Bureaucratic Reorganizations." Paper presented at the annual meeting of the Midwest Political Science Association, Chicago.

———. 1986. "The Dynamics of the 'Revolving Door' on the FCC." *American Journal of Political Science* 30 (November): 689–708.

———. 1985a. "Congressional Oversight: A Test of Two Theories." Paper presented at the annual meeting of the American Political Science Association, New Orleans.

————. 1985b. "Presidential Control of Independent Regulatory Commissions Through Appointment: The Case of the FCC." *Administration and Society* 17 (May): 61–70.

Colarulli, Guy C., and Bruce F. Berg. 1983. "Federal Legislation and Interest Group Formation." *Policy Studies Review* 3 (August): 13–20.

Cole, Richard L., and David A. Caputo. 1984. "The Public Hearing as an Effective Citizen Participation Mechanism." *American Political Science Review* 78 (June): 404–417.

————. 1979. "Presidential Control of the Senior Civil Service: Assessing the Strategies of the Nixon Years." *American Political Science Review* 73 (June): 391–413.

Conant, James K. 1988. "In the Shadow of Wilson and Brownlow: Executive Branch Reorganization in the States, 1965–1987." *Public Administration Review* 48 (September/October): 892–902.

Congressional Budgeting Office. 1981. *Supplemental Appropriations in the 1970s.* Washington, D.C.: Congressional Budgeting Office.

Conover, Pamela Johnston, Stanley Feldman, and Kathleen Knight. 1986. "Judging Inflation and Unemployment: The Origins of Retrospective Evaluations." *Journal of Politics* 48 (August): 565–588.

Cook, Constance Ewing. 1984. "Participation in Public Interest Groups: Membership Motivations." *American Politics Quarterly* 12 (October): 409–430.

Cooper, Ann. 1985. "Fowler's FCC Learns Some Hard Lessons About What It Means to Be Independent." *National Journal* 17 (April 6): 732–736.

Cooper, Joseph. 1986. "Congress and the Legislative Veto: Choices Since the Chadha Decision." In *Making Government Work,* ed. Robert S. Hunter, Wayne L. Berman, and John F. Kennedy Jr., 31–67. Boulder, Colo.: Westview Press.

————. 1985. "The Legislative Veto in the 1980s." In *Congress Reconsidered.*, ed. Larry C. Dodd and Bruce I. Oppenheimer, 364–389. 3d ed. Washington, D.C.: Congressional Quarterly Press.

————. 1956. "The Legislative Veto." *Public Policy* 7: 128–174.

Cooper, Joseph, and William F. West. 1988. "Presidential Power and Republican Government: The Theory and Practice of OMB Review of Agency Rules." *Journal of Politics* 50 (November): 864–895.

Cooper, Philip J. 1997. "Power Tools for an Effective and Responsible Presidency." *Administration & Society* 29 (November): 529–556.

————. 1988. *Public Law and Public Administration.* 2d ed. Englewood Cliffs, N.J.: Prentice-Hall.

————. 1986a. "By Order of the President: Administration by Executive Order and Proclamation." *Administration and Society* 18 (August): 233–262.

————. 1986b. "The Supreme Court, the First Amendment, and Freedom of Information." *Public Administration Review* 46 (November/December): 622–628.

————. 1984. "The Supreme Court on Governmental Immunity." *Administration and Society* 16 (November): 259–289.

Cooper, Terry L. 1987. "Hierarchy, Virtue, and the Practice of Public Administration: A Perspective for Normative Ethics." *Public Administration Review* 47 (July/August): 320–328.

Copeland, Gary W. 1985. "The Opening of Conference Committees: A New Arena for Interest Groups." Paper presented at the annual meeting of the American Political Science Association, New Orleans.

Copeland, Gary W., and Kenneth J. Meier. 1987. "Gaining Ground: The Impact of Medicaid and WIC on Infant Mortality." *American Politics Quarterly* 15 (April): 254–273.

Costle, Douglas. 1980. "In Defense of the Public Service." *PA Times* (May 1), 3ff.

Cox, Edward, Robert Fellmuth, and John Shultz. 1969. *The "Nader Report" on the Federal Trade Commission.* New York: Barron.

Craig, Barbara Hinkson. 1983. *The Legislative Veto: Congressional Control of Regulation.* Boulder, Colo.: Westview Press.

Crenshaw, Albert, and Willie Schatz. 1990.

"At the IRS, a Long Form of Problems." *Washington Post National Weekly Edition* (April 16): 20–1.

Crewson, Philip E. 1997. "Public-Service Motivation: Building Emprical Evidence of Incidence and Effect." *Journal of Public Administration Research and Theory* 7 (October): 499–518.

———. 1995. "A Comparative Analysis of Public and Private Sector Entrant Quality." *American Journal of Political Science* 39 (August): 628–639.

Crompton, John L. 1983. "Recreation Vouchers: A Case Study in Administrative Innovation and Citizen Participation." *Public Administration Review* 43 (November/December): 537–546.

Crotty, Patricia McGee. 1988. "Assessing the Role of Federal Administrative Regions: An Exploratory Analysis." *Public Administration Review* 48 (March/April): 642–648.

Crowley, Donald W. 1987. "Judicial Review of Administrative Agencies: Does Type of Agency Matter?" *Western Political Quarterly* 40 (June): 265–284.

Culhane, Paul. 1981. *Public Lands Policy.* Baltimore, Md.: Johns Hopkins University Press.

Daley, Dennis. 1984. "Controlling the Bureaucracy Among the States." *Administration and Society* 15 (February): 475–488.

David, Paul T. 1971. "Party Platforms as National Plans." *Public Administration Review* 31 (May/June): 303–315.

Davies, J. Clarence, and Barbara S. Davies. 1975. *The Politics of Pollution.* Indianapolis, Ind.: Bobbs-Merrill.

Davis, Charles, and Sandra Davis. 1988. "Analyzing Change in Public Lands Policymaking: From Subsystems to Advocacy Coalitions." *Policy Studies Journal* 17 (Fall): 3–24.

Davis, Kenneth C. 1971. *Discretionary Justice.* Urbana: University of Illinois Press.

———. 1965. *Administrative Law.* St. Paul, Minn.: West Publishing.

Davis, Otto, M. A. H. Dempster, and Aaron Wildavsky. 1966. "A Theory of the Budget Process." *American Political Science Review* 60 (September): 530–546.

deHaven-Smith, Lance. 1983. "Evidence on the Minimal Management Principle of Program Design." *Journal of Politics* 45 (August): 711–730.

deHaven-Smith, Lance, and Carl E. Van Horn. 1984. "Subgovernment Conflict in Public Policy." *Policy Studies Journal* 12 (June): 627–642.

Del Sesto, Steven L. 1980. "Nuclear Reactor Safety and the Role of the Congressman." *Journal of Politics* 42 (February): 227–242.

Demkovich, Linda E. 1982. "Team Player Schweiker May Be Paying High Price for His Loyalty to Reagan." *National Journal* 14 (May 15): 848–853.

DeMuth, Christopher C. 1984. "A Strategy for Regulatory Reform." *Regulation* 8 (March/April): 25–29.

Denhardt, Kathryn G. 1989. "The Management of Ideals: A Political Perspective on Ethics." *Public Administration Review* 49 (March/April): 187–192.

———. 1988. *The Ethics of Public Service.* Westport, Conn.: Greenwood Press.

Derthick, Martha, and Paul J. Quirk. 1985. *The Politics of Deregulation.* Washington, D.C.: The Brookings Institution.

Devine, Donald J. 1981. "Public Administration and the Reagan Era." Speech presented to the American Society for Public Administration (April 13), Detroit.

Diamond, Martin, Winston Fisk, and Herbert Garfinkel. 1970. *The Democratic Republic.* Chicago: Rand-McNally.

DiIulio, John D., Jr. 1994. "Principled Agents: The Cultural Bases of Behavior in a Federal Government Bureaucracy." *Journal of Public Administration Research and Theory* 4 (3): 277–318.

Dometrius, Nelson C., and Lee Sigelman. 1984. "Assessing Progress Toward Affirmative Action Goals in State and Local Government." *Public Administration Review* 44 (May/June): 241–246.

Downing, Paul B. 1983. "Bargaining in Pollution Control." *Policy Studies Journal* 11 (June): 577–586.

Downing, Paul B., and James N. Kimball. 1982. "Enforcing Pollution Control Laws in the U.S." *Policy Studies Journal* 11 (September): 55–66.

Downs, Anthony. 1967. *Inside Bureaucracy.* Boston: Little, Brown.

———. 1957. *An Economic Theory of Democracy.* New York: Harper & Row.

Duerst-Lahti, Georgia. 1989. "The Government's Role in Building the Women's Movement." *Political Science Quarterly* 104 (Summer): 249–268.

Durant, Robert F. 1993. *The Administrative Presidency Revisited.* Albany: State University of New York Press.

———. 1987. "Toward Assessing the Administrative Presidency: Public Lands, the BLM, and the Reagan Administration." *Public Administration Review* 47 (March/April): 180–189.

Durant, Robert F., Jerome S. Legge Jr., and Antony Moussios. 1998. "People, Profits and Service Delivery: Lessons from the Privatization of British Telcom." *American Journal of Political Science* 42 (January): 117–140.

Durant, Robert F., and William West. 1998. "Merit, Management and Federal Employment: An Analysis of U.S. Merit Systems Protection Board Decisions, FY 1988-FY 1997." Typescript, Texas A&M University.

Dye, Thomas R. 1988. "Explaining Government Contraction: A Demand-Side Model for Education in the States." *Western Political Quarterly* 41 (September): 779–790.

Easton, David. 1965. *A Systems Analysis of Political Life.* New York: Wiley.

Edwards, J. Terry, John Nalbandian, and Kenneth R. Wedel. 1981. "Individual Values and Professional Education." *Administration and Society* 13 (August): 123–133.

Eisinger, Peter K. 1982. "Black Employment in Municipal Jobs." *American Political Science Review* 76 (June): 380–392.

Eisner, Marc Allen. 1991. *Antitrust and the Triumph of Economics.* Chapel Hill: University of North Carolina Press.

Eisner, Marc Allen, and Kenneth J. Meier. 1990. "Presidential Control versus Bureaucratic Power: Explaining the Reagan Revolution in Antitrust." *American Journal of Political Science* 34 (February): 269–287.

Elling, Richard C. 1980. "State Legislative Casework and State Administrative Behavior." *Administration and Society* 12 (November): 327–357.

Ethridge, Marcus E. 1984. "Consequences of Legislative Review of Agency Regulations in Three U.S. States." *Legislative Studies Quarterly* 9 (February): 161–178.

———. 1981. "Legislative-Administrative Interaction as 'Intrusive Access.'" *Journal of Politics* 43 (May): 473–492.

Etzioni-Halevy, Eva. 1983. *Bureaucracy and Democracy: A Political Dilemma.* Boston: Routledge & Kegan Paul.

Evans, James W. 1981. "The New Administrative Ethic?" *Public Personnel Management* 10 (1): 132–139.

Farnham, Timothy J. 1995. "Forest Service Budget Requests and Appropriations: What Do Analyses of Trends Reveal?" *Policy Studies Journal* 23 (2): 253–267.

Feinberg, Lotte E. 1986. "Managing the Freedom of Information Act and Federal Information Policy." *Public Administration Review* 46 (November/December): 615–621.

Fenno, Richard. 1966. *The Power of the Purse.* Boston: Little, Brown.

Ferris, James M. 1984. "Coprovision: Citizen Time and Money Donations in Public Service Provision." *Public Administration Review* 44 (July/August): 324–333.

Finer, Herman. 1941. "Administrative Responsibility in Democratic Government." *Public Administration Review* 1 (Summer): 335–350.

Fiorina, Morris P. 1981. *Retrospective Voting in American National Elections.* New Haven, Conn.: Yale University Press.

Fisher, Louis. 1987. "The Administrative World of Chadha and Bowsher." *Public Administration Review* 47 (May/June): 213–220.

———. 1985. "Judicial Misjudgments About the Lawmaking Process: the Legislative Veto Case." *Public Administration Review* 45 (Special Issue): 705–711.

———. 1984. "One Year after INS v. Chadha: Congressional and Judicial Developments." Washington, D.C.: Congressional Research Service.

———. 1975. *Presidential Spending Power.* Princeton, N.J.: Princeton University Press.

Fleischmann, Arnold. 1989. "Politics, Administration, and Local Land-Use Regulation: Analyzing Zoning as Policy Process." *Public Administration Review* 49 (July/August): 337–344.

Fleischmann, Arnold, and Carol A. Pierannunzi. 1990. "Citizens, Development Interests, and Local Land-Use Regulation." *Journal of Politics* 52 (August): 838–853.

Fox, Charles J., and Clarke E. Cochran. 1990. "Discretion Advocacy in Public Administration Theory: Toward a Platonic Guardian Class?" *Administration and Society* 22 (August): 249–271.

Fox, Douglas. 1974. *The Politics of City and State Bureaucracy.* Pacific Palisades, Calif.: Goodyear.

———. 1971. "Congress and the Military Service Budgets in the Post War Period." *Midwest Journal of Political Science* 15 (May): 382–393.

Franke, James L., and Douglas Dobson. 1985. "Interest Groups: The Problem of Representation." *Western Political Quarterly* 38 (June): 224–237.

Frederickson, H. George. 1996a. *The Spirit of Public Administration.* San Francisco: Jossey-Bass.

———. 1996b. "Comparing the Reinventing Government Movement with the New Public Administration." *Public Administration Review* 56 (May/June): 263–270.

———. 1990. "Public Administration and Social Equity." *Public Administration Review* 50 (March/April): 228–237.

Freeman, J. Leiper. 1965. *The Political Process.* New York: Random House.

Fried, Robert. 1976. *Performance in American Bureaucracy.* Boston: Little, Brown.

Friedrich, Carl J. 1940. "Public Policy and the Nature of Administrative Responsibility." *Public Policy* 1: 3–24.

Fuchs, Edward Paul. 1988. *Presidents, Management and Regulation.* Englewood Cliffs, N.J.: Prentice-Hall.

Garand, James C. 1988. "Explaining Government Growth in the U.S. States." *American Political Science Review* 82 (September): 837–849.

Garand, James C., Catherine T. Parkhurst, and Rusanne Jourdan Seoud. 1991a. "Bureaucrats, Policy Attitudes, and Political Behavior: Extensions of the Bureau Voting Model of Government Growth." *Journal of Public Administration Research and Theory* 1 (April): 177–212.

Garand, James C., Catherine T. Parkhurst, and Rusanne Jourdan Seoud. 1991b. "Testing the Bureau Voting Model: A Research Note on Federal and State-Local Employees." *Journal of Public Administration Research and Theory* 1 (April): 229–233.

Gatlin, Douglas S., Micheal W. Giles, and Everett F. Cataldo. 1978. "Policy Support with a Target Group: The Case of School Desegregation." *American Political Science Review* 72 (September): 985–995.

General Accounting Office. 1990a. *National Health Service Corps: Program Unable to Meet Need for Physicians in Underserved Areas.* GAO/HRD-90–128. Washington, D.C.: General Accounting Office.

———. 1990b. *Drug Testing.* GAO/GGD-90–56FS. Washington, D.C.: General Accounting Office.

———. 1990c. *Performance Management: How Well is the Government Dealing with Poor Performers?.* GAO/GGD-91–7. Washington, D.C.: General Accounting Office.

———. 1990d. *The Public Service: Issues Affecting Its Quality, Effectiveness, Integrity, and Stewardship.* GAO/GGD-90–103. Washington, D.C.: General Accounting Office.

———. 1990e. *Federal Recruiting and Hiring.* GAO/GGD-90–105. Washington, D.C.: General Accounting Office.

———. 1990f. *Recruitment and Retention: Inadequate Federal Pay Cited as Primary Problem by Agency Officials.* GAO/GGD-90–117. Washington, D.C.: General Accounting Office.

———. 1989. *Accessibility, Timeliness, and Accuracy of IRS' Telephone Assistance Pro-

gram. (GAO/GGD-89–90) Washington, D.C.: General Accounting Office.

Gilbert, Charles S. 1959. "The Framework of Administrative Responsibility." *Journal of Politics* 21 (August): 373–407.

Giles, Micheal W., and Marilyn K. Dantico. 1982. "Political Participation and Neighborhood Social Context Revisited." *American Journal of Political Science* 26 (February): 144–150.

Giles, Micheal W., and Douglas S. Gatlin. 1980. "Mass-Level Compliance with Public Policy: The Case of School Desegregation." *Journal of Politics* 42 (August): 722–747.

Ginsberg, Benjamin, and John Green. 1979. "The Best Congress Money Can Buy." Paper presented at the annual meeting of the American Political Science Association, Washington, D.C.

Goetze, David. 1981. "The Shaping of Environmental Attitudes in Air Pollution Control Agencies." *Public Administration Review* 41 (July/August): 423–430.

Goggin, Malcolm, Ann O'M. Bowman, James P. Lester, and Laurence J. O'Toole Jr. 1990. *Implementation Theory and Practice.* Glenview, Ill.: Scott, Foresman/Little, Brown.

Golden, Marissa Martino. 1998. "Interest Groups in the Rule-Making Process: Who Participates? Who Gets Heard?" *Journal of Public Administration Research and Theory* 8 (April): 245–270.

Goldoff, Anna C. 1984. "The Federal Communications Commission's 'Fairness' Doctrine." *Administration and Society* 15 (February): 413–438.

Golembiewski, Robert T. 1977. "A Critique of 'Democratic Administration' and Its Supporting Ideation." *American Political Science Review* 71 (December): 1488–1507.

Goodnow, Frank J. 1900. *Politics and Administration.* New York: Macmillan.

Goodsell, Charles T. 1984. "The Grace Commission: Seeking Efficiency for the Whole People?" *Public Administration Review* 44 (May/June): 196–204.

———. 1981. "Looking Once Again at Human Service Bureaucracy." *Journal of Politics* 43 (August): 763–778.

———. 1983. *The Case for Bureaucracy.* Chatham, N.J.: Chatham House.

Gordon, Michael R. 1985. "Data on Production Inefficiencies May Spur New Debate on Defense Contracting." *National Journal* 17 (June 1): 1283–1286.

———. 1984. "Help Wanted in Weapons Testing Office But Pentagon Slow to Fill Top Job." *National Journal* 16 (October 13): 1914–1917.

Gormley, William T. 1983. *The Politics of Public Utility Regulation.* Pittsburgh, Pa.: University of Pittsburgh Press.

Gosling, James J. 1986. "Wisconsin Item-Veto Lessons." *Public Administration Review* 46 (July/August): 292–300.

Grady, Dennis O. 1989. "Economic Development and Administrative Power Theory: A Comparative Analysis of State Development Agencies." *Policy Studies Review* 8 (Winter): 322–339.

Gray, Virginia, and David Lowery. 1996. *The Population Ecology of Interest Representation.* Ann Arbor: University of Michigan Press.

Greer, Douglas F. 1981. *Business, Government and Society.* New York: Macmillan.

Gueron, Judith M., and Richard P. Nathan. 1985. "The MDRC Work/Welfare Project." *Policy Studies Review* 4 (February): 417–432.

Guess, George M. 1984. "Profitability Guardians and Service Advocates: The Evolution of Amtrak Training." *Public Administration Review* 44 (September/October): 384–392.

Gunn, Elizabeth M. 1981. "Ethics and the Public Service." *Public Personnel Management* 10 (1): 172–199.

Guy, Mary Ellen. 1989. "Minnowbrook II: Conclusions." *Public Administration Review* 49 (March/April): 219–220.

Gwyn, William F. 1973. "The British PCA: Ombudsman or Ombudsmouse?" *Journal of Politics* 24 (February): 45–69.

———. 1968. "Transferring the Ombudsman." In *Ombudsman for American Government?* ed. Stanley V. Anderson, 236–259. Englewood Cliffs, NJ: Prentice-Hall.

Haas, Lawrence J. 1987. "After Stockman." *National Journal* (June 27): 1690.

Hadwiger, Don F. 1982. *The Politics of Agricultural Research.* Lincoln: University of Nebraska Press.

Haider-Markel, Donald P. 1998. "The Politics of Social Regulatory Policy: State and Federal Hate Crime Policy and Implementation Effort." *Political Research Quarterly* 51 (March): 69–88.

Hale, George E. 1979. "Federal Courts and the State Budgetary Process." *Administration and Society* 11 (November): 357–368.

Hale, George E., and Marian Lief Palley. 1979. "Federal Grants to the States: Who Governs?" *Administration and Society* 11 (May): 3–26.

Hall, Grace, and Alan Saltzstein. 1977. "Equal Employment Opportunity for Minorities in Municipal Government." *Social Science Quarterly* 57 (March): 864–872.

Hall, Richard H. 1967. "Some Organizational Considerations in the Professional-Organizational Relationship." *Administrative Science Quarterly* 12 (December): 461–478.

Handberg, Roger. 1979. "The Supreme Court and Administrative Agencies: 1965–1978." *Journal of Contemporary Law* 6 (Fall): 161–176.

Hansen, John Mark. 1985. "The Political Economy of Group Membership." *American Political Science Review* 79 (March): 79–96.

Hansen, Wendy L. 1990. "The International Trade Commission and the Politics of Protectionism." *American Political Science Review* 84 (March): 21–43.

Hansen, Wendy L., Renee J. Johnson, and Issac Unah. 1995. "Specialized Courts, Bureaucratic Agencies, and the Politics of U.S. Trade Policy." *American Journal of Political Science* 39 (August): 529–557.

Harriman, Linda, and Jeffrey D. Straussman. 1983. "Do Judges Determine Budget Decisions?" *Public Administration Review* 43 (July/August): 343–351.

Harris, Joseph. 1964. *Congressional Control of Administration.* Washington, D.C.: The Brookings Institution.

Harris, Richard. 1989. "Federal-State Rela-

tions in the Implementation of Surface Mining Policy." *Policy Studies Review* 9 (Autumn): 69–78.

Harris, Scott A. 1977. "Issue Politicization and Policy Change." Paper presented at the Eighteenth Annual Meeting of the International Studies Association, St. Louis, Mo.

Harrison, William B. 1988. "Embattled Institution: Old and New Adversaries of the Federal Reserve System." *Social Science Quarterly* 69 (September): 646–660.

Havemann, Judith. 1987. "The Government Has Been Sorely Tested and Found Wanting." *Washington Post National Weekly Edition* (March 23): 31.

Havrilesky, Thomas. 1986. "The Effect of the Federal Reserve Reform Act on the Economic Affiliations of Directors of Federal Reserve Banks." *Social Science Quarterly* 67 (June): 393–401.

Hawley, Clifford B., and Tom S. Witt. 1986. "Discrimination and the Efficiency of an Equal Opportunity Agency." *Policy Studies Journal* 15 (September): 17–28.

Hayes, Michael T. 1981. *Lobbyists and Legislators.* New Brunswick, N.J.: Rutgers University Press.

Hays, R. Allen. 1990. "The President, Congress and the Formation of Housing Policy: A Reexamination of Redistributive Policy-Making." *Policy Studies Journal* 18 (Summer): 847–870.

Hebert, F. Ted, Jeffrey L. Brudney, and Deil S. Wright. 1983. "Gubernatorial Influence and State Bureaucracy." *American Politics Quarterly* 11 (April): 243–265.

Heclo, Hugh. 1988. "The In-and-Outer System: A Critical Assessment." *Political Science Quarterly* 103 (Spring): 37–56.

———. 1978. "Issue Networks and the Executive Establishment." In *The New American Political System,* ed. Anthony King, 87–124. Washington, D.C.: American Enterprise Institute.

———. 1977. *Government of Strangers.* Washington, D.C.: The Brookings Institution.

Hedge, David M. 1983. "Fiscal Dependency and the State Budget Process." *Journal of Politics* 45 (February): 198–208.

Hedge, David M., and Saba Jallow. 1990. "The Federal Context of Regulation: The Spatial Allocation of Federal Enforcement." *Social Science Quarterly* 71 (December): 786–801.

Hedge, David M., and Donald C. Menzel. 1985. "Loosening the Regulatory Ratchet: A Grassroots View of Environmental Deregulation." *Policy Studies Journal* 13 (March): 599–606.

Hedge, David M., Donald C. Menzel, and Mark A. Krause. 1989. "The Intergovernmental Milieu and Street-Level Implementation." *Social Science Quarterly* 70 (June): 285–299.

Hedge, David M., Donald C. Menzel, and George H. Williams. 1988. "Regulatory Attitudes and Behavior: The Case of Surface Mining Regulation." *Western Political Quarterly* 41 (June): 323–340.

Heffron, Florence, with Neil McFeeley. 1983. *The Administrative Regulatory Process.* New York: Longman.

Heidenheimer, Arnold. 1970. *Political Corruption.* New York: Holt, Rinehart and Winston.

Heimann, C. F. Larry. 1993. "Understanding the *Challenger* Disaster: Organizational Structure and the Design of Reliable Systems." *American Political Science Review* 87 (June): 421–435.

Heinz, John P., Edward O. Lauman, Robert H. Salisbury, and Robert L. Nelson. 1990. "Inner Circles or Hollow Cores? Elite Networks in National Policy Systems." *Journal of Politics* 52 (May): 356–390.

Henig, Jeffrey R. 1989. "Privatization in the United States: Theory and Practice." *Political Science Quarterly* 104 (Winter): 649–670.

Hiatt, Fred. 1985. "The Pentagon: Spend First, Think Later." *Washington Post National Weekly Edition* (February 18): 31.

Hiatt, Fred, and Rick Atkinson. 1985. "The Air Force's Bargain on Pliers." *Washington Post National Weekly Edition* (April 8): 33.

Hibbing, John, and Elizabeth Theiss-Morse. 1995. *Congress as Public Enemy.* Cambridge, England: Cambridge University Press.

Hightower, James. 1972. *Hard Tomatoes, Hard Times.* Washington, D.C.: Agribusiness Accountability Project.

Hill, Jeffrey S., and Carol S. Weissert. 1995. "Implementation and the Irony of Delegation: The Case of Low-Level Radioactive Waste Disposal." *Journal of Politics* 52 (May): 344–369.

Hill, Kim Quaile, and John Patrick Plumlee. 1984. "Policy Arenas and Budgetary Politics." *Western Political Quarterly* 37 (March): 84–99.

Hill, Larry B. 1989a. "Reconsidering American Bureaucratic Power in the Light of Recent Political Change." Paper presented at the annual meeting of the American Political Science Association, Atlanta, Ga.

Hill, Larry B. 1989b. "Refusing to Take Bureaucracy Seriously." Paper presented at the annual meeting of the Midwest Political Science Association, Chicago.

———. 1998. "Institutionalizing a Bureaucratic Monitoring Mechanism: The First Thirty Years of Hawaii's Ombudsman." Paper presented at the annual meeting of the American Political Science Association, Boston.

———. 1983. "Must Implementation Studies Be So Dismal? The Bureaucratic Impact of the Ombudsman Reforms." Paper presented at the annual meeting of the American Political Science Association, Chicago.

———. 1982. "The Citizen Participation-Representation Roles of American Ombudsmen." *Administration and Society* 13 (February): 405–434.

———. 1976. *The Model Ombudsman.* Princeton, N.J.: Princeton University Press.

Hindera, John J. 1993b. "Representative Bureaucracy: Further Evidence of Active Representation in the EEOC District Offices." *Journal of Public Administration Research and Theory* 3 (Number 4): 415–430.

Hindera, John J. 1993a. "Representative Bureaucracy: Imprimis Evidence of Active Representation in EEOC District Offices." *Social Science Quarterly* 74 (June): 95–108.

Hindera, John J., and Cheryl D. Young. 1998. "Representative Bureaucracy: Theoretical

Implications of Statistical Interactions." *Political Research Quarterly* 51 (September): 655–672.

Hodges, Donald G., and Robert F. Durant. 1989. "The Professional State Revisited: Twixt Scylla and Charybdis?" *Public Administration Review* 49 (September/October): 474–485.

Howe, Robert. 1990. "The Ill Wind Probe: Hot Air vs. Fresh Air." *Washington Post National Weekly Edition* (September 10):31.

Huckfeldt, R. Robert. 1979. "Political Participation and the Neighborhood Social Context." *American Journal of Political Science* 23 (August): 579–592.

Huddleston, Mark W. 1981. "Comparative Perspectives on Administrative Ethics." *Public Personnel Management* 10 (1): 67–76.

Huitt, Ralph K. 1966. "Congress the Durable Partner." In *Lawmakers in a Changing World*, ed. Elke Frank, 9–29. Englewood Cliffs, N.J.: Prentice-Hall.

Hult, Karen M. 1988. "Governing in Bureaucracies: The Case of Parental Notification." *Administration and Society* 20 (November): 313–333.

———. 1987. *Agency Merger and Bureaucratic Redesign*. Pittsburgh, Pa.: University of Pittsburgh Press.

Hult, Karen M., and Charles Walcott. 1990. *Governing Public Organizations: Politics, Structures, and Institutional Design*. Pacific Grove, Calif.: Brooks/Cole.

———. 1989. "Organizational Design as Public Policy." *Policy Studies Journal* 17 (Spring): 469–494.

Ingraham, Patricia W. 1991. "Political Direction and Policy Change in Three Federal Departments." In *The Managerial Presidency*, ed. James Pfiffner, 180–194. Pacific Grove, Calif.: Brooks/Cole.

———. 1987. "Building Bridges or Burning Them? The President, the Appointees, and the Bureaucracy." *Public Administration Review* 47 (September/October): 425–435.

Ingraham, Patricia W., and Carolyn Ban. 1985. "Is Neutral Competence a Myth? The Policy Environment of the Political

Executive in the Reagan Administration." Paper presented at the annual meeting of the American Political Science Association, New Orleans.

———. 1984. *Legislating Bureaucratic Change*. Albany: State University of New York Press.

Ingraham, Patricia W., and Peter W. Colby. 1982. "Political Reforms and Government Management." *Policy Studies Review* 11 (December): 304–317.

Ippolito, Dennis S. 1984. *Hidden Spending: The Politics of Federal Credit Programs*. Chapel Hill: University of North Carolina Press.

Isikoff, Michael. 1990. "A Judas in Our Midst?" *Washington Post National Weekly Edition* (August 6): 33.

Janowitz, Morris. 1960. *The Professional Soldier*. New York: Free Press of Glencoe.

Johannes, John R. 1984. "Congress, the Bureaucracy, and Casework." *Administration and Society* 16 (May): 41–70.

Johannes, John R., and James C. McAdams. 1987. "Entrepreneur or Agent: Congressmen and the Distribution of Casework." *Western Political Quarterly* 40 (September): 535–554.

Johnson, Cathy Marie. 1990. "New Wine in New Bottles: The Case of the Consumer Product Safety Commission." *Public Administration Review* 50 (January/ February): 74–81.

Johnson, Charles A., and Jon R. Bond. 1982. "Policy Implementation and Community Linkages: Hospital Abortion Services after *Roe* v. *Wade*." *Western Political Quarterly* 35 (September): 385–404.

Johnson, Roberta A., and Michael E. Kraft. 1990. "Bureaucratic Whistleblowing and Policy Change." *Western Political Quarterly* 43 (December): 849–874.

Johnson, Ronald W., and Robert E. O'Connor. 1979. "Intraagency Limitations on Policy Implementation." *Administration and Society* 11 (August): 193–215.

Jones, Bryan D. 1985. *Governing Buildings and Building Government*. Tuscaloosa: University of Alabama Press.

Jones, Bryan D., Saadia R. Greenberg, Clifford Kaufman, and Joseph Drew. 1978.

"Service Delivery Rules and the Distribution of Local Government Services." *Journal of Politics* 40 (May):332–369.

———. 1977. "Bureaucratic Response in Citizen-Initiated Contact: Environmental Enforcement in Detroit." *American Political Science Review* 71 (March): 148–165.

Jones, Charles O. 1984. *An Introduction to the Study of Public Policy.* Monterey, Calif.: Brooks/Cole.

Jones, Elise S., and Cameron P. Taylor. 1995. "Litigating Agency Change: The Impact of the Courts and Administrative Appeals Process on the Forest Service." *Policy Studies Journal* 23 (2): 310–336.

Jones, U. Lynn. 1988. "See No Evil, Hear No Evil, Speak No Evil: The Information Control Policy of the Reagan Administration." *Policy Studies Journal* 17 (Winter): 243–260.

Jos, Philip H., Mark E. Thompkins, and Steven W. Hays. 1989. "In Praise of Difficult People: A Portrait of the Committed Whistleblower." *Public Administration Review* 49 (November/December): 552–561.

Kamlet, Mark S., and David C. Mowery. 1983. "Budgetary Side Payments and Government Growth: 1953–1968." *American Journal of Political Science* 27 (November): 636–664.

Kamlet, Mark S., David C. Mowery and Tsai-Tsu Su. 1988. "Upsetting National Priorities? The Reagan Administration's Budget Strategy." *American Political Science Review* 82 (December): 1293–1307.

Kanter, Arnold. 1972. "Congress and the Defense Budget." *American Political Science Review* 66 (March): 129–143.

Karp, Jonathan and Susan Benesch. 1986. "Nice Work if You Can Get It." *Washington Post National Weekly Edition.* (September 8): 31.

Kash, Don W., and Robert W. Rycroft. 1984. *U.S. Energy Policy: Crisis and Complacency.* Norman: University of Oklahoma Press.

Kaufman, Herbert. 1985. *Time, Chance, and Organizations.* Chatham, N.J.: Chatham House.

———. 1981. "Fear of Bureaucracy: A Raging Pandemic." *Public Administration Review* 41 (January/February): 1–10.

———. 1977. *Red Tape.* Washington, D.C.: The Brookings Institution.

———. 1976. *Are Government Organizations Immortal?* Washington, D.C.: The Brookings Institution.

———. 1969. "Bureaucracy and Organized Civil Servants." In *Governing the City,* ed. Robert A. Connery and Demetrious Caraley, 41–54. New York: Praeger.

———. 1960. *The Forest Ranger.* Baltimore, Md.: Johns Hopkins University Press.

Kearney, Richard C. 1990. "Sunset: A Survey and Analysis of State Experience." *Public Administration Review* 50 (January/February): 49–57.

Kearney, Richard C., and Chandan Sinha. 1988. "Professionalism and Bureaucratic Responsiveness: Conflict of Compatibility." *Public Administration Review* 48 (January/February): 571–579.

Keiser, Lael R. 1996. "The Influence of Women's Political Power on Bureaucratic Output: The Case of Child Support Enforcement." *British Journal of Political Science,* 27(1): 136–148.

Keiser, Lael R., and Kenneth J. Meier. 1996. "Policy Design, Bureaucratic Incentives, and Public Management: The Case of Child Support Enforcement." *Journal of Public Administration Research and Theory* 6 (3): 337–364.

Keiser, Lael R., and Joe Soss. 1998. "With Good Cause: Bureaucratic Discretion and the Politics of Child Support Enforcement." *American Journal of Political Science* (October): 1133–1156.

Kellough, J. Edward. 1990a. "Federal Agencies and Affirmative Action for Blacks and Women." *Social Science Quarterly* 71 (March):83–92.

———. 1990b. "Integration in the Public Workplace: Determinants of Minority and Female Employment in Federal Agencies." *Public Administration Review* 50 (September/October): 557–566.

———. 1989. *Federal Equal Employment Opportunity Policy and Numerical Goals and Timetables.* Westport, Conn.: Praeger.

Kemp, Kathleen A. 1986. "Lawyers, Politics, and Economic Regulation." *Social Science Quarterly* 67 (June): 267–282.

———. 1984. "Accidents, Scandals, and Political Support for Regulatory Agencies." *Journal of Politics* 46 (May): 401–427.

———. 1982. "Instability in Budgeting for Federal Regulatory Agencies." *Social Science Quarterly* 63 (December): 643–660.

Kerr, James. 1965. "Congress and Space: Overview or Oversight." *Public Administration Review* 25 (March/April): 185–195.

Kessel, Reuben A. 1970. "The AMA and the Supply of Physicians." *Law and Contemporary Society* 35 (Spring): 267–283.

Kessler, Mark. 1987. "Interorganizational Environments, Attitudes, and the Policy Outputs of Public Agencies." *Administration and Society* 19 (May): 48–73.

Kettl, Donald F. 1990. "The Perils—and Prospects—of Public Administration." *Public Administration Review* 50 (July/August): 411–420.

———. 1989. "Expansion and Protection in the Budgetary Process." *Public Administration Review* 49 (May/June): 231–239.

———. 1988. *Government by Proxy: (Mis?)Managing Federal Programs.* Washington, D.C.: Congressional Quarterly Press.

———. 1986. *Leadership at the Fed.* New Haven, Conn.: Yale University Press.

Key, V. O. 1959. "Legislative Control." In *Elements of Public Administration*, ed. Fritz Morstein Marx, 312–336. Englewood Cliffs, N.J.: Prentice-Hall.

Khademian, Anne M. 1995. "Reinventing a Government Corporation: Professional Priorities and a Clear Bottom Line." *Public Administration Review* 55 (January/February): 17–28.

Kiewiet, D. Roderick, and Mathew D. McCubbins. 1988. "Presidential Influence on Congressional Appropriations Decisions." *American Journal of Political Science* 32 (August): 713–736.

———. 1985. "Congressional Appropriations and the Electoral Connection." *Journal of Politics* 47 (February): 59–82.

Kingsley, J. Donald. 1944. *Representative Bureaucracy.* Yellow Springs, Ohio: Antioch Press.

Kirst, Michael W. 1969. *Government Without Passing Laws.* Chapel Hill: University of North Carolina Press.

Knott, Jack. 1986. "The Fed Chairman as Political Executive." *Administration and Society* 18 (August): 197–232.

Knott, H. Jack, and Gary J. Miller. 1987. *Reforming Bureaucracy: The Politics of Institutional Choice.* Englewood Cliffs, N.J.: Prentice-Hall.

Kobrak, Peter. 1996. "The Social Responsibilities of a Public Entrepreneur." *Administration and Society* 28(August): 205–38.

Kosterlitz, Julie. 1989. "Mixed Reviews for Planned Sex Survey." *National Journal* (July 1): 1699.

———. 1988. "Bust Up a Winning Team?" *National Journal* (January 9): 70–74.

Krasnow, Erwin G., Lawrence D. Longley, and Herbert A. Terry. 1982. *The Politics of Broadcast Regulation.* 3d ed. New York: St. Martin's.

Krause, George A. 1996. "The Institutional Dynamics of Policy Administration: Bureaucratic Influence Over Securities Regulation." *American Journal of Political Science* 40 (November): 1083–1121.

Krislov, Samuel. 1965. *The Supreme Court in the Political Process.* New York: Macmillan.

Kuklinski, James H. 1978. "Representativeness and Elections: A Policy Analysis." *American Political Science Review* 72 (March): 165–177.

Kurtz, Howard. 1989. "The White House Used HUD as a Dumping Ground." *Washington Post National Weekly Edition* (June 26), 31.

Labaton, Stephen. 1985. "Wrong Again, Supreme Court." *Washington Post National Weekly Edition* (August 19), 10.

Lambright, W. Henry. 1976. *Governing Science and Technology.* New York: Oxford University Press.

Lambright, W. Henry, and Dianne Rahm. 1989. "Ronald Reagan and Space Policy." *Policy Studies Journal* 17 (Spring): 515–528.

Landau, Martin. 1969. "Redundancy, Rationality and the Problem of Duplication and Overlap." *Public Administration Review* 29 (July/August): 346–358.

Langbein, Laura I., and Cornelius M. Kerwin. 1987. "An Analysis of Case Processing Complexity in Public Bureaus." *Policy Studies Review* 7 (Autumn): 26–42.

Langdon, Stuart. 1981. "The Evolution of Federal Citizen Involvement Policy." *Policy Studies Review* 1 (November): 369–378.

Lanouette, William J. 1982. "IGs Say an Ounce of Prevention May Save Billions for Their Agencies." *National Journal* 14 (June 19): 1094–1097.

———. 1977. "The Revolving Door—It's Tricky to Try to Stop It." *National Journal* 9 (November 19): 1979.

Lasswell, Harold D. 1936. *Politics: Who Gets What, When, How?* New York: McGraw-Hill.

Lebovic, James H. 1995. "How Organizations Learn: U.S. Government Estimates of Foreign Military Spending." *American Journal of Political Science* 39 (November): 835–863.

Leiserson, Avery, and Fritz Morstein Marx. 1959. "The Formulation of Administrative Policy." In *Elements of Public Administration*, ed. Fritz Morstein Marx, 337–351. New York: Harper & Row.

Lerner, Allan W., and John Wanat. 1983. "Fuzziness and Bureaucracy." *Public Administration Review* 43 (November/December): 500–509.

Lerner, Michael A., with John Barry. 1985. "Sergeant York Musters Out." *Newsweek* (September 9), 23.

Lester, James P., James L. Franke, Anne Bowman, and Kenneth W. Kramer. 1983. "Hazardous Waste Politics and Public Policy." *Western Political Quarterly* 36 (June): 257–285.

Lewis, Gregory B. 1991. "Turnover and the Quiet Crisis in the Federal Service." *Public Administration Review* 51 (March/April): 145–155.

———. 1990. "In Search of the Machiavellian Milquetoasts: Comparing Attitudes of Bureaucrats and Ordinary people." *Public Administration Review* 50 (March/April): 220–227.

Lewis-Beck, Michael, and Tom W. Rice. 1985. "Government Growth in the United States." *Journal of Politics* 47 (February): 2–30.

Liedel, Mark B. 1990. "The Bloated Disservice of Congress's Constituent Service." *Washington Post National Weekly Edition* (February 5), 24.

Long, Norton E. 1993. "The Ethics and Efficacy of Resignation in Public Administration." *Administration and Society* 25 (May): 3–11.

———. 1952. "Bureaucracy and Constitutionalism." *American Political Science Review* 46 (September): 808–818.

———. 1949. "Power and Administration." *Public Administration Review* 9 (Autumn): 257–264.

Longley, Lawrence D., Herbert A. Terry, and Erwin G. Krasnow. 1983. "Citizen Groups in Broadcast Regulatory Policy Making." *Policy Studies Journal* 12 (December): 258–272.

Lovrich, Nicholas P. 1981. "Professional Ethics and the Public Interest." *Public Personnel Management* 10 (1): 87–92.

Lowery, David. 1998. "Consumer Sovereignty and Quasi-Market Failure." *Journal of Public Administration Research and Theory* 8 (April): 137–172.

———. 1982a. "Public Choice When Services Are Costs." *American Journal of Political Science* 26 (February): 57–75.

———. 1982b. "The Political Incentives of Government Contracting." *Social Science Quarterly* 63 (September): 517–529.

Lowery, David, and William D. Berry. 1983. "The Growth of Government in the United States." *American Journal of Political Science* 27 (November): 665–694.

Lowery, David, Samuel Bookheimer, and James Malachowski. 1985. "Partisanship and the Appropriations Process." *American Politics Quarterly* 13 (April): 188–199.

Lowery, David, and Virginia Gray. 1995. "The Population Ecology of Gucci Gulch, or the Natural Regulation of Interest Group Numbers in the American States." *American Journal of Political Science* 39 (February): 1–29.

———. 1990. "The Corporatist Foundations of State Industrial Policy." *Social Science Quarterly* 71 (March): 3–24.

Lowery, David, and Caryl E. Rusbult. 1986. "Bureaucratic Responses to Antibureaucratic Administrations: Federal Employee Reaction to the Reagan Election." *Administration and Society* 18 (May): 45–76.

Lowery, David, Virginia Gray, and Gregory Hager. 1989. "Public Opinion and Policy Change in the American States." *American Politics Quarterly* 17 (January): 3–31.

Lowi, Theodore. 1972. "Four Systems of Policy, Politics, and Choice." *Public Administration Review* 32 (July/August): 298–310.

———. 1969. *The End of Liberalism.* New York: Norton.

Luttbeg, Norman, and Harmon Zeigler. 1966. "Attitude Consensus and Conflict in an Interest Group." *American Political Science Review* 60 (September): 655–665.

Lynn, Laurence E. 1984. "The Reagan Administration and the Penitent Bureaucracy." In *The Reagan Presidency and the Governing of America,* ed. Lester M. Salamon and Michael S. Lund, 339–370. Washington, D.C.: The Urban Institute Press.

Lyons, William E., and David Lowery. 1989. "Governmental Fragmentation versus Consolidation: Five Public-Choice Myths About How to Create Informed, Involved, and Happy Citizens." *Public Administration Review* 49 (November/December): 533–534.

Lyons, William E., David Lowery, and Ruth Hoagland DeHoog. 1992. *The Politics of Dissatisfaction: Citizens, Services and Institutions.* Armonk, N.Y.: M. E. Sharpe.

Maass, Arthur A., and Lawrence I. Radway. 1959. "Gauging Administrative Responsibility." In *Ideas and Issues in Public Administration.,* ed. Dwight Waldo, 440–454. New York: McGraw-Hill.

MacKenzie, G. Calvin. 1981. *The Politics of Presidential Appointments.* New York: Free Press.

Madison, Christopher. 1984. "Under Wick, the USIA Has a Bigger Budget, New Digs and an Image Problem." *National Journal* 16 (June 9): 1134–1138.

Malachowski, James, Samuel Bookheimer, and David Lowery. 1987. "The Theory of the Budgetary Process in an Era of Changing Budgetary Rules: FY48–FY84." *American Politics Quarterly* 15 (July): 325–354.

Mann, Dean. 1975. "Political Incentives in U.S. Water Policy." In *What Government Does,* ed. Matthew Holden and Dennis L. Dresang, 94–123. Beverly Hills, Calif.: Sage.

———. 1968. *The Citizen and the Bureaucracy.* Berkeley, Calif.: Institute of Governmental Studies.

Mapes, Linda V. 1984. "Defense Committee Members Draw Most in Defense PAC Donations." *National Journal* 16 (October 13): 1942.

Maranto, Robert. 1998. "Thinking the Unthinkable in Public Administration: The Case for Spoils in the Federal Bureaucracy." *Administration & Society* 29 (January): 623–642.

Marcus, Alfred. 1980. "Environmental Protection Agency." In *The Politics of Regulation,* ed. James Q. Wilson, 267–303. New York: Basic Books.

Marini, Frank. 1971. *Toward a New Public Administration.* Scranton, Pa.: Chandler Publications.

Marshall, Gary S. 1998. "Whither (or Wither) OPM?" *Public Administration Review* 58 (May/June): 280–282.

Martinek, Wendy L., Kenneth J. Meier, and Lael R. Keiser. 1998. "Jackboots or Lace Panties? The Bureau of Alcohol, Tobacco, and Firearms." in *The Changing Politics of Gun Control,* ed. John M. Bruce and Clyde Wilcox, 17–44. Lanham, Md.: Rowman and Littlefield.

Martz, Larry. 1989. "Hip-Deep at HUD." *Newsweek* (July 10), 16–18.

Marvel, Mary K. 1982. "Implementation and Safety Regulation: Variations in Federal State Administration Under OSHA," *Administration and Society* 14 (May): 15–34.

Mashaw, Jerry L. 1983. *Bureaucratic Justice: Managing Social Security Disability Claims.* New Haven, Conn.: Yale University Press.

Matlack, Carol. 1987. "Ripe for a Rip-Off." *National Journal* (June 6): 1462–1463.

Mayer, Kenneth R. 1993. "Policy Disputes as a Source of Administrative Controls: Congressional Micromanagement of the Department of Defense." *Public Administration Review* 53 (July/August): 293–302.

Maynard-Moody, Steven. 1989. "Beyond Implementation: Developing an Institutional Theory of Administrative Policy Making." *Public Administration Review* 49 (March/April): 137–141.

Maynard-Moody, Steven. 1995. *The Dilemma of the Fetus.* New York: St. Martin's Press.

Mazmanian, Daniel A., and Paul A. Sabatier. 1983. *Implementation and Public Policy.* Glenview, Ill.: Scott, Foresman.

———. 1980. "A Multivariate Model of Public Policy-Making." *American Journal of Political Science* 24 (August): 439–468.

McAllister, Bill. 1989. "Scandals in the Making?" *Washington Post National Weekly Edition.* (December 11): 32.

McClosky, Herbert, Paul J. Hoffman, and Rosemary O'Hara. 1960. "Issue Conflict and Consensus Among Party Leaders and Followers." *American Political Science Review* 54 (June): 406–427.

McCool, Daniel. 1990. "Subgovernments as Determinants of Political Viability." *Political Science Quarterly* 105 (Summer): 269–294.

———. 1989. "Subgovernments and the Impact of Policy Fragmentation and Accommodation." *Policy Studies Review* 8 (Winter): 264–287.

McCubbins, Mathew D., Roger G. Noll, and Barry R. Weingast. 1989. "Structure and Process, Politics and Policy: Administrative Arrangements and Political Control of Agencies." *Virginia Law Review* 75 (March): 431–482.

McCubbins, Mathew D., and Thomas Schwartz. 1984. "Congressional Oversight Overlooked: Police Patrols versus Fire Alarms." *American Journal of Political Science* 28 (February): 165–179.

McFarlane, Deborah R. 1989. "Testing the Statutory Coherence Hypothesis: The Implementation of Federal Family Planning Policy in the States." *Administration and Society* 20 (February), 395–422.

Meier, Kenneth J. 1997. "Bureaucracy and Democracy: The Case for More Bureaucracy and Less Democracy." *Public Administration Review* 57 (May/June):193–199.

———. 1994. *The Politics of Sin: Drugs, Alcohol and Public Policy.* Armonk, N.Y.: M. E. Sharpe.

———. 1988. *The Political Economy of Regulation: The Case of Insurance.* Albany: State University of New York Press.

———. 1985. *Regulation: Politics, Bureaucracy, and Economics.* New York: St. Martin's Press.

———. 1981. "Ode to Patronage: A Critical Analysis of Two Recent Supreme Court Decisions." *Public Administration Review* 41 (September/October): 558–563.

———. 1980. "Measuring Organizational Power: Resources and Autonomy of Government Agencies." *Administration and Society* 12 (November): 357–375.

———. 1978. "Building Bureaucratic Coalitions" in *The New Politics of Food,* ed. Don F. Hadwiger and William P. Browne, 57–74. Lexington, Mass.: Lexington Books.

———. 1975. "Representative Bureaucracy and Administrative Responsiveness." Ph.D. dissertation, Syracuse University.

Meier, Kenneth J., and Gary W. Copeland. 1983. "Interest Groups and Public Policy." *Social Science Quarterly* 64 (September): 641–646.

Meier, Kenneth J., and Cathy M. Johnson. 1990. "The Politics of Demon Rum: Regulating Alcohol and Its Deleterious Consequences." *American Politics Quarterly* 18 (October): 404–429.

Meier, Kenneth J., and Lael R. Keiser. 1996. "Public Administration as a Science of the Artificial: A Methodology for Prescription." *Public Administration Review* 56 (September/October): 459–466.

Meier, Kenneth J., and Deborah R. McFarlane. 1996. "Statutory Coherence and Policy Implementation: The Case of Family Planning." *Journal of Public Policy* 15 (3): 281–298.

Meier, Kenneth J., and David R. Morgan. 1982. "Citizen Compliance with Public Policy: The National Maximum Speed Law." *Western Political Quarterly* 35 (June): 258–274.

Meier, Kenneth J., and Lloyd G. Nigro. 1976. "Representative Bureaucracy and Policy Preferences." *Public Administration Review* 36 (July/August): 458–469.

Meier, Kenneth J., and Joseph Stewart Jr. *The Politics of Hispanic Education*. Albany: State University of New York Press.

Meier, Kenneth J., Joseph Stewart Jr., and Robert E. England. 1991. "The Politics of Bureaucratic Discretion: Educational Access as an Urban Service." *American Journal of Political Science* 35 (February): 155–177.

———. 1989. *Race, Class, and Education: The Politics of Second Generation Discrimination*. Madison: University of Wisconsin Press.

Meier, Kenneth J., Robert D. Wrinkle, and J. L. Polinard. 1999a. "Equity versus Excellence in Organizations: An Application of Substantively Weighted Least Squares." *American Review of Public Administration* 29 (March): 5–18.

———. 1999b. "Representative Bureaucracy and Distributional Equity: Addressing the Hard Question." *Journal of Politics* 61 (forthcoming).

Melnick, R. Shep. 1983. *Regulation and the Courts*. Washington, D.C.: The Brookings Institution.

Menzel, Donald C. 1981. "Implementation of the Federal Surface Mining Control and Reclamation Act of 1977." *Public Administration Review* 41 (March/April): 212–219.

Menzel, Donald. 1997. "Teaching Ethics and Values in Public Administration: Are We Making a Difference?" *Public Administration Review* 57 (May/June): 224–230.

Merit Systems Protection Board. 1982. *The Other Side of Merit: Removals for Incompetence in the Federal Service*. Washington, D.C.: Merit Systems Protection Board.

Mezey, Susan Gluck. 1986. "Policymaking by the Federal Judiciary: The Effects of Judicial Review on the Social Security Disability Program." *Policy Studies Journal* 14 (March): 343–362.

Miewald, Robert D., and John C. Comer. 1986. "Complaining as Participation: The Case of the Ombudsman." *Administration and Society* 17 (February): 481–500.

Miles, Rufus E. 1978. "The Origin and Meaning of Miles' Law." *Public Administration Review* 38 (September/October): 399–403.

Miller, Arthur H. 1974. "Political Issues and Trust in Government." *American Political Science Review* 58 (September): 951–972.

Miller, Cheryl M. 1987. "The Politics of Legislative Curtailment of Administrative Rulemaking: Obstacles to Police-Patrol Oversight." *Policy Studies Review* 6 (May): 631–644.

Mitchell, Jerry. 1998. *The American Experiment with Government Corporations*. Armonk, N.Y.: M. E. Sharpe.

———. 1990. "The Policy Activities of Public Authorities." *Policy Studies Journal* 18 (Summer): 928–942.

Mitnik, Barry M. 1980. *The Political Economy of Regulation*. New York: Columbia University Press.

Mitroff, Ian L. 1974. *The Subjective Side of Science*. New York: Elsevier.

Mladenka, Kenneth R. 1981. "Citizen Demands and Urban Services: The Distribution of Bureaucratic Response in Chicago and Houston." *American Journal of Political Science* 25 (November): 693–714.

———. 1980. "The Urban Bureaucracy and the Chicago Political Machine." *American Political Science Review* 74 (December): 991–999.

Mladenka, Kenneth R., and Kim Quaile Hill. 1978. "The Distribution of Urban Police Services." *Journal of Politics* 40 (February): 112–133.

Moe, Ronald C. 1990. "Traditional Organizational Principles and the Managerial Presidency: From Phoenix to Ashes." *Public*

Administration Review 50 (March/April): 129–140.

———. 1987. "Exploring the Limits of Privatization." *Public Administration Review* 47 (November/December): 453–460.

Moe, Ronald C., and Thomas H. Stanton. 1989. "Government Sponsored Enterprises as Federal Instrumentalities: Reconciling Private Management with Public Accountability." *Public Administration Review* 49 (July/August): 321–329.

Moe, Terry M. 1985. "Control and Feedback in Economic Regulation: The Case of the NLRB." *American Political Science Review* 79 (December): 1094–1117.

———. 1982. "Regulatory Performance and Presidential Administration." *American Journal of Political Science* 26 (May): 197–224.

———. 1981. "Toward a Broader View of Interest Groups." *Journal of Politics* 43 (May): 531–543.

Moore, W. John. 1990a. "Access Denied." *National Journal* (January 20): 121–123.

———. 1990b. "Citizen Prosecutors." *National Journal* (August 18): 2006–2010.

———. 1990c. "Collaring Business." *National Journal* (April 21): 960–964.

———. 1990d. "Stoking the FTC." *National Journal* (May 19): 1217–1221.

———. 1990e. "Stopping the States." *National Journal* (July 21): 1758–1762.

———. 1986. "Mandates Without Money." *National Journal* (October 4): 2366–2370.

Morris, John C. 1997. "The Distributional Impacts of Privatization in National Water-Quality Policy." *Journal of Politics* 59 (February): 56–72.

Morrison, David C. 1988. "Not Many Old Bases Die or Fade Away." *National Journal* (March 19): 747.

Mosher, Frederick C. 1982. *Democracy and the Public Service.* New York: Oxford University Press.

———. 1979. *The GAO.* New York: Westview.

Mosher, Lawrence. 1982. "Endangered Species Act May Be Off Endangered List, at Least for 1982." *National Journal* 14 (April 24): 722–724.

Mueller, Keith J. 1988. "Federal Programs Do Expire: The Case of Health Planning." *Public Administration Review* 48 (May/June): 719–725.

Nadel, Mark V. 1971. *The Politics of Consumer Protection.* Indianapolis, Ind.: Bobbs-Merrill.

Nader, Ralph. 1972. *Whistle Blowing.* New York: Grossman.

Nalbandian, John, and J. Terry Edwards. 1983. "The Values of Public Administrators." *Review of Public Personnel Administration* (Fall): 114–127.

Nathan, Richard P. 1983. *The Administrative Presidency.* New York: Wiley.

Neiman, Max. 1989. "Government Directed Change of Everyday Life and Coproduction: The Case of Home Energy Use." *Western Political Quarterly* 42 (September): 365–390.

Nelson, Michael. 1982. "A Short, Ironic History of American National Bureaucracy." *Journal of Politics* 44 (August): 747–778.

Neustadt, Richard. 1960. *Presidential Power.* New York: Wiley.

Newcomer, Kathryn E. 1998. "The Changing Nature of Accountability: The Role of the Inspector General in Federal Agencies." *Public Administration Review* 58 (March/April): 129–136.

Newcomer, Kathryn E., Gail Johnson, Tom Naccarato, and Sam Collie. 1989. "The Presidential Management Internship Program: Looking Backward and Moving Forward." *Public Administration Review* 49 (July/August): 372–386.

Newland, Chester A. 1983. "A Mid-Term Appraisal—The Reagan Presidency." *Public Administration Review* 43 (January/February): 1–21.

Niskanen, William. 1971. *Bureaucracy and Representative Government.* Chicago: Aldine.

Nivola, Pietro S. 1978. "Distributing a Municipal Service: A Case Study of Housing Inspection." *Journal of Politics* 40 (February): 59–81.

O'Leary, Rosemary. 1994. "The Bureaucratic Politics Paradox: The Case of Wetlands Legislation in Nevada." *Journal of Public Administration Research and Theory* 4 (October): 443–468.

O'Loughlin, Michael G. 1990. "What is Bureaucratic Accountability and How Can We Measure It?" *Administration and Society* 22 (November): 275–303.

O'Toole, Lawrence J., and Robert S. Mountjoy. 1984. "Interorganizational Policy Implementation: A Theoretical Perspective." *Public Administration Review* 44 (November/December): 491–503.

O'Toole, Laurence J., Jr. 1989. "Goal Multiplicity in the Implementation Setting: Subtle Impacts and the Case of Wastewater Treatment Privatization" *Policy Studies Journal* 18 (Fall): 1–21.

Ogul, Morris S. 1976. *Congress Oversees the Bureaucracy.* Pittsburgh, Pa.: University of Pittsburgh Press.

Olson, Susan M. 1990. "Interest Group Litigation in Federal District Court: Beyond the Political Disadvantage Theory." *Journal of Politics* 52 (August): 854–882.

Ornstein, Norman J., and Shirley Elder. 1978. *Interest Groups, Lobbying and Policy Making.* Washington, D.C.: Congressional Quarterly Press.

Ornstein, Norman J., Thomas E. Mann, and Michael J. Malbin. 1990. *Vital Statistics on Congress, 1989–1990.* Washington, D.C.: Congressional Quarterly Press.

Ostrom, Vincent. 1973. *The Intellectual Crisis in American Public Administration.* Tuscaloosa: University of Alabama Press.

Page, Benjamin I., and Robert Y. Shapiro. 1983. "Effects of Public Opinion on Policy." *American Political Science Review* 77 (March): 175–190.

Pearce, Jone L., and James L. Perry. 1983. "Federal Merit Pay: A Longitudinal Analysis." *Public Administration Review* 43 (July/August): 315–325.

Pearson, William M., and Van A. Wigginton. 1986. "Effectiveness of Administrative Controls: Some Perceptions of State Legislators." *Public Administration Review* 46 (July/August): 328–331.

Percy, Stephen L. 1989. *Disability, Civil Rights, and Public Policy.* Tuscaloosa: University of Alabama Press.

Perrow, Charles. 1972. *Complex Organizations.* Glenview, Ill.: Scott, Foresman.

Perry, James L. 1988. "Making Policy by Trial and Error: Merit Pay in the Federal Service." *Policy Studies Journal* 17 (Winter): 389–405.

Perry, James L., and Lois Recascino Wise. 1990. "The Motivation Bases of Public Service." *Public Administration Review* 50 (May/June): 367–373.

Pertschuk, Michael. 1982. *Revolt Against Regulation.* Berkeley: University of California Press.

Peters, B. Guy, and Brian W. Hogwood. 1985. "In Search of the Issue Attention Cycle." *Journal of Politics* 47 (February): 238–253.

Peters, John G. 1978. "The 1977 Farm Bill: Coalitions in Congress." In *The New Politics of Food*, ed. Don F. Hadwiger and William P. Browne, 23–36. Lexington, Mass.: Lexington Books.

Peterson, Steven A. 1988. "Sources of Citizens' Bureaucratic Contacts: A Multivariate Analysis." *Administration and Society* 20 (August): 152–165.

———. 1986. "Closer Encounters of the Bureaucratic Kind: Older Americans and Bureaucracy." *American Journal of Political Science* 30 (May): 347–356.

Pfiffner, James P. 1988. *The Strategic Presidency: Hitting the Ground Running.* Homewood, Ill.: The Dorsey Press.

———. 1987a. "Political Appointees and Career Executives: The Democracy-Bureaucracy Nexus in the Third Century." *Public Administration Review* 47 (January/February): 57–65.

———. 1987b. "Nine Enemies and One Ingrate: Political Appointments during Presidential Transitions." In *The In-and-Outers*, ed. G. Calvin Mackenzie, 60–76. Baltimore, Md.: Johns Hopkins University Press.

———. 1984. "Presidential Control of the Bureaucracy." Mimeo, California State University, Fullerton.

———. 1982. "The Carter-Reagan Transition: Hitting the Ground Running." *Presidential Studies Quarterly* 13 (Fall): 623–634.

———. 1979. *The President, the Budget and Congress.* Boulder, Colo.: Westview Press.

Pierce, John C., and Nicholas P. Lovrich. 1983. "Trust in Technical Information Provided by Interest Groups." *Policy Studies Journal* 11 (June): 626–639.

Pincus, Ann. 1976. "How to Get a Government Job." *Washington Monthly* 8 (June): 22–28.

Pitsvada, Bernard T., and Frank D. Draper. 1984. "Making Sense of the Federal Budget the Old Fashioned Way—Incrementally." *Public Administration Review* 44 (September/October): 401–406.

Plant, Jeremy, and Frank J. Thompson. 1983. "Deregulation, the Bureaucracy and Employment Discrimination: The Case of the EEOC." Paper presented at the Eighth Annual Hendricks Symposium, Lincoln, Neb.

Plant, Jeremy, and Harold F. Gortner. 1981. "Ethics, Personnel Management, and Civil Service Reform." *Public Personnel Management* 10 (1): 3–10.

Plumlee, John P. 1981a. "Lawyers as Bureaucrats: The Impact of Legal Training in the Higher Civil Service." *Public Administration Review* 41 (March/April): 220–228.

———. 1981b. "Professional Training and Political Dominance in the Higher Civil Service." *Social Science Quarterly* 62 (September): 569–575.

Plumlee, John P., Jay D. Starling, and Kenneth W. Kramer. 1984. "Citizen Participation in Water Quality Planning." *Administration and Society* 16 (February): 455–474.

Poister, Theodore H. 1982. "Federal Transportation Policy for the Elderly and Handicapped." *Public Administration Review* 42 (January/February): 6–14.

Poister, Theodore H., and Gary T. Henry. 1994. "Citizen Ratings of Public and Private Service Quality: A Comparative Perspective." *Public Administration Review* 54 (March/April): 155–160.

Poveda, Tony. 1990. *The FBI in Transition: Lawlessness and Reform.* Pacific Grove, Calif.: Brooks/Cole.

Powell, Norman J., and Daniel P. Parker. 1963. *Major Aspects of American Government.* New York: McGraw-Hill.

Pressley, Sue Anne. 1985. "Hard Times at the Internal Revenue Service." *Washington Post National Weekly Edition* (July 8): 33.

Preston, Michael B. 1977. "Minority Employment and Collective Bargaining in the Public Sector." *Public Administration Review* 37 (September/October): 511–514.

Price, Don K. 1965. *The Scientific Estate.* New York: Oxford University Press.

Priest, T. B., Richard T. Sylves, and David F. Scudder. 1984. "Corporate Advice: Large Corporations and Federal Advisory Committees." *Social Science Quarterly* 65 (March): 100–111.

Priest, Dana. 1990. "Bring Back the Ponies: Overnight Mail Sometimes Takes a Day or Two." *Washington Post National Weekly Edition* (November 12): 37.

Pritchett, Herman C. 1948. *The Roosevelt Court: A Study in Judicial Politics and Values 1937–1947.* New York: Macmillan.

Quirk, Paul J. 1980. "Food and Drug Administration." in *The Politics of Regulation,* ed. James Q. Wilson. New York: Basic Books, 191–234.

Ragsdale, Lyn, and John Theis, III. 1997. "The Institutionalization of the American Presidency, 1924–92." *American Journal of Political Science* 41 (October): 1280–1319.

Rainey, Hal G. 1997. *Understanding and Managing Public Organizations.* San Francisco: Jossey-Bass.

———. 1982. "Reward Preferences Among Public and Private Managers." *American Review of Public Administration* 16 (Winter): 288–302.

Randall, Ronald. 1979. "Presidential Power versus Bureaucratic Intransigence." *American Political Science Review* 74 (September): 795–810.

Rauch, Jonathan. 1985a. "Small Business Agency Alive and Well Despite White House Attempt to Kill It." *National Journal* (August 10): 1845–1848.

———. 1985b. "Grace Commission Is Still Wooing Converts." *National Journal* 16 (April 6): 727ff.

———. 1984. "Women and Children's Food Program Is 'Off Limits' to Reagan Budget

Cutbacks." *National Journal* 15 (November 11): 2197–2199.

Ray, Bruce A. 1981. "Defense Department Spending and 'Hawkish' Voting in the House of Representatives." *Western Political Quarterly* 34 (December): 438–446.

———. 1980. "Federal Spending and the Selection of Committee Assignments in the U.S. House of Representatives." *American Journal of Political Science* 24 (August): 494–510.

Reagan, Michael D. 1987. *Regulation: The Politics of Policy.* Boston: Little, Brown.

Redford, Emmette S. 1969. *Democracy in the Administrative State.* New York: Oxford University Press.

Reeves, T. Zane. 1988. *The Politics of the Peace Corps and Vista.* Tuscaloosa: University of Alabama Press.

Regens, James L. and Robert W. Rycroft. 1981. "Administrative Discretion in Energy Policy-Making." *Journal of Politics* 43 (August): 875–888.

Rehfuss, John A. 1986. "A Representative Bureaucracy? Women and Minority Executives in California Career Service." *Public Administration Review* 46 (September/October): 454–459.

Relyea, Harold C. 1986. "Access to Government Information in the Information Age." *Public Administration Review* 46 (November/December): 635–639.

Renfrow, Patty D. 1980. "The New Independent Regulatory Commissions: The Politics of Establishment." Paper presented at the annual meeting of the Midwest Political Science Association, Chicago.

Renfrow, Patty D., and David J. Houston. 1987. "A Comparative Analysis of Rule-making Provisions in State Administrative Procedure Acts." *Policy Studies Review* 6 (May): 657–665.

Riccucci. Norma N. 1995. *Unsung Heroes: Federal Execucrats Making a Difference.* Washington, D.C.: Georgetown University Press.

Rich, Richard C. 1981. "Interaction of the Voluntary and Governmental Sectors: Toward an Understanding of the Coproduction of Municipal Services." *Administration and Society* 13 (May): 59–76.

Riedel, James A. 1972. "Citizen Participation: Myths and Realities." *Public Administration Review* 32 (March/April): 211–217.

Riehle, Thomas. 1984. "Scandals, Etc., From A to Z." *National Journal* (January 14): 92–93.

Riley, Rene T. 1986. "Revitalizing the Snake-Eaters." *National Journal* (October 25): 2566–2567.

Ringquist, Evan. 1993. *Environmental Protection at the State Level.* Armonk: N.Y.: M. E. Sharpe.

Ringuist, Evan J. 1995. "Is 'Effective Regulation' Always Oxymoronic? The States and Ambient Air Quality." *Social Science Quarterly* 76 (March): 69–87.

———. 1990. *Regulating Air and Water Quality: Politics and Progress at the State Level.* Madison: Unpublished doctoral dissertation, Department of Political Science, University of Wisconsin.

Ripley, Randall B., and Grace A. Franklin. 1991. *Congress, the Bureaucracy, and Pubic Policy.* Homewood, Ill.: Dorsey Press.

Robinson, Scott. 1998. "Shuffling Stacked Decks: Congressional Manipulation of Administrative Procedures." Mimeo, Texas A&M University.

Robson, William. 1964. *The Governors and the Governed.* Baton Rouge: Louisiana State University Press.

Rodgers, Harrell R., and Charles S. Bullock. 1976. *From Coercion to Compliance.* Lexington, Mass.: Lexington Books.

Rohr, John. 1989. *Ethics for Bureaucrats.* 2nd ed. New York: Marcel Decker.

Romzek, Barbara. 1985. "The Effects of Public Service Recognition, Job Security, and Staff Reductions on Organizational Involvement." *Public Administration Review* 45 (March/April): 282–291.

Romzek, Barbara S. 1990. "Employee Investment and Commitment: The Ties that Bind." *Public Administration Review* 50 (May/June): 374–382.

Romzek, Barbara S., and Melvin J. Dubnick. 1987. "Accountability in the Public Sector:

Lessons for the *Challenger* Tragedy." *Public Administration Review* 47 (May/June): 227–238.

Romzek, Barbara, and J. Stephen Hendricks. 1982. "Organizational Involvement and Representative Bureaucracy: Can We Have It Both Ways?" *American Political Science Review* 76 (March):75–82.

Romzek, Barbara, and Patricia Ingraham. 1998. "Crosspressures of Accountability: Initiative, Command, and Failure in the Ron Brown Plane Crash." Paper presented at the annual meeting of the American Political Science Association, Boston.

Rose, Richard. 1985. *Public Employment in Western Nations.* Cambridge, England: Cambridge University Press.

Rosen, Bernard. 1981. "Uncertainty in the Senior Executive Service." *Public Administration Review* 41 (March/April): 203–207.

Rosen, Bernard. 1986. "Crises in the U.S. Civil Service." *Public Administration Review* 46 (May/June): 207–215.

Rosenbloom, David H. 1994. "Fuzzy Law from the High Court." *Public Administration Review* 54 (November/December): 503–506.

———. 1973. "The Civil Service Commission's Decision to Authorize the Use of Goals and Timetables in the Federal Equal Employment Opportunity Program." *Western Political Quarterly* 26 (June): 236–251.

Rosenburg, Neil D. 1990. "Drug Use Entrenched Among Workers." *The Milwaukee Journal* (August 17): A1.

Rosener, Judy B. 1982. "Making Bureaucrats Responsive: A Study of the Impact of Citizen Participation and Staff Recommendations on Regulatory Decision Making." *Public Administration Review* 42 (July/August): 339–345.

Rosenfeld, Raymond A. 1984. "An Expansion and Application of Kaufman's Model of Red Tape." *Western Political Quarterly* 37 (December): 603–620.

Rourke, Francis E. 1984. *Bureaucracy, Politics, and Public Policy,* 3d ed. Boston: Little, Brown.

Rowan, Carl T. 1975. "The IRS Needs to Be Abuse Proof." *Houston Post* (October 8): 2c.

Rowat, Donald C. 1968. "The Spread of the Ombudsman Idea." In *Ombudsman for American Government?* , ed. Stanley V. Anderson, 7–36. Englewood Cliffs, N.J.: Prentice-Hall.

Rubin, Irene S. 1985. *Shrinking the Federal Government.* New York: Longman.

Russell, Christine. 1985. "What Else Are We Going to Do with All That Useless Vaccine?" *Washington Post National Weekly Edition* (June 17): 33.

Sabatier, Paul A. 1991. "Interest Group Membership and Organization: Multiple Theories." In *The Politics of Interests: Interest Groups Transformed* , ed. Mark P. Petracca, 99–129. Boulder, Colo.: Westview Press.

———. 1988. "An Advocacy Coalition Framework of Policy Change and the Role of Policy-Oriented Learning Therein." *Policy Sciences* 21 (No.2–3): 129–168.

———. 1975. "Social Movements and Regulatory Agencies." *Policy Sciences* 6 (September): 301–342.

Sabatier, Paul A., and Susan Hunter. 1989. "The Incorporation of Causal Perceptions into Models of Elite Belief Systems." *Western Political Quarterly* 42 (September): 229–262.

Sabatier, Paul A., and Daniel Mazmanian. 1981. "Relationships Between Governing Boards and Professional Staff." *Administration and Society* 13 (August): 207–248.

Sabatier, Paul A., and Susan M. McLaughlin. 1990. "Belief Congruence between Interest-Group Leaders and Members: An Empirical Analysis of Three Theories and a Suggested Synthesis." *Journal of Politics* 52 (August): 914–938.

———. 1988. "Belief Congruence of Governmental and Interest Group Elites with their Constituencies." *American Politics Quarterly* 16 (January): 61–98.

Sabatier, Paul A., Neil Pelky, Susan McLaughlin, and Cherie Wolfe. 1985. "Longitudinal Analysis of Permit Review by Regional Land Use Agencies." Paper presented at the annual meeting of the American Political Science Association, New Orleans.

Sabatier, Paul, and Matthew Zafonte. 1999. "Are Bureaucrats and Scientists Members of Advocacy Coalitions?" In *An Advocacy Coalition Lens on Environmental Policy,* ed. Paul Sabatier. Cambridge, Mass.: MIT Press.

Salamon, Lester M., and Gary L. Wamsley. 1975. "The Federal Bureaucracy: Responsive to Whom?" Paper presented at the annual meeting of the Midwest Political Science Association, Chicago.

Salisbury, Robert. H. 1984. "Interest Representation: The Domination of Institutions." *American Political Science Review* 78 (March): 64–76.

Saltzstein, Grace Hall. 1989. "Black Mayors and Police Policies." *Journal of Politics* 51 (August): 525–541.

———. 1986a. "Female Mayors and Women in Municipal Jobs." *American Journal of Political Science* 30 (February): 140–164.

———. 1986b. "Institutional Barriers to Employment in Bureaucracy: The Residual Effects of Organizational Reform." *Administration and Society* 18 (May): 77–90.

———. 1983. "Personnel Directors and Female Employment Representation." *Social Science Quarterly* 64 (December): 734–746.

———. 1979. "Representative Bureaucracy and Bureaucratic Responsibility." *Administration and Society* 10 (February): 465–476.

Sanford, Terry. 1967. *Storm Over the States.* New York: McGraw-Hill.

Sawyer, Kathy. 1985. "The Mess at the IRS." *Washington Post National Weekly Edition* (November 11): 6–7.

Schattschneider, E. E. 1960. *The Semi-Sovereign People.* New York: Holt, Rinehart and Winston.

Scher, Seymour. 1960. "Congressional Committee Members as Independent Agency Overseers." *American Political Science Review* 54 (December): 911–920.

Schick, Allen. 1971. "Toward the Cybernetic State." In *Public Administration in a Time of Turbulence* , ed. Dwight Waldo, 214–233. Scranton, Pa.: Chandler Publishing.

Schmidt, Diane E. 1995. "The Presidential Appointment Process, Task Environment Pressures, and Regional Office Case Processing." *Political Research Quarterly* 48 (June): 381–401.

Schmidt, Warren H., and Barry Z. Posner. 1987. "Values and Expectations of City Managers in California." *Public Administration Review* 47 (September/October): 404–409.

Schneider, Saundra K. 1988. "Intergovernmental Influences on Medicaid Program Expenditures." *Public Administration Review* 48 (July/August): 756–763.

———.1987. "Influences on State Professional Licensure Policy." *Public Administration Review* 47 (November/December): 479–484.

Schneider, Saundra K., William G. Jacoby and Jerrell D. Coggborn. 1997. "The Structure of Bureaucratic Decisions in the American States." *Public Administration Review* 57 (May/June): 240–249.

Scholz, John T., and Feng Heng Wei. 1986. "Regulatory Enforcement in a Federalist System." *American Political Science Review* 80 (December): 1249–1270.

Scholz, John, and B. Dan Wood. 1998. "Controlling the IRS: Principals, Principles, and Public Administration." *American Journal of Political Science* 42 (January): 141–162.

Scholzman, Kay Lehman. 1984. "What Accent the Heavenly Chorus? Political Equality and the American Pressure System." *Journal of Politics* 46 (November): 1006–1032.

Schrage, Michael. 1985. "Is This What They Mean by Successor Technology?" *Washington Post National Weekly Edition* (November 11): 23.

Schumaker, Paul. 1975. "Policy Responsiveness to Protest Group Demands." *Journal of Politics* 37 (May): 488–521.

Schutz, Howard G. 1983. "Effects of Increased Citizen Membership on Occupational Licensing Boards in California." *Policy Studies Journal* 11 (March): 504–516.

Scicchitano, Michael J., David M. Hedge, and Patricia Metz. 1989. "The States and Deregulation: The Case of Surface Mining." *Policy Studies Review* 9 (Autumn): 120–131.

Seidenstat, Paul. 1996. "Privatization: Trends, Interplay of Forces, and Lessons Learned." *Policy Studies Journal* 24 (3): 464–470.

Seidman, Harold, and Robert Gilmour. 1986. *Politics, Position, and Power.* 4th ed. New York: Oxford University Press.

Selden, Sally Coleman. 1997. *The Promise of Representative Bureaucracy.* Armonk, N.Y.: M. E. Sharpe.

Shapiro, Michael. 1969. "Rational Political Man." *American Political Science Review* 63 (December): 1106–1119.

Shapiro, Martin. 1988. *Who Guards the Guardians? Judicial Control of Administration.* Athens: University of Georgia Press.

Sharp, Elaine. 1984. "Citizen Demand Making in the Urban Context." *American Journal of Political Science* 28 (November): 654–670.

———. 1982. "Citizen Initiated Contacting of Government Officials and Socioeconomic Status." *American Political Science Review* 76 (March): 109–115.

Sheehan, Reginald S. 1990. "Administrative Agencies and the Court: A Reexamination of the Impact of Agency Type on Decisional Outcomes." *Western Political Quarterly* 43 (December): 875–886.

Sherwood, Frank P., and Lee J. Breyer. 1987. "Executive Personnel Systems in the States." *Public Administration Review* 47 (September/October): 410–416.

Shimberg, Benjamin, Barbara F. Esser, and Daniel H. Druger. 1973. *Occupational Licensing: Practices and Policies.* Washington, D.C.: Public Affairs Press.

Shover, Neal, Donald A. Clelland, and John Lynxwiler. 1986. *Enforcement or Negotiation: Construction a Regulatory Bureaucracy.* Albany: State University of New York Press.

Shull, Steven A. 1978. "Presidential-Congressional Support for Agencies and for Each Other." *Journal of Politics* 40 (August): 753–760.

Shull, Steven A., and David Garland. 1995. "Presidential Influence versus Agency Characteristics in Explaining Policy Implementation." *Policy Studies Review* 14 (1&2): 49–70.

Sickels, Robert J. 1974. *Presidential Transitions.* Englewood Cliffs, N.J.: Prentice-Hall.

Simon, Herbert. 1998. "Why Public Administration?" *Journal of Public Administration Research and Theory* 8 (January): 1–12.

Sinclair, Ward. 1987. "Here's a Way to Ease the Budget Crunch." *Washington Post National Weekly Edition* (November 9): 33.

Slaughter, Cynthia. 1986. "Sunset and Occupational Regulation: A Case Study." *Public Administration Review* 46 (May/June): 241–245.

Smith, Kevin B. 1994. "Policy, Markets and Bureaucracy: Reexamining School Choice." *Journal of Politics* 52 (May): 475–491.

Snow, C. P. 1961. *Science and Government.* Cambridge, Mass.: Harvard University Press.

Spurrier, Robert L. 1983. "Paying the Piper in Federal Civil Rights Litigation." *Public Administration Review* 43 (May/June): 199–208.

Stanley, David T. 1984. "Civil Service Reform, Then and Now." In *Legislating Bureaucratic Change,* ed. Patricia W. Ingraham and Carolyn Ban, 258–263. Albany: State University of New York Press.

———. 1965. *Changing Administrations.* Washington, D.C.: The Brookings Institution.

Starobin, Paul. 1990. "Foggy Forecasts." *National Journal* (May 19): 1212–1215.

Stehr, Steven D. 1997. "Top Bureaucrats and the Distribution of Influence in Reagan's Executive Branch." *Public Administration Review* 57 (January/February): 75–82.

Stein, Lana. 1987. "Merit Systems and Political Influence: The Case of Local Government." *Public Administration Review* 47 (May/June): 263–271.

———. 1986. "Representative Local Government: Minorities in the Municipal Work Force." *Journal of Politics* 48 (August): 694–716.

Steinbach, Carol F. 1989. "Programmed for Plunder." *National Journal* (September 16): 2259–2262.

Stephens, David. 1983. "President Carter, The Congress and NEA: Creating the Department of Education." *Political Science Quarterly* 98 (Winter): 641–663.

Stewart, Joseph, James E. Anderson, and Zona Taylor. 1982. "Presidential and Congressional Support for 'Independent' Regulatory Commissions." *Western Political Quarterly* 35 (September): 318–326.

Stewart, Joseph, and Charles S. Bullock. 1981. "Implementing Equal Educational Opportunity Policy." *Administration and Society* 12 (February): 427–446.

Stigler, George J. 1971. "The Theory of Economic Regulation." *Bell Journal of Economics and Management Science* 2 (Spring): 3–21.

Stimson, James A., Michael B. MacKuen, and Robert S. Erikson. 1995. "Dynamic Representation." *American Political Science Review* 89 (September): 543–585.

Stokes, Bruce. 1985. "A Target of the Right and Left, AID Administrator Keeps Surviving." *Washington Post National Weekly Edition* (February 9): 31.

Stokey, Edith, and Richard Zeckhauser. 1978. *A Primer for Policy Analysis.* New York: Norton.

Stone, Clarence N. 1985. "Efficiency versus Social Learning: A Reconsideration of the Implementation Process." *Policy Studies Review* 4 (February): 484–496.

————. 1977. "Paternalism Among Social Agency Employees." *Journal of Politics* 39 (August): 794–804.

Stover, Robert V., and Don W. Brown. 1975. "Understanding Compliance and Noncompliance with the Law." *Social Science Quarterly* 56 (December): 363–375.

Straussman, Jeffrey D. 1986. "Courts and Public Purse Strings: Have Portraits of Budgeting Missed Something?" *Public Administration Review* 46 (July/August): 345–351.

Sullivan, Robert R. 1970. "The Role of the President in Shaping Lower Level Policymaking Processes." *Polity* 3 (Winter): 201–221.

Sussman, Barry. 1985. "The Public Perceives a Stalemate in Reagan's War on Waste." *Washington Post National Weekly Edition* (September 2): 37.

Swardson, Anne. 1985. "IRS Says You Owe $2 Million? Probably Just Another Snafu." *Washington Post National Weekly Edition* (May 13): 32.

Taggart, William A. 1985. "Air Quality Control Expenditures in the American States." *Journal of Politics* 47 (May): 704–714.

Tanenhaus, Joseph. 1960. "Supreme Court Attitudes Toward Federal Administrative Agencies." *Journal of Politics* 22 (August): 502–524.

Temples, James R. 1982. "The Nuclear Regulatory Commission and the Politics of Regulatory Reform." *Public Administration Review* 42 (July/August): 355–362.

Terry, Larry D. 1998. "Administrative Leadership, Neo-Managerialism, and the Public Management Movement." *Public Administration Review* 58 (May/June): 194–200.

————. 1990. "Leadership in the Administrative State: The Concept of Administrative Conservatorship." *Administration and Society* 21 (February): 395–413.

Teske, Paul, Mark Schneider, Michael Mintrom, and Samuel Best. 1993. "Establishing the Micro Foundations of a Macro Theory: Information, Movers and the Competitive Local Market for Public Goods." *American Political Science Review* 87 (September): 702–713.

Theobald, Robin. 1997. "Enhancing Public Service Ethics: More Culture, Less Bureaucracy?" *Administration and Society* 29 (September): 490–503.

Thielemann, Gregory S., and Joseph Stewart Jr. 1996. "A Demand-side Perspective on the Importance of Representative Bureaucracy: AIDS, Ethnicity, Gender and Sexual Orientation." *Public Administration Review* 56 (March/April): 168–173.

Thomas, Craig W. 1993. "Reorganizing Public Organizations: Alternatives, Objectives, Evidence." *Journal of Public Administration Research and Theory* 3 (October): 457–80.

Thomas, John Clayton. 1982. "Citizen Initiated Contacts with Government Agencies." *American Journal of Political Science* 26 (August): 504–522.

Thomas, Rich. 1987. "Uncle Sam the Cosigner." *Newsweek* (June 8): 50–52.

Thomas, Robert D., and Robert B. Handberg. 1974. "Congressional Budgeting for Eight Agencies." *American Journal of Political Science* 18 (February): 179–187.

Thompson, Frank J. 1984. "Deregulation at the EEOC: Prospects and Implications." *Review of Public Personnel Administration* 4 (Summer): 41–56.

———. 1982a. "Deregulation by the Bureaucracy: OSHA and the Augean Quest for Error Correction." *Public Administration Review* 42 (May/June): 202–212.

———. 1982b. "Bureaucratic Discretion and the National Health Service Corps." *Political Science Quarterly* 97 (Fall): 427–445.

Thompson, Frank J., and Michael J. Scicchitano. 1987. "State Implementation and Federal Enforcement Priorities: Safety versus Health in OSHA and the States." *Administration and Society* 19 (May): 95–124.

———. 1985. "State Implementation Effort and Federal Regulatory Policy." *Journal of Politics* 47 (May): 686–703.

Thompson, Joel A. 1987. "Agency Requests, Gubernatorial Support, and Budget Success in States Legislatures Revisited." *Journal of Politics* 49 (August): 756–774.

Thurow, Lester. 1980. *The Zero-Sum Society.* New York: Basic Books.

Tibbles, Lance, and John H. Holland. 1970. *Buffalo Citizens Administrative Service.* Berkeley, Calif.: Institute for Governmental Studies.

Tierney, John T. 1984. "Government Corporations and Managing the Public's Business." *Political Science Quarterly* 99 (Spring): 73–92.

Tobin, Richard J. 1982. "Recalls and the Remediation of Hazardous or Defective Consumer Products." *Journal of Consumer Affairs* 16 (Winter): 278–306.

Truman, David B. 1951. *The Governmental Process.* New York: Knopf.

Tufte, Edward. 1978. *Political Control of the Economy.* Princeton, N.J.: Princeton University Press.

Tullock, Gordon. 1965. *The Politics of Bureaucracy.* Washington, D.C.: Public Affairs Press.

Uslaner, Eric M., and Ronald E. Weber. 1983. "Party Congruence and American State Elites." *Journal of Politics* 45 (February): 183–196.

Van Riper, Paul P. 1958. *History of the United States Civil Service.* Evanston, Ill.: Row, Peterson and Company.

Vasu, Michael Lee. 1979. *Politics and Planning.* Chapel Hill: University of North Carolina Press.

Vaughn, Robert G. 1988. "The Performance of the United States Merit Systems Protection Board." *Policy Studies Journal* 17 (Winter): 352–369.

Vedlitz, Arnold, and James A. Dyer. 1984. "Bureaucratic Response to Citizen Contacts." *Journal of Politics* 46 (November): 1207–1216.

Verba, Sidney, and Norman Nie. 1972. *Participation in America.* New York: Harper & Row.

Vig, Norman J., and Michael E. Kraft. 1984. *Environmental Policy in the Eighties.* Washington, D.C.: Congressional Quarterly Press.

Vittes, M. Elliot. 1985. "Value Tradeoffs and Productivity: The Transpoliticization of the U.S. Postal Service." *Policy Studies Review* 4 (February): 504–511.

Volcker, Paul A. 1989. *Leadership for America: Rebuilding the Public Service.* Washington, D.C.: National Commission on the Public Service.

Walcott, Charles, and Karen M. Hult. 1987. "Organizing the White House: Structure, Environment, and Organizational Governance." *American Journal of Political Science* 31 (February): 109–125.

Waldo, Dwight. 1971. *Public Administration in a Time of Turbulence.* Scranton, Pa.: Chandler Publications.

Walsh, Louise D. 1989. "The IRS' Faulty Filing Skills: The Clerical Kind." *Washington*

Post National Weekly Edition (February 27): 33.

Wamsley, Gary L., Charles T. Goodsell, John A. Rohr, Camilla M. Stivers, Orion F. White, and James F. Wolf. 1987. "The Public Administration and the Governance Process: Refocusing the American Dialogue." In *A Centennial History of the American Administrative State,* ed. Ralph Clark Chandler, 291–317. New York: The Free Press.

Wanat, John. 1974. "Bases of Budgetary Incrementalism." *American Political Science Review* 68 (December): 1221–1228.

Wanat, John, Karen Burke, and Marilyn Snodell. 1984. "Legislators as Budget Initiators and Lobbyists." *American Politics Quarterly* 12 (October): 389–408.

Washington Post Poll. 1982. Reported in "The Business Climate." *Public Opinion* (November): 22.

Waterman, Richard W. 1989. *Presidential Influence and the Administrative State.* Knoxville: University of Tennessee Press.

Watson, Douglas. 1975. "SBA Violating No Politics Regulation." *Washington Post* (April 13): A9.

Weber, Max. 1946. *From Max Weber: Essays in Sociology.* H.H. Gerth and C. Wright Mills, trans. New York: Oxford University Press.

Weingast, Barry R., and Mark J. Moran. 1983. "Bureaucratic Discretion or Congressional Control? Regulatory Policymaking by the Federal Trade Commission." *Journal of Political Economy* 91 (5): 765–800.

Weisskopf, Michael. 1985. "A Ship in Every Port, a Vote in Every Committee." *Washington Post National Weekly Edition* (September 2): 12.

Welborn, David M. 1977. *The Governance of Federal Regulatory Agencies.* Knoxville: University of Tennessee Press.

Welborn, David M., and Anthony E. Brown. 1980. "Power and Politics in Federal Regulatory Commissions." *Administration and Society* 12 (May): 37–68.

Welch, Susan, and John G. Peters. 1983. "Private Interests and Public Interests." *Journal of Politics* 45 (May): 378–396.

Welch, W. P. 1982. "Campaign Contributions and Legislative Voting: Milk Money and Dairy Price Supports." *Western Political Quarterly* 35 (December): 478–495.

Welch, William M. 1989. "VA Employees Took Gratuities." *Madison Capital Times* (January 31): 5.

Wenner, Lettie McSpadden. 1983. "Interest Group Litigation and Environmental Policy." *Policy Studies Review* 11 (June): 671–683.

———. 1973. "Attitudes of Water Pollution Control Officials." DeKalb: Center for Governmental Studies, University of Northern Illinois.

West, William F. 1995. *Controlling the Bureaucracy.* Armonk, N.Y.: M. E. Sharpe.

———. 1988. "The Growth of Internal Conflict in Administrative Regulation." *Public Administration Review* 48 (July/August): 773–782.

———. 1985. *Administrative Rulemaking: Politics and Processes.* Westport, Conn.: Greenwood Press.

———. 1984. "Restructuring Administrative Discretion: The Pursuit of Rationality and Responsiveness." *American Journal of Political Science* 28 (May): 340–360.

———. 1983. "Institutionalizing Rationality in Regulatory Administration." *Public Administration Review* 43 (July/August): 326–334.

West, William F., and Joseph Cooper. 1989. "Legislative Influence v. Presidential Dominance: Competing Models of Bureaucratic Control." *Political Science Quarterly* 104 (Winter): 581–606.

———. 1983. "The Congressional Veto and Administrative Rulemaking." *Political Science Quarterly* 98 (Summer): 285–304.

West, William, and Robert F. Durant. 1998. "MSPB" typescript, Texas A&M University.

White, Leonard D. 1959. *The Republican Era.* New York: Macmillan.

———. 1954. *The Jacksonians.* New York: Macmillan.

———. 1951. *The Jeffersonians.* New York: Macmillan.

———. 1948. *The Federalists*. New York: Macmillan.

Williams, Walter. 1990. "Cutting Off Our Nose in Spite of Our Needs." *Washington Post National Weekly Edition* (October 22): 26.

Willison, David H. 1986. "Judicial Review of Administrative Decisions: Agency Cases Before the Court of Appeals for the District of Columbia, 1981–84." *American Politics Quarterly* 14 (October): 317–327.

Wilsford, David. 1984. "Exit and Voice: Strategies for Change in Bureaucratic-Legislative Policymaking." *Policy Studies Review* 12 (March): 431–444.

Wilson, James Q. 1989. *Bureaucracy*. New York: Basic Books.

———. 1973. *Political Organizations*. New York: Basic Books.

Wilson, Woodrow. 1887. "The Study of Administration." *Political Science Quarterly* 2 (June): 197–222.

Wines, Michael. 1983a. "From Doctors to Dairy Farmers, Critics Gunning for FTC." *National Journal* 15 (January 29): 221–223.

———. 1983b. "Auchter's Record at OSHA Leaves Labor Outraged, Business Satisfied." *National Journal* 15 (October 10): 2008–2013.

Winn, Mylon. 1989. "Black Administrators and Racial Roadblocks in Public Organizations: Problems and Recourse." *International Journal of Public Administration* 12 (5): 797–819.

Wise, Charles R. 1989. "Wither Federal Organizations: The Air Safety Challenge and Federal Management's Response." *Public Administration Review* 49 (January/February): 17–28.

Wise, Charles, and Rosemary O'Leary. 1997. "Intergovernmental Relations and Federalism in Environmental Management and the Role of the Courts." *Public Administration Review* 57 (March/April): 150–159.

Witte, John F. 1985. *The Politics and Development of the Federal Income Tax*. Madison: University of Wisconsin Press.

Wlezien, Christopher. 1995. "The Public as Thermostat: Dynamics of Preferences for Spending." *American Journal of Political Science* 39 (November): 981–1000.

Wohlstetter, Priscilla. 1989. "The Politics of Legislative Oversight: Monitoring Educational Reform in Six States." *Policy Studies Review* 9 (Autumn): 50–65.

Wolf, Patrick. 1997. "Why Must We Reinvent the Federal Government? Putting Development Historical Claims to the Test." *Journal of Public Administration Research and Theory* 7 (July): 353–388.

Wolin, Sheldon. 1960. *Politics and Vision*. Boston: Little, Brown.

Wolman, Harold. 1971. *The Politics of Federal Housing*. New York: Dodd, Mead.

Wood, B. Dan, and Richard W. Waterman. 1994. *Bureaucratic Dynamics: The Role of Bureaucracy in a Democracy*. Boulder, Colo.: Westview.

———. 1992. "Modeling Federal Implementation as a System." *American Journal of Political Science* 36 (February): 40–67.

———. 1990. "Does Politics Make a Difference at the EEOC?" *American Journal of Political Science* 34 (May): 503–530.

———. 1988. "Principals, Bureaucrats, and Responsiveness in Clean Air Enforcements." *American Political Science Review* 82 (March): 213–234.

Wood, B. Dan, and Richard W. Waterman. 1991. "The Dynamics of Political Control of the Bureaucracy." *American Political Science Review* 85 (September): 801–828.

Woodhouse, Edward J. 1985. "External Influences on Productivity: EPA's Implementation of TSCA." *Policy Studies Review* 4 (February): 497–503.

Woodiwiss, Michael. 1988. *Crime, Crusades, and Corruption: Prohibitions in the United States, 1900–1987*. London: Pinter Publishers.

Wright, Gerald C., and Michael B. Berkman. 1986. "Candidates and Policy in United States Senate Elections." *American Political Science Review* 80 (June): 566–588.

Wright, John R. 1985. "PACs, Contributions, and Roll Calls." *American Political Science Review* 79 (June): 400–414.

Wrinkle, Robert D., and Kenneth J. Meier.

1998. "Regulating Agriculture." In *Regulation and Consumer Protection*, ed. Kenneth J. Meier, E. Thomas Garman, and Lael R. Keiser, 121–142. Houston: Dame Publications.

Yandle, Bruce. 1986. "Federal Trade Commission Output and Costs: Cycling through the Zone of Political Wrath." *Social Science Quarterly* 67 (September): 517–533.

———. 1982. "A Social Regulation Controversy." *Social Science Quarterly* 63 (March): 58–69.

Yantek, Thom, and Kenneth D. Gartrell. 1988. "Political Climate and Corporate Mergers: When Politics Affects Economics." *Western Political Quarterly* 41 (June): 309–322.

Yarmolinsky, Adam. 1971. *The Military Establishment*. New York: Harper & Row.

Yarwood, Dean L., and Ben M. Enis. 1982. "Advertising and Publicity Programs in the Executive Branch of National Government." *Public Administration Review* 42 (January/February): 36–46.

Yoo, Jae-Won, and Deil S. Wright. 1993. "Public Policy and Intergovernmental Relations: Measuring Perceived Change(s) in National Influence the Effects of the Federalism Decade." *Policy Studies Journal* 21 (4): 687–699.

Young, John D. 1983. "Reflections on the Root Causes of Fraud, Abuse and Waste in Federal Social Programs." *Public Administration Review* 43 (July/August): 362–369.

Zeigler, L. Harmon. 1983. "Interest Groups in the States." In *Politics in the American States*, eds. Virginia Gray, Herbert Jacob, and Kenneth N. Vines. Boston: Little, Brown.

Zeigler, L. Harmon, and G. Wayne Peak. 1972. *Interest Groups in American Society*. Englewood Cliffs, N.J.: Prentice-Hall.

Zentner, Joseph L. 1972. "Presidential Transitions and the Perpetuation of Programs." *Western Political Quarterly* 15 (March): 5–15.

INDEX

NOTES

NOTES

NOTES

NOTES

NOTES

NOTES

NOTES

NOTES

NOTES

NOTES